# Othello, the Moor of Venice

## Texts and Contexts

WILLIAM SHAKESPEARE

# *Othello, the Moor of Venice*

## Texts and Contexts

—————————————— ⇥⇤ ——————————————

Edited by

# KIM F. HALL

Fordham University

*Bedford / St. Martin's*     BOSTON ◆ NEW YORK

*For Bedford/St. Martin's*

*Editorial Assistant:* Marisa Feinstein
*Production Supervisor:* Andrew Ensor
*Senior Marketing Manager:* Jenna Bookin Barry
*Project Management:* DeMasi Design and Publishing, Inc.
*Text Design:* Claire Seng-Niemoller
*Cover Design:* Donna L. Dennison
*Cover Art: The Marriage Feast at Cana*, detail of banqueting table with man in a
   green robe and dwarf with a parrot, c. 1562. Oil on canvas by Veronese (Paolo
   Caliari), 1528–88 © Louvre, Paris, France/Peter Willi/The Bridgeman Art
   Library; *Lace Border*, Italian (Venice), 1600's. V&A Images/Victoria and Albert
   Museum.
*Composition:* Stratford Publishing Services, Inc.
*Printing and Binding:* Haddon Craftsmen, an RR Donnelley & Sons Company

*President:* Joan E. Feinberg
*Editorial Director:* Denise B. Wydra
*Editor in Chief:* Karen S. Henry
*Director of Marketing:* Karen Melton Soeltz
*Director of Editing, Design, and Production:* Marcia Cohen
*Manager, Publishing Services:* Emily Berleth

Library of Congress Control Number: 200692274

Manufactured in the United States of America.

2   1   0   9   8   7
f   e   d   c   b   a

*For information, write:* Bedford/St. Martin's, 75 Arlington Street, Boston, MA 02116
(617-399-4000)

ISBN-10: 0-312-39898-0
ISBN-13: 978-0-312-39898-9

Published and distributed outside North America by

PALGRAVE MACMILLAN

Houndmills, Basingstoke, Hampshire RG21 2XS and London
Companies and representatives throughout the world.

ISBN-10: 1-4039-4633-7
ISBN-13: 978-1-4039-4633-1

A catalog record for this book is available from the British Library.

# *About the Series*

Shakespeare wrote his plays in a culture unlike, though related to, the culture of the emerging twenty-first century. The Bedford Shakespeare Series resituates Shakespeare within the sometimes alien context of the sixteenth and seventeenth centuries while inviting students to explore ways in which Shakespeare, as text and as cultural icon, continues to be part of contemporary life. Each volume frames a Shakespearean play with a wide range of written and visual material from the early modern period, such as homilies, polemical literature, emblem books, facsimiles of early modern documents, maps, woodcut prints, court records, other plays, medical tracts, ballads, chronicle histories, and travel narratives. Selected to reveal the many ways in which Shakespeare's plays were connected to the events, discourses, and social structures of his time, these documents and illustrations also show the contradictions and the social divisions in Shakespeare's culture and in the plays he wrote. Engaging critical introductions and headnotes to the primary materials help students identify some of the issues they can explore by reading these texts with and against one another, setting up a two-way traffic between the Shakespearean text and the social world these documents help to construct.

Jean E. Howard
Columbia University
Series Editor

# *About This Volume*

――――――――――――――――――――――――――― >< ―――――――――――――――――――――――――――

Obviously, no book or series can deliver all of early modern culture; however, *Othello: Texts and Contexts* makes available a compelling variety of verbal and visual cultural materials in accessible form. The chapters situate
readers within concerns about race, religion, geography, emotion, marriage,
and the military that *Othello* shared with the early modern world.

The Bedford Texts and Contexts series draws much of its energy from a
school of criticism known as New Historicism that was first widely used and
discussed in the 1980s. New Historicism has since had a seismic impact on
the teaching of early modern literature, making a host of new texts and
questions available for students. New Historicism proposes that all narratives do significant cultural work; that is, stories, descriptions, and images
grapple with the hopes, dreams, anxieties, and obsessions of a society. In this
view, literature exists not in isolation from social questions but as a dynamic
participant in the messy processes of cultural formation. Furthermore, this
critical school uses the tools of analysis generally applied to literature —
questions of imagery, genre, plot, and language — with equal vigor to all
narratives from private journals to public speeches. New Historicism, then,
proposes that text and context are equal partners in the production of culture. Questions of interpretation are best answered by combining rigorous
textual analysis with investigations into the debates, historical events, and

social movements that shaped people's lives when the text was written. Although most scholarly movements value students as active learners, New Historicism encourages students to be scholars and cultural detectives — exploring archives and historical narratives to uncover the relationship between a particular text and its cultural moment.

Dialogue with Feminist, post-colonial, ethnic studies, and other more overtly political schools of criticism made New Historicism a powerful tool for addressing not just the lives of cultural elites but also those at the margins of early culture. This dialogue also raised specific questions about gender, cultural dominance, colonial aspiration, and race that make *Othello* an ideal, if daunting, play for contextual analysis. The texts made available in this volume give a sense of the texture and variety of early modern thinking on key issues of identity, subjectivity, and ethnic and religious conflict. Most of them stand out among the hundreds of possibilities because they offer either especially clear or particularly interesting perspectives on these aspects of early modern culture. In a few cases there are clear echoes of the text in the play; in most others, there is no evidence that Shakespeare knew of the work. Actually, in some cases Shakespeare would not have had access to the text. This more capacious sense of context distinguishes this volume from a source study, which would only interest itself in texts that Shakespeare would know. Rather, the volume opts for opening a window into the circulation of ideas in the culture, rather than narrowly examining the author's relation to specific texts used for the play. Some offerings, such as the selections from William Whately's *The Bride-bush* and Thomas Coryate's commentary on Venice, have been subject to much scholarly scrutiny; others, like the excerpts from Robert and Thomas Digges' *Stratioticos* and *The Cuckold's Haven*, have not been frequently read with *Othello*. Nonetheless, each selection offers a different avenue into the play that would have been available to an early modern audience, if not to Shakespeare himself.

In addition to the variety of written materials, including military manuals, treatises about emotions, sermons, edicts, and poetry, the volume includes an important range of visual materials: paintings, engravings, portraits, woodcuts, and miniatures. While the commentary on these images points out specific details and suggests possible ways of reading them, these suggestions are not definitive. Students will benefit from scrutinizing the images further and from actively incorporating their own ideas about the images into their analyses of the play.

This volume is unusual in the Bedford series in including both a "pretext," Cinthio's *Gli Hecatommithi*, written before the completion of *Othello*, and a final chapter on responses to the play that post-date Shakespeare.

Cinthio's version of the play's important predecessor gives readers an opportunity to see Shakespeare as an appropriator himself and thus to understand "context" as multi-directional and densely layered. Although all of Shakespeare's major plays have reached beyond the stage and into other media, few have done so with the force of *Othello*. The documents in the final chapter reveal the play itself as an important context for cultural discussions of race and interracial desire. While I could have limited the volume to early modern texts, I feel strongly that the history of appropriations and revisions of *Othello* too powerfully influences modern conceptions of the play and interracial desire in general to be overlooked.

I anticipate, and even hope, that readers will question my decision to include actual texts of minstrel *Othello*s. Setting loose racial imagery into the world is never an easy decision. The minstrel texts I read for this edition are without a doubt racist, grotesque, and personally demeaning: it would have been much easier to ignore their haunting laughter and keep them buried in the archive rather than lose sleep over giving them new life and legitimacy in this volume. But silence does not teach, and a violent play about racial intermarriage should not be taught with what David Pilgrim has called "thick naiveté" about our racial past.

While working on this volume, I witnessed multiple scholarly attempts to recuperate blackface minstrelsy, attempts that normalize and flatten out its racism by divorcing it from actual black experience. Hearing writers attempt to inoculate the virulence of minstrelsy by asserting that the role of Othello was initially performed in blackface, I feel even more certain of the importance of students seeing for themselves the links with — and the important differences between — Richard Burbage's "blackening up" to play his Othello in 1604 and performances like T. D. Rice's *Otello*. Placing *Othello* in the context of these encounters I hope will liberate the students to ask hard questions about literature, culture, and our responsibilities to each other as readers and citizens.

*Editing* can be a fascinatingly contradictory term, often connoting exclusion and limitation. Of necessity, editing a volume such as this excludes and interprets, but it does so in service of an original meaning of "to edit," which is *ēdere*, to put forth or give to the world. Neither the categories employed nor the contextual materials selected are definitive; the volume is intended to provoke broader thinking and inspire readers to take advantage of the great variety of early modern materials now available in both print and electronic forms. Rather than thinking of this volume as the last word on *Othello*, I hope that you will find in it the tools for creating your own dialogue with the play.

## EDITORIAL POLICY

Most of the texts transcribed and edited for this volume are the editions that appeared closest to the date of the play's first performance, although on occasion I deviated from that practice in favor of an edition that had a particular resonance with the play. I consulted original documents, microfilm, and electronic versions of the originals. This series does not wish to overwhelm a reader with lengthy notes that significantly alter the reader's experience of the text, so the annotated documents do not contain complete scholarly apparatus, but rather are lightly annotated to enhance reader understanding and enjoyment. The texts have been modernized according to the following principles:

1. Spelling has been modernized and regularized to American usage; however, to retain some flavor of early modern language, archaic verb endings (e.g., *-eth*) have been retained and archaic words, especially those referring to certain ethnic and religious groups, are retained and glossed. Wherever possible, I used the preferred spelling from the *Oxford English Dictionary (OED)* for obsolete words and annotated obsolete and archaic words in accordance with the *OED*. Some names and place names have been changed to reflect modern spellings, others (particularly names not found in the *Dictionary of National Biography [DNB]*) appear as in the original documents. Foreign words, phrases, or citations not already translated in the original have been translated. In some cases, I omitted sections of foreign text that did not add significantly to the sense of a passage.

2. Punctuation has been lightly modernized. I have, in the interests of readability, altered punctuation to clarify meanings. That is, I have at times cut up longer sentences, added semi-colons and other modern forms of punctuation, and introduced paragraph breaks to break up long sections of text and to emphasize points. The originals contain no quotation marks, and I have punctuated obvious quotations according to modern usage.

3. Early modern texts used capitalization and italics as a form of emphasis; I have in most cases followed the capitalization and italicization of the original texts except in cases where modernizing the punctuation called for additional capitalization.

4. The titles of early modern texts have been modernized according to the above principles in both the Introduction and the headnotes. Those sections use a shortened form of the title. The selection's source footnote uses the more commonly used full title, but eschews the more delightfully lengthy titles.

5. In citing sixteenth- and seventeenth-century texts, page numbers have been given where they exist. When they do not exist, signature numbers

have been given. Signature numbers are a now-obsolete method of pagination used in early printing and indicate how a book was made. Large sheets of paper were folded into two, creating a *folio* or *F* volume; into four, creating a *quarto* or *Q* volume; or into eight, creating an *octavo* or *O* volume. These folded pages were stitched or "gathered" to form a book. Printers used a letter to identify all of the pages printed on the original large sheet, a number to indicate page order in the "gathering," and "r" (for *recto*) or "v" (for *verso*) to indicate the front and back sides of a page respectively. (At times the "recto" side is unmarked. Thus, a page marked C3 indicates that the page comes from the third gathering, third page, and a page marked B3v indicates the second gathering, the back of the third page.)

6. Quotations from other early modern printed texts have also been modernized according to the principles above. In the case of well-known printed works, the editorial policy of the edition cited has been used. Act, scene, and line references to *Othello* are from David Bevington's edition reprinted in this volume. References to other plays by Shakespeare are to *The Riverside Shakespeare*.

ACKNOWLEDGMENTS

I am profoundly grateful to the series editor, Jean E. Howard, for her intellectual leadership and level head and to Karen S. Henry, Editor in Chief, for her encouragement and patience with the project's progress. The volume benefited from Edward Pechter, University of Victoria, and Virginia Mason Vaughan, Clark University, who offered thoughtful readings at different stages, as well as from the following readers: Rebecca Bach, University of Alabama, Birmingham; Frances E. Dolan, University of California, Davis; Julia Reinhard Lupton, University of California, Irvine; Steven Mullaney, University of Michigan; William H. Sherman, University of York; Ian Smith, Lafayette College; and Daniel Vitkus, Florida State University.

Thanks also to the Bedford/St. Martin's staff, especially to Emily Berleth for bringing the production together, to Linda DeMasi of DeMasi Design and Publishing, and to freelance editors Janet Renard for conscientious copyediting and Jennifer Blanksteen for her heroic efforts in locating illustrations and securing permissions. Paul H. D. Kaplan and Scott Redford offered crucial help with the artwork, and Fred Wilson has my heartfelt thanks for allowing the use of his work in this volume.

Over the years a number of students researched, transcribed, and collaborated with me on this edition: Soyica Diggs, Luis Ramos, Regina McAloney, Lauren Puccio, Andrew Tumminia, and Melissa Whalen. I am indebted to Heather Blatt for her translations, her eye for detail, and her organizational skills. Colleagues from both Georgetown and Fordham University have been very generous with advice and encouragement. The Sister Scholars of New York are a constant source of wisdom and insight: Jennifer L. Morgan and Farah Jasmine Griffin in particular offered vital assistance.

Work on this volume proceeded during several major personal and professional transitions, and I thank the many friends and colleagues who helped me sort out knotty issues with both. To name all of the individuals who offered encouragement, support, and suggestions would take a volume in itself, but special thanks go to Patricia Akhimie, Denise Albanese, John Michael Archer, Frank Boyle, Jennifer deVere Brody, Yvette Christiansë, Lila Coleburn, Anne Cubilie, Pamela A. Fox, Christopher Gogwilt, Lalitha Gopalan, Susan Greenfield, Margo Hendricks, Sharon Holland, Stephen Hopkins, M. Lindsay Kaplan, Arthur Little, Joyce Green MacDonald, Fawzia Mustapha, Nicola Pitchford, Phyllis Rackin, Michael Ragussis, Constance M. Razza, Francesca Royster, Bruce Smith, Ian Smith, Christine So, Ayana Thompson, and Irma Watkins-Owen. The staffs of the Folger Shakespeare Library (particularly Luellen DeHaven, Rachel Doggett, Bettina Smith, Betsy Walsh, and Georgiana Ziegler), the Newberry Library, and the Warburg Institute offered vital support. I would also like to thank my first Shakespeare teacher, Mr. Vernon Rey, and my students.

Also too numerous to list, my family — particularly my parents, Lawrence and Vera Hall — and what my grandmother used to call our "family connections" have been an enduring source of inspiration and support for me even when they don't quite know why I spend so much time in the library. Sadly, my work on this volume coincided with the deaths of several family members and friends, some of whom I would like to remember here: Carolyn Bowen, Freddie Bowen Jr., David Kadlec, James Slevin, Annie Bell Smith, and VanDyke Smith.

This edition is dedicated to the memory of my beloved aunt, Ada Burnell Cole, an Emilia who would have spoken up immediately.

Kim F. Hall
Fordham University

# Contents

><

## → *2. Cultural Geography* 228

# Illustrations

————————————————>‹————————————————

# *Othello, the Moor of Venice*

## Texts and Contexts

# Introduction

><

>'Tis a pageant
>To keep us in false gaze. (1.3.20–21)

*Othello* might just be Shakespeare's most agonizing play. Viewers and editors insist that the play, especially its final scene, is somehow unbearable, yet they clearly cannot look away from the unfolding tragedy. Of the play's ending, influential Shakespeare editor H. H. Furness writes, "I do not shrink from saying that I wish this tragedy had never been written" (300 n80). Director Margaret Webster recalls hearing a girl in the audience of a 1943 performance whispering, "Oh God, don't let him kill her . . . don't let him kill her" (115). It is one of *Othello*'s peculiar ironies that a play so dependent on the spectacle of its hero's blackness and on various forms of "seeing" has proved so unbearable for its audience to watch. The often excruciating dilemmas of the characters are made all the more painful because what each character — and the audience — sees is so obviously driven by powerful cultural commonplaces, by stories about love, sexuality, race, and gender. The play tantalizes the audience with the possibility that the characters might transcend these shaping conceptions even as it recirculates them in various forms. Characters generate narratives both to explain themselves and to influence others' actions and reactions. These narratives prove peculiarly effective, provoking readers to ask along with critic Stephen Greenblatt, "Why does anyone submit to another's narrative at all?" (*Renaissance* 237).

The specter of the known haunts *Othello*: each character both articulates and resists cultural norms and commonplaces. Othello steps onto the stage and into a world of discourse; when he enters in 1.2, the audience already knows tales of "the Moor," not only from characters onstage but also from cultural beliefs. So, too, Desdemona is subject to powerful cultural beliefs about the nature of women. Iago, the model of dangerous eloquence, is the character who most frequently rehearses the "common sense" of the culture (Stallybrass 139; see also Omi and Winant 59). However, Iago is just the most obvious voice of these beliefs. The story of Othello and Desdemona draws upon many other narratives that early modern culture told itself — and that contemporary culture brings to its readings of the play. *Othello* not only simultaneously articulates and resists the cultural commonplaces and norms of its own time but actually helps create the "common sense" of race in the Western world. Every time we read or see *Othello*, we must ask what stories we bring to the experience, what histories and beliefs shape our responses to the play. This edition explores the "common sense" of early modern life. Each section includes documents that comment on what early modern readers and audiences might have thought about race and place (cultural geography), marriage and the household, masculinity and military life, and the passions. This introduction provides an overview of these issues and discusses changing responses to the play over time.

## Stories of Race and Place

The English nobility and foreign dignitaries arriving at King James I's Whitehall Palace on November 1, 1604, to see the Shakespeare's company recently renamed King's Men (formerly the Chamberlain's Men) perform a new tragedy would have already known the story of the ill-fated marriage between the noble-born Venetian Disdemona[1] and her Moorish husband. A version had been told years earlier in a widely read collection of stories known as Cinthio's *Hecatommithi*. This edition begins with Cinthio's tale of an ensign that falls in love with his commander's wife, Disdemona, and schemes to separate her from her unnamed Moorish husband. While reading this version, you might want to consider how Shakespeare makes his

---

[1] Shakespeare spells out the wife's name slightly differently than Cinthio. See the headnote on Cinthio, p. 31.

audience rethink what they knew of Cinthio's tale of sexual jealousy and misalliance.

The full title of Shakespeare's play is *The Tragedy of Othello, the Moor of Venice*, and the opening dialogue refers to the main character not as Othello but (as in Cinthio) "the Moor." Although the play offers a range of roles for Othello — wooer, soldier, and husband — other characters most frequently identify him as a "Moor." The meaning of *Moor* and, consequently, the nature of Othello's color and race have been the subjects of lively dispute since the eighteenth century. Bringing a Moor to the early modern stage was hardly novel; many stories circulated about Moors during Shakespeare's time, and the play takes advantage of a complicated — and contradictory — web of associations with the term. Although earlier critics spent a great deal of time trying to pin down Othello's precise racial and ethnic origins, contemporary critics generally understand *Moor* as an extremely malleable term used to mark geographic and religious differences (see Bartels, "*Othello* and Africa" 61–62; Barthelemy, *Black Face* 5–12; D'Amico, *Moor*; Neill, *Putting History* 269–74; Vaughan 56–58). While sharing the common connotations of "alien" or "foreigner," the word "can mean . . . non-black Muslim, black Christian, or black Muslim" (Barthelemy, *Black Face* 7). In all of its permutations, however, the word *Moor* represents Christian Europe's most profound "other," almost always "imagined in terms of polluting sexual contacts with European others" (Gillies 25). Just as the play draws upon ambivalent cultural attitudes toward Moors, the cultures marked by the term could be "admired and reviled at almost the same time" (D'Amico, *Moor* 4). Often the geographic, cultural, and political resonances of a specific image of a racial other can be discerned by paying close attention to language and context, but the word *Moor* is tied up in so many cultural threads that this is not always possible.

Despite the overall ambiguity of *Moor*, one can safely say that in the long tradition of (usually male) Moors on the English stage, the Moor is most frequently and profoundly connected to Islam (the religion most feared by Christian Europe) and to Christian conceptions of blackness.[2] These links were so intertwined that a Moor not associated with either would have to deny any relationship with his literary brethren (Barthelemy, *Black Face* 17). Othello is clearly drawn from multiple traditions, a "stranger / Of here and everywhere" (1.1.137–38). He is "a hybrid who might be associated, in the minds of Shakespeare's audience, with a whole set of related terms — *Moor,*

---

[2] Unfortunately, there is no comparably rich tradition of female stage Moors. For some discussion of female Moors, see Andrea, "Black Skin"; Barthelemy, *Black Face*; Boose, "Getting"; K. Hall, "Guess" and "Object"; MacDonald, *Women*.

*Turk, Ottomite, Saracen, Mahometan, Egyptian, Judean, Indian* — all constructed in opposition to Christian faith and virtue" (Vitkus, *Turning Turk* 90). Allied with the problem of definition is the question of how many early moderns would have actually seen an African or anyone else they considered a Moor. Although for many reasons, this question defies a definitive answer, no longer can one confidently assert that inhabitants of early modern Europe experienced Muslims, Arabs, or Africans only through books (Lester; Said). Recent scholarship bolsters Nabil Matar's argument that "throughout the Elizabethan and Stuart periods Britons had extensive interaction with Turks and Moors" (17). For example, the 1600 visit of a Moroccan ambassador with his entourage occasioned many comments in London, some describing the visitors using many of the same terms found in *Othello* (Harris). Besides such official encounters, both Londoners and other English who were increasingly traveling abroad would have had multiple contacts with strangers. Levantine (countries that border the Eastern Mediterranean) and Atlantic networks of commerce and trade, Mediterranean piracy, and other forms of exchange created classes of people who were, as historian Ira Berlin notes, truly cosmopolitan, and who had extensive contacts with inhabitants from a range of countries and nations in port cities, urban centers, ships and trade routes (Berlin 17; see also Matar 44–82).

Like Othello, blacks in England were already associated with a number of stories about themselves told by others. Anthony Barthelemy notes that actual encounters were profoundly shaped by the literary and popular traditions that preceded them, while Ruth Cowhig argues for a more "schizophrenic" reaction: "the everyday Londoner would have two conflicting views of blacks, one of their savagery out of travel books and from the stage and the other of their basic humanity as fellow citizens in the streets" ("Blacks" 7). Scholars are thus unclear about how actual English experience of black and brown peoples in England influenced their depictions on stage.

Debates about the precise identity of Moors have largely been superseded by larger questions about the significance of race to the play. Some argue that, as a Moor, Othello was not considered "black" in a modern sense and thus that the play is not about race in ways familiar to modern audiences; others argue that "race" as a concept only took hold in the West in the eighteenth century and that it is thus anachronistic to place *Othello* in this framework. Still others, declining to comment on the viability of race as a concept, produce readings that make race secondary to the play's interest in jealousy and marriage. This volume holds not only that *Othello* is about race but also that it has helped question and define race and interracial desire for centuries. The play's central role in Western representations of interracial desire is one of the reasons that it feels familiar and modern to contemporary audiences even though, as we shall see, very different conceptions of race coexisted in the period. This edition attempts the high-wire act of holding on to the modern notions of race we bring to the play while at the same time pointing to the many ways in which race looked different to *Othello*'s early modern audience.

What does it mean to say that the play is about race? In the early modern period, the word *race* referred not to the linking of character with physical appearance, but to family and lineage (Hendricks 183–85; Liu 565). These meanings indicate that early modern notions of race, like modern ones, were at heart driven by questions of affinity and community. Even for early moderns, however, race was not simply about biological difference or distrust of outsiders. For both early modern and contemporary thinkers, "race-thinking" is an exclusionary logic that narrows and contains difference in ways that legitimate a person's own cultural norms. Rather than simply expressing individual prejudice (which it can do), race-thinking legitimates the unequal distribution of resources, sets political priorities, and understands communities as always in opposition with each other (S. Hall, "Subjects"). The many facets of early modern notions of race mean that, when examining race in the play and the documents that follow, it is fruitful to think beyond notions of color or physiognomy; rather, consider that race may include religion, geography, family, nationality, body shape and adornment, speech, sexuality, and habits of consumption. In other words, go beyond noting the racism that various characters (or Shakespeare himself) exhibit toward Othello and examine more broadly the ways in which the text evinces race-thinking: How are ideas of human difference used to solidify or naturalize structures of power, hierarchy, and social order? How does the language of race overlap and transform languages of sexuality and gender?

The logic of race-thinking is primarily constituted by and revealed through language. For example, the play presents Othello and Desdemona within a charged linguistic opposition of black and white that is both racial and moral. Othello's lament in Act 3 — "Her name, that was as fresh / As Dian's visage, is now begrimed and black / As mine own face" (3.3.403–5) — equates his loss of reputation (and, allegedly, his wife's virtue) with his own dark face, a move that relies on an idea of blackness as a mark of inferiority and sin. Feminist critic Michelle Wallace argues that the "unrelenting logic of dualism, or polar opposition — such as black and white, good and evil, male and female — is basic to the discourse of the dominant culture" (60) and fundamental to a culture's more negative thinking about race and gender. During the Renaissance, the rhetoric of black and white became a key language used by the English to articulate new relationships to physical and cultural differences. A constellation of beliefs drawn from the Bible, medical tradition, aphorism, visual arts, and ethnography came together to create an early modern language of race, one that gave the English a specifically hierarchical way of understanding their culture's relation to the world. Within this black/white division, the words *black* and *white* (or *fair*) refer not just to a moral state but also to cultural or physical differences. Shakespeare continually plays with this dichotomy, forcing splits, ruptures, and reconceptualizations of the black/white division, demanding that the audience contend with its seemingly inexorable logic (Parker 95). The Duke consoles Brabantio about the loss of his daughter using just such wordplay: "If virtue no delighted beauty lack / your son-in-law is far more fair than black" (1.3.291–92). At such moments, a reader must consider both the obvious forms of the opposition ("more fair than black") and the subtler (for example, the color symbolism in the more curious line "If virtue no delighted beauty lack"). While *delighted* certainly means "delightful" (as modern editors contend), it might also have a secondary meaning of "delighted" or darkened, making both lines suggest the collapse of dark/light divisions. Dark/light imagery is also important in many illustrations of the play such as the engraving by Henry Singleton (Figure 1). Readers might wish to consider other occasions when black/white imagery speaks to the play's emphasis on "belonging and estrangement" (Neill, *Putting History* 207). Attention to this rhetorical opposition then forces other questions about dark/light imagery. How does the language of "fair" shape conceptions of Desdemona and femininity? (See Loomba, "Sexuality"; Neely; Newman.) Is it possible that the repeated calls for "light" in the play do more than amplify stage directions for an indoor theater?

A language of conversion animates much of the race-thinking in the play. *Othello* is a drama of transformation that strikes at the heart of early modern concerns about the nature and stability of the self. Othello is not meant to be associated with any single racializing or religious category; he is rather a prism in reverse, concentrating a spectrum of narratives about Moors, Turks, Africans, and possibly Indians into a single figure. Clearly the most striking transformation or conversion is Othello's change from noble Christian (already converted) to "circumcisèd dog" (5.2.365), also spoken of as "turning Turk"; however, *Othello* "exhibits a conflation of various images of conversion — transformations from Christian to Turk, from virgin to whore, from good to evil, and from gracious virtue to black damnation" (Vitkus, *Turning* 78). Conversion speaks to anxieties over the mutability of identity — the ability of the self to become radically "other," indeed the other that is most feared — and suspicion of the convert is rife in Renaissance texts. Critic Michael Neill reminds readers that it is Othello's very indeterminacy that renders him troubling (*Putting* 272); however, Othello's

FIGURE 1 *Engraving of Act 5.2, by Henry Singleton (1839?). The many illustrations of* Othello *take pains to emphasize the black/white contrast running through the play. Typically these illustrations focus on the murder and place sources of light (lamps, candles, etc.) near Desdemona, creating an idealized, almost divine innocence. In some images, like the Wright/Engleheart engraving (p. 17), it looks almost as if she has a halo. The nineteenth-century audiences' desire for a divinely innocent Desdemona was often at odds with the at times assertive and frank woman of Shakespeare's play. Performances often cut scenes that showed these qualities, making the heroine much more passive than in the original.*

"conversion" is only the most obvious focus of the play's larger concerns with the possibility of sudden and dangerous transformation.

To speak of race in *Othello* is also to speak of cultural geography, or place. In addition to denoting religion, the terms *Turk* and *Moor* were associated

## INDIAN / JUDEAN?

At what may be the play's most dramatic moment, Othello's suicide, Othello refers to himself as "one whose hand, / Like the base Indian, threw a pearl away / Richer than all his tribe (5.2.356–58). At least that's what he says in the Quarto (Q1), published in 1622. In the first collection of Shakespeare's works, known as the First Folio (F), published in 1623, Othello compares himself to "the base *Judean.*" This is but one of many differences between the two earliest printed texts of *Othello.* Not published for a good twenty years after its first performance, *Othello* has a vexing history in print: Q1 and F were published within a year of each other, and scholars have long puzzled over the significant discrepancies between the two. Q1 has more complete stage directions and contains more than fifty oaths not seen in F, whereas F is longer than Q1 by some 160 lines. There are well over a thousand differences between the two texts; while many are minor discrepancies, others produce differences in characterization and language.

Previous generations of textual scholars attempted to find one authoritative version that most accurately represented their sense of "Shakespeare"; more recent criticism has come to see *Othello* as a "multiple-text play." Rather than trying to judge the accuracy of a single text over others, these editors suggest that each text has something to teach us about theatrical and reading practices. Scott McMillin reminds readers that "all successful Elizabethan plays existed in multiple scripts over their lifetimes" (41; see also Sanders) and suggests that Q1's unusual features may reflect the actors' interpretations of their roles. Leah Marcus has argued that Q1 and F contain very different constructions of race and female virtue. In her view, F ratchets up the racial conflict by "deliberately intensi[fying] what looks from our modern perspective like racist elements in the play" (23). Additionally, Thomas Berger makes a case for special attention to yet another text, the second Quarto (Q2), in which the editor has combined features of F and Q1, creating what is known as a composite text, arguing that this editor's work offers insight into early modern processes of revision and textuality.

Most editors choose Q1's "Indian," suggesting that "Judean" is an error introduced during the process of typesetting and arguing that "Indian" refers to travel accounts that insist that foreign others, particularly Africans and Indians, did not know how to value precious goods (or at least those precious to Europeans). So, too, the proverbial saying "Black men are pearls in women's eyes" links black men, pearls, and desire. Fewer advocate for F's "Judean," which may allude to the biblical Herod, who in a jealous rage has his "jewel of a wife" killed, or to Judas Iscariot's rejection of Christ. "Judean" also resonates thematically with the later line "circumcisèd dog" (5.2.365; see Honigmann 342–43; Sohmer 234–37). Natasha Korda has suggested that both readings rely on an alleged inability to assess value (see an example of this in

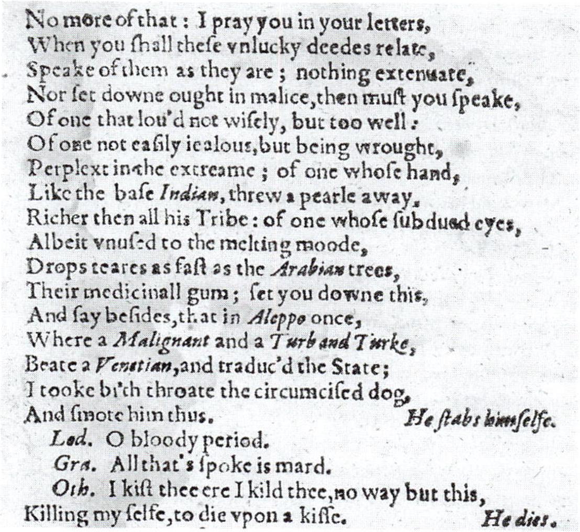

No more of that : I pray you in your letters,
When you shall these vnlucky deedes relate,
Speake of them as they are ; nothing extenuate,
Nor set downe ought in malice, then must you speake,
Of one that lou'd not wisely, but too well :
Of one not easily iealous, but being wrought,
Perplext in the extreame ; of one whose hand,
Like the base *Indian*, threw a pearle away,
Richer then all his Tribe : of one whose subdued eyes,
Albeit vnusd to the melting moode,
Drops teares as fast as the *Arabian* trees,
Their medicinall gum ; set you downe this,
And say besides, that in *Aleppo* once,
Where a *Malignant* and a *Turb and Turke*,
Beate a *Venetian*, and traduc'd the State ;
I tooke b'th throate the circumcised dog,
And smote him thus.                               *He stabs himselfe.*
    *Lod.* O bloody period.
    *Gra.* All that's spoke is mard.
    *Oth.* I kist thee ere I kild thee, no way but this,
Killing my selfe, to die vpon a kisse.            *He dies.*

FIGURE 2   *Quarto* Othello *(Q1) 5.2 (1622)*

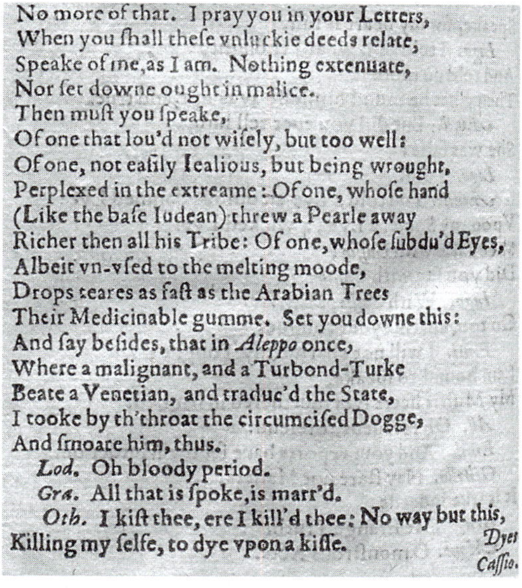

No more of that. I pray you in your Letters,
When you shall these vnluckie deeds relate,
Speake of me, as I am. Nothing extenuate,
Nor set downe ought in malice.
Then must you speake,
Of one that lou'd not wisely, but too well :
Of one, not easily Iealious, but being wrought,
Perplexed in the extreame : Of one, whose hand
(Like the base Iudean) threw a Pearle away
Richer then all his Tribe : Of one, whose subdu'd Eyes,
Albeit vn-vsed to the melting moode,
Drops teares as fast as the Arabian Trees
Their Medicinable gumme. Set you downe this :
And say besides, that in *Aleppo* once,
Where a malignant, and a Turbond-Turke
Beate a Venetian, and traduc'd the State,
I tooke by th'throat the circumcised Dogge,
And smoate him, thus.
    *Lod.* Oh bloody period.
    *Gra.* All that is spoke, is marr'd.
    *Oth.* I kist thee, ere I kill'd thee : No way but this,
Killing my selfe, to dye vpon a kisse.        *Dyes*
                                              *Cassio.*

FIGURE 3   *Folio* Othello *(F) 5.2 (1623)*

---

**INDIAN / JUDEAN?** (continued)

the reading from Peter Martyr, Chapter 2), a conceptualization that may be a distinguishing feature of the racial other in the period (113). Even while accepting "base Indian" as the authoritative line, a reader might use the discrepancy to think about the easy transferability of racializing images between groups (see Andreas, "Curse"; Matar 83–107). Thus, *Othello*'s ending might draw simultaneously from multiple layers of race-thinking about Moors, Turks, Indians, and Jews.

---

with far-off locales that were often centers of what the English called *traffic*; trade, navigation, and/or pilgrimage brought together an international cast of peoples in urban centers across Europe and the Middle East. *Othello*'s final vivid image of violent ethnic conflict set in locales far from Jacobean London ("say besides that in Aleppo once, / Where a malignant and turbaned Turk / Beat a Venetian and traduced the state" [5.2.362–64]) draws its dramatic force from the audience's long-standing fascination with stories from exotic places as well the ongoing fear of and fascination with the threat of Islam and the Ottoman empire in the Mediterranean. Although performed at court and in London playhouses, *Othello* takes the Mediterranean world as its larger stage, and place becomes as important as character in understanding the play's conflicts. Indeed, a reader might pay careful attention to how location and character mimic each other. Why, for example, identify Cassio as a Florentine or tell the story of a maid named Barbary at a crucial moment of dramatic tension?

Like people, objects travel, generating histories that reshape one's sense of what they are and often giving impressions of different cultures. Trade, the driving force of most early modern travel, relies on the exchange of goods; indeed, objects like Othello's handkerchief traveled with as much (or more) frequency as people. From the first decades of trade with Africa, Portuguese travelers brought home not just raw goods but also items shaped by African craftsmen (Mark, *Africans*). In early modern England, such traveling objects bore the weight of what Europeans thought they knew about the "other." They represented cultural differences, understood through the lens of European culture. However, the compelling wonder of these objects also warned against greed and possessiveness. Objects such as maps and luxurious cloth were beginning to fill elite homes and may have made their way onto the stage (Boose, "Othello's Handkerchief"; Harris and Korda 1–31; Sofer, *Stage*). Andrew Sofer reminds readers that props are objects in

## THE OTTOMAN EMPIRE IN EARLY MODERN EUROPE

Othello's vision of his suicide as a "turbaned Turk" who beats a Venetian spoke vividly to early modern fears of Islamic control. The Ottoman empire was the largest empire in Europe, with military and political structures that posed a profound threat to Christian Europe. A modern map (Figure 4) shows the extent of the Ottoman empire in the early seventeenth century. According to Fernand Braudel, "that empire covered a good half of the Mediterranean region; it was an anti-Christendom, balancing the weight of the West" (13). Not only did "Turks" control significant parts of the Mediterranean coast, but the Mediterranean waters were filled with both Ottoman naval vessels and pirate ships that attacked European vessels, taking hostages or slaves. Even though England is much farther north, seafarers reported heated battles off the English coast (see Chapter 4, p. 313). As the closest major European city to the empire, and the imperial governor of lands such as Cyprus that were in the heart of Ottoman territory, Venice had particular strategic importance. Notice how the western edges of the Ottoman empire almost surround the Italian peninsula.

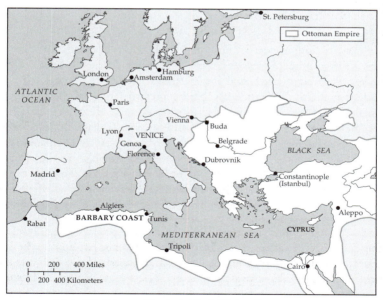

FIGURE 4  *Map of the Ottoman Empire in Early Modern Europe*

motion, manipulated by actors and having many lives (*Stage*, 11–29). Objects become important carriers of stories told onstage. They not only help actors tell stories but "speak" (Teague) of travels and memory and point our attention to alternative histories and unnoticed relationships.

The linen of *Othello*'s handkerchief is woven into the play's concerns with cultural difference, sexuality, and mutual obligation. It vexes because it seems to carry so much weight and so many stories. Initially a simple love token (in Cinthio, it is a "handkerchief embroidered most delicately [or curiously] in the Moorish fashion" [p. 37]),[3] it becomes both more and less familiar as the play progresses. It is embroidered with strawberries, a very popular English motif (Boose, "Othello's Handkerchief"; Frye; Ross), but its meanings accumulate with its movement on the stage, becoming a chief sign of Othello's difference and possibly undermining his protestations in 1.3 that he used no witchcraft in attaining Desdemona's love:

> That handkerchief
> Did an Egyptian to my mother give.
> She was a charmer, and could almost read
> The thoughts of people. She told her, while she kept it
> 'Twould make her amiable, and subdue my father
> Entirely to her love.   (3.4.51–56)

Critics propose many possible meanings for the handkerchief: discussions often cast its significance within a conflict between domestic and foreign codes. While Othello's account of its origin associates the handkerchief with exotic foreignness, sexual intrigue, and witchcraft, more local connotations make the embroidered object represent female virginity (Boose, "Othello's Handkerchief"), female sexuality (Boose, "Othello's Handkerchief; Newman), women's textile arts and agency (Callaghan, "Looking"; Frye), the disciplining forces of civility (Stallybrass), female companionship (Sofer, "Felt Absences"), and England's fetishized trade in textiles (Yachnin). Searching for one "true" meaning or locating the handkerchief in one realm at the expense of others, however, undermines the productive oscillation of meaning in the play and reaffirms the sense of Othello's absolute difference from the Venetians.

For example, although witchcraft in Othello's account is orientalized, which is to say that it is made part of a Western mythology of an exotic, sensuous, and mysterious East, one might also remember that early moderns shared with many seventeenth-century African cultures a profound belief in

---

[3] For the implications of the different translations of the Cinthio's description, see Korda 124–25.

witchcraft (Mark, *Africans* 23; Mafe 54–57; Orlin, *Private Matters* 207–15). Indeed, King James I was known for his fear of the supernatural. Likewise, Europeans and many African cultures shared a patriarchal interest in controlling women's sexuality. Othello's inconsistent accounts of the handkerchief's origins: that it was either "an antique token / My father gave my mother" (5.2.223–24) as a sign of love, or that it was given to his mother by an Egyptian "charmer" who "could almost read / The thoughts of people" (3.4.53–54), also seem to combine fear of uncontrolled female sexuality and witchcraft. Rather than being either foreign or domestic, "the associative threads used to describe the handkerchief . . . would seem to pull in two directions: one toward the familiar and domestic, the other toward the exoticizing and strange" (Korda 125). Thus, the handkerchief should be a potent reminder for readers of how unstable the differences were that Englishmen drew between themselves and others. Like significant words in the play, the handkerchief moves within a wide circuit of meaning. Among the difficult questions readers might ask concerning this object are: What is the effect of having two stories about the handkerchief's origins? How do the accounts of its origins differ, and who are the original owners in each? How does each character interact with the handkerchief? How does the handkerchief connect or stand in for specific characters? Desdemona laments that she would have sooner lost her "purse / Full of crusadoes" (3.4.19–20) — with what other things (tangible and intangible) is the handkerchief compared? How are Thomas Rymer and Paula Vogel's responses to the play (given in Chapter 6) shaped by their view of the handkerchief's importance?

## Stories of Marriage and the Household

Mary Beth Rose argues, "The Elizabethan and Jacobean periods witnessed major transformations in the social construction of gender, the conceptualization of the position of woman, and the ideology of the family" (2; see also Callaghan, *Romeo and Juliet* 15–27; Howell; Stone). In opposition to a Catholic view that celibacy was the highest good for both sexes, Protestant authorities advocated conjugal or married love over celibacy and began to focus on the married couple as an independent unit. In theory this new emphasis on married love valued the individual's choice of a mate more highly; thus, it strained the authority of parents over children and provoked lively conversation about the powers of parents versus the wishes of their marriageable children. So, too, ideologies of married love led to new articulations of the woman's role in marriage. While marriage and the place of women are defined in many spheres — the church, the legal system, and the state as well as custom — the stories that circulate about "Woman" — that she is lecherous, untrustworthy, and inherently unfaithful — can seem depressingly similar across all realms. These are the stories that come to blind Othello to Desdemona's clear innocence and that force Emilia into initial complicity with Iago's betrayal. They are also the stories that early modern women increasingly resisted, particularly the newly literate women of the age.

Just as possession of the handkerchief accelerates the play's action, possession of women and their honor, "an essence that's not seen" (4.1.16), shapes its gender relations. Desdemona begins the public defense of her marriage by reminding Brabantio of her "divided duty" (1.3.183) and the necessarily shifting allegiances of women. Her prompt "I am hitherto your daughter. But here's my husband" (1.3.187) concisely encapsulates the early modern woman's primary roles and an ideal of orderly movement from one household to the next. A woman was primarily defined by her status within the household as a wife, mother, daughter, or servant. Her transition in status was in effect a realignment of loyalties and obedience, and readers should note carefully what the characters, particularly the women, say about female obedience. Scholars debate whether women's subservience within the family allowed for much freedom in choosing marriage partners; nonetheless, women and their families had common aims for marriage: social prestige, economic security, children, and companionship. When Iago mentions Desdemona's past rejection of men of similar "clime, complexion, and degree" (3.3.247), he taps into the audience's sense that marriage partners should match in material and immaterial ways. Historian Olwen Hulfton concludes, "For both sexes, the goal was not merely marriage, but the right marriage, joining the worthy couple in a 'fitting match,' an instructive concept in which appropriateness was the criterion" (65). An appropriate marriage paired people not simply by age, social status, and religion but also by temperament and moral qualities. Unhappiness as well as disorder within and without the home would result from inappropriate matches, warned the (mostly male) commentators on marriage. It is useful to note, within the play, how characters view the many differences between Othello and Desdemona. Patriarchal marriages create bonds between men as well as affirm male possession of women's sexuality, but *Othello* troubles this pattern: the marriage in fact destroys Othello's connection to Brabantio, and Othello is never sure of his "possession" of Desdemona. What role does Othello's Moorishness play in this disruption?

From its opening the play interlaces its depictions of love and household affairs with foreign danger. An early modern audience would have been well aware of the correspondence between Othello's alleged infiltration of Brabantio's household and purported threats to Venetian holdings in the Mediterranean. The image of Venice under siege by demonic others parallels the early modern perception that marriage was meant to protect a couple from the devil's constant attacks, an onslaught of evil that the *Homily on Matrimony* (read at every marriage ceremony in England) calls "the dangers of the troublous sea of the world" (Klein 24). Most early modern commentators are emphatic that prayer and domestic tranquillity are the only means of guarding against a world beset by sin and against the emotions that can potentially engulf everyone. Unfortunately, women were often seen as more susceptible to temptation and therefore as the source of danger in the marriage. Ania Loomba notes that "Jacobean drama implicitly connected female disobedience with a degenerate social order" ("Sexuality" 163) During the sixteenth and seventeenth centuries marital sex came to be seen more positively (Wiesner 58); still, women's sexuality was viewed with suspicion. From the tavern to the church, the dangers of women's excessive sexuality and the need for male control of his own (as well as his wife's) passions would have been central to discussions of marriage. So, too, issues of female "propriety" and property come together in male fears about possession of women, a fear that gnaws at Othello, who bemoans the inability of marriage to secure a wife's affections: "Oh, curse of marriage, / That we can call these delicate creatures ours / And not their appetites!" (3.3.285–87). Consider how often the play's language links sexuality with chaos or disorder. Bianca raises other questions regarding female sexuality and independence. How do other characters react to her possession (and commodification) of her own sexuality?

The binding of women's "chaste" speech with their sexual behavior is central to the gendered meanings of honor and honesty in *Othello*. While the word *honest* for a man refers almost entirely to his truthfulness, a woman's honor rests almost entirely on "chastity" of body, mind, and mouth; *honesty* for her refers just as often to chastity as to veracity (Muldrew, "'Mutual Assent'" 53). Laura Gowing points to the gendered meanings of honor, arguing, "In association with ideas of morals, of reputation, and of credit, it was a powerful tool in the daily negotiation of gender relations" (113). The combined domestic and military worlds in the play force the gendered meanings of concepts like "honor," "credit," and "reputation" into powerful collision. It is a chain of associations that Othello cannot break; he is forced to choose between Iago's "honesty" and Desdemona's: "I think my wife be honest and think she is not; / I think that thou art just and think thou art not" (3.3.401–2). Peter Stallybrass notes the relation between speech, sexuality, and acting in public: "Silence, the closed mouth, is made a sign of chastity. And silence and chastity are, in turn, homologous to women's enclosure in the house" (127). Nonetheless, all of the women in *Othello* are compelled to speak out in public — often against male authority. How then does the play interpret Desdemona's eloquent and frank avowals of love as well as the speech of other women in the play? How does Othello's choice to strangle Desdemona on her marriage bed comment on ideals of chaste speech?

Cuckoldry and sexual jealousy were continual subjects of jest for early moderns. Onstage these topics primarily inhabit the world of comedy, which by definition concerns itself with obstacles to the marriage of young lovers. Indeed, several critics note that, like *Romeo and Juliet*, *Othello* structurally begins as a comedy and turns into a tragedy (Comensoli; Snyder, *Comic Matrix*). Just as in comedy, a young couple marries (or desires to marry) against the father's wishes. Brabantio, the *senex* or blocking father, and Roderigo, the comic dupe, are figures imported from classical comedy. Such generic hybridity, along with the focus on sexuality, has kept many critics from ranking the play as highly as "purer" tragedies like *Hamlet* and *King Lear*. However, rather than seeing the single-minded exploration of jealously and adultery as evidence of Shakespeare's faulty stagecraft, one might use such evaluations to think about how classic definitions of genre might fail to accommodate important groups and concerns. For example, the idea that tragedy focuses on the fall of nobles and princes (usually male) might lead to the conclusion that narratives of women, of people of color, and of lower classes cannot evoke the requisite terror and pity in an audience.

*Othello*'s concerns align it quite closely with the emerging genre of domestic tragedy (Helgerson; Lieblein; Orlin, *Private Matters* 246–50). Unlike traditional tragedy, in which a combination of personal flaws and fatal circumstance brings about the fall of a noble man or prince, domestic tragedy focuses on the destruction of households and domestic spaces, often among the gentry or the middling sort.

Although marriage primarily marked an individual's public entry into the community — and elite couples in particular lived their married lives under the scrutiny of others — the ongoing early modern debates over the nature of love and marriage coincided with an increase in private space within the household (Fumerton; Orlin, *Private Matters*; Ziegler). These social changes form the basis for the interweaving of public and private in *Othello*. Most of *Othello* takes place in highly public spaces, with an audience onstage as well as off, which means that the few moments of "privacy" or intimacy (real or imagined) increase in significance. The couple's most intimate onstage moment is Desdemona's murder. Indeed, the murder can be seen as a perversion of marriage. The first time the audience sees the marriage bed, there is death instead of a consummation. Instead of a public affirmation of community, the community witnesses the horror of Desdemona's death and Othello's ultimate alienation from Venetian society.

Desdemona's death makes clear that the marriage bed is the site of early modern fears of pollution by miscegenation, female sexuality, and unbridled emotions. Critic Valerie Traub notes that only in death can Othello safely see Desdemona as a sexual being, "after she is permanently immobilized and sacramentally elevated" (131). Michael Neill argues that "the spectacle of the violated marriage bed" dominated the first illustrations of *Othello*. Artworks like the Singleton engraving seen earlier (Figure 1) and the John Massey Wright/Timothy Stansfield Engleheart engraving in Figure 5 foregrounded "not merely the perverse exoticism of the scene, but its aspect of forbidden disclosure" (Neill, *Putting History* 238, 40). The bedchamber is also the only

FIGURE 5 *In this John Massey Wright/Timothy Stansfield Engleheart engraving of Act 5. 2, Emilia is literally closer to Desdemona than Othello is, and her dress suggests that she is already in mourning. What does this image of Desdemona's death suggest about the bonds between women?*

female space in a play dominated by masculine political and military settings. Andrew Sofer points out that Emilia's undressing of Desdemona "creates an extraordinary intimacy between the two women (even as it must have focused the audience's attention to the male body beneath the female apparel)" (*Stage Life* 22; see also Grennan). Readers might want to compare Desdemona's intimacy with Emilia with her relation to her husband. Although Iago charges Emilia to "get you home," the only home we see is Desdemona's and that only at her death.

Most domestic tragedies take place within the English household; unusually, Shakespeare places his domestic tragedy in Cyprus. Why move the marriage to Cyprus, the site of competing dangers (internal and external enemies) and loyalties (marriage and the military)? Interestingly, work on early modern women writers reveals close affinities between *Othello* and Elizabeth Cary's domestic tragedy, *The Tragedy of Mariam, the Fair Queen of Jewry*, which, although published in 1613, was probably written contemporaneously with *Othello* (see Ferguson and Weller 5–5, 41–47). This tale of the jealous prince Herod, who murders his innocent wife, Mariam, shares (and possibly influenced) *Othello*'s interest in race, marriage, and women's speech.

Servants play key roles in domestic tragedies — as they do in early modern households and in *Othello*. Iago's complaints about "service" in the play's opening alert the audience to the importance of subordinates and loyalty (Neill, "His Master's"). The fidelity required in relations of household service mirrors that required in marriage and the military; both spheres depend on expectations of loving obedience and both are undermined by worry that "underlings" will bond with each other against a master. In *Othello* these arenas often intersect, and servants are key avenues between them. For example, having lost his rank, Cassio desires that Emilia will "Procure [him] some access" (3.1.33) to Desdemona in order to obtain her help in restoring his place with Othello. Like *service*, *office* becomes a term that draws together military and marital order. A reader might note where the play articulates the responsibilities of masters and subordinates. How might one compare Iago and Emilia's relations of service?

## Masculinity and Military Life

Iago's complaint about the changing nature of military advancement that goes "not by old gradation, where each second / Stood heir to th' first" (1.1.38–39), echoes Thomas Lodge's sense of a vast change in early modern military life: "All things are changed. The means, the men and arms, / Our stratagems now differ from the old" (*A Fig for Momus* E1r). Changes in the "means, the men and arms" of war appear throughout *Othello*. The specificity of the play's depiction of military life — Iago's anger at being passed over for promotion, his disdain for Cassio's "bookish theoric," the drinking and brawling among the soldiers — would have been quite recognizable to the literate in the audience, some of whom might have been immersed in the vast outpouring of literature on military practice in the time. It also would have a familiar ring for the officers and soldiers in London who "were a common constituent of playhouses which themselves served in close proximity to the sites of London's musters of its citizen militia" (de Somogyi 6).

Iago's envy of Cassio springs from Cassio's very character, not just his promotion. Cassio is not only an arithmetician, he is a "proper man" (1.3.375) or a gentleman, both qualities that allowed new forms of mobility in military and social circles (Whigham 46–47). Cassio's use of *courtesy* ("'tis my breeding / That gives me this bold show of courtesy" [2.1.100–01]) both fatally differentiates him from Iago and locates him within a specific idea of the gentleman. The gentleman or courtier was considered to have exceptional gifts of wit, eloquence, manners, and learning: *courtesy*, the outward manifestation of these qualities, surfaces as a point of comparison or anxiety for both Othello and Iago. Iago reveals to the audience his envy of Cassio, who "hath a daily beauty in his life / That makes me ugly" (5.1.19–20). And, although Elizabethan writers began to argue that one could attain this ideal through education and rhetorical training rather than through birth (Whigham 2), Othello seems to suggest that his race excludes him from such advancement despite evidence of his high status: "Haply, for I am black / And have not those soft parts of conversation / That chamberers have" (3.3.280–82). The reader might consider why Shakespeare made Cassio a focal point of Othello's jealousy. What is Cassio's role in Othello's courtship of Desdemona? How would you compare Cassio's, Othello's, and Iago's treatment of women? What forms do courtesy and propriety take in the play? Obviously in an aural arena like the stage, the eloquence demanded of courtesy would draw attention. How do Shakespeare's characters view their own abilities to speak and persuade?

To Shakespeare's audience, Cassio's eloquence might have provoked perceptions of both Italian deceit (Whigham 176–78) and failed masculinity. Early modern writers frequently idealized the military as an ultimately masculine, antidomestic space, and we can see an opposition between the military and the domestic when Iago condemns Cassio as "A fellow almost damned in a fair wife, / That never set a squadron in the field / Nor the division of a battle knows / More than a spinster" (1.1.22–25). Although it is certainly a common misogynist or woman-hating tactic for men to denigrate other men by equating them with women, Iago's ridicule of Cassio through associations with women (implying that he is both uxorious ["damned in a fair wife"] and unworldly ["a spinster"]) indirectly reinforces the image of the military as a wholly masculine arena. Patricia Cahill notes that military texts "imagine the domain of the military as the site of idyllic homosociality, a site that is capable of being sexualized and in which men gain privileged access to the love of other men" (16).

However, even as the soldiers in the play rely on a masculine ideal, their language and the play itself continually show the correspondence and overlap of the hierarchies and emotional bonds in domestic life and in the military. What concepts or terms (e.g., *love* or *duty*) do you see used in both spheres? If the friendship between Desdemona and Emilia demonstrates the possibility of female intimacy across hierarchy within the household, Iago's account of Cassio's dream, albeit false, suggests that the military world relied on a fragile balance of intimacy and obedience. The image of Cassio kissing Iago and Iago's vow to obey Othello raise questions about the play's representation of bonds between men. What is the relation between male bonding and misogyny? What tensions are there between military and domestic life?

## "Floodgate and O'erbearing Nature": Passions

The military and marriage are social institutions dependent on the regulation of passion. Establishing order in relations among men is key in military texts, but self-control is equally important. Thus, the jealousy that so unhinges Othello threatens his command both in his household and over Cyprus. The passion that shakes his "very frame" (5.2.46) portends a greater collapse of social order. Although wrenching emotions are intrinsic to tragedy, *Othello* seems to exhibit more extremes of passion and to focus more on one single emotion than almost any other Shakespearean play. While it is tempting to read *Othello* as the story of a great love brought down by internal insecurity and outside subversion, at least some in the early modern audience might well have seen romantic love itself at the root of the problem. The idea of romantic love as a force that would conclude with a strong marriage would have been a relatively new concept in early modern Europe. Most of *Othello*'s audience would have seen romantic love as a passion leading to a dangerous loss of control.

*Othello*'s exploration of the extremes of feeling, often represented as overwhelming or monstrous, coincides with a burgeoning interest in emotions — most often referred to as the "passions" — and the self in the seventeenth century (Roach; Newbold 17–26). The modern word *emotion* derives from the Latin *emovere* ("to move out or stir up"); however, the word used in early modern England, *passions*, derives from the Latin *pati* ("to suffer"); this etymological association also captures the difference between the Renaissance response to the emotional world and our own (Roach 28). Passions were to be controlled lest they unleash their harm into the world. Almost every articulation of the passions in *Othello* and the contextual documents speaks to early modern fears that one might utterly lose oneself, degenerate into a monster of feeling. Intimations that emotions can be easily manipulated and, once so, are almost too powerful to overcome, are embedded in the play from Brabantio's accusation that Othello "Abused her [Desdemona's] delicate youth with drugs or minerals / That weakens motion" (1.2.75–76), to Emilia and Desdemona's discussion of Othello's jealousy in 3.4. That Othello imagines his change from moderate, noble soldier to jealous murderer as a conversion (or reconversion) to a "turbaned Turk" argues for the utterly transformative power of passion. What might be the link between the play's attention to "turning" as religious conversion (discussed in Chapter 1) and other metamorphoses wrought by the power of passion?

Passion's transformative power also makes theater perilous. Theater's main elements — acting, imagination, rhetoric, and eloquence — all had the capacity to transform both audience and actors, sometimes in dangerous ways. *Othello* is highly self-conscious about these elements, and it is instructive to pay particular attention to moments in which characters refer to language or performance. Iago is one of the most theatrical performers in Shakespeare's works; consequently, he often uses self-consciously rhetorical or theatrical language. For example, there are several references in the play to shows and signs, or symbols. What does Iago mean when he says, "I must show out a flag and sign of love, / Which is indeed but sign" (1.1.158–59)?

While the emotional state that leads Othello to murder is marked by physical change as well as by language, the evidence for Iago's motivations and emotions is entirely rhetorical; that is, he says that he is angry at being overlooked for promotion, jealous of Othello, and envious of Cassio, but are anger, jealousy, and envy really his motivating passions? Iago's singular ability to stir grand passions at times masks his own relationship to them. Iago is the only character who tells the audience directly what he is thinking and feeling, but what is his relationship to that audience? Can viewers trust the many stories Iago tells them after witnessing his ability to interpret actions for his own purposes? Critic Stephen Greenblatt sees Iago as an exemplar of a Renaissance quality of "improvisation": "the ability both to capitalize on the unforeseen and to transform given materials into one's own scenario" (*Renaissance* 227) in order to insinuate oneself into another's consciousness. Iago's "opportunistic grasp" of already established structures seems key to understanding his dramatic function; it also makes clearer why he is the character who mouths most of the stories Europe told itself about race and gender as well as most of the play's proverbial wisdom. However, Iago's ability to turn endlessly to narrative and use it for his own purposes also raises questions about his identity and its relationship to narrative and role-playing as revealed in deceptively plain lines like "I am not what I am" (1.1.67). What does it mean to say, "Were I the Moor I would not be Iago (1.1.59)? Are these merely statements of absolute difference, suggestions of a self divided, or images of a more existential emptiness, a self-cancellation? (See Greenblatt, *Renaissance* 235–37.) Is there a way to compare these statements of divided identity with Othello's final self-division in 5.2?

The play's investments in emotions and theatricality might also speak to the problem of "double-time" in *Othello*. The idea of double-time was developed to explain what Steve Sohmer calls the play's "abundant manifestations of shifty time" (216).[4] Scholars have long noted the play's inconsistent time references and some point out that the play's fast-paced movement scarcely allows time for actions that the audience might assume to have happened (such as the marriage's consummation) or actions that are referred to (Desdemona's adultery). Is it Othello's heightened emotion that makes him overlook the constraints of time?

## *Othello* over Time

From its first appearance on stage, *Othello* was remarkable for its ability to draw audiences into its almost unbearable pathos. In a rare early commentary from 1610, an Oxford spectator writes that the actors "drew tears not only by their speech, but also by their action. Indeed Desdemona, though always excellent, moved us especially in her death when, as she lay on her bed, her face itself implored the pity of the audience" (quoted in Rosenburg 5). Paradoxically, the play's very ability to move some spectators repulsed others: its roots in domestic tragedy, with its combination of quotidian household moments and heroic gestures, alternately moved and disturbed viewers. Othello's insistence on his own dignity tapped into a strain of audience unease with being made to feel profound empathy for a black man and the murderer of an innocent woman. Still other critics felt that *Othello* generated too much grandeur for a play on domestic violence. What

---

[4] For a detailed discussion of the double-time scheme, see Sohmer. For an equally detailed rebuttal, see Bradshaw. For an insightful view of critical concerns with the marriage's consummation, see Neill, *Putting*, chapter 9, esp. 249–50.

accounts for the "intensity of engagement" with this play (Pechter 12)? Why do some find it a "fundamentally intolerable experience" that is almost unbearable to sit through?

*Othello* appeals as much to the passions as to the mind and thus is seen at times as not measuring up to the poetic heights of Shakespeare's other major tragedies such as *Hamlet*. Almost uniquely among the major plays, performances of *Othello* rarely include actual reconfigurations of existing scenes. The script is frequently cut, however: Othello's "trance," his eaves-dropping on Iago and Cassio, Bianca's railings, and the Willow scene have at various times disappeared under concerns that they are "hateful" or "distasteful" and "not to be spoken." From the Restoration on, these deleted scenes reflect critical/theatrical anxieties over active women, passion, and race (see Pechter; Siemon). The play's frank depictions of sexuality (particularly female desire), comic interludes, violent intensity, and emphasis on color all come to be read as inconsistent with high-minded notions of the poetry of Shakespearean tragedy (see K. Hall, "*Othello*"; Loomba, *Race*; Neill, *Putting History* 245–48; Singh). However, when reading such early critiques, it is important to keep in mind the ways in which racist thinking aligns white women and black peoples in general, particularly in complaints that they are overly emotional and too sexual, that is, outside the Eurocentric norms of civility.

Given the play's popularity and the novel prominence of love between a black man and white woman, it is not surprising that *Othello*'s stage history contains several milestones. The first woman on the English stage may have appeared as Desdemona in 1660.[5] Ironically, the appearance of actresses on the English stage coincides with the diminution of women's roles in *Othello*: Desdemona becomes a more passive victim (Dash 115; see Siemon), and the desire and independence of the three female characters — Desdemona, Emilia, and Bianca — fade under the intensity of the Iago-Othello dynamic. In the twentieth century, playwrights Paula Vogel (*Desdemona: A Play about a Handkerchief*, 1979) and Anne-Marie McDonald (*Good Night Desdemona, Good Morning Juliet*, 1998) reworked Shakespeare's text to put onstage a consistently assertive Desdemona as much in love with the life of adventure Othello offers as with Othello himself. Although the first black theater company in the United States, the African Theater, included *Othello* in its repertoire in 1822, Ira Aldridge is generally hailed as the first black Shakespearean actor (see Figure 8 on p. 26). In the 1830s, Aldridge became the first

---

[5] The actress is unnamed. She is assumed to be either Anne Marshall or Margaret Hughes (Leonard 13).

actor of African descent to appear in a major performance of Shakespeare as well as one of the innovators of a naturalistic approach to acting (Hill 19).[6]

Enduring innovations in *Othello*'s stage history address questions of Othello's difference and the performance of his passion. Jyotsna Singh argues that critical and theatrical histories have difficulty "reconciling Othello's role as a tragic hero with his blackness" (288), and it is important to read this difficulty in historical context. Transatlantic slavery, with its denigration of African peoples and racist caricatures, translated blackness into both commodity and comedy, making it almost impossible to see Othello as simultaneously noble and black.[7] During the eighteenth century, Othello's color became an important part of questions of nobility. Albeit written tongue-in-cheek, poet Anna Seward's response to the play — "we cannot with-hold our esteem and pity from the man, who, giving way to suspicious appearances, murders his innocent wife" (131n.) — hits at a central problem: How can we still see Othello as noble after he murders Desdemona? Later this quandary devolved into two subsidiary questions: (1) How is an essentially noble man reduced to incoherence (the trance) and horrific violence ("I will chop her into messes")? (2) Can an African man be perceived as noble and alluring?

Despite ongoing discussion about the meanings of Othello's color, that the actor playing Othello would perform him as "black" seems not to have been questioned until the era of transatlantic slavery. In the beginning of the nineteenth century, actor Edmund Kean inaugurated what has been known as the "Bronze Age" of *Othello*: arguing that it was a "gross error to make Othello either black or negro" (qtd. in Kaul 8), Kean played him as a "tawny" Arab (Figure 6.)[8] While there was some disagreement with his assessment, this portrayal fit into dominant racial sentiments of the era, and the tradition of Othello as Arab or even Indian was to last for another century. The Victorian theater's concerns with historical accuracy and the culture's investment in a strict racial hierarchy turned many performances and editions of *Othello* into quasi-ethnographic attempts to understand his "true" racial origins. For example, in his strikingly physical and passionate performances in Europe and the United States, Italian actor Tomasso Salvini (Figure 7) played Othello as "tawny," yet he had the character cut his own

---

[6] This truncated history refers to performances in major venues in the United States and Europe.

[7] That the long tradition of rendering black lives comic interferes with the ability to see blackness as noble or tragic can be seen in responses to black performances of Shakespeare. One reviewer from the *Washington Post* wrote in 1884 that "a Richard with a seal-brown skin and a typically African cast of countenance is calculated to excite the merriment of the most lugubrious" (quoted in Hill 2). For an account of how black images change in response to historical conditions, see Riggs.

[8] Edelstein argues that Kean's bronze Othello speaks to American conceptions of the mulatto in the period (183).

FIGURE 6  *Edmund Kean as Othello by John William Gear.*

FIGURE 7  *Tomasso Salvini as Othello by F. Armytage*

throat instead of stab himself on the grounds that it "was more in accordance with the custom of the people of Africa" (quoted in Carlson 79). The career of Ira Aldridge, the first African-descended man to play Othello on a major stage, brought an end to the bronze age (Figure 8).

In the twentieth century, *Othello* became an even more potent index of race and race relations in culture and theater. Sir Lawrence Olivier onstage and Orson Welles in film provocatively rejected bronze-age representations: both actors purposefully emulated their (limited) understandings of black men and offered performances that placed race relations in the foreground. Unfortunately, their recuperation of the tradition seemed to rely on a rejection of Othello's essential nobility. In particular, Welles's imitation of blackness (the last major blackface performance in a U.S. film) was often condemned as caricatured and offensive. Actor-activist Paul Robeson's watershed performance of *Othello* in 1943 changed the way *Othello* would be performed in major theaters for the rest of the century (see Figure 9). Although *Othello* is popularly known as Shakespeare's "American play," no African American actor had played the title role on a major U.S. stage until this production. (Ira Aldridge performed as Othello extensively in Europe

FIGURE 8 *Ira Aldridge as Othello.*

FIGURE 9 *Paul Robeson, and his co-star Mary Ure during their final rehearsal of* Othello *(1959) in the Shakespeare Memorial Theater's hundredth season. Robeson, who received fifteen curtain calls, was the first black man to play Othello at Stratford on Avon.*

to great acclaim but was not allowed to appear onstage in the United States.) Actor Earle Hyman remembered that "all of us in the audience knew we were seeing Shakespeare's *Othello* for the first time" (23).

After Robeson's performance, the role of Othello in the United States was played primarily by black actors (with the exception of Welles) until Patrick Stewart's 1997 appearance at the Shakespeare Theater in Washington, D.C. (see Figure 10). This historic "photo-negative" production, directed by Jude Kelly, reversed racial roles: Stewart, a white actor famous in both elite and popular venues, appeared with an all-black cast. Notable also in the performance was actress Francelle Dorn's portrayal of Emilia as a victim of spousal abuse and Kelly's color-coded staging of the Venetians as an

FIGURE 10 *Patrick Stewart and Patrice Johnson in* Othello *(1997). Stage and screen actor Patrick Stewart played Othello in Jude Kelly's "photo-negative"* Othello *at the Shakespeare Theater Company in 1997. The production used black actors in all of the roles except Othello.*

occupying army (Albanese; Potter 179–84). Kelly's production took place a year after playwright August Wilson's controversial denunciation of the practice of color-blind or nontraditional casting (casting against the racial expectations or directives of the script) and was thus the occasion for many theater critics to take up contemporary concerns in the theatrical community about multiculturalism and cross-racial casting.[9] Wilson argued that color-blind casting is a tool of cultural imperialism, one that casts African Americans "in the role of mimics" and denies African American history and cultural productions both culturally and economically (72).

While major African-descended actors like Aldridge, Robeson, James Earl Jones, and Laurence Fishburne (the first African American actor to play Othello in a major film) have made the role of Othello quintessentially black (Royster), other critics and writers are uneasy with such untroubled naturalization of the part. Actor-director Hugh Quarshie suggests, "Of all the parts in the canon, perhaps Othello is the one which should most definitely *not* be played by a black actor" (emphasis added; see also Kwei-Armah), and Sheila Rose Bland has argued that blackface performance would in fact remind the audience that Othello is Shakespeare's caricature of a black man (33; see also Potter 167–72).

While issues of jealousy, love, and alienation resonate with audiences and creative writers across the globe, postcolonial writers have seen in *Othello's* clash of cultures the potential for speaking to very specific racial and colonial histories. For example, the questioning of racial intermarriage strikes a powerful chord within the United States' long history of antimiscegenation laws. Paul Robeson's accounts of his role indicate that his own experiences with racism and Jim Crow profoundly affected his performance: "For the first two weeks in every scene I played with Desdemona that girl couldn't get near me, I was backin' away from her all the time. I was like a plantation hand in the parlor, that clumsy" (152, see also 154–55). South African director Janet Suzman's groundbreaking 1987 production of *Othello* featuring Tony winner John Kani was specifically envisioned as a reflection of the apartheid state. Suzman said, "I wanted to see if Shakespeare without changing a single word could be a protest play. And it turned out to be exactly that." Both Derek Walcott and Tayeb Salih read Othello as an emblem of the postcolonial subject, the diasporic African, forever alienated from both his home and his adopted lands. When seeing the play for the first time after leaving Guadeloupe, Maryse Condé felt that Iago powerfully reflected the dangers awaiting her as a colonial subject in France.

Film and video versions of *Othello* are particularly adept at situating the play in scenes of contemporary racial conflict. Tim Blake Nelson's 2001 film, *O*, makes Othello a star African American college athlete at an elite southern

[9] Wilson's speech was followed by a debate with critic Robert Brustein over color-blind casting. For more details, see *American Theatre*, September and October 1996. *African American Review* (31:4 [1997]) devoted its special issue on theater to issues raised in Wilson's lecture. For a discussion of color-blind casting in relation to this specific performance, see Albanese.

prep school, while Geoffrey Sax's 2001 BBC version uses the brutal 1993 murder of black teenager Steven Lawrence in London as the central context while casting Othello as a recently promoted police commissioner. Paradoxically, situating *Othello* in situations of modern racial conflict seems to both raise and resist the oft-asked question "Is *Othello* racist?" Modern criticism has been quite insightful in identifying stereotypes about Moors in the play (see Vaughan 63–70), but there is little agreement on whether the play subverts or upholds these stereotypes and on whether Shakespeare shared his culture's negative attitudes toward Moors. Writing out of a history of South African apartheid, Martin Orkin argued that the play can in certain contexts be antiracist, a position vehemently disagreed with by Michael Neill (Orkin 188; Neill, *Putting* 246–48). Virginia Vaughan captures the contradictions in the play in saying, "I think this play is racist and I think it is not" (70). Instead of trying to decide whether or not the play is racist, this edition prefers to ask how it reflects and stimulates race-thinking across time. In that spirit, it asks the reader to consider what it means to claim the play as racist, nonracist, or antiracist. What in the play or in a particular performance of it encourages one response or another? How does the answer affect a reader's response to the play or its appearance in the classroom and on the stage?

Shakespeare's play made Cinthio's already popular tale legendary, and the signs of *Othello* permeate popular culture. During the now infamous "night of the white Bronco" in the summer of 1994, CBS news anchor Dan Rather commented that the tragic end of the marriage of O.J. and Nicole Brown Simpson reminded him of *Othello*. Thus, *Othello* became the story used to frame an emerging drama. Barbara Hodgdon reminds us that Rather did not have to reach far for a metaphor that appeared to capture cultural anxieties about race and sexuality, particularly one that addressed U.S. anxieties about black men's access to white women (41; see also Albanese 239–40). One can find less explosive — and seemingly romanticized — signs of *Othello* everywhere. An exclusive chocolate chain carries chocolates named "Othello" and "Desdemona," one with a dark chocolate center, the other with a white creme center; so, too, a high-end marketer of household goods produced a cookbook with a recipe for the Othello cookie (named in other venues "the monster"). All of these acts of naming assume that even people who have never read the play "know" *Othello*.

The documents included in this volume ask readers to consider the role of language and narratives in shaping human relations, and to consider what it means to think one "knows" a story or person. Shakespeare's dramas are never his alone — they are part of the intricate network of ideas, language, and actions that constituted early modern culture; they become ours, too, as we encounter them along with our individual experiences and changing historical circumstances. Chapter 6, Encounters with *Othello*, shows how completely texts are embedded in history and offers a peek into the processes of interpretation in which everyone partakes; the documents in this chapter may make a mysterious process more understandable, if never completely clear. It is my hope that attention to *Othello* in relation to the documents in this volume will help readers become more self-conscious about the histories they bring to the play and to their encounters with differences, whatever those might be.

## An *Othello* Pre-text

→ CINTHIO

## *From* Gli Hecatommithi                                              *1566*

Most English readers knew Giovanni Battista Giraldi (1504–1573) by his classical pseudonym, Cinthio. Cinthio was a significant figure in Italian Renaissance literature, known for both his plays and his theories of drama. *De Gli Hecatommithi di M. Giovanbattista giraldi Cinthio nobile ferrarese* (*The Hecatommithi*), published in 1566, was a popular collection of over one hundred novellas, or stories, divided into ten groups called decades, each addressing a different topic. The third decade is titled "The Unfaithfulness of Husbands and of Wives," and its seventh story is the account of a marriage between a Venetian noblewoman, Disdemona, and an unnamed Moor of Venice who murders her at the instigation of his Ensign. The narrator, Curzio, tells the story as an example that "it sometimes happens that without any fault at all, a faithful and loving lady, through the insidious plots of a villainous mind, and the frailty of one who believes more than he need, is murdered by her faithful husband" (Bullough 242).

Shakespeare was clearly attentive to Cinthio's work at this time (another section of *The Hecatommithi* provides the main plot for *Measure for Measure*, which is close in date to *Othello*), but it is difficult to say for certain how he gained access to the narratives. Scholars find verbal echoes of both the original Italian and a French translation by Gabriel Chappuys, published in *Premier Volume des Cents Excellentes Nouvelles* in 1584. Others speculate that there was an English translation, now lost to us. The first surviving English translation was printed in 1855.

As this story of sexual jealousy and misplaced revenge moves from two to three dimensions, from narrative to stage, you will see many changes. Unlike

Geoffrey Bullough, ed., *Narrative and Dramatic Sources of Shakespeare* (London: Routledge and Kegan Paul; Columbia University Press, 1957–75), 241–52.

*Measure for Measure*, which adds an important subplot to the Cinthio original, *Othello* focuses tightly on the original cast of characters (albeit attributing to them very different motivations). His characters have more knowledge of events and less ambiguous motivations than in Shakespeare's play. For example, in the play, Emilia does not put all of the pieces together until after Desdemona's death, while Cinthio's maid knows "everything" and, out of fear of her husband, hides the truth as events unfold. Interestingly, Cinthio's story emphasizes how much work and scheming it takes to bring the disaster about, but how does Shakespeare's play represent Iago's improvisations? Together, Cinthio's narrative and Shakespeare's play show the different and at times conflicting attitudes toward Moors in the early modern period (see Chapter 1). What assumptions does each text make about Moors? When you move from the story to the play, compare the scenes in which the Ensign/Iago first plants doubt in the Moor/Othello and the interactions between Othello and Desdemona. How does the play deal with Othello's jealousy? Why does Shakespeare have Emilia, rather than Iago, steal the handkerchief? Cinthio's version gives only one character a name, the wife, whose name is spelled "Disdemona" ("unfortunate one" in Greek), not the "Desdemona" of Shakespeare's play.

## THE THIRD DECADE, STORY 7

*A Moorish Captain takes to wife a Venetian lady, and his Ensign accuses her to her husband of adultery; he desires the Ensign to kill the man whom he believes to be the adulterer; the Captain kills his wife and is accused by the Ensign. The Moor does not confess, but on clear indications of his guilt he is banished; and the scoundrelly Ensign, thinking to injure others, brings a miserable end on himself.*

The ladies would have had great pity for the fate of the Florentine woman had her adultery not made her appear worthy of the severest punishment; and it seemed to them that the gentleman's patience had been unusually great. Indeed they declared that it would be hard to find any other man who, discovering his wife in such a compromising situation, would not have slain both of the sinners outright. The more they thought about it the more prudently they considered him to have behaved.

After this discussion, Curzio, on whom all eyes were turned as they waited for him to begin his story, said: I do not believe that either men or women are free to avoid amorous passion, for human nature is so disposed to it that even against our will it makes itself powerfully felt in our souls. Nevertheless, I believe that a virtuous lady has the power, when she feels herself burning with such a desire, to resolve rather to die than through dishonorable lust to stain that modesty which ladies should preserve as untainted as white ermine. And I believe that they err less who, free from the holy bonds of matrimony, offer their bodies to the delight of every man, than does a married woman who commits adultery with one person only. But as this woman suffered well-deserved punishment for her fault, so it sometimes happens that without any fault at all, a faithful and loving lady, through the insidious plots (*tesele*) of a villainous mind, and the frailty of one who believes more than he need, is murdered by her faithful husband; as you will clearly perceive by what I am about to relate to you.

There was once in Venice a Moor, a very gallant man, who, because he was personally valiant and had given proof in warfare of great prudence and skillful energy, was very dear to the Signoria, who in rewarding virtuous actions ever advance the interests of the Republic. It happened that a virtuous Lady of wondrous beauty called Disdemona, impelled not by female appetite but by the Moor's good qualities, fell in love with him, and he, vanquished by the Lady's beauty and noble mind, likewise was enamored of her. So propitious was their mutual love that, although the Lady's relatives did all they could to make her take another husband, they were united in marriage and lived together in such concord and tranquillity while they remained in Venice, that never a word passed between them that was not loving.

It happened that the Venetian lords made a change in the forces that they used to maintain in Cyprus; and they chose the Moor as Commandant of the soldiers whom they sent there.[1] Although he was pleased by the honor offered him (for such high rank and dignity is given only to noble and loyal men who have proved themselves most valiant), yet his happiness was lessened when he considered the length and dangers of the voyage, thinking that Disdemona would be much troubled by it. The Lady, who had no other happiness on earth but the Moor, and was very pleased with the recognition of his merits that her husband had received from so noble and powerful a Republic, could hardly wait for the hour when he would set off with his men, and she would accompany him to that honorable post. It grieved her greatly to see the Moor troubled; and, not knowing the reason for it, one day while they were dining together she said to him: "Why is it, my Moor, that after being given such an honorable rank by the Signoria, you are so melancholy?"

The Moor said to Disdemona: "The love I bear you spoils my pleasure at the honor I have received, because I see that one of two things must happen: either I must take you with me in peril by sea, or, so as not to cause you this hardship, I must leave you in Venice. The first alternative must inevitably

Notes to this selection are reprinted from Bullough.
[1] No reason is given, no mention of the Turkish menace.

weigh heavily on me, since every fatigue you endured and every danger we met would give me extreme anxiety. The second, having to leave you behind, would be hateful to me, since, parting from you I should be leaving my very life behind."

"Alas, husband," said Disdemona, hearing this, "What thoughts are these passing through your mind? Why do you let such ideas perturb you? I want to come with you wherever you go, even if it meant walking through fire in my shift instead of, as it will be, crossing the water with you in a safe, well-furnished galley. If there really are to be dangers and fatigues, I wish to share them with you; and I should consider myself very little beloved if, rather than have my company on the sea, you were to leave me in Venice, or persuaded yourself that I would rather stay here in safety than be in the same danger as yourself. Get ready then for the voyage in the cheerfulness that befits the high rank you hold."

Then the Moor joyously threw his arms round his wife's neck and said, with a loving kiss: "God keep us long in this love, my dear wife!" Shortly afterward, having donned his armor and made all ready for the journey, he embarked in the galley with his lady and all his train; then, hoisting sail, they set off, and with a sea of the utmost tranquillity arrived safely in Cyprus.

The Moor had in his company an Ensign of handsome presence but the most scoundrelly nature in the world. He was in high favor with the Moor, who had no suspicion of his wickedness; for although he had the basest of minds, he so cloaked the vileness hidden in his heart with high sounding and noble words, and by his manner, that he showed himself in the likeness of a Hector or an Achilles. This false man had likewise taken to Cyprus his wife, a fair and honest young woman. Being an Italian she was much loved by the Moor's wife, and spent the greater part of the day with her.

In the same company there was also a Corporal who was very dear to the Moor. This man went frequently to the Moor's house and often dined with him and his wife. The Lady, knowing him so well liked by her husband, gave him proofs of the greatest kindness, and this was much appreciated by the Moor.

The wicked Ensign, taking no account of the faith he had pledged to his wife, and of the friendship, loyalty and obligations he owed the Moor, fell ardently in love with Disdemona, and bent all his thoughts to see if he could manage to enjoy her; but he did not dare openly show his passion, fearing that if the Moor perceived it he might straightway kill him. He sought therefore in various ways, as deviously as he could, to make the Lady aware that he desired her. But she, whose every thought was for the Moor, never gave a thought to the Ensign or anybody else. And all the things he did to arouse her feelings for him had no more effect than if he had not tried them.

Whereupon he imagined that this was because she was in love with the Corporal; and he wondered how he might remove the latter from her sight. Not only did he turn his mind to this, but the love which he had felt for the Lady now changed to the bitterest hate, and he gave himself up to studying how to bring it about that, once the Corporal were killed, if he himself could not enjoy the Lady, then the Moor should not have her either. Turning over in his mind divers schemes, all wicked and treacherous, in the end he determined to accuse her of adultery, and to make her husband believe that the Corporal was the adulterer. But knowing the singular love of the Moor for Disdemona, and his friendship for the Corporal, he recognized that, unless he could deceive the Moor with some clever trick, it would be impossible to make him believe either charge. Wherefore he set himself to wait until time and place opened a way for him to start his wicked enterprise.

Not long afterward the Moor deprived the Corporal of his rank for having drawn his sword and wounded a soldier while on guard-duty. Disdemona was grieved by this and tried many times to reconcile the Moor with him. Whereupon the Moor told the rascally Ensign that his wife importuned him so much for the Corporal that he feared he would be obliged to reinstate him. The evil man saw in this a hint for setting in train the deceits he had planned, and said: "Perhaps Disdemona has good cause to look on him so favorably!" "Why is that?" asked the Moor. "I do not wish," said the Ensign, "to come between man and wife, but if you keep your eyes open you will see for yourself." Nor for all the Moor's inquiries would the Ensign go beyond this: nonetheless his words left such a sharp thorn in the Moor's mind, that he gave himself up to pondering intensely what they could mean. He became quite melancholy, and one day, when his wife was trying to soften his anger toward the Corporal, begging him not to condemn to oblivion the loyal service and friendship of many years just for one small fault, especially since the Corporal had been reconciled to the man he had struck, the Moor burst out in anger and said to her, "There must be a very powerful reason why you take such trouble for this fellow, for he is not your brother, nor even a kinsman, yet you have him so much at heart!"

The lady, all courtesy and modesty, replied: "I should not like you to be angry with me. Nothing else makes me do it but sorrow to see you deprived of so dear a friend as you have shown that the Corporal was to you. He has not committed so serious an offense as to deserve such hostility. But you Moors are so hot by nature that any little thing moves you to anger and revenge."

Still more enraged by these words the Moor answered: "Anyone who does not believe that may easily have proof of it! I shall take such revenge for any wrongs done to me as will more than satisfy me!" The lady was terrified by these words, and seeing her husband angry with her, quite against his habit, she said humbly: "Only a very good purpose made me speak to you about this, but rather than have you angry with me I shall never say another word on the subject."

The Moor, however, seeing the earnestness with which his wife had again pleaded for the Corporal, guessed that the Ensign's words had been intended to suggest that Disdemona was in love with the Corporal, and he went in deep depression to the scoundrel and urged him to speak more openly. The Ensign, intent on injuring this unfortunate lady, after pretending not to wish to say anything that might displease the Moor, appeared to be overcome by his entreaties and said: "I must confess that it grieves me greatly to have to tell you something that must be in the highest degree painful to you; but since you wish me to tell you, and the regard that I must have of your honor as my master spurs me on, I shall not fail in my duty to answer your request. You must know therefore that it is hard for your Lady to see the Corporal in disgrace for the simple reason that she takes her pleasure with him whenever he comes to your house. The woman has come to dislike your blackness."

These words struck the Moor's heart to its core; but in order to learn more (although he believed what the Ensign had said to be true, through the suspicion already sown in his mind) he said, with a fierce look: "I do not know what holds me back from cutting out that outrageous tongue of yours which has dared to speak such insults against my Lady!" Then the Ensign: "Captain," he said, "I did not expect any other reward for my loving service; but since my duty and my care for your honor have carried me so far, I repeat that the matter stands exactly as you have just heard it, and if your Lady, with a false show of love for you, has so blinded your eyes that you have not seen what you ought to have seen, that does not mean that I am not speaking the truth. For this Corporal has told me all, like one whose happiness does not seem complete until he has made someone else acquainted with it."[2] And he added: "If I had not feared your wrath, I should, when he told me, have given him the punishment he deserved by killing him. But since letting you know what concerns you more than anyone else brings me so undeserved a reward, I wish that I had kept silent, for by doing so I should not have fallen into your displeasure."

Then the Moor, in the utmost anguish, said, "If you do not make me see with my own eyes[3] what you have told me, be assured, I shall make you realize that it would have been better for you had you been born dumb." "To prove it

[2] Iago invents an erotic dream.
[3] "Give me the ocular proof."

would have been easy," replied the villain, "when he used to come to your house; but now when, not as it should have been, but for the most trivial cause, you have driven him away, it cannot but be difficult for me, for although I fancy that he still enjoys Disdemona whenever you give him the opportunity, he must do it much more cautiously than he did before, now that he knows you have turned against him. Yet I do not lose hope of being able to show you what you do not wish to believe." And with these words they parted.

The wretched Moor, as if struck by the sharpest of darts, went home to wait for the day when the Ensign would make him see that which must make him miserable for ever. But no less trouble did the Ensign suffer by his knowledge of the Lady's chastity, for it did not seem possible to find a way of making the Moor believe what he had falsely told him, till, his thoughts twisting and turning in all directions, the scoundrel thought of a new piece of mischief.

The Moor's wife often went, as I have said, to the house of the Ensign's wife, and stayed with her a good part of the day; wherefore seeing that she sometimes carried with her a handkerchief embroidered most delicately in the Moorish fashion, which the Moor had given her and which was treasured by the Lady and her husband too, the Ensign planned to take it from her secretly, and thereby prepare her final ruin. He had a little girl of three years old, much loved by Disdemona. One day, when the unfortunate Lady had gone to pass some time at the villain's house, he took the child in his arms and carried her to the Lady, who took her and pressed her to her breast. The deceiver, who had great sleight of hand, lifted the handkerchief from her girdle so warily that she did not notice it; and he took his leave of her in great joy.[4]

Disdemona, knowing nothing of it, went back home and, being occupied with other thoughts, did not miss the handkerchief. But a few days later, she looked for it, and not finding it she became afraid that the Moor might ask for it, as he often did. The wicked Ensign, seizing a suitable opportunity, went to the Corporal's room, and with cunning malice left the handkerchief at the head of his bed. The Corporal did not notice it till the next morning when, getting out of bed, he put his foot upon the handkerchief, which had fallen to the floor. Not being able to imagine how it had come into his house, and knowing that it was Disdemona's, he determined to give it back to her. So he waited till the Moor had gone out, then went to the back door and knocked. Fortune, it seems, had conspired with the Ensign to bring about the death of the unhappy lady; for just then the Moor came home, and hearing a knock on the door went to the window and shouted angrily:

[4] Shakespeare omits the child and makes Desdemona drop the handkerchief.

"Who is knocking?" The Corporal, hearing the Moor's voice and fearing that he might come down and attack him, fled without answering. The Moor ran down the stairs, and opening the outside door went out into the street and looked around, but could see nobody. Then returning full of evil passion, he asked his wife who had knocked on the door below.

The Lady replied truthfully that she did not know. The Moor then said, "It looked to me like the Corporal." "I do not know," she said, "whether it was he or somebody else." The Moor restrained his fury, though he was consumed with rage. He did not want to do anything before consulting the Ensign, to whom he went at once and told him what had occurred, praying him to find out from the Corporal all that he could about it. Delighted with what had happened, the Ensign promised to do so. Accordingly he spoke to the Corporal one day while the Moor was standing where he could see them as they talked; and chatting of quite other matters than the Lady, he laughed heartily and, displaying great surprise, he moved his head about and gestured with his hands, acting as if he were listening to marvels. As soon as the Moor saw them separate he went to the Ensign to learn what the other had told him; and the Ensign, after making him entreat him for a long time, finally declared: "He has hidden nothing from me. He tells me that he has enjoyed your wife every time you have given them the chance by your absence. And on the last occasion she gave him the handkerchief which you gave her as a present when you married her." The Moor thanked the Ensign and it seemed obvious to him that if he found that the Lady no longer had the handkerchief, then all must be as the Ensign claimed.

Wherefore one day after dinner, while chatting with the Lady on various matters, he asked her for the handkerchief. The unhappy woman, who had greatly feared this, grew red in the face at the request, and to hide her blushes (which the Moor well noted), she ran to the chest, pretending to look for it. After much search, "I do not know," she said, "why I cannot find it; perhaps you have had it?" "If I had had it," said he, "why should I ask for it? But you will look more successfully another time."[5]

Leaving her, the Moor began to think how he might kill his wife, and the Corporal too, in such a way that he would not be blamed for it.[6] And since he was obsessed with this, day and night, the Lady inevitably noticed that he was not the same toward her as he was formerly. Many times she said to him, "What is the matter with you? What is troubling you? Whereas you used to be the gayest of men, you are now the most melancholy man alive!"

The Moor invented various excuses, but she was not at all satisfied, and

[5] Othello is more demanding.
[6] Iago plays a bigger part here.

although she knew no act of hers which could have so perturbed the Moor, she nevertheless feared that through the abundance of lovemaking which he had with her he might have become tired of her. Sometimes she would say to the Ensign's wife, "I do not know what to make of the Moor. He used to be all love toward me, but in the last few days he has become quite another man, and I fear greatly that I shall be a warning to young girls not to marry against their parents' wishes; and Italian ladies will learn by my example not to tie themselves to a man whom Nature, Heaven, and manner of life separate from us. But because I know that he is very friendly with your husband, and confides in him, I beg you, if you have learned anything from him which you can tell me, that you will not fail to help me." She wept bitterly as she spoke.[7]

The Ensign's wife, who knew everything (for her husband had wished to use her as an instrument in causing the Lady's death, but she had never been willing to consent), did not dare, for fear of her husband, to tell her anything. She said only: "Take care not to give your husband any reason for suspicion, and try your hardest to make him realize your love and loyalty.[8] "That indeed I do," said Disdemona, "but it does not help."

In the meantime the Moor sought in every way to get more proof of that which he did not wish to discover, and prayed the Ensign to contrive to let him see the handkerchief in the Corporal's possession; and although that was difficult for the villain, he promised nonetheless to make every effort to give him this testimony.

The Corporal had a woman at home who worked the most wonderful embroidery on lawn,[9] and seeing the handkerchief and learning that it belonged to the Moor's wife, and that it was to be returned to her, she began to make a similar one before it went back. While she was doing so, the Ensign noticed that she was working near a window where she could be seen by whoever passed by on the street. So he brought the Moor and made him see her,[10] and the latter now regarded it as certain that the most virtuous Lady was indeed an adulteress. He arranged with the Ensign to kill her and the Corporal, and they discussed how it might be done. The Moor begged the Ensign to kill the Corporal, promising to remain eternally grateful to him. The Ensign refused to undertake such a thing, as being too difficult and dangerous, for the Corporal was as skillful as he was courageous; but after much entreaty, and being given a large sum of money, he was persuaded to say that he would tempt Fortune.[11]

---

[7] Desdemona begs Iago to help her.
[8] Emilia hints that he is jealous and tries to convince Othello that his wife is honest.
[9] Bianca combines the functions of this woman and the courtesan.
[10] Othello sees her give it back to Cassio.
[11] Iago needs no bribe.

Soon after they had resolved on this, the Corporal, issuing one dark night from the house of a courtesan with whom he used to amuse himself, was accosted by the Ensign, sword in hand, who directed a blow at his legs to make him fall down; and he cut the right leg entirely through, so that the wretched man fell. The Ensign was immediately on him to finish him off, but the Corporal, who was valiant and used to blood and death, had drawn his sword, and wounded as he was he set about defending himself, while shouting in a loud voice: "I am being murdered!"

At that the Ensign, hearing people come running, including some of the soldiers who were quartered thereabouts, began to flee, so as not to be caught there; then, turning back he pretended to have run up on hearing the noise. Mingling with the others, and seeing the leg cut off, he judged that if the Corporal were not already dead, he soon would die of the wound, and although he rejoiced inwardly, he outwardly grieved for the Corporal as if he had been his own brother.

In the morning, news of the affray was spread throughout the city and reached the ears of Disdemona,[12] whereupon, being tender-hearted and not thinking that evil would come to her by it, she showed the utmost sorrow at the occurrence. On this the Moor put the worst possible construction. Seeking out the Ensign, he said to him: "Do you know, my imbecile of a wife is in such grief about the Corporal's accident that she is nearly out of her mind!" "How could you expect anything else?" said the other, "since he is her very life and soul?"

"Soul indeed!" replied the Moor, "I'll drag the soul from her body, for I couldn't think myself a man if I didn't rid the world of such a wicked creature."

They were discussing whether the Lady should perish by poison or the dagger, and not deciding on either of them, when the Ensign said: "A method has come into my head that will satisfy you and that nobody will suspect.[13] It is this: the house where you are staying is very old, and the ceiling of your room has many cracks in it. I suggest that we beat Disdemona with a stocking filled with sand until she dies. Thus there will not appear on her any sign of the blows. When she is dead, we shall make part of the ceiling fall; and we'll break the Lady's head, making it seem that a rafter has injured it in falling, and killed her. In this way nobody will feel any suspicion of you, for everyone will think that she died accidentally."[14]

The cruel plan pleased the Moor, and they waited for a suitable opportu-

[12] Desdemona is dead before morning.
[13] Othello suggests poison, Iago strangulation.
[14] Othello makes no preparations to avoid discovery.

nity. One night the Moor concealed the Ensign in a closet which opened off the bedchamber, and when the husband and wife were in bed, the Ensign, in accordance with their plan, made some sort of noise. Hearing it the Moor said to his wife:

"Did you hear that noise?"

"Yes, I heard it," she replied.

"Get up," said the Moor, "and see what it is."

The unfortunate Disdemona got out of bed, and as soon as she was near the closet, the Ensign came out and, being strong and muscular, he gave her a frightful blow in the small of her back, which made the Lady fall down at once, scarcely able to draw her breath. With the little voice she had she called on the Moor to help her. But he, jumping out of bed, said to her, "You wicked woman, you are having the reward of your infidelity. This is how women are treated who, pretending to love their husbands, put horns on their heads."[15]

The wretched Lady, hearing this and feeling herself near to death (for the Ensign had given her another blow), called on Divine Justice to witness to her fidelity, since earthly justice failed; and as she called on God to help her, a third blow struck her, and she lay still, slain by the impious Ensign. Then, placing her in the bed, and breaking her skull, he and the Moor made the ceiling fall as they had previously planned, and the Moor began to call for help, that the house was falling. Hearing his cries the neighbors ran in and found the bed, and the Lady dead under the rafters — which made everyone grieve, for they knew what a good life she had led.

Next day Disdemona was buried, amid the universal mourning of the people. But God, the just observer of men's hearts, did not intend such vile wickedness to go without proper punishment. He ordained that the Moor, who had loved the Lady more than his life, on finding himself deprived of her should feel such longing that he went about like one beside himself, searching for her in every part of the house. Realizing now that the Ensign was the cause of his losing his Lady and all joy in life, he held the villain in such abhorrence that he could not bear even to see him; and if he had not been afraid of the inviolable justice of the Venetian lords, he would have slain him openly. Not being able to do this with safety, he took away his rank and would not have him in his company, whereupon such a bitter hatred sprang up between them that no greater or more deadly feud could be imagined.

---

[15] Contrast Othello's attempt at a ritual murder. On horns, see chapter 3, p. 286. [Hall]

The Ensign, that worst of all scoundrels, therefore set all his mind to injuring the Moor, and seeking out the Corporal, who had now recovered and went about with a wooden leg instead of the one that had been cut off, he said to him, "It is time you got your revenge for the leg you lost. If you will come to Venice with me, I shall tell you who the miscreant was, for here I dare not tell you, for many reasons; and I am willing to bear witness for you in court."

The Corporal, who felt himself deeply wronged but did not know the real truth, thanked the Ensign and came with him to Venice. When they arrived there the Ensign told him that it was the Moor who had cut off his leg because of a suspicion he had formed that he was Disdemona's lover, and that for the same reason he had murdered her, and afterward made it known that the fallen ceiling had killed her. Hearing this, the Corporal accused the Moor to the Signoria, both of cutting off his leg and of causing the Lady's death, and called as witness the Ensign, who said that both accusations were true, for the Moor had approached him and tried to induce him to commit both crimes; and that, having then killed his wife through the bestial jealousy that he had conceived in his mind, he had told him how he had killed her.

When the Signoria learned of the cruelty inflicted by the Barbarian upon a citizen of Venice, they ordered the Moor to be apprehended in Cyprus and to be brought to Venice, where with many tortures they tried to discover the truth. But enduring with great steadfastness of mind every torment, he denied everything so firmly that nothing could be extorted from him. Although by his constancy he escaped death, he was, however, after many days in prison, condemned to perpetual exile, in which he was finally slain by Disdemona's relatives, as he richly deserved.

The Ensign returned to his own country; and not giving up his accustomed behavior, he accused one of his companions, saying that the latter had sought to have him murder one of his enemies, who was a nobleman. The accused man was arrested and put to the torture, and when he denied that what his accuser said was true, the Ensign too was tortured, to compare their stories; and he was tortured so fiercely that his inner organs were ruptured. Afterward he was let out of prison and taken home, where he died miserably.[16] Thus did God avenge the innocence of Disdemona. And all these events were told after his death by the Ensign's wife, who knew the facts, as I have told them to you. . . .

---

[16] Cf. the tortures promised for Iago.

# PART ONE

>‹

## WILLIAM SHAKESPEARE
### *Othello, the Moor of Venice*

*Edited by David Bevington*

# Othello, the Moor of Venice

><-

SCENE: *Venice; a seaport in Cyprus*]

## ACT 1, SCENE 1°

*Enter Roderigo and Iago.*

RODERIGO:
    Tush, never tell me!° I take it much unkindly
    That thou, Iago, who hast had my purse
    As if the strings were thine, shouldst know of this.°
IAGO:    'Sblood,° but you'll not hear me.
    If ever I did dream of such a matter,    5
    Abhor me.
RODERIGO:
    Thou toldst me thou didst hold him° in thy hate.
IAGO:    Despise me
    If I do not. Three great ones of the city,
    In personal suit to make me his lieutenant,    10
    Off-capped to him; and by the faith of man,
    I know my price, I am worth no worse a place.
    But he, as loving his own pride and purposes,
    Evades them with a bombast circumstance°
    Horribly stuffed with epithets of war,°    15
    And, in conclusion,
    Nonsuits° my mediators. For, "Certes,"° says he,
    "I have already chose my officer."
    And what was he?
    Forsooth, a great arithmetician,°    20
    One Michael Cassio, a Florentine,
    A fellow almost damned in a fair wife,°
    That never set a squadron in the field
    Nor the division of a battle° knows
    More than a spinster° — unless the bookish theoric,°    25

---

ACT 1, SCENE 1. Location: Venice. A street.  **1. never tell me:** (An expression of incredulity, like "tell me another one.")  **3. this:** i.e., Desdemona's elopement.  **4. 'Sblood:** by His (Christ's) blood.  **7. him:** Othello.  **14. bombast circumstance:** wordy evasion. (*Bombast* is cotton padding.)  **15. epithets of war:** military expressions.  **17. Nonsuits:** rejects the petition of.  **Certes:** certainly.  **20. arithmetician:** i.e., a man whose military knowledge is merely theoretical, based on books of tactics.  **22. A . . . wife:** (Cassio does not seem to be married, but his counterpart in Shakespeare's source does have a woman in his house. See also 4.1.128.)  **24. division of a battle:** disposition of a military unit.  **25. a spinster:** i.e., a housewife, one whose regular occupation is spinning.  **theoric:** theory.

Wherein the togaed consuls° can propose°
As masterly as he. Mere prattle, without practice
Is all his soldiership. But he, sir, had th'election;
And I, of whom his° eyes had seen the proof
At Rhodes, at Cyprus, and on other grounds                    30
Christened and heathen, must be beleed and calmed°
By debitor and creditor.° This countercaster,°
He, in good time,° must his lieutenant be,
And I — God bless the mark!° — his Moorship's ancient.°

RODERIGO:
By heaven, I rather would have been his hangman.°              35

IAGO:
Why, there's no remedy. 'Tis the curse of service;
Preferment° goes by letter and affection,°
And not by the old gradation,° where each second
Stood heir to th' first. Now, sir, be judge yourself
Whether I in any just term° am affined°                        40
To love the Moor.

RODERIGO:    I would not follow him then.

IAGO:    Oh, sir, content you.°
I follow him to serve my turn upon him.
We cannot all be masters, nor all masters                      45
Cannot be truly° followed. You shall mark
Many a duteous and knee-crooking knave
That, doting on his own obsequious bondage,
Wears out his time, much like his master's ass,
For naught but provender, and when he's old, cashiered.°       50
Whip me° such honest knaves. Others there are
Who, trimmed in forms and visages of duty,°

---

26. **togaed consuls:** toga-wearing counselors or senators.  **propose:** discuss.  29. **his:** Othello's.  31. **beleed and calmed:** left to leeward without wind, becalmed. (A sailing metaphor.) 32. **debitor and creditor:** (A name for a system of bookkeeping, here used as a contemptuous nickname for Cassio.)  **countercaster:** i.e., bookkeeper, one who tallies with *counters*, or "metal disks." (Said contemptuously.)  33. **in good time:** opportunely, i.e., forsooth.  34. **God bless the mark:** (Perhaps originally a formula to ward off evil; here an expression of impatience.) **ancient:** standard-bearer, ensign (below lieutenant in rank). [Hall]  35. **his hangman:** the executioner of him.  37. **Preferment:** promotion.  **letter and affection:** personal influence and favoritism.  38. **old gradation:** step-by-step seniority, the traditional way.  40. **term:** respect.  **affined:** bound.  43. **content you:** don't you worry about that.  46. **truly:** faithfully.  50. **cashiered:** dismissed from service.  51. **Whip me:** whip, as far as I'm concerned. 52. **trimmed . . . duty:** dressed up in the mere form and show of dutifulness.

Keep yet their hearts attending on themselves,
And, throwing but shows of service on their lords,
Do well thrive by them, and when they have lined their coats,°     55
Do themselves homage.° These fellows have some soul,
And such a one do I profess myself. For, sir,
It is as sure as you are Roderigo,
Were I the Moor I would not be Iago.°
In following him, I follow but myself —     60
Heaven is my judge, not I for love and duty,
But seeming so for my peculiar° end.
For when my outward action doth demonstrate
The native° act and figure° of my heart
In compliment extern,° 'tis not long after     65
But I will wear my heart upon my sleeve
For daws° to peck at. I am not what I am.°

RODERIGO:
What a full° fortune does the thick-lips° owe°
If he can carry 't thus!°

IAGO:                                    Call up her father.
Rouse him, make after him, poison his delight,     70
Proclaim him in the streets; incense her kinsmen,
And, though he in a fertile climate dwell,
Plague him with flies.° Though that his joy be joy,°
Yet throw such changes of vexation° on't
As it may lose some color.°     75

RODERIGO:
Here is her father's house. I'll call aloud.

IAGO:
Do, with like timorous° accent and dire yell

---

55. **lined their coats:** i.e., stuffed their purses.   56. **Do themselves homage:** i.e., attend to self-interest solely.   59. **Were . . . Iago:** i.e., if I were able to assume command, I certainly would not choose to remain a subordinate, or, I would keep a suspicious eye on a flattering subordinate. 62. **peculiar:** particular, personal.   64. **native:** innate.  **figure:** shape, intent.  65. **compliment extern:** outward show (conforming in this case to the inner workings and intention of the heart).   67. **daws:** small crowlike birds, proverbially stupid and avaricious.  **I am not what I am:** i.e., I am not one who wears his heart on his sleeve.   68. **full:** swelling.  **thick-lips:** (Elizabethans often applied the term "Moor" to Negroes.)  **owe:** own.  69. **carry't thus:** carry this off.   72–73. **though . . . flies:** though he seems prosperous and happy now, vex him with misery.   73. **Though . . . be joy:** Although he seems fortunate and happy. (Repeats the idea of line 72.)   74. **changes of vexation:** vexing changes.   75. **As . . . color:** that may cause it to lose some of its first gloss.   77. **timorous:** frightening.

As when, by night and negligence, the fire°
Is spied in populous cities.

RODERIGO:
What ho, Brabantio! Signor Brabantio, ho!                              80

IAGO:
Awake! What ho, Brabantio! Thieves, thieves, thieves!
Look to your house, your daughter, and your bags!
Thieves, thieves!

*Brabantio [enters] above, [at a window].*°

BRABANTIO:
What is the reason of this terrible summons?
What is the matter there?                                             85

RODERIGO:
Signor, is all your family within?

IAGO:
Are your doors locked?

BRABANTIO:                    Why, wherefore ask you this?

IAGO:
Zounds,° sir, you're robbed. For shame, put on your gown!
Your heart is burst; you have lost half your soul.
Even now, now, very now, an old black ram
Is tupping° your white ewe. Arise, arise!                             90
Awake the snorting° citizens with the bell,
Or else the devil° will make a grandsire of you.
Arise, I say!

BRABANTIO:    What, have you lost your wits?

RODERIGO:
Most reverend signor, do you know my voice?                           95

BRABANTIO:    Not I. What are you?

RODERIGO:    My name is Roderigo.

BRABANTIO:    The worser welcome.
I have charged thee not to haunt about my doors.
In honest plainness thou hast heard me say                          100
My daughter is not for thee; and now, in madness,

---

78. **As . . . fire:** as when a fire, having gained hold by negligence at night.    83. **s.d. *at a window:*** (This stage direction, from the Quarto, probably calls for an appearance on the gallery above and rearstage.)    88. **Zounds:** by His (Christ's) wounds.    91. **tupping:** covering, copulating with. (Said of sheep.)    92. **snorting:** snoring.    93. **the devil:** (The devil was conventionally pictured as black.)

Being full of supper and distemp'ring° drafts,
Upon malicious bravery° dost thou come
To start° my quiet.

RODERIGO:
Sir, sir, sir —

BRABANTIO:      But thou must needs be sure                    105
My spirits and my place have in their power°
To make this bitter to thee.

RODERIGO:                          Patience, good sir.

BRABANTIO:
What tell'st thou me of robbing? This is Venice;
My house is not a grange.°

RODERIGO:                          Most grave Brabantio,
In simple° and pure soul I come to you.                       110

IAGO:    Zounds, sir, you are one of those that will not serve God if the devil
bid you. Because we come to do you service and you think we are ruffi-
ans, you'll have your daughter covered with a Barbary° horse; you'll have
your nephews° neigh to you; you'll have coursers for cousins and jennets
for germans.°                                                 115

BRABANTIO:    What profane wretch art thou?

IAGO:    I am one, sir, that comes to tell you your daughter and the Moor are
now making the beast with two backs.°

BRABANTIO:
Thou art a villain.

IAGO:                          You are — a senator.°

BRABANTIO:
This thou shalt answer.° I know thee, Roderigo.               120

RODERIGO:
Sir, I will answer anything. But I beseech you,
If 't be your pleasure and most wise° consent —
As partly I find it is — that your fair daughter,
At this odd-even and dull watch o'th' night,°
Transported with° no worse nor better guard                   125

---

102. **distemp'ring**: intoxicating.   103. **Upon malicious bravery**: with hostile intent to defy me.   104. **start**: startle, disrupt.   106. **My . . . power**: my temperament and my authority of office have it in their power.   109. **grange**: isolated country house.   110. **simple**: sincere. 113. **Barbary**: from northern Africa (and hence associated with Othello).   114. **nephews**: i.e., grandsons.   114–15. **you'll . . . germans**: you'll consent to have powerful horses for kinfolks and small Spanish horses for near relatives.   118. **making the beast with two backs**: copulating. [Hall]   119. **a senator**: (Said with mock politeness, as though the word itself were an insult.)   120. **answer**: be held accountable for.   122. **wise**: well-informed.   124. **At . . . night**: at this hour that is between day and night, neither the one nor the other.   125. **with**: by.

But with a knave° of common hire, a gondolier,
To the gross clasps of a lascivious Moor —
If this be known to you and your allowance°
We then have done you bold and saucy° wrongs.
But if you know not this, my manners tell me                    130
We have your wrong rebuke. Do not believe
That, from° the sense of all civility,°
I thus would play and trifle with your reverence.°
Your daughter, if you have not given her leave,
I say again, hath made a gross revolt,                          135
Tying her duty, beauty, wit,° and fortunes
In an extravagant and wheeling stranger
Of here and everywhere.° Straight° satisfy yourself.
If she be in her chamber or your house,
Let loose on me the justice of the state                        140
For thus deluding you.
BRABANTIO: [*calling*]    Strike on the tinder,° ho!
Give me a taper! Call up all my people!
This accident° is not unlike my dream.
Belief of it oppresses me already.                              145
Light, I say, light!                              *Exit* [*above*].
IAGO:                 Farewell, for I must leave you.
It seems not meet° nor wholesome to my place°
To be producted° — as, if I stay, I shall —
Against the Moor. For I do know the state,
However this may gall° him with some check,°                    150
Cannot with safety cast° him, for he's embarked°
With such loud° reason to the Cyprus wars,
Which even now stands in act,° that, for their souls,°
Another of his fathom° they have none
To lead their business; in which regard,°                       155
Though I do hate him as I do hell pains,

---

126. **But with a knave:** than by a low fellow, a servant.    128. **and your allowance:** and has your permission.    129. **saucy:** insolent.    132. **from:** contrary to.    **civility:** good manners, decency. 133. **your reverence:** (1) the respect due to you; (2) Your Reverence.    136. **wit:** intelligence. 137–38. **In . . . everywhere:** to a wandering and vagabond foreigner of uncertain origins. 140. **Straight:** straightaway.    142. **tinder:** charred linen ignited by a spark from flint and steel, used to light torches or *tapers* (lines 143, 168).    144. **accident:** occurrence, event.    147. **meet:** fitting.    **place:** position (as ensign).    148. **producted:** produced (as a witness).    150. **gall:** rub; oppress.    **check:** rebuke.    151. **cast:** dismiss.    **embarked:** engaged.    152. **loud:** urgent. 153. **stands in act:** have started.    **for their souls:** to save their souls.    154. **fathom:** i.e., ability, depth of experience.    155. **in which regard:** out of regard for which.

Yet for necessity of present life°
I must show out a flag and sign of love,
Which is indeed but sign. That you shall surely find him,
Lead to the Sagittary° the raisèd search,°                          160
And there will I be with him. So farewell.                          *Exit.*

*Enter [below] Brabantio [in his nightgown]° with servants and torches.*

BRABANTIO:
It is too true an evil. Gone she is;
And what's to come of my despisèd time°
Is naught but bitterness. Now, Roderigo,
Where didst thou see her? — Oh, unhappy girl! —                     165
With the Moor, say'st thou? — Who would be a father! —
How didst thou know 'twas she? — Oh, she deceives me
Past thought! — What said she to you? — Get more tapers.
Raise all my kindred. — Are they married, think you?
RODERIGO:    Truly, I think they are.                               170
BRABANTIO:
Oh, heaven! How got she out? Oh, treason of the blood!
Fathers, from hence trust not your daughters' minds
By what you see them act. Is there not charms°
By which the property° of youth and maidhood
May be abused?° Have you not read, Roderigo,                        175
Of some such thing?
RODERIGO:                    Yes, sir, I have indeed.
BRABANTIO:
Call up my brother. — Oh, would you had had her! —
Some one way, some another. — Do you know
Where we may apprehend her and the Moor?
RODERIGO:
I think I can discover° him, if you please                          180
To get good guard and go along with me.
BRABANTIO:
Pray you, lead on. At every house I'll call;
I may command° at most. — Get weapons, ho!

---

157. **life:** livelihood.    160. **Sagittary:** (An inn or house where Othello and Desdemona are staying, named for its sign of Sagittarius, or Centaur.)    **raisèd search:** search party roused out of sleep.    161. **s.d.** *nightgown:* dressing gown. (This costuming is specified in the Quarto text.)    163. **time:** i.e., remainder of life.    173. **charms:** spells.    174. **property:** special quality, nature.    175. **abused:** deceived.    180. **discover:** reveal, uncover.    183. **command:** demand assistance.

And raise some special officers of night. —
On, good Roderigo. I'll deserve° your pains.               *Exeunt.*    185

## ACT I, SCENE 2°

*Enter Othello, Iago, attendants with torches.*

IAGO:
Though in the trade of war I have slain men,
Yet do I hold it very stuff° o'th' conscience
To do no contrived° murder. I lack iniquity
Sometimes to do me service. Nine or ten times
I had thought t'have yerked° him° here under the ribs.               5
OTHELLO:
'Tis better as it is.
IAGO:                    Nay, but he prated,
And spoke such scurvy and provoking terms
Against your honor
That, with the little godliness I have,
I did full hard forbear him.° But, I pray you, sir,               10
Are you fast married? Be assured of this,
That the magnifico° is much beloved,
And hath in his effect° a voice potential°
As double as the Duke's. He will divorce you,
Or put upon you what restraint or grievance               15
The law, with all his might to enforce it on,
Will give him cable.°
OTHELLO:                    Let him do his spite.
My services which I have done the seigniory°
Shall out-tongue his complaints. 'Tis yet to know° —
Which, when I know that boasting is an honor,               20
I shall promulgate — I fetch my life and being
From men of royal siege,° and my demerits°

185. **deserve:** show gratitude for.   ACT I, SCENE 2. Location: Venice. Another street, before
Othello's lodgings.   2. **very stuff:** essence, basic material. (Continuing the metaphor of
*trade* from line 1.)   3. **contrived:** premeditated.   5. **yerked:** stabbed.   **him:** i.e., Roderigo.
10. **I . . . him:** I restrained myself with great difficulty from assaulting him.   12. **magnifico:**
Venetian grandee, i.e., Brabantio.   13. **in his effect:** at his command.   **potential:** powerful.
17. **cable:** i.e., scope.   18. **seigniory:** Venetian government.   19. **yet to know:** not yet widely
known.   22. **siege:** i.e., rank. (Literally, a seat used by a person of distinction.)   **demerits:**
deserts.

May speak unbonneted° to as proud a fortune
As this that I have reached. For know, Iago,
But that I love the gentle Desdemona,                                    25
I would not my unhousèd° free condition
Put into circumscription and confine°
For the sea's worth.° But, look, what lights come yond?

*Enter Cassio [and officers]° with torches.*

IAGO:
Those are the raisèd father and his friends.
You were best go in.
OTHELLO:              Not I. I must be found.               30
My parts, my title, and my perfect soul°
Shall manifest me rightly. Is it they?
IAGO:    By Janus,° I think no.
OTHELLO:
The servants of the Duke? And my lieutenant?
The goodness of the night upon you, friends!               35
What is the news?
CASSIO:              The Duke does greet you, General,
And he requires your haste-post-haste appearance
Even on the instant.
OTHELLO:              What is the matter, think you?
CASSIO:
Something from Cyprus, as I may divine.°
It is a business of some heat.° The galleys               40
Have sent a dozen sequent° messengers
This very night at one another's heels,
And many of the consuls,° raised and met,
Are at the Duke's already. You have been hotly called for;
When, being not at your lodging to be found,               45
The Senate hath sent about° three several° quests
To search you out.
OTHELLO:              'Tis well I am found by you.

---

23. **unbonneted:** without removing the hat, i.e., on equal terms (? Or "with hat off," "in all due modesty.")   26. **unhousèd:** unconfined, undomesticated.   27. **circumscription and confine:** restriction and confinement.   28. **the sea's worth:** all the riches at the bottom of the sea.   28. s.d. *officers:* (The Quarto text specifies, "*Enter* Cassio *with lights, Officers, and torches.*")   31. **My . . . soul:** my natural gifts, my position or reputation, and my unflawed conscience.   33. **Janus:** Roman two-faced god of beginnings.   39. **divine:** guess.   40. **heat:** urgency.   41. **sequent:** successive.   43. **consuls:** senators.   46. **about:** all over the city.   **several:** separate.

I will but spend a word here in the house
And go with you.             *[Exit.]*

CASSIO:           Ancient, what makes° he here?

IAGO:

Faith, he tonight hath boarded° a land carrack.°       50
If it prove lawful prize,° he's made forever.

CASSIO:

I do not understand.

IAGO:         He's married.

CASSIO:          To who?

*[Enter Othello.]*

IAGO:

Marry,° to — Come, Captain, will you go?

OTHELLO:

Have with you.°

CASSIO:

Here comes another troop to seek for you.         55

*Enter Brabantio, Roderigo, with officers and torches.°*

IAGO:

It is Brabantio. General, be advised.°
He comes to bad intent.

OTHELLO:       Holla! stand there!

RODERIGO:

Signor, it is the Moor.

BRABANTIO:       Down with him, thief!

*[They draw on both sides.]*

IAGO:

You, Roderigo! Come, sir, I am for you.

OTHELLO:

Keep up° your bright swords, for the dew will rust them.     60
Good signor, you shall more command with years
Than with your weapons.

---

49. **makes:** does.    50. **boarded:** gone aboard and seized as an act of piracy. (With sexual suggestion.)    **carrack:** large merchant ship.    51. **prize:** booty.    53. **Marry:** (An oath, originally "by the Virgin Mary"; here used with wordplay on *married*.)    54. **Have with you:** i.e., let's go.    55. s.d. *officers and torches:* (The Quarto text calls for *"others with lights and weapons."*)    56. **be advised:** be on your guard.    60. **Keep up:** keep in the sheath.

BRABANTIO:
  O thou foul thief, where hast thou stowed my daughter?
  Damned as thou art, thou hast enchanted her!
  For I'll refer me to all things of sense,°              65
  If she in chains of magic were not bound
  Whether a maid so tender, fair, and happy,
  So opposite to marriage that she shunned
  The wealthy curlèd darlings of our nation,
  Would ever have, t'incur a general mock,           70
  Run from her guardage° to the sooty bosom
  Of such a thing as thou — to fear, not to delight.
  Judge me the world, if 'tis not gross in sense°
  That thou hast practiced on her with foul charms,
  Abused her delicate youth with drugs or minerals°     75
  That weakens motion.° I'll have't disputed on;°
  'Tis probable, and palpable to thinking.
  I therefore apprehend and do attach° thee
  For an abuser° of the world, a practicer
  Of arts inhibited° and out of warrant.° —         80
  Lay hold upon him! If he do resist,
  Subdue him at his peril.
OTHELLO:                 Hold your hands,
  Both you of my inclining° and the rest.
  Were it my cue to fight, I should have known it
  Without a prompter. — Whither will you that I go     85
  To answer this your charge?
BRABANTIO:     To prison, till fit time
  Of law and course of direct session°
  Call thee to answer.
OTHELLO:            What if I do obey?
  How may the Duke be therewith satisfied,        90
  Whose messengers are here about my side
  Upon some present business of the state
  To bring me to him?
OFFICER:           'Tis true, most worthy signor.

---

65. **I'll . . . sense:** I'll submit my case to one and all.   71. **guardage:** guardianship.   73. **gross in sense:** obvious.   75. **minerals:** i.e., poisons.   76. **weakens motion:** impair the vital faculties.   **disputed on:** argued in court by professional counsel, debated by experts.   78. **attach:** arrest.   79. **abuser:** deceiver.   80. **arts inhibited:** prohibited arts, black magic.   **out of warrant:** illegal.   83. **inclining:** following, party.   88. **course of direct session:** regular or specially convened legal proceedings.

The Duke's in council, and your noble self,
I am sure, is sent for.
BRABANTIO:                    How? The Duke in council?                    95
In this time of the night? Bring him away.°
Mine's not an idle° cause. The Duke himself,
Or any of my brothers of the state,
Cannot but feel this wrong as 'twere their own;
For if such actions may have passage free,°                              100
Bondslaves and pagans shall our statesmen be.          *Exeunt.*

## ACT 1, SCENE 3°

*Enter Duke [and] Senators [and sit at a table, with lights], and Officers.° [The Duke and Senators are reading dispatches.]*

DUKE:
There is no composition° in these news
That gives them credit.
FIRST SENATOR:    Indeed, they are disproportioned.°
My letters say a hundred and seven galleys.
DUKE:
And mine, a hundred and forty.
SECOND SENATOR:                    And mine, two hundred.          5
But though they jump° not on a just° account —
As in these cases, where the aim° reports,
'Tis oft with difference — yet do they all confirm
A Turkish fleet, and bearing up to Cyprus.
DUKE:
Nay, it is possible enough to judgment.                                  10
I do not so secure me in the error,
But the main article I do approve°
In fearful sense.
SAILOR: (*within*)    What ho, what ho, what ho!

*Enter Sailor.*

96. **away:** right along.    97. **idle:** trifling.    100. **may . . . free:** are allowed to go unchecked.
**Act 1, Scene 3. Location:** Venice. A council chamber.    **s.d.** *Enter . . . Officers:* (The Quarto text calls for the Duke and senators to *"set at a Table with lights and Attendants."*)    1. **composition:** consistency.    3. **disproportioned:** inconsistent.    6. **jump:** agree.    **just:** exact.    7. **the aim:** conjecture.    11–12. **I do not . . . approve:** I do not take such (false) comfort in the discrepancies that I fail to perceive the main point, i.e., that the Turkish fleet is threatening.

OFFICER:    A messenger from the galleys.
DUKE:    Now, what's the business?                                    15
SAILOR:
The Turkish preparation° makes for Rhodes.
So was I bid report here to the state
By Signor Angelo.
DUKE:
How say you by° this change?
FIRST SENATOR:                       This cannot be
By no assay° of reason. 'Tis a pageant°                              20
To keep us in false gaze.° When we consider
Th'importancy of Cyprus to the Turk,
And let ourselves again but understand
That, as it more concerns the Turk than Rhodes,
So may he with more facile question bear it,°                        25
For that° it stands not in such warlike brace,°
But altogether lacks th'abilities°
That Rhodes is dressed in° — if we make thought of this,
We must not think the Turk is so unskillful°
To leave that latest° which concerns him first,                      30
Neglecting an attempt of ease and gain
To wake and wage° a danger profitless.
DUKE:
Nay, in all confidence, he's not for Rhodes.
OFFICER:    Here is more news.

*Enter a Messenger.*

MESSENGER:
The Ottomites, reverend and gracious,                               35
Steering with due course toward the isle of Rhodes,
Have there injointed them° with an after° fleet.
FIRST SENATOR:
Ay, so I thought. How many, as you guess?

---

16. **preparation:** fleet prepared for battle.   19. **by:** about.   20. **assay:** test.   **pageant:** mere show.   21. **in false gaze:** looking the wrong way.   25. **So may . . . it:** so also he (the Turk) can more easily capture it (Cyprus).   26. **For that:** since.   **brace:** state of defense.   27. **th'abilities:** the means of self-defense.   28. **dressed in:** equipped with.   29. **unskillful:** deficient in judgment.   30. **latest:** last.   32. **wake and wage:** stir up and risk.   37. **injointed them:** joined themselves.   **after:** second, following.

MESSENGER:
Of thirty sail; and now they do restem
Their backward course,° bearing with frank appearance°   40
Their purposes toward Cyprus. Signor Montano,
Your trusty and most valiant servitor,°
With his free duty° recommends° you thus,
And prays you to believe him.
DUKE:   'Tis certain then for Cyprus.   45
Marcus Luccicos, is not he in town?
FIRST SENATOR:   He's now in Florence.
DUKE:
Write from us to him, post-post-haste. Dispatch.
FIRST SENATOR:
Here comes Brabantio and the valiant Moor.

*Enter Brabantio, Othello, Cassio, Iago, Roderigo, and officers.*

DUKE:
Valiant Othello, we must straight° employ you   50
Against the general enemy° Ottoman.
[*To Brabantio*] I did not see you; welcome, gentle° signor.
We lacked your counsel and your help tonight.
BRABANTIO:
So did I yours. Good Your Grace, pardon me;
Neither my place° nor aught I heard of business   55
Hath raised me from my bed, nor doth the general care
Take hold of me, for my particular° grief
Is of so floodgate° and o'erbearing nature
That it engluts° and swallows other sorrows
And it is still itself.°
DUKE:                    Why, what's the matter?   60
BRABANTIO:
My daughter! Oh, my daughter.
DUKE AND SENATORS:                    Dead?
BRABANTIO:                              Ay, to me.

---

39–40. **restem . . . course:** retrace their original course.   40. **frank appearance:** undisguised intent.   42. **servitor:** officer under your command.   43. **free duty:** freely given and loyal service.   **recommends:** commends himself and reports to.   50. **straight:** straightaway.   51. **general enemy:** universal enemy to all Christendom.   52. **gentle:** noble.   55. **place:** official position.   57. **particular:** personal.   58. **floodgate:** i.e., overwhelming (as when floodgates are opened).   59. **engluts:** engulfs.   60. **is still itself:** remains undiminished.

She is abused,° stol'n from me, and corrupted
By spells and medicines bought of mountebanks;
For nature so preposterously to err,
Being not deficient,° blind, or lame of sense,°                    65
Sans° witchcraft could not.

DUKE:
Whoe'er he be that in this foul proceeding
Hath thus beguiled your daughter of herself
And you of her, the bloody book of law
You shall yourself read in the bitter letter                       70
After your own sense° — yea, though our proper° son
Stood in your action.°

BRABANTIO:                    Humbly I thank Your Grace.
Here is the man, this Moor, whom now it seems
Your special mandate for the state affairs
Hath hither brought.

ALL:                          We are very sorry for't.              75

DUKE: [to Othello]
What, in your own part, can you say to this?

BRABANTIO:    Nothing, but this is so.

OTHELLO:
Most potent, grave, and reverend signors,
My very noble and approved° good masters:
That I have ta'en away this old man's daughter,                    80
It is most true; true, I have married her.
The very head and front° of my offending
Hath this extent, no more. Rude° am I in my speech,
And little blessed with the soft phrase of peace;
For since these arms of mine had seven years' pith,°               85
Till now some nine moons wasted,° they have used
Their dearest° action in the tented field;
And little of this great world can I speak
More than pertains to feats of broils° and battle,
And therefore little shall I grace my cause                        90

---

62. abused: deceived.   65. deficient: defective.   lame of sense: deficient in sensory perception.   66. Sans: without.   71. After . . . sense: according to your own interpretation.   our
proper: my own.   72. Stood . . . action: were under your accusation.   79. approved: proved,
esteemed.   82. head and front: height and breadth, entire extent.   83. Rude: unpolished.
85. since . . . pith: i.e., since I was seven. (*Pith* means "strength, vigor.")   86. Till . . . wasted:
until some nine months ago (since when Othello has evidently not been on active duty, but in
Venice).   87. dearest: most valuable.   89. broils: skirmishes. [Hall]

In speaking for myself. Yet, by your gracious patience,
I will a round° unvarnished tale deliver
Of my whole course of love — what drugs, what charms,
What conjuration, and what mighty magic,
For such proceeding I am charged withal,°                     95
I won his daughter.

BRABANTIO:          A maiden never bold;
Of spirit so still and quiet that her motion
Blushed at herself;° and she, in spite of nature,
Of years,° of country, credit,° everything,
To fall in love with what she feared to look on!             100
It is a judgment maimed and most imperfect
That will confess° perfection so could err
Against all rules of nature, and must be driven
To find out practices° of cunning hell
Why this should be. I therefore vouch° again                 105
That with some mixtures powerful o'er the blood,°
Or with some dram conjured to this effect,°
He wrought upon her.

DUKE:               To vouch this is no proof,
Without more wider° and more overt test°
Than these thin habits° and poor likelihoods°               110
Of modern seeming° do prefer° against him.

FIRST SENATOR: But Othello, speak.
Did you by indirect and forcèd courses°
Subdue and poison this young maid's affections?
Or came it by request and such fair question°               115
As soul to soul affordeth?

OTHELLO:               I do beseech you,
Send for the lady to the Sagittary
And let her speak of me before her father.
If you do find me foul in her report,
The trust, the office I do hold of you                        120

---

92. **round:** plain.   95. **withal:** with.   97–98. **her . . . herself:** i.e., she blushed easily at herself. (*Motion* can suggest the impulse of the soul or of the emotions, or physical movement.)   99. **years:** i.e., difference in age.   **credit:** virtuous reputation.   102. **confess:** concede (that).   104. **practices:** plots.   105. **vouch:** assert.   106. **blood:** passions.   107. **dram . . . effect:** dose made by magical spells to have this effect.   109. **more wider:** fuller.   **test:** testimony.   110. **habits:** garments, i.e., appearances.   **poor likelihoods:** weak inferences.   111. **modern seeming:** commonplace assumption.   **prefer:** bring forth.   113. **forcèd courses:** means used against her will.   115. **question:** conversation.

Not only take away, but let your sentence
Even fall upon my life.

DUKE:                    Fetch Desdemona hither.

OTHELLO: [*to Iago*]

Ancient, conduct them. You best know the place.

[*Exeunt Iago and attendants.*]

And, till she come, as truly as to heaven
I do confess the vices of my blood,°
So justly° to your grave ears I'll present                                    125
How I did thrive in this fair lady's love,
And she in mine.

DUKE:   Say it, Othello.

OTHELLO:

Her father loved me; oft invited me,                                        130
Still° question'd me the story of my life
From year to year — the battles, sieges, fortunes
That I have passed.
I ran it through, even from my boyish days
To th' very moment that he bade me tell it,                                 135
Wherein I spoke of most disastrous chances,
Of moving accidents° by flood and field,
Of hairbreadth scapes i'th'imminent deadly breach,°
Of being taken by the insolent foe
And sold to slavery, of my redemption thence,                              140
And portance° in my travels' history,
Wherein of antres° vast and deserts idle,°
Rough quarries,° rocks, and hills whose heads touch heaven,
It was my hint° to speak — such was the process —
And of the Cannibals that each other eat,                                   145
The Anthropophagi,° and men whose heads
Do grow beneath their shoulders. These things to hear
Would Desdemona seriously incline;
But still the house affairs would draw her thence,
Which ever as she could with haste dispatch                                 150
She'd come again, and with a greedy ear
Devour up my discourse. Which I, observing,

125. **blood:** passions, human nature.   126. **justly:** truthfully, accurately.   131. **Still:** continually.   137. **moving accidents:** stirring happenings.   138. **i'th'imminent . . . breach:** in death-threatening gaps made in a fortification.   141. **portance:** conduct.   142. **antres:** caverns. **idle:** barren, desolate.   143. **Rough quarries:** rugged rock formations.   144. **hint:** occasion, opportunity.   146. **Anthropophagi:** man-eaters. (A term from Pliny's *Natural History*.)

Took once a pliant° hour, and found good means
To draw from her a prayer of earnest heart
That I would all my pilgrimage dilate,°                        155
Whereof by parcels° she had something heard,
But not intentively.° I did consent,
And often did beguile her of her tears,
When I did speak of some distressful stroke
That my youth suffered. My story being done,           160
She gave me for my pains a world of sighs.
She swore, in faith, 'twas strange, 'twas passing° strange,
'Twas pitiful, 'twas wondrous pitiful.
She wished she had not heard it, yet she wished
That heaven had made her° such a man. She thanked me,   165
And bade me, if I had a friend that loved her,
I should but teach him how to tell my story,
And that would woo her. Upon this hint° I spake.
She loved me for the dangers I had passed,
And I loved her that she did pity them.                      170
This only is the witchcraft I have used.
Here comes the lady. Let her witness it.

*Enter Desdemona, Iago, [and] attendants.*

DUKE:
I think this tale would win my daughter too.
Good Brabantio,
Take up this mangled matter at the best.°                    175
Men do their broken weapons rather use
Than their bare hands.
BRABANTIO:                    I pray you, hear her speak.
If she confess that she was half the wooer,
Destruction on my head if my bad blame
Light on the man! — Come hither, gentle mistress.        180
Do you perceive in all this noble company
Where most you owe obedience?
DESDEMONA:                          My noble father,
I do perceive here a divided duty.

153. **pliant:** well-suiting.   155. **dilate:** relate in detail.   156. **by parcels:** piecemeal.   157. **intentively:** with full attention, continuously.   162. **passing:** exceedingly.   165. **made her:** (1) created her to be (2) made for her.   168. **hint:** opportunity. (Othello does not mean that she was dropping hints.)   175. **Take . . . best:** make the best of a bad bargain.

To you I am bound for life and education;°
My life and education both do learn° me                                      185
How to respect you. You are the lord of duty;°
I am hitherto your daughter. But here's my husband,
And so much duty as my mother showed
To you, preferring you before her father,
So much I challenge° that I may profess                                     190
Due to the Moor my lord.
BRABANTIO:    God be with you! I have done.
Please it Your Grace, on to the state affairs.
I had rather to adopt a child than get° it.
Come hither, Moor.          [*He joins the hands of Othello and Desdemona.*]   195
I here do give thee that with all my heart°
Which, but thou hast already, with all my heart°
I would keep from thee. — For your sake,° jewel,
I am glad at soul I have no other child,
For thy escape° would teach me tyranny,                                     200
To hang clogs° on them. — I have done, my lord.
DUKE:
Let me speak like yourself,° and lay a sentence°
Which, as a grece° or step, may help these lovers
Into your favor.
When remedies are past, the griefs are ended                               205
By seeing the worst, which late on hopes depended.°
To mourn a mischief° that is past and gone
Is the next° way to draw new mischief on.
What cannot be preserved when fortune takes,
Patience her injury a mock'ry makes.°                                       210
The robbed that smiles steals something from the thief;
He robs himself that spends a bootless grief.°

184. **education:** upbringing.  185. **learn:** teach.  186. **of duty:** to whom duty is due.  190. **challenge:** claim.  194. **get:** beget.  196. **with all my heart:** wherein my whole affection has been engaged.  197. **with all my heart:** willingly, gladly.  198. **For your sake:** because of you.  200. **escape:** elopement.  201. **clogs:** (Literally, blocks of wood fastened to the legs of criminals or animals to inhibit escape.)  202. **like yourself:** i.e., as you would, in your proper temper.  **lay a sentence:** apply a maxim.  203. **grece:** step.  205–06. **When . . . depended:** when all hope of remedy is past, our sorrows are ended by realizing that the worst has already happened which lately we hoped would not happen.  207. **mischief:** misfortune, injury.  208. **next:** nearest.  209–10. **What . . . makes:** when fortune takes away what cannot be saved, patience makes a mockery of fortune's wrongdoing.  212. **spends a bootless grief:** indulges in unavailing grief.

BRABANTIO:
So let the Turk of Cyprus us beguile,
We lose it not, so long as we can smile.
He bears the sentence well that nothing bears                              215
But the free comfort which from thence he hears,
But he bears both the sentence and the sorrow
That, to pay grief, must of poor patience borrow.°
These sentences, to sugar or to gall,
Being strong on both sides, are equivocal.°                                220
But words are words. I never yet did hear
That the bruisèd heart was piercèd through the ear.°
I humbly beseech you, proceed to th'affairs of state.

DUKE:   The Turk with a most mighty preparation makes for Cyprus.
Othello, the fortitude° of the place is best known to you; and though we   225
have there a substitute° of most allowed° sufficiency, yet opinion, a sovereign mistress of effects, throws a more safer voice on you.° You must
therefore be content to slubber° the gloss of your new fortunes with this
more stubborn and boisterous expedition.°

OTHELLO:
The tyrant custom, most grave senators,                                    230
Hath made the flinty and steel couch of war
My thrice-driven° bed of down. I do agnize°
A natural and prompt alacrity
I find in hardness,° and do undertake
These present wars against the Ottomites.                                  235
Most humbly therefore bending to your state,°
I crave fit disposition for my wife,
Due reference of place and exhibition,
With such accommodation and besort
As levels with her breeding.°                                              240

215–18. He bears . . . borrow: a person can easily be comforted by your maxim that enjoys its platitudinous comfort without having to experience the misfortune that occasions sorrow, but anyone whose grief bankrupts his poor patience is left with your saying and his sorrow, too. (*Bears the sentence* also plays on the meaning, "receives judicial sentence.") 219–20. These . . . equivocal: these fine maxims are equivocal, being equally appropriate to happiness or bitter-ness. 222. piercèd . . . ear: relieved by mere words reaching it through the ear. 225. fortitude: strength. 226. substitute: deputy. allowed: acknowledged. 226–27. opinion . . . on you: general opinion, an important determiner of affairs, chooses you as the best man. 228. slub-ber: soil, sully. 229. stubborn . . . expedition: rough and violent expedition, for which haste is needed. 232. thrice-driven: thrice sifted, winnowed. agnize: know in myself, acknowl-edge. 234. hardness: hardship. 236. bending . . . state: bowing or kneeling to your author-ity. 238–40. Due . . . breeding: proper respect for her place (as my wife) and maintenance, with such suitable provision and attendance as befits her upbringing.

DUKE:
  Why at her father's.
BRABANTIO:                    I will not have it so.
OTHELLO:
  Nor I.
DESDEMONA:    Nor I. I would not there reside,
  To put my father in impatient thoughts
  By being in his eye. Most gracious Duke,          245
  To my unfolding° lend your prosperous° ear;
  And let me find a charter° in your voice,
  T'assist my simpleness.
DUKE:    What would you, Desdemona?
DESDEMONA:
  That I did love the Moor to live with him,          250
  My downright violence and storm of fortunes°
  May trumpet to the world. My heart's subdued
  Even to the very quality° of my lord.
  I saw Othello's visage in his mind,
  And to his honors and his valiant parts°          255
  Did I my soul and fortunes consecrate.
  So that, dear lords, if I be left behind
  A moth° of peace, and he go to the war,
  The rites° for which I love him are bereft me,
  And I a heavy° interim shall support          260
  By his dear° absence. Let me go with him.
OTHELLO:
  Let her have your voice.°
  Vouch with me, heaven, I therefor beg it not
  To please the palate of my appetite,
  Nor to comply with heat° — the young affects°          265
  In me defunct° — and proper° satisfaction,
  But to be free° and bounteous to her mind.
  And heaven defend° your good souls that you think°

246. **my unfolding:** what I shall unfold or say. **prosperous:** favorable. 247. **charter:** privilege, authorization. 251. **My . . . fortunes:** my plain and total breach of social custom. 253. **quality:** moral and spiritual identity. 255. **parts:** qualities. 258. **moth:** i.e., one who consumes merely. 259. **rites:** rites of love. (With a suggestion, too, of "rights," sharing.) 260. **heavy:** burdensome. 261. **dear:** grievous. 262. **voice:** consent. 265. **heat:** sexual passion. **young affects:** passions of youth, adolescent desires. 266. **defunct:** done with, at an end. **proper:** personal. 267. **free:** generous. 268. **defend:** forbid. **think:** should think.

I will your serious and great business scant
When she is with me. No, when light-winged toys                                    270
Of feathered Cupid seel° with wanton dullness
My speculative and officed instruments,°
That my disports corrupt and taint my business,°
Let huswives° make a skillet of my helm,
And all indign° and base adversities                                                            275
Make head° against my estimation!°

DUKE:
Be it as you shall privately determine,
Either for her stay or going. Th'affair cries haste,
And speed must answer it.

A SENATOR:                                     You must away tonight.

DESDEMONA:
Tonight, my lord?

DUKE:                                This night.

OTHELLO:                                     With all my heart.                                    280

DUKE:
At nine i'th' morning here we'll meet again.
Othello, leave some officer behind,
And he shall our commission bring to you,
With such things else of quality and respect°
As doth import° you.

OTHELLO:                                So please Your Grace, my ancient;                         285
A man he is of honesty and trust.
To his conveyance I assign my wife,
With what else needful Your Good Grace shall think
To be sent after me.

DUKE:                                Let it be so.
Good night to everyone. [*To Brabantio*] And, noble signor,                          290
If virtue no delighted° beauty lack,
Your son-in-law is far more fair than black.

FIRST SENATOR:
Adieu, brave Moor. Use Desdemona well.

---

**271. seel:** i.e., make blind (as in falconry, by sewing up the eyes of the hawk during training). **272. My . . . instruments:** my eyes, whose function is to see. **273. That . . . business:** in such a way that my sexual pastimes interfere with my official duties. **274. huswives:** housewives; also hussies. [Hall] **275. indign:** unworthy, shameful. **276. Make head:** raise an army. **estimation:** reputation. **284. of quality and respect:** of importance and relevance. **285. import:** concern. **291. delighted:** capable of delighting.

BRABANTIO:
Look to her, Moor, if thou hast eyes to see.
She has deceived her father, and may thee.                                                    295
*Exeunt [Duke, Brabantio, Cassio, Senators, and officers].*

OTHELLO:
My life upon her faith! — Honest Iago,
My Desdemona must I leave to thee.
I prithee, let thy wife attend on her,
And bring them after in the best advantage.°
Come, Desdemona. I have but an hour                                                          300
Of love, of worldly matters and direction,°
To spend with thee. We must obey the time.°          *Exit [with Desdemona].*

RODERIGO:   Iago —
IAGO:   What sayst thou, noble heart?
RODERIGO:   What will I do, think'st thou?                                                   305
IAGO:   Why, go to bed, and sleep.
RODERIGO:   I will incontinently° drown myself.
IAGO:   If thou dost, I shall never love thee after. Why, thou silly gentle-
man?
RODERIGO:   It is silliness to live when to live is torment; and then have we a           310
prescription° to die when death is our physician.
IAGO:   Oh, villainous!° I have looked upon the world for four times seven
years, and, since I could distinguish betwixt a benefit and an injury, I
never found man that knew how to love himself. Ere I would say I would
drown myself for the love of a guinea hen,° I would change° my human-           315
ity with a baboon.
RODERIGO:   What should I do? I confess it is my shame to be so fond,° but
it is not in my virtue° to amend it.
IAGO:   Virtue? A fig!° 'Tis in ourselves that we are thus or thus. Our bodies
are our gardens, to the which our wills are gardeners; so that if we will       320
plant nettles or sow lettuce, set hyssop° and weed up thyme, supply it
with one gender° of herbs or distract it with° many, either to have it
sterile with idleness° or manured with industry — why, the power and

---

299. **in . . . advantage:** at the most favorable opportunity.   301. **direction:** instructions.
302. **the time:** the urgency of the present crisis.   307. **incontinently:** immediately, without
self-restraint.   311. **prescription:** (1) right based on long-established custom (2) doctor's
prescription.   312. **villainous:** i.e., what perfect nonsense.   315. **guinea hen:** (A slang term
for a prostitute.)   **change:** exchange.   317. **fond:** infatuated.   318. **virtue:** strength, nature.
319. **fig:** (To give a fig is to thrust the thumb between the first and second fingers in a vulgar
and insulting gesture.)   321. **hyssop:** an herb of the mint family.   322. **gender:** kind.   **distract it with:** divide it among.   323. **idleness:** want of cultivation.

corrigible authority° of this lies in our wills. If the beam° of our lives had
not one scale of reason to poise° another of sensuality, the blood° and base-  325
ness of our natures would conduct us to most preposterous conclusions.
But we have reason to cool our raging motions,° our carnal stings, our
unbitted° lusts, whereof I take this that you call love to be a sect or scion.°

RODERIGO:   It cannot be.

IAGO:   It is merely a lust of the blood and a permission of the will. Come,  330
be a man. Drown thyself? Drown cats and blind° puppies. I have professed me thy friend, and I confess me knit to thy deserving with cables
of perdurable° toughness. I could never better stead° thee than now. Put
money in thy purse. Follow thou the wars; defeat thy favor° with an
usurped° beard. I say, put money in thy purse. It cannot be long that Des-  335
demona should continue her love to the Moor — put money in thy
purse — nor he his to her. It was a violent commencement in her, and
thou shalt see an answerable sequestration° — put but money in thy
purse. These Moors are changeable in their wills° — fill thy purse with
money. The food that to him now is as luscious as locusts° shall be to him  340
shortly as bitter as coloquintida.° She must change for youth; when she is
sated with his body, she will find the error of her choice. She must have
change, she must. Therefore put money in thy purse. If thou wilt needs
damn thyself, do it a more delicate way than drowning. Make° all the
money thou canst. If sanctimony° and a frail vow betwixt an erring° bar-  345
barian and a supersubtle Venetian be not too hard for my wits and all the
tribe of hell, thou shalt enjoy her. Therefore make money. A pox of°
drowning thyself! It is clean out of the way.° Seek thou rather to be
hanged in compassing° thy joy than to be drowned and go without her.

RODERIGO:   Wilt thou be fast° to my hopes if I depend on the issue?°  350

IAGO:   Thou art sure of me. Go, make money. I have told thee often, and I
retell thee again and again, I hate the Moor. My cause is hearted;° thine

---

324. corrigible authority: power to correct.   beam: balance.   325. poise: counterbalance.
blood: natural passions.   327. motions: appetites.   328. unbitted: unbridled, uncontrolled.
sect or scion: cutting or offshoot.   331. blind: i.e., newborn and helpless.   333. perdurable:
very durable.   stead: assist.   334. defeat thy favor: disguise your face.   335. usurped: (The
suggestion is that Roderigo is not man enough to have a beard of his own.)   338. an answerable sequestration: a corresponding cutting off or estrangement.   339. wills: carnal appetites.
340. locusts: fruit of the carob tree (see Matthew 3:4), or perhaps honeysuckle.   341. coloquintida: colocynth or bitter apple, a purgative.   344. Make: raise, collect.   345. sancti-
mony: (1) an aura of goodness (2) love-worship.   erring: wandering, vagabond, unsteady.
347. A pox of: a plague or curse on. [Hall]   348. clean . . . way: entirely unsuitable as a course
of action.   349. compassing: encompassing, embracing.   350. fast: true.   issue: (successful)
outcome.   352. hearted: fixed in the heart, heartfelt.

hath no less reason. Let us be conjunctive° in our revenge against him. If
thou canst cuckold him, thou dost thyself a pleasure, me a sport. There
are many events in the womb of time which will be delivered. Traverse,°     355
go, provide thy money. We will have more of this tomorrow. Adieu.

RODERIGO:   Where shall we meet i'th' morning?

IAGO:   At my lodging.

RODERIGO:   I'll be with thee betimes.° [*He starts to leave.*]

IAGO:   Go to,° farewell. — Do you hear, Roderigo?     360

RODERIGO:   What say you?

IAGO:   No more of drowning, do you hear?

RODERIGO:   I am changed.

IAGO:   Go to, farewell. Put money enough in your purse.

RODERIGO:   I'll sell all my land.     *Exit.*     365

IAGO:   Thus do I ever make my fool my purse;
For I mine own gained knowledge should profane
If I would time expend with such a snipe°
But for my sport and profit. I hate the Moor;
And it is thought abroad° that 'twixt my sheets     370
He's done my office.° I know not if 't be true;
But I, for mere suspicion in that kind,
Will do as if for surety.° He holds me well;°
The better shall my purpose work on him.
Cassio's a proper° man. Let me see now:     375
To get his place and to plume up° my will
In double knavery — How, how? — Let's see:
After some time, to abuse° Othello's ear
That he° is too familiar with his° wife.
He hath a person and a smooth dispose°     380
To be suspected, framed° to make women false.
The Moor is of a free and open° nature,
That thinks men honest that but seem to be so,
And will as tenderly° be led by the nose
As asses are.     385

---

353. **conjunctive:** united.   355. **Traverse:** (A military marching term.)   359. **betimes:** early.
360. **Go to:** (An expression of impatience or jollying along others.)   368. **snipe:** woodcock,
i.e., fool.   370. **it is thought abroad:** it is rumored.   371. **my office:** i.e., my sexual function as
husband.   373. **do . . . surety:** act as if on certain knowledge.   **holds me well:** regards me
favorably.   375. **proper:** handsome.   376. **plume up:** put a feather in the cap of, i.e., glorify,
gratify.   378. **abuse:** deceive.   379. **he:** Cassio.   **his:** Othello's.   380. **dispose:** disposition.
381. **framed:** formed, made.   382. **free and open:** frank and unsuspecting.   384. **tenderly:**
readily.

I have't. It is engender'd. Hell and night
Must bring this monstrous birth to the world's light.                    [*Exit.*]

## ACT 2, SCENE I°

*Enter Montano and two Gentlemen.*

MONTANO:
    What from the cape can you discern at sea?
FIRST GENTLEMAN:
    Nothing at all. It is a high-wrought flood.°
    I cannot, twixt the heaven and the main,°
    Descry a sail.
MONTANO:
    Methinks the wind hath spoke aloud at land;                              5
    A fuller blast ne'er shook our battlements.
    If it hath ruffianed° so upon the sea,
    What ribs of oak, when mountains° melt on them,
    Can hold the mortise?° What shall we hear of this?
SECOND GENTLEMAN:
    A segregation° of the Turkish fleet.                                    10
    For do but stand upon the foaming shore,
    The chidden° billow seems to pelt the clouds;
    The wind-shaked surge, with high and monstrous mane,°
    Seems to cast water on the burning Bear°
    And quench the guards of th'ever-fixèd pole.                            15
    I never did like molestation° view
    On the enchafèd° flood.
MONTANO:
    If that° the Turkish fleet
    Be not ensheltered and embayed,° they are drowned;
    It is impossible to bear it out.°                                       20

Act 2, Scene 1. Location: A seaport in Cyprus. An open place near the quay.   2. high-wrought flood: very agitated sea.   3. main: ocean. (Also at line 41.)   7. ruffianed: raged.   8. mountains: i.e., of water.   9. hold the mortise: hold their joints together. (A *mortise* is the socket hollowed out in fitting timbers.)   10. segregation: dispersion.   12. chidden: i.e., rebuked, repelled (by the shore), and thus shot into the air.   13. monstrous mane: (The surf is like the mane of a wild beast.)   14. the burning Bear: i.e., the constellation Ursa Minor or the Little Bear, which includes the polestar (and hence regarded as the *guards of th'ever-fixèd pole* in the next line; sometimes the term *guards* is applied to the two "pointers" of the Big Bear or Dipper, which may be intended here.)   16. like molestation: comparable disturbance.   17. enchafèd: angry.   18. If that: if.   19. embayed: sheltered by a bay.   20. bear it out: survive, weather the storm.

*Enter a [Third] Gentleman.*

THIRD GENTLEMAN:    News, lads! Our wars are done.
The desperate tempest hath so banged the Turks
That their designment halts.° A noble ship of Venice
Hath seen a grievous wreck° and sufferance°
On most part of their fleet.                                            25
MONTANO:    How? Is this true?
THIRD GENTLEMAN:    The ship is here put in,
A Veronesa;° Michael Cassio,
Lieutenant to the warlike Moor Othello,
Is come on shore: the Moor himself at sea,                              30
And is in full commission here for Cyprus.
MONTANO:
I am glad on't. 'Tis a worthy governor.
THIRD GENTLEMAN:
But this same Cassio, though he speak of comfort
Touching the Turkish loss, yet he looks sadly°
And prays the Moor be safe, for they were parted                       35
With foul and violent tempest.
MONTANO:                                      Pray heaven he be,
For I have served him, and the man commands
Like a full° soldier. Let's to the seaside, ho!
As well to see the vessel that's come in
As to throw out our eyes for brave Othello,                            40
Even till we make the main and th'aerial blue°
An indistinct regard.°
THIRD GENTLEMAN:    Come, let's do so,
For every minute is expectancy°
Of more arrivance.°

*Enter Cassio.*

CASSIO:
Thanks, you the valiant of this warlike isle,                          45
That so approve° the Moor! Oh, let the heavens
Give him defense against the elements,
For I have lost him on a dangerous sea.

---

23. **designment halts:** enterprise is crippled. (Literally, "is lame.")  **24. wreck:** shipwreck.
**sufferance:** damage, disaster.  **28. Veronesa:** from Verona (and perhaps in service with
Venice).  **34. sadly:** gravely.  **38. full:** perfect.  **41. the main . . . blue:** the sea and the sky.
**42. An indistinct regard:** indistinguishable in our view.  **43. is expectancy:** gives expectation.
**44. arrivance:** arrival.  **46. approve:** admire, honor.

MONTANO:    Is he well shipped?

CASSIO:
His bark is stoutly timbered, and his pilot          50
Of very expert and approved allowance;°
Therefore my hopes, not surfeited to death,
Stand in bold cure.°          [*A cry*] *within:* "A sail, a sail, a sail!"

CASSIO:    What noise?

A GENTLEMAN:
The town is empty. On the brow o'th' sea°          55
Stand ranks of people, and they cry "A sail!"

CASSIO:
My hopes do shape him for the governor.°          [*A shot within.*]

SECOND GENTLEMAN:
They do discharge their shot of courtesy;°
Our friends at least.

CASSIO:                    I pray you, sir, go forth,
And give us truth who 'tis that is arrived.          60

SECOND GENTLEMAN:    I shall.          *Exit.*

MONTANO:
But, good Lieutenant, is your general wived?

CASSIO:
Most fortunately. He hath achieved a maid
That paragons° description and wild fame,°
One that excels the quirks° of blazoning° pens,          65
And in th'essential vesture of creation
Does tire the engineer.°

*Enter [Second] Gentleman.*

How now? Who has put in?°

SECOND GENTLEMAN:
'Tis one Iago, ancient to the General.

CASSIO:
He's had most favorable and happy speed.
Tempests themselves, high seas, and howling winds,          70

---

51. **approved allowance:** tested reputation.    52–53. **not . . . cure:** not worn thin through repeated application or delayed fulfillment, strongly persist.    55. **brow o'th' sea:** cliff-edge.    57. **My . . . governor:** I hope and imagine this ship to be Othello's.    58. **discharge . . . courtesy:** fire a salute in token of respect and courtesy.    64. **paragons:** surpasses.    **wild fame:** extravagant report.    65. **quirks:** witty conceits.    **blazoning:** setting forth as though in heraldic language.    66–67. **And in . . . engineer:** and in her real, God-given, beauty, (she) defeats any attempt to praise her. (An *engineer* is one who devises, here a poet.)    67. **put in:** i.e., to harbor.

The guttered° rocks and congregated sands —
Traitors ensteeped° to clog the guiltless keel —
As° having sense of beauty, do omit°
Their mortal° natures, letting go safely by
The divine Desdemona.

MONTANO:                    What is she?                    75

CASSIO:

She that I spake of, our great captain's captain,
Left in the conduct of the bold Iago,
Whose footing here anticipates our thoughts
A sennight's speed.° Great Jove, Othello guard,
And swell his sail with thine own powerful breath,          80
That he may bless this bay with his tall° ship,
Make love's quick pants in Desdemona's arms,
Give renewed fire to our extincted spirits,
And bring all Cyprus comfort!

*Enter Desdemona, Iago, Roderigo, and Emilia.*

                            Oh, behold,
The riches of the ship is come on shore.                    85
You men of Cyprus, let her have your knees.

                    [*The gentlemen make curtsy to Desdemona.*]

Hail to thee, lady! And the grace of heaven
Before, behind thee, and on every hand
Enwheel thee round!

DESDEMONA:             I thank you, valiant Cassio.
What tidings can you tell me of my lord?                    90

CASSIO:

He is not yet arrived; nor know I aught
But that he's well and will be shortly here.

DESDEMONA:

Oh, but I fear — How lost you company?

CASSIO:

The great contention of the sea and skies
Parted our fellowship.

                            (*Within*) "A sail, a sail!" [*A shot.*]

                    But hark. A sail!                       95

---

71. **guttered:** jagged, trenched.    72. **ensteeped:** lying under water.    73. **As:** as if.    **omit:** forbear to exercise.    74. **mortal:** deadly.    78–79. **Whose . . . speed:** whose arrival here has happened a week sooner than we expected.    81. **tall:** tall-masted.

SECOND GENTLEMAN:
They give their greeting to the citadel.
This likewise is a friend.

CASSIO: See for the news! *[Exit Second Gentleman.]*
Good Ancient, you are welcome. [*Kissing Emilia.*] Welcome, mistress.
Let it not gall your patience, good Iago,
That I extend° my manners; 'tis my breeding° 100
That gives me this bold show of courtesy.

IAGO:
Sir, would she give you so much of her lips
As of her tongue she oft bestows on me,
You would have enough.

DESDEMONA: Alas, she has no speech!° 105

IAGO: In faith, too much.
I find it still,° when I have list° to sleep.
Marry, before Your Ladyship, I grant,
She puts her tongue a little in her heart
And chides with thinking.°

EMILIA: You have little cause to say so. 110

IAGO:
Come on, come on. You are pictures out of doors,°
Bells° in your parlors, wildcats in your kitchens,°
Saints in your injuries,° devils being offended,
Players in your huswifery, and huswives in your beds.°

DESDEMONA: Oh, fie upon thee, slanderer! 115

IAGO:
Nay, it is true, or else I am a Turk.°
You rise to play, and go to bed to work.

EMILIA:
You shall not write my praise.

IAGO: No, let me not.

DESDEMONA:
What wouldst thou write of me, if thou shouldst praise me?

---

100. **extend:** give scope to. **breeding:** training in the niceties of etiquette. 105. **she has no**
**speech:** i.e., she's not a chatterbox, as you allege. 107. **still:** always. **list:** desire. 110. **with**
**thinking:** i.e., in her thoughts only. 111. **pictures out of doors:** i.e., as pretty as pictures, and
silently well-behaved in public. 112. **Bells:** i.e., jangling, noisy, and brazen. **in your**
**kitchens:** i.e., in domestic affairs. (Ill tempered or spiteful at home. [Hall]) 113. **Saints . . .**
**injuries:** i.e., putting on airs of sanctity and innocence when wronged by others. 114. **Play-**
**ers . . . beds:** play-actors at domesticity and truly energetic only as lovers in bed. 116. **a Turk:**
an infidel, not to be believed.

IAGO:

Oh, gentle lady, do not put me to't,                                    120
For I am nothing if not critical.°

DESDEMONA:

Come on, essay.° — There's one gone to the harbor?

IAGO:  Ay, madam.

DESDEMONA:

I am not merry, but I do beguile
The thing I am° by seeming otherwise.                                   125
Come, how wouldst thou praise me?

IAGO:

I am about it, but indeed my invention
Comes from my pate as birdlime does from frieze° —
It plucks out brains and all. But my Muse labors°
And thus she is delivered:                                              130
If she be fair and wise, fairness and wit,
The one's for use, the other useth it.°

DESDEMONA:

Well praised! How if she be black° and witty?

IAGO:

If she be black, and thereto have a wit,
She'll find a white that shall her blackness fit.°                      135

DESDEMONA:

Worse and worse.

EMILIA:                        How if fair and foolish?

IAGO:

She never yet was foolish that was fair,
For even her folly° help'd to an heir.°

DESDEMONA:   These are old fond° paradoxes to make fools laugh i'th'ale-
house. What miserable praise hast thou for her that's foul° and foolish?   140

IAGO:

There's none so foul and foolish thereunto,°

---

121. **critical:** censorious.  122. **essay:** try.  125. **The thing I am:** i.e., my anxious self.
128. **Comes . . . frieze:** comes out of my head with as much difficulty as birdlime (a sticky substance used to catch birds) comes out of frieze (a type of coarse woolen cloth).  129. **labors:**
(1) exerts herself (2) prepares to deliver a child. (With a following pun on *delivered* in line 130.)
132. **The one's . . . it:** i.e., her cleverness will make use of her beauty.  133. **black:** dark-
complexioned, brunette.  135. **She'll . . . fit:** she will find a fair-complexioned mate suited to
her dark complexion. (Punning on *wight*, person, and contrasting *white* and *black*, with suggestion of sexual coupling.)  138. **folly:** (With added meaning of "lechery, wantonness.")  **to an
heir:** i.e., to bear a child.  139. **fond:** foolish.  140. **foul:** ugly.  141. **thereunto:** in addition.

But does foul° pranks which fair and wise ones do.

DESDEMONA:   Oh, heavy ignorance! Thou praisest the worst best. But what praise couldst thou bestow on a deserving woman indeed, one that, in the authority of her merit, did justly put on the vouch° of very malice itself?    145

IAGO:

She that was ever fair, and never proud,
Had tongue at will,° and yet was never loud,
Never lacked gold and yet went never gay,°
Fled from her wish and yet said, "Now I may,"°    150
She that being angered, her revenge being nigh,
Bade her wrong stay° and her displeasure fly,
She that in wisdom never was so frail
To change the cod's head for the salmon's tail,°
She that could think and ne'er disclose her mind,    155
See suitors following and not look behind,
She was a wight, if ever such wight were —

DESDEMONA:   To do what?

IAGO:

To suckle fools and chronicle small beer.°

DESDEMONA:   Oh, most lame and impotent conclusion! Do not learn of    160
him, Emilia, though he be thy husband. How say you, Cassio? Is he not a most profane and liberal° counselor?

CASSIO:   He speaks home,° madam. You may relish° him more in° the soldier than in the scholar.

[*Cassio and Desdemona stand together, conversing intimately.*]

IAGO: [*aside*]   He takes her by the palm. Ay, well said,° whisper. With as    165
little a web as this will I ensnare as great a fly as Cassio. Ay, smile upon her, do; I will gyve° thee in thine own courtship.° You say true;° 'tis so, indeed. If such tricks as these strip you out of your lieutenantry, it had been better you had not kissed your three fingers so oft, which now again

---

142. **foul:** sluttish.   145. **put . . . vouch:** compel the approval.   148. **Had . . . will:** was never at a loss for words.   149. **gay:** extravagantly clothed.   150. **Fled . . . may:** avoided temptation where the choice was hers.   152. **Bade . . . stay:** i.e., resolved to put up with her injury and bade her anger to cease.   154. **To . . . tail:** i.e., to be selfishly demanding and ambitious. (The fish's lower body, below the rib cage, has fewest bones and is generally the succulent portion. With sexual implication as well: *cod's head* can be slang for "penis," and *tail* for "pudendum.")   159. **To . . . beer:** i.e., to breastfeed babies and keep track of trivial matters. [Hall]   162. **profane and liberal:** irreverent and licentious.   163. **home:** right to the target. (A term from fencing.)   **relish:** appreciate.   **in:** in the character of.   165. **well said:** well done.   167. **gyve:** fetter, shackle.   **courtship:** courtesy, show of courtly manners.   **You say true:** i.e., that's right, go ahead.

you are most apt to play the sir° in. Very good; well kissed! An excellent   170
courtesy! 'Tis so, indeed. Yet again your fingers to your lips? Would they
were clyster pipes° for your sake! [*Trumpet within.*] The Moor! I know his
trumpet.

CASSIO:   'Tis truly so.

DESDEMONA:   Let's meet him and receive him.   175

CASSIO:   Lo, where he comes!

*Enter Othello and attendants.*

OTHELLO:
Oh, my fair warrior!

DESDEMONA:                My dear Othello!

OTHELLO:
It gives me wonder great as my content
To see you here before me. O my soul's joy,
If after every tempest come such calms,   180
May the winds blow till they have wakened death,
And let the laboring bark climb hills of seas
Olympus-high, and duck again as low
As hell's from heaven! If it were now to die,
'Twere now to be most happy, for I fear   185
My soul hath her content so absolute
That not another comfort like to this
Succeeds in unknown fate.°

DESDEMONA:                The heavens forbid
But that our loves and comforts should increase
Even as our days do grow!   190

OTHELLO:   Amen to that, sweet powers!
I cannot speak enough of this content.
It stops me here; it is too much of joy.
And this, and this, the greatest discords be                [*They kiss.*]°
That e'er our hearts shall make!   195

IAGO: [*aside*]   Oh, you are well tuned now!
But I'll set down° the pegs that make this music,
As honest as I am.°

OTHELLO:   Come, let us to the castle.

---

170. **the sir:** i.e., the fine gentleman.   172. **clyster pipes:** tubes used for enemas and douches.
188. **Succeeds . . . fate:** i.e., can follow in the unknown future.   194. **s.d.** *They kiss:* (The
direction is from the Quarto.)   197. **set down:** loosen (and hence untune the instrument).
198. **As . . . I am:** for all my supposed honesty.

News, friends! Our wars are done, the Turks are drowned.        200
How does my old acquaintance of this isle? —
Honey, you shall be well desired° in Cyprus;
I have found great love amongst them. Oh, my sweet,
I prattle out of fashion,° and I dote
In mine own comforts. — I prithee, good Iago,        205
Go to the bay and disembark my coffers.°
Bring thou the master° to the citadel;
He is a good one, and his worthiness
Does challenge° much respect. — Come, Desdemona. —
Once more, well met at Cyprus!        210

*Exeunt Othello and Desdemona [and all but Iago and Roderigo].*

IAGO: [*to a departing attendant*]   Do thou meet me presently at the harbor.
[*To Roderigo*] Come hither. If thou be'st valiant — as, they say, base men°
being in love have then a nobility in their natures more than is native to
them — list° me. The Lieutenant tonight watches on the court of guard.°
First, I must tell thee this: Desdemona is directly in love with him.        215

RODERIGO:   With him? Why, 'tis not possible.

IAGO:   Lay thy finger thus,° and let thy soul be instructed. Mark me with
what violence she first loved the Moor, but° for bragging and telling her
fantastical lies. To love him still for prating? Let not thy discreet heart
think it. Her eye must be fed; and what delight shall she have to look on        220
the devil? When the blood is made dull with the act of sport,° there
should be, again to inflame it and to give satiety a fresh appetite, loveli-
ness in favor,° sympathy° in years, manners, and beauties — all which the
Moor is defective in. Now, for want of these required conveniences,° her
delicate tenderness will find itself abused,° begin to heave the gorge,° dis-        225
relish and abhor the Moor. Very nature° will instruct her in it and compel
her to some second choice. Now, sir, this granted — as it is a most preg-
nant° and unforced position — who stands so eminent in the degree of°
this fortune as Cassio does? A knave very voluble,° no further con-
scionable° than in putting on the mere form of civil and humane°        230

---

202. **desired:** sought after.    204. **out of fashion:** indecorously, incoherently.    206. **coffers:**
chests, baggage.    207. **master:** ship's captain.    209. **challenge:** lay claim to, deserve.    212. **base
men:** even ignoble men.    214. **list:** listen to.    **court of guard:** guardhouse. (Cassio is in
charge of the watch.)    217. **thus:** i.e., on your lips.    218. **but:** only.    221. **the act of sport:**
sex.    223. **favor:** appearance.    **sympathy:** correspondence, similarity.    224. **required conveniences:** things conducive to compatibility.    225. **abused:** cheated, revolted.    **heave the
gorge:** experience nausea.    226. **Very nature:** her very instincts.    227–28. **pregnant:** evident,
cogent.    228. **in . . . of:** as next in line for.    229. **voluble:** facile, glib.    229–30. **con-
scionable:** conscientious, conscience-bound.    230. **humane:** polite, courteous.

seeming for the better compassing of his salt° and most hidden loose affection.° Why, none, why, none. A slipper° and subtle knave, a finder out of occasions, that has an eye can stamp° and counterfeit advantages,° though true advantage never present itself; a devilish knave. Besides, the knave is handsome, young, and hath all those requisites in him that folly°   235
and green° minds look after. A pestilent complete knave, and the woman hath found him° already.

RODERIGO:   I cannot believe that in her. She's full of most blessed condition.°

IAGO:   Blessed fig's end!° The wine she drinks is made of grapes. If she had been blessed, she would never have loved the Moor. Blessed pudding!°   240
Didst thou not see her paddle with the palm of his hand? Didst not mark that?

RODERIGO:   Yes, that I did; but that was but courtesy.

IAGO:   Lechery, by this hand. An index° and obscure° prologue to the history of lust and foul thoughts. They met so near with their lips that their   245
breaths embraced together. Villainous thoughts, Roderigo! When these mutualities° so marshal the way, hard at hand° comes the master and main exercise, th'incorporate° conclusion. Pish! But, sir, be you ruled by me. I have brought you from Venice. Watch you° tonight; for the command, I'll lay't upon you.° Cassio knows you not. I'll not be far from you.   250
Do you find some occasion to anger Cassio, either by speaking too loud, or tainting° his discipline, or from what other course you please, which the time shall more favorably minister.°

RODERIGO:   Well.

IAGO:   Sir, he's rash and very sudden in choler,° and haply° may strike at   255
you. Provoke him that he may, for even out of that will I cause these of Cyprus to mutiny,° whose qualification° shall come into no true taste° again but by the displanting of Cassio. So shall you have a shorter journey to your desires by the means I shall then have to prefer° them, and the impediment most profitably removed, without the which there were   260
no expectation of our prosperity.

---

231. **salt:** licentious.   232. **affection:** passion.   **slipper:** slippery.   233. **an eye can stamp:** an eye that can coin, create.   **advantages:** favorable opportunities.   235. **folly:** wantonness.   236. **green:** immature.   237. **found him:** sized him up, perceived his intent.   238. **condition:** disposition.   239. **fig's end:** (See 1.3.319 for the vulgar gesture of the fig.)   240. **pudding:** sausage.   244. **index:** table of contents.   **obscure:** veiled, hidden.   247. **mutualities:** exchanges, intimacies.   **hard at hand:** closely following.   248. **th'incorporate:** the carnal.   249. **Watch you:** stand watch.   249–50. **for . . . you:** I'll arrange for you to be appointed, given orders; or, I'll put you in charge.   252. **tainting:** disparaging.   253. **minister:** provide.   255. **choler:** wrath.   **haply:** perhaps.   257. **mutiny:** riot.   **qualification:** pacification.   **true taste:** i.e., acceptable state.   259. **prefer:** advance.

RODERIGO:    I will do this, if you can bring it to any opportunity.
IAGO:    I warrant° thee. Meet me by and by° at the citadel. I must fetch his
    necessaries ashore. Farewell.
RODERIGO:    Adieu.                                                *Exit.*    265
IAGO:
     That Cassio loves her, I do well believe't;
     That she loves him, 'tis apt° and of great credit.°
     The Moor, howbeit that I endure him not,
     Is of a constant, loving, noble nature,
     And I dare think he'll prove to Desdemona                          270
     A most dear husband. Now, I do love her too,
     Not out of absolute lust — though peradventure
     I stand accountant° for as great a sin —
     But partly led to diet° my revenge
     For that I do suspect the lusty Moor                               275
     Hath leaped into my seat, the thought whereof
     Doth, like a poisonous mineral, gnaw my innards;
     And nothing can or shall content my soul
     Till I am evened with him, wife for wife,
     Or failing so, yet that I put the Moor                             280
     At least into a jealousy so strong
     That judgment cannot cure. Which thing to do,
     If this poor trash of Venice, whom I trace°
     For° his quick hunting, stand the putting on,°
     I'll have our Michael Cassio on the hip,°                          285
     Abuse° him to the Moor in the rank garb° —
     For I fear Cassio with my nightcap° too —
     Make the Moor thank me, love me, and reward me
     For making him egregiously an ass
     And practicing upon° his peace and quiet                           290
     Even to madness. 'Tis here, but yet confused.
     Knavery's plain face is never seen till used.                *Exit.*

---

263. **warrant:** assure.  **by and by:** immediately.  267. **apt:** probable.  **credit:** credibility.
273. **accountant:** accountable.  274. **diet:** feed.  283. **trace:** i.e., pursue, dog; or, keep hungry
(?) or perhaps *trash*, a hunting term, meaning to put weights on a hunting dog in order to slow
him down.  284. **For:** to make more eager for.  **stand . . . on:** responds properly when I
incite him to quarrel.  285. **on the hip:** at my mercy, where I can throw him. (A wrestling
term.)  286. **Abuse:** slander.  **rank garb:** coarse manner, gross fashion.  287. **with my
nightcap:** i.e., as a rival in my bed, as one who gives me cuckold's horns.  290. **practicing
upon:** plotting against.

## ACT 2, SCENE 2°

*Enter Othello's Herald with a proclamation.*

HERALD: It is Othello's pleasure, our noble and valiant general, that, upon
certain tidings now arrived, importing the mere perdition° of the Turkish
fleet, every man put himself into triumph:° some to dance, some to make
bonfires, each man to what sport and revels his addiction° leads him. For,
besides these beneficial news, it is the celebration of his nuptial. So much     5
was his pleasure should be proclaimed. All offices° are open, and there is
full liberty of feasting from this present hour of five till the bell have told
eleven. Heaven bless the isle of Cyprus and our noble general Othello!

*Exit.*

## ACT 2, SCENE 3°

*Enter Othello, Desdemona, Cassio, and attendants.*

OTHELLO:
Good Michael, look you to the guard tonight.
Let's teach ourselves that honorable stop°
Not to outsport° discretion.

CASSIO:
Iago hath direction what to do,
But notwithstanding, with my personal eye     5
Will I look to't.

OTHELLO:            Iago is most honest.
Michael, good-night. Tomorrow with your earliest°
Let me have speech with you. [*To Desdemona*] Come, my dear love,
The purchase made, the fruits are to ensue;
That profit's yet to come 'tween me and you.° —     10
Good night.                    *Exit [Othello, with Desdemona and attendants].*

*Enter Iago.*

CASSIO: Welcome, Iago. We must to the watch.

---

Act 2, Scene 2. Location: Cyprus. **2. mere perdition:** complete destruction. **3. triumph:**
public celebration. **4. addiction:** inclination. **6. offices:** rooms where food and drink are
kept. Act 2, Scene 3. Location: Cyprus. The citadel. **2. stop:** restraint. **3. outsport:** cel-
ebrate beyond the bounds of. **7. with your earliest:** at your earliest convenience. **9–10. The
purchase . . . you:** i.e., though married, we haven't yet consummated our love. (Possibly, too,
Othello is referring to pregnancy. At all events, his desire for sexual union is manifest.)

IAGO:   Not this hour,° Lieutenant; 'tis not yet ten o'th' clock. Our general cast° us thus early for the love of his Desdemona; who° let us not therefore blame. He hath not yet made wanton the night with her, and she is    15
sport for Jove.

CASSIO:   She's a most exquisite lady.

IAGO:   And, I'll warrant her, full of game.

CASSIO:   Indeed, she's a most fresh and delicate creature.

IAGO:   What an eye she has! Methinks it sounds a parley° to provocation.    20

CASSIO:   An inviting eye, and yet methinks right modest.

IAGO:   And when she speaks, is it not an alarum° to love?

CASSIO:   She is indeed perfection.

IAGO:   Well, happiness to their sheets! Come, lieutenant, I have a stoup° of wine, and here without° are a brace° of Cyprus gallants that would fain    25
have a measure° to the health of black Othello.

CASSIO:   Not tonight, good Iago. I have very poor and unhappy brains for drinking. I could well wish courtesy would invent some other custom of entertainment.

IAGO:   Oh, they are our friends; but one cup: I'll drink for you.°    30

CASSIO:   I have drunk but one cup tonight, and that was craftily qualified° too, and behold, what innovation° it makes here.° I am unfortunate in the infirmity and dare not task my weakness with any more.

IAGO:   What, man? 'Tis a night of revels. The gallants desire it.

CASSIO:   Where are they?    35

IAGO:   Here at the door. I pray you, call them in.

CASSIO:   I'll do't, but it dislikes me.°                                    *Exit.*

IAGO:

If I can fasten but one cup upon him,
With that which he hath drunk tonight already,
He'll be as full of quarrel and offense°                                     40
As my young mistress' dog. Now, my sick fool Roderigo,
Whom love hath turned almost the wrong side out,
To Desdemona hath tonight caroused°

---

**13. Not this hour:** not for an hour yet.   **14. cast:** dismissed.   **15. who:** i.e., Othello.
**20. sounds a parley:** calls for a conference, issues an invitation.   **22. alarum:** signal calling men to arms. (Continuing the military metaphor of *parley*, line 20.)   **24. stoup:** measure of liquor, two quarts.   **25. without:** outside.   **brace:** pair.   **25–26. fain have a measure:** gladly drink a toast.   **30. for you:** in your place. (Iago will do the steady drinking to keep the gallants company while Cassio has only one cup.)   **31. qualified:** diluted.   **32. innovation:** disturbance, insurrection.   **here:** i.e., in my head.   **37. it dislikes me:** i.e., I'm reluctant.   **40. offense:** readiness to give or take offense.   **43. caroused:** drunk off.

Potations pottle-deep;° and he's to watch.°
Three lads of Cyprus — noble swelling° spirits,                45
That hold their honors in a wary distance,°
The very elements° of this warlike isle —
Have I tonight flustered with flowing cups,
And they watch° too. Now, 'mongst this flock of drunkards
Am I to put our Cassio in some action                          50
That may offend the isle. — But here they come.

*Enter Cassio, Montano, and gentlemen; [servants following with wine].*

If consequence do but approve my dream,°
My boat sails freely both with wind and stream.°
CASSIO:   'Fore God, they have given me a rouse° already.
MONTANO:   Good faith, a little one; not past a pint, as I am a soldier.   55
IAGO:   Some wine, ho!
[ *He sings.*]   "And let me the cannikin° clink, clink,
        And let me the cannikin clink, clink,
            A soldier's a man,
            Oh, man's life's but a span;°                      60
        Why, then, let a soldier drink."
Some wine, boys!
CASSIO:   'Fore God, an excellent song.
IAGO:   I learned it in England, where indeed they are most potent in pot-
    ting.° Your Dane, your German, and your swag-bellied Hollander —   65
    drink, ho! — are nothing to your English.
CASSIO:   Is your Englishman so exquisite in his drinking?
IAGO:   Why, he drinks you,° with facility, your Dane° dead drunk; he
    sweats not° to overthrow your Almain;° he gives your Hollander a vomit
    ere the next pottle can be filled.                          70
CASSIO:   To the health of our general!
MONTANO:   I am for it, Lieutenant, and I'll do you justice.°

---

44. **pottle-deep:** to the bottom of the tankard.   **watch:** stand watch.   45. **swelling:** proud.
46. **hold . . . distance:** i.e., are extremely sensitive of their honor.   47. **elements:** lifeblood.
49. **watch:** are members of the guard.   52. **If . . . dream:** if subsequent events will only confirm my dreams and hopes.   53. **stream:** current.   54. **rouse:** full draft of liquor.   57. **canni-
kin:** small drinking vessel.   60. **span:** brief span of time. (Compare Psalm 39:5 as rendered in
the Book of Common Prayer: "Thou hast made my days as it were a span long.")   64–65. **pot-
ting:** drinking.   68. **drinks you:** drinks.   **your Dane:** your typical Dane.   69. **sweats not:**
i.e., need not exert himself.   **Almain:** German.   72. **I'll . . . justice:** i.e., I'll drink as much
as you.

IAGO: O sweet England! [*He sings.*]

> "King Stephen was and-a worthy peer,
>> His breeches cost him but a crown;
> He held them sixpence all too dear,          75
>> With that he called the tailor lown.°

> He was a wight of high renown,
>> And thou art but of low degree.
> 'Tis pride° that pulls the country down;
>> Then take thine auld° cloak about thee."          80

Some wine, ho!

CASSIO: 'Fore God, this is a more exquisite song than the other.

IAGO: Will you hear't again?

CASSIO: No, for I hold him to be unworthy of his place that does those things. Well, God's above all; and there be souls must be saved, and there   85 be souls must not be saved.

IAGO: It's true, good Lieutenant.

CASSIO: For mine own part — no offense to the General, nor any man of quality° — I hope to be saved.

IAGO: And so do I too, Lieutenant.          90

CASSIO: Ay; but, by your leave, not before me; the lieutenant is to be saved before the ancient. Let's have no more of this; let's to our affairs. — God forgive us our sins! — Gentlemen, let's look to our business. Do not think, gentlemen, I am drunk. This is my ancient; this is my right hand, and this is my left. I am not drunk now. I can stand well enough, and   95 speak well enough.

GENTLEMEN: Excellent well.

CASSIO: Why, very well, then; you must not think then that I am drunk.

                                                          *Exit.*

MONTANO:
   To th' platform, masters. Come, let's set the watch.°   [*Exeunt Gentlemen.*]

IAGO:
   You see this fellow that is gone before.          100
   He's a soldier fit to stand by Caesar
   And give direction; and do but see his vice.

---

76. **lown:** lout, rascal.   79. **pride:** i.e., extravagance in dress.   80. **auld:** old.   89. **quality:** rank.   99. **set the watch:** mount the guard.

'Tis to his virtue a just equinox,°
The one as long as th'other. 'Tis pity of him.
I fear the trust Othello puts him in,                                    105
On some odd time of his infirmity,
Will shake this island.

MONTANO:                          But is he often thus?

IAGO:
'Tis evermore the prologue to his sleep.
He'll watch the horologe a double set,°
If drink rock not his cradle.

MONTANO:                          It were well                            110
The General were put in mind of it.
Perhaps he sees it not, or his good nature
Prizes the virtue that appears in Cassio
And looks not on his evils. Is not this true?

*Enter Roderigo.*

IAGO: [*aside to him*]   How now, Roderigo?                              115
I pray you, after the Lieutenant; go.                    [*Exit Roderigo.*]

MONTANO:
And 'tis great pity that the noble Moor
Should hazard such a place as his own second
With° one of an engraffed° infirmity.
It were an honest action to say so                                       120
To the Moor.

IAGO:                    Not I, for this fair island.
I do love Cassio well and would do much
To cure him of this evil.               [*Cry within:* "Help! Help!"]
                    But hark! what noise?

*Enter Cassio, pursuing° Roderigo.*

CASSIO:   Zounds, you rogue! You rascal!

MONTANO:   What's the matter, Lieutenant?

CASSIO:   A knave teach me my duty? I'll beat the knave into a twiggen°     125
bottle.

---

103. **just equinox:** exact counterpart. (*Equinox* is an equal length of days and nights.) 109. **watch . . . set:** stay awake twice around the clock, or *horologe.* 118–19. **hazard . . . With:** risk giving such an important position as his second in command to. 119. **engraffed:** engrafted, inveterate. 123. **s.d.** *pursuing:* (The Quarto text reads, *"driuing in."*) 126. **twiggen:** wicker-covered. (Cassio vows to assail Roderigo until his skin resembles wickerwork or until he has driven Roderigo through the holes in a wickerwork.)

RODERIGO:   Beat me?

CASSIO:   Dost thou prate, rogue?                    [*He strikes Roderigo.*]

MONTANO:   Nay, good Lieutenant. [*Restraining him.*] I pray you, sir, hold        130
   your hand.

CASSIO:   Let me go, sir, or I'll knock you o'er the mazard.°

MONTANO:   Come, come, you're drunk.

CASSIO:   Drunk?                              [*They fight.*]

IAGO: [*aside to Roderigo*]
   Away, I say. Go out and cry a mutiny.°              [*Exit Roderigo.*]    135
   Nay, good lieutenant — God's will, gentlemen —
   Help, ho! — Lieutenant — sir — Montano — sir —
   Help, masters!° — Here's a goodly watch indeed!         [*A bell rings.*]°
   Who's that which rings the bell? — Diablo,° ho!
   The town will rise.° God's will, Lieutenant, hold!                140
   You'll be ashamed forever.

*Enter Othello and attendants* [*with weapons*].

OTHELLO:
   What is the matter here?

MONTANO:                     Zounds, I bleed still.
   I am hurt to th' death. He dies! [*He thrusts at Cassio.*]

OTHELLO:                        Hold, for your lives!

IAGO:
   Hold, ho! Lieutenant — sir — Montano — gentlemen —
   Have you forgot all sense of place and duty?                    145
   Hold! The General speaks to you. Hold, for shame!

OTHELLO:
   Why, how now, ho! From whence ariseth this?
   Are we turned Turks, and to ourselves do that
   Which heaven hath forbid the Ottomites?°
   For Christian shame put by this barbarous brawl!               150
   He that stirs next to carve for° his own rage
   Holds his soul light;° he dies upon his motion.°
   Silence that dreadful bell. It frights the isle

---

132. **mazard:** i.e., head. (Literally, a drinking vessel.)   135. **mutiny:** riot.   138. **masters:** sirs.
138. **s.d.** *A bell rings:* (This direction is from the Quarto, as are *Exit Roderigo* at line 117. *They fight* at line 135, and *with weapons* at line 143 s.d.)   139. **Diablo:** the devil.   140. **rise:** grow riotous.   148–49. **to ourselves . . . Ottomites:** inflict on ourselves the harm that heaven has prevented the Turks from doing (by destroying their fleet).   151. **carve for:** i.e., indulge, satisfy with his sword.   152. **Holds . . . light:** i.e., places little value on his life.   **upon his motion:** if he moves.

From her propriety.° What is the matter, masters?
Honest Iago, that looks dead with grieving,                              155
Speak. Who began this? On thy love, I charge thee.

IAGO:

I do not know. Friends all but now, even now,
In quarter and in terms° like bride and groom
Devesting them° for bed; and then, but now —
As if some planet had unwitted men —                                    160
Swords out, and tilting one at others' breasts
In opposition bloody. I cannot speak°
Any beginning to this peevish odds;°
And would in action glorious I had lost
Those legs that brought me to a part of it!                             165

OTHELLO:

How comes it, Michael, you are thus forgot?°

CASSIO:

I pray you, pardon me. I cannot speak.

OTHELLO:

Worthy Montano, you were wont be° civil;
The gravity and stillness° of your youth
The world hath noted, and your name is great                            170
In mouths of wisest censure.° What's the matter,
That you unlace° your reputation thus
And spend your rich opinion° for the name
Of a night-brawler? Give me answer to it.

MONTANO:

Worthy Othello, I am hurt to danger.                                    175
Your officer, Iago, can inform you —
While I spare speech, which something° now offends° me —
Of all that I do know; nor know I aught
By me that's said or done amiss this night,
Unless self-charity be sometimes a vice,                                180
And to defend ourselves it be a sin
When violence assails us.

OTHELLO:                              Now, by heaven,

---

154. **propriety:** proper state or condition.   158. **In quarter . . . terms:** in conduct and speech.
159. **Devesting them:** undressing themselves.   162. **speak:** explain.   163. **peevish odds:**
childish quarrel.   166. **are thus forgot:** you have forgotten yourself? [Hall]   168. **wont be:**
accustomed to be.   169. **stillness:** sobriety.   171. **censure:** judgment.   172. **unlace:** undo, lay
open (as one might loose the strings of a purse containing reputation).   173. **opinion:** reputation.   177. **something:** somewhat.   **offends:** pains.

My blood° begins my safer guides° to rule,
And passion, having my best judgment collied,°
Essays° to lead the way. Zounds, if I stir,                                    185
Or do but lift this arm, the best of you
Shall sink in my rebuke. Give me to know
How this foul rout° began, who set it on;
And he that is approved in° this offense,
Though he had twinned with me, both at a birth,                                190
Shall lose me. What? In a town of° war,
Yet wild, the people's hearts brim full of fear,
To manage° private and domestic quarrel?
In night, and on the court and guard of safety?°
'Tis monstrous. Iago, who began't?                                            195
MONTANO: [*To Iago*]
    If partially affined, or leagued in office,°
    Thou dost deliver more or less than truth,
    Thou art no soldier.
IAGO:                        Touch me not so near.
    I had rather have this tongue cut from my mouth
    Than it should do offense to Michael Cassio;                              200
    Yet, I persuade myself, to speak the truth
    Shall nothing wrong him. Thus it is, General:
    Montano and myself being in speech,
    There comes a fellow crying out for help,
    And Cassio following with determined sword                                205
    To execute upon him.° Sir, this gentleman        [*indicating Montano*]
    Steps in to Cassio and entreats his pause.°
    Myself the crying fellow did pursue,
    Lest by his clamor — as it so fell out —
    The town might fall in fright. He, swift of foot,                         210
    Outran my purpose, and I returned, the rather°
    For that I heard the clink and fall of swords
    And Cassio high in oath, which till tonight
    I ne'er might say before. When I came back —
    For this was brief — I found them close together                          215

---

183. **blood:** passion (of anger).  **guides:** i.e., reason.  184. **collied:** darkened.  185. **Essays:**
undertakes.  188. **rout:** riot.  189. **approved in:** found guilty of.  191. **town of:** town gar-
risoned for.  193. **manage:** undertake.  194. **on . . . safety:** at the main guardhouse or headquarters and on watch.  196. **If . . . office:** if made partial by personal relationship or by your
being fellow officers.  206. **execute upon him:** (1) proceed violently against him (2) execute
him.  207. **his pause:** him to stop.  211. **rather:** sooner.

At blow and thrust, even as again they were
When you yourself did part them.
More of this matter cannot I report.
But men are men; the best sometimes forget.°
Though Cassio did some little wrong to him,                    220
As men in rage strike those that wish them best,°
Yet surely Cassio, I believe, received
From him that fled some strange indignity,
Which patience could not pass.°

OTHELLO:                                    I know, Iago,
Thy honesty and love doth mince this matter,
Making it light to Cassio. Cassio, I love thee,                    225
But nevermore be officer of mine.

*Enter Desdemona, attended.*

Look if my gentle love be not raised up.
I'll make thee an example.

DESDEMONA:
What is the matter, dear?

OTHELLO:                              All's well now, sweeting;                    230
Come away to bed. [*To Montano*] Sir, for your hurts,
Myself will be your surgeon.° — Lead him off.          [*Montano is led off.*]
Iago, look with care about the town
And silence those whom this vile brawl distracted.
Come, Desdemona. 'Tis the soldiers' life                    235
To have their balmy slumbers waked with strife.

                              *Exit [with all but Iago and Cassio].*

IAGO:   What, are you hurt, Lieutenant?

CASSIO:   Ay, past all surgery.

IAGO:   Marry, God forbid!

CASSIO:   Reputation, reputation, reputation! Oh, I have lost my reputation!    240
I have lost the immortal part of myself, and what remains is bestial. My
reputation, Iago, my reputation!

IAGO:   As I am an honest man, I thought you had received some bodily
wound; there is more sense in that than in reputation. Reputation is an
idle and most false imposition,° oft got without merit and lost without    245

---

219. **forget:** forget themselves.    221. **those . . . best:** i.e., even those who are well disposed
toward them.    224. **pass:** pass over, overlook.    232. **be your surgeon:** i.e., make sure you
receive medical attention.    245. **false imposition:** thing artificially imposed and of no real
value.

deserving. You have lost no reputation at all, unless you repute yourself such a loser. What, man, there are ways to recover° the General again. You are but now cast in his mood° — punishment more in policy° than in malice, even so as one would beat his offenseless dog to affright an imperious lion.° Sue° to him again and he's yours.                                                    250

CASSIO:   I will rather sue to be despised than to deceive so good a commander with so slight,° so drunken, and so indiscreet an officer. Drunk? And speak parrot?° And squabble? Swagger? Swear? And discourse fustian with one's own shadow? O thou invisible spirit of wine, if thou hast no name to be known by, let us call thee devil!                                            255

IAGO:   What was he that you followed with your sword? What hath he done to you?

CASSIO:   I know not.

IAGO:   Is't possible?

CASSIO:   I remember a mass of things, but nothing distinctly; a quarrel, but    260
nothing wherefore.° Oh, God, that men should put an enemy in their mouths to steal away their brains! That we should, with joy, pleasance, revel, and applause,° transform ourselves into beasts!

IAGO:   Why, but you are now well enough. How came you thus recovered?

CASSIO:   It hath pleased the devil drunkenness to give place to the devil    265
wrath. One unperfectness shows me another, to make me frankly despise myself.

IAGO:   Come, you are too severe a moraler.° As the time, the place, and the condition of this country stands, I could heartily wish this had not befallen; but since it is as it is, mend it for your own good.                          270

CASSIO:   I will ask him for my place again; he shall tell me I am a drunkard. Had I as many mouths as Hydra,° such an answer would stop them all. To be now a sensible man, by and by a fool, and presently a beast! Oh strange! Every inordinate° cup is unblessed, and the ingredient is a devil.

IAGO:   Come, come, good wine is a good familiar creature, if it be well    275
used. Exclaim no more against it. And, good Lieutenant, I think you think I love you.

CASSIO:   I have well approved° it, sir. I drunk!

---

247. **recover:** regain favor with.   248. **cast in his mood:** dismissed in a moment of anger. **in policy:** done for expediency's sake and as a public gesture.   249–50. **would . . . lion:** i.e., would make an example of a minor offender in order to deter more important and dangerous offenders.   250. **Sue:** petition.   252. **slight:** worthless.   253. **speak parrot:** talk nonsense, rant. (*Discourse fustian,* lines 254–55, has much the same meaning.)   261. **wherefore:** why. 263. **applause:** desire for applause.   268. **moraler:** moralizer.   272. **Hydra:** the Lernaean Hydra, a monster with many heads and the ability to grow two heads when one was cut off, slain by Hercules as the second of his twelve labors.   274. **inordinate:** immoderate.   278. **approved:** proved by experience.

IAGO:   You or any man living may be drunk at a time,° man. I'll tell you
what you shall do. Our general's wife is now the general — I may say so       280
in this respect, for that° he hath devoted and given up himself to the con-
templation, mark, and denotement° of her parts° and graces. Confess
yourself freely to her; importune her help to put you in your place again.
She is of so free,° so kind, so apt, so blessed a disposition, that she holds it
a vice in her goodness not to do more than she is requested. This broken       285
joint between you and her husband entreat her to splinter;° and, my fortunes against any lay° worth naming, this crack of your love shall grow
stronger than it was before.

CASSIO:   You advise me well.

IAGO:   I protest,° in the sincerity of love and honest kindness.                290

CASSIO:   I think it freely;° and betimes in the morning I will beseech the
virtuous Desdemona to undertake for me. I am desperate of my fortunes
if they check° me here.

IAGO:   You are in the right. Good night, Lieutenant. I must to the watch.

CASSIO:   Good night, honest Iago.                                *Exit Cassio.*    295

IAGO:
And what's he then that says I play the villain,
When this advice is free° I give, and honest,
Probal° to thinking, and indeed the course
To win the Moor again? For 'tis most easy
Th'inclining° Desdemona to subdue°                                              300
In any honest suit; she's framed as fruitful°
As the free elements.° And then for her
To win the Moor — were't to renounce his baptism,
All seals° and symbols of redeemèd sin —
His soul is so enfettered to her love                                           305
That she may make, unmake, do what she list,
Even as her appetite° shall play the god
With his weak function.° How am I then a villain,
To counsel Cassio to this parallel° course

---

279. **at a time:** at one time or another.   281. **for that:** that.   282. **mark, and denotement:**
(Both words mean "observation.")   **parts:** qualities.   284. **free:** generous.   286. **splinter:** bind
with splints.   287. **lay:** stake, wager.   290. **protest:** insist, declare.   291. **freely:** unreservedly.
293. **check:** repulse.   297. **free:** (1) free from guile (2) freely given.   298. **Probal:** probable,
reasonable.   300. **Th'inclining:** the favorably disposed.   **subdue:** persuade.   301. **framed as
fruitful:** created as generous.   302. **free elements:** i.e., earth, air, fire, and water, unrestrained
and spontaneous.   304. **seals:** tokens.   307. **her appetite:** her desire, or, perhaps his desire for
her.   308. **function:** exercise of faculties (weakened by his fondness for her).   309. **parallel:**
i.e., seemingly in his best interests but at the same time threatening.

Directly to his good? Divinity of hell!°                                    310
When devils will the blackest sins put on,°
They do suggest° at first with heavenly shows,
As I do now. For whiles this honest fool
Plies Desdemona to repair his fortune,
And she for him pleads strongly to the Moor,                                315
I'll pour this pestilence into his ear,
That she repeals him° for her body's lust;
And by how much she strives to do him good,
She shall undo her credit with the Moor.
So will I turn her virtue into pitch,°                                      320
And out of her own goodness make the net
That shall enmesh them all.

*Enter Roderigo.*

                    How now, Roderigo?
RODERIGO:   I do follow here in the chase, not like a hound that hunts, but
    one that fills up the cry.° My money is almost spent; I have been tonight
    exceedingly well cudgeled; and I think the issue° will be I shall have so   325
    much° experience for my pains, and so, with no money at all and a little
    more wit, return again to Venice.
IAGO:
    How poor are they that have not patience!
    What wound did ever heal but by degrees?
    Thou know'st we work by wit, and not by witchcraft,                       330
    And wit depends on dilatory time.
    Does't not go well? Cassio hath beaten thee,
    And thou, by that small hurt, hast cashiered° Cassio.
    Though other things grow fair against the sun,
    Yet fruits that blossom first will first be ripe.°                        335
    Content thyself awhile. By the Mass, 'tis morning!
    Pleasure and action make the hours seem short.
    Retire thee; go where thou art billeted.
    Away, I say! Thou shalt know more hereafter.

310. **Divinity of hell!:** inverted theology of hell (which seduces the soul to its damnation)!
311. **put on:** further, instigate.   312. **suggest:** tempt.   317. **repeals him:** attempts to get him
restored.   320. **pitch:** ie., (1) foul blackness (2) a snaring substance.   324. **fills up the cry:**
merely takes part as one of the pack.   325. **issue:** outcome.   325–26. **so much:** just so much
and no more.   333. **cashiered:** dismissed from service.   334–35. **Though . . . ripe:** i.e., plans
that are well prepared and set expeditiously in motion will soonest ripen into success.

Nay, get thee gone.                                    *Exit Roderigo.*
                    Two things are to be done.                                340
My wife must move° for Cassio to her mistress;
I'll set her on;
Myself the while to draw the Moor apart
And bring him jump° when he may Cassio find
Soliciting his wife. Ay, that's the way.                                     345
Dull not device° by coldness° and delay.                        *Exit.*

## Act 3, Scene 1°

*Enter Cassio [and] Musicians.*

CASSIO:
Masters,° play here, I will content your pains° —
Something that's brief; and bid "Good morrow, general."      [*They play.*]

[*Enter*] *Clown.*

CLOWN:  Why, masters, have your instruments been in Naples, that they
speak i'the nose° thus?
A MUSICIAN:  How, sir, how?                                                   5
CLOWN:  Are these, I pray you, wind instruments?
A MUSICIAN:  Ay, marry, are they, sir.
CLOWN:  O! thereby hangs a tail.
A MUSICIAN:  Whereby hangs a tale, sir?
CLOWN:  Marry, sir, by many a wind instrument° that I know. But, mas-    10
ters, here's money for you. [*He gives money.*] And the General so likes your
music that he desires you, for love's sake, to make no more noise with it.
A MUSICIAN:  Well, sir, we will not.
CLOWN:  If you have any music that may not° be heard, to't again; but, as
they say, to hear music the General does not greatly care.                    15
A MUSICIAN:  We have none such, sir.
CLOWN:  Then put up your pipes in your bag, for I'll away. Go; vanish into
air, away!                                                *Exeunt Musicians.*

---

341. **move:** plead.    344. **jump:** precisely.    346. **device:** plot.    **coldness:** lack of zeal.    **Act
3, Scene 1. Location:** Before the chamber of Othello and Desdemona.    1. **Masters:** Good
sirs.    **content your pains:** reward your efforts.    4. **speak i'th' nose:** (1) sound nasal (2) sound
like one whose nose has been attacked by syphilis. (Naples was popularly supposed to have a
high incidence of venereal disease.)    10. **wind instrument:** (With a joke on flatulence. The
*tail,* line 8, that hangs nearby the *wind instrument* suggests the penis.)    14. **may not:** cannot.

CASSIO:   Dost thou hear, mine honest friend?

CLOWN:   No, I hear not your honest friend; I hear you.                          20

CASSIO:   Prithee, keep up thy quillets.° There's a poor piece of gold for
thee. [ *He gives money.*] If the gentlewoman that attends the General's wife
be stirring, tell her there's one Cassio entreats her a little favor of speech.°
Wilt thou do this?

CLOWN:   She is stirring, sir: if she will stir° hither, I shall seem° to notify   25
unto her.

CASSIO:
Do, good my friend.                                              *Exit Clown.*

*Enter Iago.*

                    In happy time,° Iago.

IAGO:   You have not been a bed, then?

CASSIO:   Why, no. The day had broke
Before we parted. I have made bold, Iago,                              30
To send in to your wife. My suit to her
Is that she will to virtuous Desdemona
Procure me some access.

IAGO:   I'll send her to you presently;
And I'll devise a mean to draw the Moor                               35
Out of the way, that your converse and business
May be more free.

CASSIO:
I humbly thank you for 't.                                    *Exit [Iago].*
                    I never knew
A Florentine° more kind and honest.

*Enter Emilia.*

EMILIA:
Good morrow, good Lieutenant. I am sorry                              40
For your displeasure;° but all will sure be well.
The General and his wife are talking of it,
And she speaks for you stoutly.° The Moor replies
That he you hurt is of great fame° in Cyprus

---

21. keep . . . quillets: refrain from quibbling.   23. a little . . . speech: the favor of a brief talk.
25. stir: bestir herself. (With a play on *stirring*, "rousing herself from rest.")   seem: deem it
good, think fit.   27. In happy time: i.e., well met.   39. Florentine: i.e., even a fellow
Florentine. (Iago is a Venetian; Cassio is a Florentine.)   41. displeasure: fall from favor.
43. stoutly: spiritedly.   44. fame: reputation, importance.

And great affinity,° and that in wholesome wisdom 45
He might not but refuse you; but he protests° he loves you,
And needs no other suitor but his likings
To take the safest occasion by the front°
To bring you in again.

CASSIO:                    Yet I beseech you,
If you think fit, or that it may be done, 50
Give me advantage of some brief discourse
With Desdemona alone.

EMILIA:                    Pray you, come in.
I will bestow you where you shall have time
To speak your bosom° freely.

CASSIO:   I am much bound to you.                    [*Exeunt.*] 55


## Act 3, Scene 2°

*Enter Othello, Iago, and Gentlemen.*

OTHELLO: [ *giving letters* ]
These letters give, Iago, to the pilot,
And by him do my duties° to the Senate.
That done, I will be walking on the works;°
Repair° there to me.

IAGO:                    Well, my good lord, I'll do't.

OTHELLO:
This fortification, gentlemen, shall we see't? 5

GENTLEMEN.
We'll wait upon° your lordship.                    *Exeunt.*


## Act 3, Scene 3°

*Enter Desdemona, Cassio, and Emilia.*

DESDEMONA:
Be thou assured, good Cassio, I will do
All my abilities in thy behalf.

---

**45. affinity:** kindred, family connection. **46. protests:** insists. **48. occasion . . . front:** opportunity by the forelock. **54. bosom:** inmost thoughts. **Act 3, Scene 2. Location:** The citadel. **2. do my duties:** convey my respects. **3. works:** breastworks, fortifications. **4. Repair:** return, come. **6. wait upon:** attend. **Act 3, Scene 3. Location:** The garden of the citadel.

EMILIA:
Good madam, do. I warrant it grieves my husband
As if the cause were his.

DESDEMONA:
Oh, that's an honest fellow. Do not doubt, Cassio,                    5
But I will have my lord and you again
As friendly as you were.

CASSIO:                                    Bounteous madam,
Whatever shall become of Michael Cassio,
He's never any thing but your true servant.

DESDEMONA:
I know't. I thank you. You do love my lord;                          10
You have known him long, and be you well assured
He shall in strangeness° stand no farther off
Than in a politic° distance.

CASSIO:                                    Ay, but, lady,
That policy may either last so long,
Or feed upon such nice and waterish diet,°                           15
Or breed itself so out of circumstance,°
That, I being absent and my place supplied,°
My general will forget my love and service.

DESDEMONA:
Do not doubt° that. Before Emilia here
I give thee warrant° of thy place. Assure thee,                      20
If I do vow a friendship I'll perform it
To the last article. My lord shall never rest.
I'll watch him tame° and talk him out of patience;°
His bed shall seem a school, his board° a shrift;°
I'll intermingle every thing he does                                 25
With Cassio's suit. Therefore be merry, Cassio,
For thy solicitor° shall rather die
Than give thy cause away.°

*Enter Othello and Iago [at a distance].*

---

12. **strangeness:** aloofness.   13. **politic:** required by wise policy.   15. **Or . . . diet:** or sustain
itself at length upon such trivial and meager technicalities.   16. **breed . . . circumstance:** continually renew itself so out of chance events, or yield so few chances for my being pardoned.
17. **supplied:** filled by another person.   19. **doubt:** fear.   20. **warrant:** guarantee.   23. **watch
him tame:** tame him by keeping him from sleeping. (A term from falconry.)   **out of patience:**
past his endurance.   24. **board:** dining table.   **shrift:** confessional.   27. **solicitor:** advocate.
28. **away:** up.

EMILIA:   Madam, here comes my lord.
CASSIO:   Madam, I'll take my leave.                                    30
DESDEMONA:   Why, stay, and hear me speak.
CASSIO:
    Madam, not now; I am very ill at ease,
    Unfit for mine own purposes.
DESDEMONA:   Well, do your discretion.°                    *Exit Cassio.*
IAGO:   Ha! I like not that.                                            35
OTHELLO:   What dost thou say?
IAGO:
    Nothing, my lord; or if — I know not what.
OTHELLO:
    Was not that Cassio parted from my wife?
IAGO:
    Cassio, my lord? No, sure, I cannot think it,
    That he would steal away so guiltylike,                             40
    Seeing you coming.
OTHELLO:   I do believe 'twas he.
DESDEMONA: [*joining them*]   How now, my lord?
    I have been talking with a suitor here,
    A man that languishes in your displeasure.
OTHELLO:   Who is't you mean?                                           45
DESDEMONA:
    Why, your lieutenant, Cassio. Good my lord,
    If I have any grace or power to move you,
    His present reconciliation take;°
    For if he be not one that truly loves you,
    That errs in ignorance and not in cunning,°                         50
    I have no judgment in an honest face.
    I prithee, call him back.
OTHELLO:   Went he hence now?
DESDEMONA:   Yes, faith, so humbled
    That he hath left part of his grief with me                         55
    To suffer with him. Good love, call him back.
OTHELLO:
    Not now, sweet Desdemona. Some other time.
DESDEMONA:   But shall't be shortly?
OTHELLO:   The sooner, sweet, for you.                                  60

---

34. **do your discretion:** do as you think fit.   49. **His . . . take:** let him be reconciled to you right away.   51. **in cunning:** wittingly.

DESDEMONA:  Shall't be tonight at supper?

OTHELLO:  No, not tonight.

DESDEMONA:  Tomorrow dinner,° then?

OTHELLO:  I shall not dine at home.
I meet the captains at the citadel.                                                  65

DESDEMONA:
Why, then, tomorrow night; or Tuesday morn,
On Tuesday noon, or night, on Wednesday morn.
I prithee, name the time, but let it not
Exceed three days. In faith, he's penitent;
And yet his trespass, in our common reason° —                        70
Save that, they say, the wars must make example
Out of her best° — is not almost° a fault
T'incur a private check.° When shall he come?
Tell me, Othello. I wonder in my soul
What you would ask me that I should deny,                              75
Or stand so mamm'ring on.° What? Michael Cassio,
That came a wooing with you, and so many a time,
When I have spoke of you dispraisingly,
Hath ta'en your part — to have so much to do
To bring him in!° By'r Lady, I could do much —                        80

OTHELLO:
Prithee, no more. Let him come when he will;
I deny thee nothing.

DESDEMONA:  Why, this is not a boon.
'Tis as I should entreat you wear your gloves,
Or feed on nourishing dishes, or keep you warm,                     85
Or sue to you to do a peculiar° profit
To your own person. Nay, when I have a suit
Wherein I mean to touch° your love indeed,
It shall be full of poise and difficult weight,°
And fearful to be granted.                                                            90

OTHELLO:  I will deny thee nothing.
Whereon,° I do beseech thee, grant me this,
To leave me but a little to myself.

---

63. **dinner:** (The noontime meal.)   70. **common reason:** everyday judgments.   71–72. **Save . . . best:** were it not that, as the saying goes, military discipline requires making an example of the very best men. (*Her* refers to wars as a singular concept.)   72. **not almost:** scarcely.   73. **a private check:** even a private reprimand.   76. **mamm'ring on:** wavering or muttering about. 80. **bring him in:** restore him to favor.   86. **peculiar:** particular, personal.   88. **touch:** test. 89. **poise . . . weight:** delicacy and weightiness.   92. **Whereon:** in return for which.

DESDEMONA:
 Shall I deny you? No. Farewell, my lord.
OTHELLO:
 Farewell, my Desdemona. I'll come to thee straight.°          95
DESDEMONA:
 Emilia, come. Be as your fancies° teach you;
 Whate'er you be, I am obedient.                    *Exit [with Emilia].*
OTHELLO:
 Excellent wretch!° Perdition catch my soul,
 But I do love thee! and when I love thee not,
 Chaos is come again.°                                       100
IAGO:   My noble lord —
OTHELLO:   What dost thou say, Iago?
IAGO:
 Did Michael Cassio, when you wooed my lady,
 Know of your love?
OTHELLO:
 He did, from first to last. Why dost thou ask?              105
IAGO:
 But for a satisfaction of my thought;
 No further harm.
OTHELLO:              Why of thy thought, Iago?
IAGO:
 I did not think he had been acquainted with her.
OTHELLO:
 Oh, yes; and went between us very oft.
IAGO:   Indeed?                                              110
OTHELLO:
 Indeed? Ay, indeed. Discern'st thou aught in that?
 Is he not honest?
IAGO:   Honest, my lord?
OTHELLO:   Honest. Ay, honest.
IAGO:   My lord, for aught I know.                           115
OTHELLO:   What dost thou think?
IAGO:   Think, my lord?
OTHELLO:
 "Think, my lord?" By heaven, thou echo'st me,

---

95. **straight:** straightaway.   96. **fancies:** inclinations.   98. **wretch:** (A term of affectionate endearment.)   99–100. **And . . . again:** i.e., my love for you will last forever, until the end of time when chaos will return. (But with an unconscious, ironic suggestion that, if anything should induce Othello to cease loving Desdemona, the result would be chaos.)

As if there were some monster in thy thought
Too hideous to be shown. Thou dost mean something.                    120
I heard thee say even now, thou lik'st not that,
When Cassio left my wife. What didst not like?
And when I told thee he was of my counsel°
In my whole course of wooing, thou cried'st, "Indeed?"
And didst contract and purse° thy brow together                       125
As if thou then hadst shut up in thy brain
Some horrible conceit.° If thou dost love me,
Show me thy thought.
IAGO:      My lord, you know I love you.
OTHELLO:    I think thou dost;                                          130
   And, for° I know thou art full of love and honesty,
   And weigh'st thy words before thou giv'st them breath,
   Therefore these stops° of thine fright me the more;
   For such things in a false disloyal knave
   Are tricks of custom,° but in a man that's just                     135
   They're close dilations, working from the heart
   That passion cannot rule.°
IAGO:                       For Michael Cassio,
   I dare be sworn I think that he is honest.
OTHELLO:
   I think so too.
IAGO:              Men should be what they seem;
   Or those that be not, would they might seem none!°                  140
OTHELLO:
   Certain men should be what they seem.
IAGO:
   Why then, I think Cassio's an honest man.
OTHELLO:    Nay, yet there's more in this.
   I prithee, speak to me as to thy thinkings,
   As thou dost ruminate, and give thy worst of thoughts              145
   The worst of words.
IAGO:                  Good my lord, pardon me.
   Though I am bound to every act of duty,
   I am not bound to that° all slaves are free to.°

---

123. **of my counsel:** in my confidence.  125. **purse:** knit.  127. **conceit:** fancy.  131. **for:** because.  133. **stops:** pauses.  135. **of custom:** customary.  136–37. **They're . . . rule:** they are secret or involuntary expressions of feeling that are too strong to be kept back.  137. **For:** as for.  140. **seem none:** not seem at all, not seem to be honest.  148. **that:** that which.  **free to:** free with respect to.

Utter my thoughts? Why, say they are vile and false,
As where's that palace whereinto foul things                    150
Sometimes intrude not? Who has a breast so pure
But some uncleanly apprehensions
Keep leets and law days,° and in sessions sit
With meditations lawful?°

OTHELLO:

Thou dost conspire against thy friend,° Iago,                   155
If thou but think'st him wronged and mak'st his ear
A stranger to thy thoughts.

IAGO:                              I do beseech you,
Though I perchance am vicious° in my guess —
As I confess it is my nature's plague
To spy into abuses, and oft my jealousy°                        160
Shapes faults that are not — that your wisdom then,
From one° that so imperfectly conceits,°
Would take no notice, nor build yourself a trouble
Out of his scattering° and unsure observance.
It were not for your quiet nor your good,                       165
Nor for my manhood, honesty, and wisdom,
To let you know my thoughts.

OTHELLO:                              What dost thou mean?

IAGO:

Good name in man and woman, dear my lord,
Is the immediate° jewel of their souls.
Who steals my purse steals trash; 'tis something, nothing;     170
'Twas mine, 'tis his, and has been slave to thousands;
But he that filches from me my good name
Robs me of that which not enriches him
And makes me poor indeed.

OTHELLO:   By heaven, I'll know thy thoughts.                   175

IAGO:

You cannot, if° my heart were in your hand,
Nor shall not, whilst 'tis in my custody.

OTHELLO:   Ha?

---

153. **Keep leets and law days:** i.e., hold court, set up their authority in one's heart. (*Leets* are a kind of manor court; *law days* are the days courts sit in session, or those sessions.)  153–54. **and . . . lawful:** i.e., and coexist in a kind of spiritual conflict with virtuous thoughts.  155. **thy friend:** i.e., Othello.  158. **vicious:** wrong.  160. **jealousy:** suspicious nature.  162. **one:** i.e., myself, Iago.  **conceits:** judges, conjectures.  164. **scattering:** random.  169. **immediate:** essential, most precious.  176. **if:** even if.

IAGO:   Oh, beware, my lord, of jealousy.
It is the green-eyed monster, which doth mock                              180
The meat it feeds on.° That cuckold lives in bliss
Who, certain of his fate, loves not his wronger;°
But, oh, what damnèd minutes tells° he o'er
Who dotes, yet doubts; suspects, yet fondly loves!
OTHELLO:   Oh, misery!                                                    185
IAGO:
Poor and content is rich, and rich enough,°
But riches fineless° is as poor as winter
To him that ever fears he shall be poor.
Good God, the souls of all my tribe defend
From jealousy!                                                           190
OTHELLO:   Why, why is this?
Think'st thou I'd make a life of jealousy,
To follow still the changes of the moon
With fresh suspicions?° No! To be once in doubt
Is once° to be resolved.° Exchange me for a goat                          195
When I shall turn the business of my soul
To such exsufflicate and blown° surmises
Matching thy inference.° 'Tis not to make me jealous
To say my wife is fair, feeds well, loves company,
Is free of speech, sings, plays, and dances well;                        200
Where virtue is, these are more virtuous.
Nor from mine own weak merits will I draw
The smallest fear or doubt of her revolt,°
For she had eyes, and chose me. No, Iago,
I'll see before I doubt; when I doubt, prove;                             205
And on the proof, there is no more but this —
Away at once with love or jealousy.

---

180–81. which . . . feeds on: (Jealousy mocks both itself and the sufferer of jealousy; it is self-devouring and is its own punishment.)   181–82. That . . . wronger: A cuckolded husband who knows his wife to be unfaithful can at least take comfort in knowing the truth, so that he will not continue to love her or to befriend her lover. (Othello echoes this sentiment in lines 205–07, when he vows that he would end uncertainty and cease to love an unfaithful wife.)   183. tells: counts.   186. Poor . . . enough: to be content with what little one has is the greatest wealth of all. (Proverbial.)   187. fineless: boundless.   193–94. To follow . . . suspicions?: to be constantly imagining new causes for suspicion, changing incessantly like the moon?   195. once: once and for all.   resolved: free of doubt, having settled the matter.   197. exsufflicate and blown: inflated and blown up or flyblown, hence, loathsome, disgusting.   198. inference: description or allegation.   203. doubt . . . revolt: fear of her unfaithfulness.

IAGO:

I am glad of this, for now I shall have reason
To show the love and duty that I bear you
With franker spirit. Therefore, as I am bound,                    210
Receive it from me. I speak not yet of proof.
Look to your wife; observe her well with Cassio.
Wear your eyes thus, not° jealous nor secure.°
I would not have your free and noble nature,
Out of self-bounty,° be abused.° Look to't.                       215
I know our country disposition well;
In Venice they do let God see the pranks
They dare not show their husbands; their best conscience
Is not to leave't undone, but keep't unknown.

OTHELLO:    Dost thou say so?                                     220

IAGO:

She did deceive her father, marrying you;
And when she seemed to shake and fear your looks,
She lov'd them most.

OTHELLO:                    And so she did.

IAGO:                              Why, go to,° then!
She that, so young, could give out such a seeming,°
To seel° her father's eyes up close as oak,°                      225
He thought 'twas witchcraft! But I am much to blame.
I humbly do beseech you of your pardon
For too much loving you.

OTHELLO:    I am bound° to thee forever.

IAGO:

I see this hath a little dashed your spirits.                     230

OTHELLO:

Not a jot, not a jot.

IAGO:                    I'faith, I fear it has.
I hope you will consider what is spoke
Comes from my love. But I do see you're moved.
I am to pray you not to strain my speech
To grosser issues° nor to larger reach°                           235
Than to suspicion.

---

213. **not:** neither.  **secure:** free from uncertainty.  215. **self-bounty:** inherent or natural goodness and generosity.  **abused:** deceived.  223. **go to:** (An expression of impatience.) 224. **seeming:** false appearance.  225. **seel:** blind. (A term from falconry.)  **oak:** (A close-grained wood.)  229. **bound:** indebted. (But perhaps with ironic sense of "tied.")  235. **issues:** significances.  **reach:** meaning, scope.

OTHELLO:   I will not.

IAGO:   Should you do so, my lord,
My speech should fall into such vile success°
Which my thoughts aimed not. Cassio's my worthy friend.          240
My lord, I see you're moved.

OTHELLO:                              No, not much moved.
I do not think but Desdemona's honest.°

IAGO:
Long live she so! and long live you to think so!

OTHELLO:
And yet, how nature erring from itself —

IAGO:
Ay, there's the point! As — to be bold with you —          245
Not to affect° many proposèd matches
Of her own clime, complexion, and degree,°
Whereto we see in all things nature tends —
Foh! One may smell in such a will° most rank,
Foul disproportion,° thoughts unnatural.          250
But pardon me. I do not in position°
Distinctly speak of her, though I may fear
Her will, recoiling° to her better° judgment,
May fall to match you with her country forms°
And happily repent.°

OTHELLO:                    Farewell, farewell!          255
If more thou dost perceive, let me know more.
Set on thy wife to observe. Leave me, Iago.

IAGO: [going]   My lord, I take my leave.

OTHELLO:
Why did I marry? This honest creature doubtless
Sees and knows more, much more, than he unfolds.          260

IAGO: [returning]
My lord, I would I might entreat Your Honor
To scan° this thing no farther. Leave it to time.
Although 'tis fit that Cassio have his place —
For, sure, he fills it up with great ability —

---

239. success: effect, result.   242. honest: chaste.   246. affect: prefer, desire.   247. clime . . .
degree: country, temperament or skin color, and social position.   249. will: sensuality, appetite.   250. disproportion: abnormality.   251. in position: in making this argument or prop-
osition.   253. recoiling: reverting.   better: i.e., more natural and reconsidered.   254. fall . . .
forms: undertake to compare you with Venetian norms of handsomeness.   255. happily
repent: haply repent her marriage.   262. scan: scrutinize.

Yet, if you please to hold him off awhile,                                                  265
You shall by that perceive him and his means.°
Note if your lady strain his entertainment°
With any strong or vehement importunity;
Much will be seen in that. In the meantime,
Let me be thought too busy° in my fears —                                                    270
As worthy cause I have to fear I am —
And hold her free,° I do beseech Your Honor.
OTHELLO:   Fear not my government.°
IAGO:   I once more take my leave.                                *Exit.*
OTHELLO:
This fellow's of exceeding honesty,                                                          275
And knows all qualities,° with a learnèd spirit,
Of human dealings. If I do prove her haggard,°
Though that her jesses° were my dear heartstrings,
I'd whistle her off and let her down the wind°
To prey at fortune.° Haply, for° I am black                                                  280
And have not those soft parts of conversation°
That chamberers° have, or for I am declined
Into the vale of years — yet that's not much —
She's gone. I am abused,° and my relief
Must be to loathe her. Oh, curse of marriage,                                                285
That we can call these delicate creatures ours
And not their appetites! I had rather be a toad
And live upon the vapor of a dungeon
Than keep a corner in the thing I love
For others' uses. Yet, 'tis the plague of great ones;                                       290
Prerogatived° are they less than the base.°
'Tis destiny unshunnable, like death.

---

266. **his means:** the method he uses (to regain his post).   267. **strain his entertainment:** urge his reinstatement.   270. **busy:** officious.   272. **hold her free:** regard her as innocent. 273. **government:** self-control, conduct.   276. **qualities:** natures, types.   277. **haggard:** wild (like a wild female hawk).   278. **jesses:** straps fastened around the legs of a trained hawk. 279. **I'd . . . wind:** i.e., I'd let her go forever. (To release a hawk downwind was to turn it loose.)   280. **prey at fortune:** fend for herself in the wild.   **Haply, for:** perhaps because. 281. **soft . . . conversation:** pleasing social graces.   282. **chamberers:** drawing-room gallants. 284. **abused:** deceived.   291. **Prerogatived:** privileged (to have honest wives).   **the base:** ordinary citizens. (Socially prominent men are especially prone to the common destiny of being cuckolded and to the public shame that goes with it.)

Even then this forkèd° plague is fated to us
When we do quicken.° Look where she comes.

*Enter Desdemona and Emilia.*

If she be false, oh, then heaven mocks itself!                    295
I'll not believe't.
DESDEMONA:            How now, my dear Othello?
Your dinner, and the generous° islanders
By you invited do attend° your presence.
OTHELLO:
I am to blame.
DESDEMONA:            Why do you speak so faintly?
Are you not well?                                                300
OTHELLO:
I have a pain upon my forehead here.
DESDEMONA:
Faith, that's with watching.° 'Twill away again. [*She offers her handkerchief.*]
Let me but bind it hard, within this hour
It will be well.
OTHELLO:            Your napkin° is too little:
Let it alone.° Come, I'll go in with you.                        305
                    [*He puts the handkerchief from him, and it drops.*]
DESDEMONA:
I am very sorry that you are not well.        *Exit* [*with Othello*].
EMILIA: [ *picking up the handkerchief* ]
I am glad I have found this napkin.
This was her first remembrance from the Moor.
My wayward° husband hath a hundred times
Wooed me to steal it, but she so loves the token —              310
For he conjured her she should ever keep it —
That she reserves it evermore about her
To kiss and talk to. I'll have the work ta'en out,°
And give't Iago. What he will do with it

---

293. **forkèd:** (An allusion to the horns of the cuckold.)   294. **quicken:** receive life. (*Quicken* may also mean to swarm with maggots as the body festers, as in 4.2.69, in which case lines 293–94 suggest that *even then,* in death, we are cuckolded by *forkèd* worms.)   297. **generous:** noble.   298. **attend:** await.   302. **watching:** too little sleep.   304. **napkin:** handkerchief.   305. **Let it alone:** i.e., never mind.   309. **wayward:** capricious.   313. **work ta'en out:** design of the embroidery copied.

Heaven knows, not I;                                                     315
I nothing but to please his fantasy.°

*Enter Iago.*

IAGO:
How now? What do you here alone?
EMILIA:
Do not you chide. I have a thing for you.
IAGO:
You have a thing for me? It is a common thing° —
EMILIA:    Ha?                                                          320
IAGO:    To have a foolish wife.
EMILIA:
Oh, is that all? What will you give me now
For that same handkerchief?
IAGO:    What handkerchief?
EMILIA:    What handkerchief?                                           325
Why, that the Moor first gave to Desdemona;
That which so often you did bid me steal.
IAGO:    Hath stolen it from her?
EMILIA:
No, faith. She let it drop by negligence,
And to th'advantage° I, being there, took't up.                        330
Look, here 'tis.
IAGO:                A good wench! Give it me.
EMILIA:
What will you do with't, that you have been so earnest
To have me filch it?
IAGO: [*snatching it*]     Why, what is that to you?
EMILIA:
If it be not for some purpose of import,
Give't me again. Poor lady, she'll run mad                             335
When she shall lack° it.
IAGO:                        Be not acknown on't.°
I have use for it. Go, leave me.                    *Exit Emilia.*
I will in Cassio's lodging lose° this napkin

---

**316. fantasy:** whim.   **319. common thing:** (With bawdy suggestion; *common* suggests coarseness and availability to all comers, and *thing* is a slang term for the pudendum.)   **330. to th'advantage:** taking the opportunity.   **336. lack:** miss.   **Be . . . on't:** do not confess knowledge of it, keep out of this.   **338. lose:** (The Folio spelling, "loose," is a normal spelling for "lose," but it may also contain the idea of "let go," "release.")

And let him find it. Trifles light as air
Are to the jealous confirmations strong                    340
As proofs of Holy Writ. This may do something.
The Moor already changes with my poison.
Dangerous conceits° are in their natures poisons,
Which at the first are scarce found to distaste,°
But with a little act° upon the blood                      345
Burn like the mines of sulphur.

*Enter Othello.*

                                    I did say so.
Look where he comes! Not poppy nor mandragora°
Nor all the drowsy syrups of the world,
Shall ever medicine thee to that sweet sleep
Which thou owed'st° yesterday.
OTHELLO:                        Ha, ha, false to me?      350
IAGO:
Why, how now, General? No more of that.
OTHELLO:
Avaunt! Begone! Thou hast set me on the rack.
I swear 'tis better to be much abused
Than but to know't a little.
IAGO:                          How now, my lord?
OTHELLO:
What sense had I of her stolen hours of lust?             355
I saw't not, thought it not, it harmed not me.
I slept the next night well, fed well, was free° and merry;
I found not Cassio's kisses on her lips.
He that is robbed, not wanting° what is stolen,
Let him not know't and he's not robbed at all.            360
IAGO:   I am sorry to hear this.
OTHELLO:
I had been happy if the general camp,
Pioneers° and all, had tasted her sweet body,
So° I had nothing known. Oh, now, forever
Farewell the tranquil mind! Farewell content!            365
Farewell the plumèd troops and the big° wars

---

343. **conceits**: fancies, ideas.   344. **distaste**: be distasteful.   345. **act**: action, working.
347. **mandragora**: an opiate made of the mandrake root.   350. **thou owed'st**: you did own.
357. **free**: carefree.   359. **wanting**: missing.   363. **Pioneers**: diggers of mines, the lowest
grade of soldiers.   364. **So**: provided.   366. **big**: mighty.

That makes ambition virtue! Oh, farewell!
Farewell the neighing steed and the shrill trump,
The spirit-stirring drum, th'ear-piercing fife,
The royal banner, and all quality,°                          370
Pride,° pomp, and circumstance° of glorious war!
And, O you mortal engines,° whose rude throats
Th'immortal Jove's dread clamors° counterfeit,
Farewell! Othello's occupation's gone.

IAGO:    Is't possible, my lord?                              375

OTHELLO:
Villain, be sure thou prove my love a whore!
Be sure of it. Give me the ocular proof,
Or, by the worth of mine eternal soul,
Thou hadst been better have been born a dog
Than answer my waked wrath.

IAGO:                              Is 't come to this?         380

OTHELLO:
Make me to see't; or at the least, so prove it
That the probation° bear no hinge nor loop
To hang a doubt on, or woe upon thy life!

IAGO:    My noble lord —

OTHELLO:
If thou dost slander her and torture me,                      385
Never pray more; abandon all remorse;°
On horror's head horrors accumulate;°
Do deeds to make heaven weep, all earth amazed;°
For nothing canst thou to damnation add
Greater than that.

IAGO:                    O grace! O heaven forgive me!         390
Are you a man? Have you a soul or sense?
God b'wi'you; take mine office. O wretched fool!°
That lov'st to make thine honesty a vice!°
O monstrous world! Take note, take note, O world,
To be direct and honest is not safe.                          395

---

370. quality: character, essential nature.   371. Pride: rich display.   circumstance: pageantry.
372. mortal engines: i.e., cannon. (*Mortal* means "deadly.")   373. Jove's dread clamors:
i.e., thunder.   382. probation: proof.   386. remorse: pity, penitent hope for salvation.
387. horrors accumulate: add still more horrors.   388. amazed: confounded with horror.
392. O wretched fool: (Iago addresses himself as a fool for having carried honesty too far.)
393. vice: failing, something overdone.

I thank you for this profit,° and from hence°
I'll love no friend, sith° love breeds such offence.°
OTHELLO:    Nay, stay. Thou shouldst be° honest.
IAGO:
  I should be wise, for honesty's a fool
  And loses that° it works for.
OTHELLO:                    By the world,                    400
  I think my wife be honest and think she is not;
  I think that thou art just and think thou art not.
  I'll have some proof. Her name, that was as fresh
  As Dian's° visage, is now begrimed and black
  As mine own face. If there be cords, or knives,          405
  Poison, or fire, or suffocating streams,
  I'll not endure it. Would I were satisfied!
IAGO:
  I see, sir, you are eaten up with passion.
  I do repent me that I put it to you.
  You would be satisfied?
OTHELLO:                    Would? Nay, and I will.          410
IAGO:
  And may; but how? How satisfied, my lord?
  Would you, the supervisor,° grossly gape on?
  Behold her topped?
OTHELLO:                    Death and damnation! Oh!
IAGO:
  It were a tedious difficulty, I think,
  To bring them to that prospect. Damn them then,°          415
  If ever mortal eyes do see them bolster°
  More° than their own.° What then? How then?
  What shall I say? Where's satisfaction?
  It is impossible you should see this,
  Were they as prime° as goats, as hot as monkeys,          420
  As salt° as wolves in pride,° and fools as gross

---

396. **profit:** profitable instruction.  **hence:** henceforth.  397. **sith:** since.  **offense:** i.e., harm to the one who offers help and friendship.  398. **Thou shouldst be:** it appears that you are. (But Iago replies in the sense of "ought to be.")  400. **that:** what.  404. **Dian:** Diana, goddess of the moon and of chastity.  412. **supervisor:** onlooker.  415. **Damn them then:** i.e., they would have to be really incorrigible.  416. **bolster:** go to bed together, share a bolster.  417. **More:** other.  **own:** own eyes.  420. **prime:** lustful.  421. **salt:** wanton, sensual.  **pride:** heat.

As ignorance made drunk. But yet I say,
If imputation and strong circumstances°
Which lead directly to the door of truth
Will give you satisfaction, you may have't. 425

OTHELLO:
Give me a living reason she's disloyal.

IAGO:
I do not like the office.
But, sith I am entered in this cause so far,
Pricked° to't by foolish honesty and love,
I will go on. I lay with Cassio lately, 430
And being troubled with a raging tooth
I could not sleep. There are a kind of men
So loose of soul that in their sleeps will mutter
Their affairs. One of this kind is Cassio.
In sleep I heard him say, "Sweet Desdemona, 435
Let us be wary, let us hide our loves!"
And then, sir, would he grip and wring my hand,
Cry, "O sweet creature!," and then kiss me hard,
As if he plucked up kisses by the roots
That grew upon my lips; then laid his leg 440
Over my thigh, and sighed, and kissed, and then
Cried, "Cursèd fate that gave thee to the Moor!"

OTHELLO:
Oh, monstrous! Monstrous!

IAGO:                                Nay, this was but his dream.

OTHELLO:
But this denoted a foregone conclusion.°
'Tis a shrewd doubt,° though it be but a dream. 445

IAGO:
And this may help to thicken other proofs
That do demonstrate thinly.

OTHELLO:                        I'll tear her all to pieces.

IAGO:
Nay, but be wise. Yet we see nothing done;
She may be honest yet. Tell me but this:
Have you not sometimes seen a handkerchief 450

---

423. imputation . . . circumstances: strong circumstantial evidence.   429. Pricked: spurred.
444. foregone conclusion: previous experience or action.   445. shrewd doubt: suspicious
circumstance.

Spotted with strawberries° in your wife's hand?

OTHELLO:

I gave her such a one. 'Twas my first gift.

IAGO:

I know not that; but such a handkerchief —
I am sure it was your wife's — did I today
See Cassio wipe his beard with.

OTHELLO:                                     If it be that —                          455

IAGO:

If it be that, or any that was hers,
It speaks against her with the other proofs.

OTHELLO:

Oh, that the slave° had forty thousand lives!
One is too poor, too weak for my revenge.
Now do I see 'tis true. Look here, Iago,                          460
All my fond° love thus do I blow to heaven.
'Tis gone.
Arise, black vengeance, from the hollow hell!
Yield up, O love, thy crown and hearted° throne
To tyrannous hate! Swell, bosom, with thy freight,°          465
For 'tis of aspics'° tongues!

IAGO:    Yet be content.°

OTHELLO:    O! blood, blood, blood!

IAGO:

Patience, I say. Your mind perhaps may change.

OTHELLO:

Never, Iago. Like to the Pontic Sea,°                          470
Whose icy current and compulsive course
Ne'er feels retiring ebb, but keeps due on
To the Propontic° and the Hellespont,°
Even so my bloody thoughts with violent pace
Shall ne'er look back, ne'er ebb to humble love,                          475
Till that a capable° and wide revenge
Swallow them up. Now, by yond marble° heaven,

451. Spotted with strawberries: embroidered with a strawberry pattern. 458. the slave: i.e., Cassio. 461. fond: foolish. (But also suggesting "affectionate.") 464. hearted: fixed in the heart. 465. freight: burden. 466. aspics': venomous serpents'. 467. content: calm. 470. Pontic Sea: Black Sea. 473. Propontic: Sea of Marmora, between the Black Sea and the Aegean. Hellespont: Dardanelles, straits where the Sea of Marmora joins with the Aegean. 476. capable: ample, comprehensive. 477. marble: i.e., gleaming, polished, and indifferent to human suffering.

[*Kneeling*] In the due reverence of a sacred vow
I here engage my words.

IAGO:                              Do not rise yet.

[*He kneels.*]° Witness, you ever-burning lights above,          480
You elements that clip° us round about,
Witness that here Iago doth give up
The execution° of his wit,° hands, heart,
To wrongèd Othello's service. Let him command,
And to obey shall be in me remorse,°                             485
What bloody business ever.°                    [*They rise.*]

OTHELLO:                       I greet thy love,
Not with vain thanks, but with acceptance bounteous,
And will upon the instant put thee to't.°
Within these three days let me hear thee say
That Cassio's not alive.

IAGO:                          My friend is dead;               490
'Tis done at your request. But let her live.

OTHELLO:
Damn her, lewd minx!° Oh, damn her, damn her!
Come, go with me apart. I will withdraw.
To furnish me with some swift means of death
For the fair devil. Now art thou my lieutenant.                 495

IAGO:   I am your own forever.                     *Exeunt.*


## ACT 3, SCENE 4°

*Enter Desdemona, Emilia, and Clown.*

DESDEMONA:   Do you know, sirrah,° where Lieutenant Cassio lies?°
CLOWN:   I dare not say he lies anywhere.
DESDEMONA:   Why, man?
CLOWN:   He is a soldier, and for me to say a soldier lies, 'tis stabbing.
DESDEMONA:   Go to. Where lodges he?                             5
CLOWN:   To tell you where he lodges is to tell you where I lie.
DESDEMONA:   Can anything be made of this?


---

480. s.d. *He kneels:* (In the Quarto text, Iago kneels here after Othello has knelt at line 477.)
481. **clip:** encompass.   483. **execution:** exercise, action.   **wit:** mind.   485. **remorse:** pity
(for Othello's wrongs).   486. **ever:** soever.   488. **to't:** to the proof.   492. **minx:** wanton.
ACT 3, SCENE 4. **Location:** Before the citadel.   1. **sirrah:** (A form of address to an inferior.)
**lies:** lodges. (But the Clown makes the obvious pun.)

CLOWN:   I know not where he lodges, and for me to devise a lodging and say he lies here, or he lies there, were to lie in mine own throat.°

DESDEMONA:   Can you inquire him out, and be edified by report?          10

CLOWN:   I will catechize the world for him; that is, make questions, and by them answer.

DESDEMONA:   Seek him, bid him come hither. Tell him I have moved my lord° on his behalf, and hope all will be well.

CLOWN:   To do this is within the compass of man's wit, and therefore I will          15
attempt the doing it.                                        *Exit Clown.*

DESDEMONA:
Where should I lose that handkerchief, Emilia?

EMILIA:   I know not, madam.

DESDEMONA:
Believe me, I had rather have lost my purse
Full of crusadoes;° and but my noble Moor          20
Is true of mind and made of no such baseness
As jealous creatures are, it were enough
To put him to ill thinking.

EMILIA:                                        Is he not jealous?

DESDEMONA:
Who, he? I think the sun where he was born
Drew all such humors° from him.

EMILIA:                                        Look where he comes.          25

*Enter Othello.*

DESDEMONA:
I will not leave him now till Cassio
Be called to him. — How is't with you, my lord?

OTHELLO:
Well, my good lady. [*Aside.*] Oh, hardness to dissemble! —
How do you, Desdemona?

DESDEMONA:                        Well, my good lord.

OTHELLO:
Give me your hand. [*She gives her hand.*] This hand is moist, my lady.          30

DESDEMONA:
It yet hath felt no age nor known no sorrow.

---

9. **lie . . . throat:** lie egregiously and deliberately.   13–14. **moved my lord:** petitioned Othello.
20. **crusadoes:** Portuguese gold coins.   25. **humors:** (Refers to the four bodily fluids thought to determine temperament.)

OTHELLO:
    This argues° fruitfulness° and liberal° heart;
    Hot, hot, and moist. This hand of yours requires
    A sequester° from liberty, fasting and prayer,
    Much castigation,° exercise devout;°                35
    For here's a young and sweating devil here
    That commonly rebels. 'Tis a good hand,
    A frank° one.
DESDEMONA:    You may indeed say so,
    For 'twas that hand that gave away my heart.
OTHELLO:
    A liberal hand. The hearts of old gave hands,         40
    But our new heraldry is hands,° not hearts.
DESDEMONA:
    I cannot speak of this. Come now, your promise.
OTHELLO:    What promise, chuck?°
DESDEMONA:
    I have sent to bid Cassio come speak with you.
OTHELLO:
    I have a salt and sorry rheum° offends me;         45
    Lend me thy handkerchief.
DESDEMONA:    Here, my lord.                *[She offers a handkerchief.]*
OTHELLO:
    That which I gave you.
DESDEMONA:           I have it not about me.
OTHELLO:    Not?
DESDEMONA:    No, faith, my lord.             50
OTHELLO:
    That's a fault. That handkerchief
    Did an Egyptian to my mother give.
    She was a charmer,° and could almost read
    The thoughts of people. She told her, while she kept it
    'Twould make her amiable° and subdue my father       55

---

32. **argues:** gives evidence of. **fruitfulness:** generosity, amorousness, and fecundity. **liberal:** generous and sexually free. 34. **sequester:** sequestration. 35. **castigation:** corrective discipline. **exercise devout:** i.e., prayer, religious meditation, etc. 38. **frank:** generous, open. (With sexual suggestion.) 40–41. **The hearts . . . hands:** i.e., in former times, people would give their hearts when they gave their hands to something, but in our decadent present age the joining of hands no longer has that spiritual sense. 43. **chuck:** (A term of endearment.) 45. **salt . . . rheum:** distressful head cold or watering of the eyes. 53. **charmer:** sorceress. 55. **amiable:** desirable.

Entirely to her love, but if she lost it
Or made a gift of it, my father's eye
Should hold her loathèd, and his spirits should hunt
After new fancies.° She, dying, gave it me,
And bid me, when my fate would have me wived,                    60
To give it her.° I did so; and take heed on't;
Make it a darling like your precious eye.
To lose't or give't away, were such perdition°
As nothing else could match.

DESDEMONA:                          Is 't possible?

OTHELLO:
'Tis true; there 's magic in the web° of it.                    65
A sibyl, that had numbered in the world
The sun to course two hundred compasses,°
In her prophetic fury° sewed the work;°
The worms were hallowed that did breed the silk,
And it was dy'd in mummy° which the skillful               70
Conserved of° maidens' hearts.

DESDEMONA:                          I'faith! Is't true?

OTHELLO:
Most veritable. Therefore look to't well.

DESDEMONA:
Then would to God that I had never seen't!

OTHELLO:     Ha? Wherefore?

DESDEMONA:
Why do you speak so startingly and rash?°                    75

OTHELLO:
Is't lost? Is't gone? Speak, is't out o'th' way?°

DESDEMONA:     Heaven bless us!

OTHELLO:     Say you?

DESDEMONA:
It is not lost; but what an if° it were?

OTHELLO:     How?                                                 80

DESDEMONA:
I say, it is not lost.

59. fancies: loves.   61. her: i.e., to my wife.   63. perdition: loss; ruin. [Hall]   65. web: fabric, weaving.   67. compasses: annual circlings. (The *sibyl*, or prophetess, was two hundred years old.)   68. prophetic fury: frenzy of prophetic inspiration.   work: embroidered pattern.
70. mummy: medicinal or magical preparation drained from mummified bodies.   71. Conserved of: prepared or preserved out of.   75. startingly and rash: disjointedly and impetuously, excitedly.   76. out o'th' way: lost, misplaced.   79. an if: if.

OTHELLO:                Fetch 't, let me see 't!
DESDEMONA:
  Why, so I can, sir, but I will not now.
  This is a trick to put me from my suit.
  Pray you, let Cassio be received again.
OTHELLO:
  Fetch me the handkerchief. My mind misgives.                    85
DESDEMONA:   Come, come,
  You'll never meet a more sufficient° man.
OTHELLO:
  The handkerchief!
DESDEMONA:                I pray, talk° me of Cassio.
OTHELLO:   The handkerchief!
DESDEMONA:                      A man that all his time
  Hath founded his good fortunes on your love,°                   90
  Shared dangers with you —
OTHELLO:   The handkerchief!
DESDEMONA:   I'faith, you are to blame.
OTHELLO:   Zounds!                              *Exit Othello.*
EMILIA:   Is not this man jealous?                                 95
DESDEMONA:   I ne'er saw this before.
  Sure, there's some wonder in this handkerchief.
  I am most unhappy° in the loss of it.
EMILIA:
  'Tis not a year or two shows us a man.°
  They are all but° stomachs, and we all but food;                100
  They eat us hungerly,° and when they are full
  They belch us.

  *Enter Iago and Cassio.*

                Look you, Cassio and my husband.
IAGO: [*to Cassio*]
  There is no other way; 'tis she must do't.
  And, lo, the happiness!° Go and importune her.
DESDEMONA:
  How now, good Cassio! What's the news with you?                 105

---

87. **sufficient:** able, complete.   88. **talk:** talk to.   89–90. **A man . . . love:** A man who throughout his career has relied on your favor for his advancement.   98. **unhappy:** (1) unfortunate (2) sad.   99. **'Tis . . . man:** A year or two is not enough time for us women to know what men really are.   100. **but:** nothing but.   101. **hungerly:** hungrily.   104. **the happiness:** in happy time, fortunately met.

CASSIO:

Madam, my former suit. I do beseech you
That by your virtuous° means I may again
Exist and be a member of his love
Whom I, with all the office° of my heart,
Entirely honor. I would not be delayed.                              110
If my offense be of such mortal° kind
That nor my service past, nor° present sorrows,
Nor purposed merit in futurity
Can ransom me into his love again,
But to know so must be my benefit;°                                  115
So shall I clothe me in a forced content,
And shut myself up in° some other course,
To fortune's alms.°

DESDEMONA:            Alas! thrice-gentle Cassio,
My advocation° is not now in tune.
My lord is not my lord; nor should I know him,                       120
Were he in favor° as in humor° altered.
So help me every spirit sanctified°
As I have spoken for you all my best
And stood within the blank° of his displeasure
For my free° speech! You must awhile be patient.                    125
What I can do I will, and more I will
Than for myself I dare. Let that suffice you.

IAGO:

Is my lord angry?

EMILIA:              He went hence but now,
And certainly in strange unquietness.

IAGO:

Can he be angry? I have seen the cannon                             130
When it hath blown his ranks into the air,
And like the devil from his very arm
Puffed his own brother — and is he angry?
Something of moment° then. I will go meet him;

---

107. **virtuous:** (1) efficacious (2) morally good.   109. **office:** loyal service.   111. **mortal:** fatal.
112. **nor . . . nor:** neither . . . nor.   115. **But . . . benefit:** merely to know that my case is hope-
less will have to content me (and will be better than uncertainty).   117. **And shut . . . in:** commit
myself to.   118. **To fortune's alms:** throwing myself on the mercy of fortune.   119. **advoca-
tion:** advocacy.   121. **favor:** appearance.  **humor:** mood.   122. **So . . . sanctified:** so help me
all the heavenly host.   124. **within the blank:** within point-blank range. (The *blank* is the center of the target.)   125. **free:** frank.   134. **of moment:** of immediate importance, momentous.

There's matter in't indeed, if he be angry.                                    135
DESDEMONA:
   I prithee, do so.                                    *Exit [Iago].*
        Something, sure, of state,°
Either from Venice, or some unhatched practice°
Made demonstrable here in Cyprus to him,
Hath puddled° his clear spirit; and in such cases
Men's natures wrangle with inferior things,                                    140
Though great ones are their object. 'Tis even so;
For let our finger ache, and it indues°
Our other, healthful members even to a sense
Of pain. Nay, we must think men are not gods,
Nor of them look for such observancy°                                    145
As fits the bridal.° Beshrew me° much, Emilia,
I was, unhandsome° warrior as I am,
Arraigning his unkindness with° my soul;
But now I find I had suborned the witness,°
And he's indicted falsely.
EMILIA:              Pray heaven it be                                    150
State matters, as you think, and no conception
Nor no jealous toy° concerning you.
DESDEMONA:
   Alas the day! I never gave him cause.
EMILIA:
   But jealous souls will not be answered so;
They are not ever jealous for the cause,
But jealous for° they're jealous. It is a monster                                    155
Begot upon itself,° born on itself.
DESDEMONA:
   Heaven keep that monster from Othello's mind!
EMILIA:   Lady, amen.
DESDEMONA:
   I will go seek him. Cassio, walk hereabout.                                    160
If I do find him fit, I'll move your suit

---

136. **of state:** concerning state affairs.   137. **unhatched practice:** as yet unexecuted or undiscovered plot.   139. **puddled:** muddied.   142. **indues:** endows, brings to the same condition. 145. **observancy:** attentiveness.   146. **bridal:** wedding (when a bridegroom is newly attentive to his bride).  **Beshrew me:** (A mild oath.)  147. **unhandsome:** insufficient, unskillful. 148. **with:** before the bar of.   149. **suborned the witness:** induced the witness to give false testimony.  152. **toy:** fancy.  156. **for:** because.  157. **Begot upon itself:** generated solely from itself.

And seek to effect it to my uttermost.

CASSIO:
I humbly thank Your Ladyship.                    *Exit [Desdemona with Emilia].*

*Enter Bianca.*

BIANCA:
Save° you, friend Cassio!

CASSIO:                              What make° you from home?
How is't with you, my most fair Bianca?                                        165
I' faith, sweet love, I was coming to your house.

BIANCA:
And I was going to your lodging, Cassio.
What, keep a week away? Seven days and nights?
Eightscore-eight° hours? And lovers' absent hours
More tedious than the dial° eightscore times?                                  170
Oh, weary reck'ning!

CASSIO:                              Pardon me, Bianca.
I have this while with leaden thoughts been pressed;
But I shall, in a more continuate° time,
Strike off this score° of absence. Sweet Bianca,
                    [*giving her Desdemona's handkerchief*]
Take me this work out.°

BIANCA:                              Oh, Cassio, whence came this?                175
This is some token from a newer friend.°
To the felt absence now I feel a cause.
Is't come to this? Well, well.

CASSIO:                              Go to, woman!
Throw your vile guesses in the devil's teeth,
From whence you have them. You are jealous now                                 180
That this is from some mistress, some remembrance.
No, by my faith, Bianca.

BIANCA:                              Why, whose is it?

CASSIO:
I know not, neither. I found it in my chamber.
I like the work well. Ere it be demanded° —
As like° enough it will — I would have it copied.                             185

---

164. **Save:** God save.   **make:** do.   169. **Eightscore-eight:** one hundred sixty-eight, the number of hours in a week.   170. **the dial:** a complete revolution of the clock.   173. **continuate:** uninterrupted.   174. **Strike ... score:** settle this account.   175. **Take ... out:** copy this embroidery for me.   176. **friend:** mistress.   184. **demanded:** inquired for.   185. **like:** likely.

Take it and do't, and leave me for this time.
BIANCA:    Leave you? Wherefore?
CASSIO:
   I do attend here on the General,
   And think it no addition,° nor my wish,
   To have him see me womaned.                                        190
BIANCA:    Why, I pray you?
CASSIO:    Not that I love you not.
BIANCA:    But that you do not love me.
   I pray you, bring° me on the way a little,
   And say if I shall see you soon at night.                          195
CASSIO:
   'Tis but a little way that I can bring you,
   For I attend here; but I'll see you soon.
BIANCA:
   'Tis very good. I must be circumstanced.°                *Exeunt omnes.*

# ACT 4, SCENE 1°

*Enter Othello and Iago.*

IAGO:
   Will you think so?
OTHELLO:                    Think so, Iago?
IAGO:                                    What,
   To kiss in private?
OTHELLO:              An unauthorized kiss!
IAGO:
   Or to be naked with her friend in bed
   An hour or more, not meaning any harm?
OTHELLO:
   Naked in bed, Iago, and not mean harm?                            5
   It is hypocrisy against the devil.
   They that mean virtuously and yet do so,
   The devil their virtue tempts, and they tempt heaven.
IAGO:
   If they do nothing, 'tis a venial° slip.
   But if I give my wife a handkerchief —                            10

---

189. **addition:** i.e., addition to my reputation.    194. **bring:** accompany.    198. **be circumstanced:** be governed by circumstance, yield to your conditions.    ACT 4, SCENE 1. **Location:** Before the citadel.    9. **venial:** pardonable.

OTHELLO:   What then?

IAGO:
Why then, 'tis hers, my lord, and being hers,
She may, I think, bestow't on any man.

OTHELLO:
She is protectress of her honor too.
May she give that?                                                    15

IAGO:
Her honor is an essence that's not seen;
They have it° very oft that have it not.
But, for the handkerchief —

OTHELLO:
By heaven, I would most gladly have forgot it.
Thou said'st — Oh, it comes o'er my memory        20
As doth the raven o'er the infectious house,°
Boding to all — he had my handkerchief.

IAGO:
Ay, what of that?

OTHELLO:                         That's not so good now.

IAGO:                                                        What,
If I had said I had seen him do you wrong?
Or heard him say — as knaves be such abroad,       25
Who having, by their own importunate suit,
Or voluntary dotage of some mistress,
Convincèd or supplied them, cannot choose
But they must blab° —

OTHELLO:                         Hath he said anything?

IAGO:
He hath, my lord; but, be you well assured,          30
No more than he'll unswear.

OTHELLO:                         What hath he said?

IAGO:
Faith, that he did — I know not what he did.

OTHELLO:   What? What?

IAGO:
Lie —

---

17. **They have it:** i.e., they enjoy a reputation for it.   21. **raven . . . house:** (Allusion to the belief that the raven hovered over a house of sickness or infection, such as one visited by the plague.)   25–29. **as . . . blab:** since there are rascals enough who, having seduced a woman either through their own importunity or through the woman's willing infatuation, cannot keep quiet about it.

OTHELLO:   With her?

IAGO:                                  With her, on her; what you will.

OTHELLO:   Lie with her? Lie on her? We say "lie on her" when they belie°   35
her. Lie with her? Zounds, that's fulsome.° — Handkerchief — confes-
sions — handkerchief! To confess and be hanged for his labor — first to
be hanged and then to confess.° — I tremble at it. Nature would not
invest herself in such shadowing passion without some instruction.° It is
not words° that shakes me thus. Pish! Noses, ears, and lips. — Is't pos-   40
sible? — Confess — handkerchief! — O devil!                *Falls in a trance.*

IAGO:   Work on,
My medicine, work! Thus credulous fools are caught,
And many worthy and chaste dames even thus,
All guiltless, meet reproach. — What, ho! My lord!                          45
My lord, I say! Othello!

*Enter Cassio.*

                              How now, Cassio!

CASSIO:   What's the matter?

IAGO:
My lord is fall'n into an epilepsy.
This is his second fit. He had one yesterday.

CASSIO:
Rub him about the temples.

IAGO:                                  No, forbear.                          50
The lethargy° must have his° quiet course.
If not, he foams at mouth, and by and by
Breaks out to savage madness. Look, he stirs.
Do you withdraw yourself a little while.
He will recover straight. When he is gone,                                  55
I would on great occasion° speak with you.               [*Exit Cassio.*]
How is it, General? have you not hurt your head?

OTHELLO:
Dost thou mock me?°

---

35. **belie:** slander.   36. **fulsome:** foul.   37–38. **first . . . to confess:** (Othello reverses the
proverbial *confess and be hanged;* Cassio is to be given no time to confess before he dies.)
38–39. **Nature . . . instruction:** i.e., without some foundation in fact, nature would not have
dressed herself in such an overwhelming passion that comes over me now and fills my mind
with images, or in such a lifelike fantasy as Cassio had in his dream of lying with Desdemona.
40. **words:** mere words.   51. **lethargy:** coma.   **his:** its.   56. **on great occasion:** on a matter
of great importance.   58. **mock me:** (Othello takes Iago's question about hurting his head to
be a mocking reference to the cuckold's horns.)

IAGO:                 I mock you not, by heaven.
  Would you would bear your fortune like a man!

OTHELLO:
  A hornèd man's a monster and a beast.                    60

IAGO:
  There's many a beast then in a populous city,
  And many a civil° monster.

OTHELLO:    Did he confess it?

IAGO:    Good sir, be a man.
  Think every bearded fellow that's but yoked°            65
  May draw with you.° There's millions now alive
  That nightly lie in those unproper° beds
  Which they dare swear peculiar.° Your case is better.°
  Oh, 'tis the spite of hell, the fiend's arch-mock,
  To lip° a wanton in a secure° couch                70
  And to suppose her chaste! No, let me know,
  And knowing what I am, I know what she shall be.°

OTHELLO:    Oh, thou art wise. 'Tis certain.

IAGO:    Stand you awhile apart;
  Confine yourself but in a patient list.°             75
  Whilst you were here o'erwhelmed with your grief —
  A passion most unsuiting such a man —
  Cassio came hither. I shifted him away,
  And laid good 'scuse upon your ecstasy,°
  Bade him anon return and here speak with me,       80
  The which he promised. Do but encave° yourself
  And mark the fleers,° the gibes, and notable scorns
  That dwell in every region of his face;
  For I will make him tell the tale anew,
  Where, how, how oft, how long ago, and when       85
  He hath and is again to cope° your wife.
  I say, but mark his gesture. Marry, patience!
  Or I shall say you're all-in-all in spleen,°
  And nothing of a man.

---

62. **civil:** i.e., dwelling in a city.   65. **yoked:** (1) married (2) put into the yoke of infamy and cuckoldry.   66. **draw with you:** pull as you do, like oxen who are yoked, i.e., share your fate as cuckold.   67. **unproper:** not exclusively their own.   68. **peculiar:** private, their own.   **better:** i.e., because you know the truth.   70. **lip:** kiss.   **secure:** free from suspicion.   72. **And . . . shall be:** and, knowing myself to be a cuckold, I'll know for certain that she's a whore.   75. **in . . . list:** within the bounds of patience.   78–79. **I shifted . . . ecstasy:** I got him out of the way, using your fit as my excuse for doing so.   81. **encave:** conceal.   82. **fleers:** sneers.   86. **cope:** encounter with, have sex with.   88. **all-in-all in spleen:** utterly governed by passionate impulses.

OTHELLO:                       Dost thou hear, Iago?
  I will be found most cunning in my patience;                    90
  But — dost thou hear? — most bloody.
IAGO:                                   That's not amiss;
  But yet keep time° in all. Will you withdraw?      [*Othello stands apart.*]
  Now will I question Cassio of Bianca,
  A huswife° that by selling her desires
  Buys herself bread and clothes. It is a creature              95
  That dotes on Cassio — as 'tis the strumpet's plague
  To beguile many and be beguiled by one.
  He, when he hears of her, cannot restrain°
  From the excess of laughter. Here he comes.

*Enter Cassio.*

  As he shall smile, Othello shall go mad;                     100
  And his unbookish° jealousy must conster°
  Poor Cassio's smiles, gestures, and light behaviors
  Quite in the wrong. — How do you now, Lieutenant?
CASSIO:
  The worser that you give me the addition°
  Whose want° even kills me.                                    105
IAGO:
  Ply Desdemona well and you are sure on't.
  [*Speaking lower*] Now, if this suit lay in Bianca's power,
  How quickly should you speed!
CASSIO: [*laughing*]    Alas! poor caitiff!°
OTHELLO: [*aside*]    Look how he laughs already!                      110
IAGO:
  I never knew woman love man so.
CASSIO:
  Alas, poor rogue! I think i'faith, she loves me.
OTHELLO: [*aside*]
  Now he denies it faintly, and laughs it out.
IAGO:
  Do you hear, Cassio?
OTHELLO:                       Now he importunes him
  To tell it o'er. Go to!° Well said,° well said.                115

---

92. **keep time:** keep yourself steady (as in music).   94. **huswife:** hussy.   98. **restrain:** refrain.   101. **his unbookish:** Othello's uninstructed.   **conster:** construe.   104. **addition:** title.
105. **Whose want:** the lack of which.   109. **caitiff:** wretch.   115. **Go to:** (An expression of remonstrance.)   **Well said:** well done. (Sarcastic.)

IAGO:
    She gives it out that you shall marry her.
    Do you intend it?
CASSIO:  Ha, ha, ha!
OTHELLO: [*aside*]  Do you triumph, Roman?° Do you triumph?
CASSIO:  I marry her? What? A customer?° Prithee, bear some charity to    120
    my wit;° do not think it so unwholesome. Ha, ha, ha!
OTHELLO: [*aside*]  So, so, so, so! They laugh that win.°
IAGO:  Faith, the cry° goes that you shall marry her.
CASSIO:  Prithee, say true.
IAGO:  I am a very villain else.°    125
OTHELLO: [*aside*]  Have you scored me?° Well.
CASSIO:  This is the monkey's own giving out. She is persuaded I will
    marry her out of her own love and flattery,° not out of my promise.
OTHELLO: [*aside*]  Iago beckons° me. Now he begins the story.
CASSIO:  She was here even now; she haunts me in every place. I was the    130
    other day talking on the seabank° with certain Venetians, and thither
    comes the bauble,° and, by this hand,° she falls me thus about my neck —
                               [*He embraces Iago.*]
OTHELLO: [*aside*]  Crying, "Oh, dear Cassio!" as it were; his gesture imports it.
CASSIO:  So hangs and lolls and weeps upon me, so shakes and pulls me.
    Ha, ha, ha!    135
OTHELLO: [*aside*]  Now he tells how she plucked him to my chamber. Oh, I
    see that nose of yours, but not that dog I shall throw it to.°
CASSIO:  Well, I must leave her company.
IAGO:  Before me,° look where she comes.

*Enter Bianca [with Othello's handkerchief].*

CASSIO:  'Tis such another fitchew!° Marry, a perfumed one. — What do    140
    you mean by this haunting of me?
BIANCA:  Let the devil and his dam° haunt you! What did you mean by
    that same handkerchief you gave me even now? I was a fine fool to take

---

119. **Roman:** (The Romans were noted for their triumphs or triumphal processions.)    120. **A customer?:** who, I, the whore's customer? (Or, *customer* could mean "prostitute.").    120–21. **bear . . . wit:** be more charitable to my judgment.    122. **They . . . win:** i.e., they that laugh last laugh best.    123. **cry:** rumor.    125. **I . . . else:** call me a complete rogue if I'm not telling the truth.    126. **scored me:** scored off me, beaten me, made up my reckoning, branded me.    128. **flattery:** self-flattery, self-deception.    129. **beckons:** signals to.    131. **seabank:** seashore.    132. **bauble:** plaything.  **by this hand:** I make my vow.    137. **not . . . to:** (Othello imagines himself cutting off Cassio's nose and throwing it to a dog.)    139. **Before me:** i.e., on my soul.    140. **'Tis . . . fitchew!:** what a whore she is, just like all the others! (*Fitchew*, or "polecat," was a common term of contempt for a courtesan or prostitute.)    142. **dam:** mother.

it. I must take out the work? A likely piece of work,° that you should find
it in your chamber and know not who left it there! This is some minx's        145
token, and I must take out the work? There; give it your hobbyhorse.°
[*She gives him the handkerchief.*] Wheresoever you had it, I'll take out no
work on't.

CASSIO:  How now, my sweet Bianca? How now? How now?

OTHELLO: [*aside*]  By heaven, that should be° my handkerchief!              150

BIANCA:  If you'll come to supper tonight, you may; if you will not, come
when you are next prepared for.°                                          *Exit.*

IAGO:  After her, after her.

CASSIO:  Faith, I must. She'll rail in the streets else.

IAGO:  Will you sup there?                                                   155

CASSIO:  Faith, I intend so.

IAGO:  Well, I may chance to see you, for I would very fain speak with you.

CASSIO:  Prithee come. Will you?

IAGO:  Go to.° Say no more.                                     [*Exit Cassio.*]

OTHELLO: [*advancing*]  How shall I murder him, Iago?                        160

IAGO:  Did you perceive how he laughed at his vice?

OTHELLO:  Oh, Iago!

IAGO:  And did you see the handkerchief?

OTHELLO:  Was that mine?

IAGO:  Yours, by this hand. And to see how he prizes the foolish woman        165
your wife! She gave it him, and he hath given it his whore.

OTHELLO:  I would have him nine years a-killing. A fine woman! A fair
woman! A sweet woman!

IAGO:  Nay, you must forget that.

OTHELLO:  Ay, let her rot and perish, and be damned tonight, for she shall    170
not live. No, my heart is turned to stone; I strike it, and it hurts my hand.
Oh, the world hath not a sweeter creature! She might lie by an emperor's
side and command him tasks.

IAGO:  Nay, that's not your way.°

OTHELLO:  Hang her! I do but say what she is. So delicate with her needle!    175
An admirable musician! Oh, she will sing the savageness out of a bear. Of
so high and plenteous wit and invention!°

IAGO:  She's the worse for all this.

OTHELLO:  Oh, a thousand, a thousand times! And then, of so gentle a
condition!°
                                                                            180

---

144. **A likely . . . work:** A fine story.  146. **hobbyhorse:** harlot.  150. **should be:** must be.
152. **when . . . for:** when I'm ready for you (i.e., never).  159. **Go to:** (An expression of remonstrance.)  174. **your way:** i.e., the way you should think of her.  177. **invention:** imagination.
179–80. **gentle a condition:** wellborn and well-bred.

IAGO:    Ay, too gentle.°

OTHELLO:    Nay, that's certain. But yet the pity of it, Iago! Oh, Iago, the pity of it, Iago!

IAGO:    If you are so fond° over her iniquity, give her patent° to offend, for if it touch not you it comes near nobody.                                              185

OTHELLO:    I will chop her into messes.° Cuckold me!

IAGO:    Oh, 'tis foul in her.

OTHELLO:    With mine officer?

IAGO:    That's fouler.

OTHELLO:    Get me some poison, Iago, this night. I'll not expostulate    190
with her, lest her body and beauty unprovide° my mind again. This night,
Iago.

IAGO:    Do it not with poison. Strangle her in her bed, even the bed she
hath contaminated.

OTHELLO:    Good, good! The justice of it pleases. Very good.               195

IAGO:    And for Cassio, let me be his undertaker.° You shall hear more by
midnight.

OTHELLO:

Excellent good. [*A trumpet within.*] What trumpet is that same?

IAGO:    I warrant, something from Venice.

*Enter Lodovico, Desdemona, and attendants.*

'Tis Lodovico. This comes from the Duke.                                    200
See, your wife's with him.

LODOVICO:

God save you, worthy General!

OTHELLO:                                    With all my heart,° sir.

LODOVICO: [ *giving him a letter*]    The Duke and the senators of Venice greet
you.

OTHELLO:

I kiss the instrument of their pleasures.        [*He opens the letter, and reads.*]    205

DESDEMONA:

And what's the news, good cousin Lodovico?

IAGO:

I am very glad to see you, signor.
Welcome to Cyprus.

---

181. **gentle:** generous, yielding (to other men).    184. **fond:** foolish.    **patent:** license.
186. **messes:** portions of meat, i.e., bits.    191. **unprovide:** weaken, disarm.    196. **be his
undertaker:** undertake to dispatch him.    202. **With all my heart:** i.e., I thank you most
heartily.

LODOVICO:
   I thank you. How does Lieutenant Cassio?
IAGO:   Lives, sir.

210

DESDEMONA:
   Cousin, there's fall'n between him and my lord
   An unkind° breach; but you shall make all well.
OTHELLO:   Are you sure of that?
DESDEMONA:   My lord?
OTHELLO: [*reads*]   "This fail you not to do, as you will —"

215

LODOVICO:
   He did not call; he's busy in the paper.
   Is there division twixt my lord and Cassio?
DESDEMONA:
   A most unhappy one. I would do much
   T'atone° them, for the love I bear to Cassio.
OTHELLO:   Fire and brimstone!

220

DESDEMONA:   My lord?
OTHELLO:   Are you wise?
DESDEMONA:
   What, is he angry?
LODOVICO:            Maybe the letter moved him;
   For, as I think, they do command him home,
   Deputing Cassio in his government.°

225

DESDEMONA:   By my troth, I am glad on't.°
OTHELLO:   Indeed?
DESDEMONA:   My lord?
OTHELLO:   I am glad to see you mad.°
DESDEMONA:   Why, sweet Othello —

230

OTHELLO: [*striking her*]   Devil!
DESDEMONA:   I have not deserved this.
LODOVICO:
   My lord, this would not be believed in Venice,
   Though I should swear I saw't. 'Tis very much.°
   Make her amends, she weeps.
OTHELLO:              Oh, devil, devil!

235

   If that the earth could teem° with woman's tears,

---

212. **unkind:** unnatural, contrary to their natures; hurtful.   219. **T'atone:** to reconcile.   225. **government:** office.   226. **on't:** of it.   229. **I am . . . mad:** i.e., I am glad to see that you are insane enough to rejoice in Cassio's promotion. (? Othello bitterly plays on Desdemona's *I am glad.*)   234. **very much:** too much, outrageous.   236. **teem:** breed, be impregnated.

Each drop she falls° would prove a crocodile.°
Out of my sight!
DESDEMONA:     I will not stay to offend you.     *[Going.]*
LODOVICO:   Truly, an obedient lady.
I do beseech Your Lordship, call her back.     240
OTHELLO: [*calling*]   Mistress!
DESDEMONA: [*returning*]   My lord?
OTHELLO:   What would you with her, sir?°
LODOVICO:   Who, I, my lord?
OTHELLO:

Ay, you did wish that I would make her turn.     245
Sir, she can turn, and turn, and yet go on
And turn again; and she can weep, sir, weep;
And she's obedient, as you say, obedient,°
Very obedient. — Proceed you in your tears. —
Concerning this, sir — Oh, well-painted passion!° —     250
I am commanded home. — Get you away;
I'll send for you anon. — Sir, I obey the mandate,
And will return to Venice. — Hence! avaunt!     *[Exit Desdemona.]*
Cassio shall have my place. And, sir, tonight
I do entreat that we may sup together.     255
You are welcome, sir, to Cyprus. — Goats and monkeys!°     *Exit.*
LODOVICO:

Is this the noble Moor whom our full Senate
Call all in all sufficient? Is this the nature
Whom passion could not shake? Whose solid virtue
The shot of accident nor dart of chance     260
Could neither graze nor pierce?
IAGO:     He is much changed.
LODOVICO:

Are his wits safe? Is he not light of brain?
IAGO:

He's that he is. I may not breathe my censure
What he might be. If what he might he is not,
I would to heaven he were!°

237. **falls:** lets fall. **crocodile:** (Crocodiles were supposed to weep hypocritical tears for their victims.) 243. **What ... sir?** (Othello implies that Desdemona is pliant and will do a *turn,* lines 243–45, for any man.) 248. **obedient:** (With much the same sexual connotation as *turn* in lines 243–45.) 250. **passion:** i.e., grief. 256. **Goats and monkeys:** (See 3.3.419.) 263–65. **I may ... were!** I dare not venture an opinion as to whether he's of unsound mind, as you suggest, but, if he isn't, then it might be better to wish he were in fact insane, since only that could excuse his wild behavior!

LODOVICO:                          What! strike his wife!                          265
IAGO:
   Faith, that was not so well; yet would I knew
   That stroke would prove the worst!
LODOVICO:                                    Is it his use?°
   Or did the letters work upon his blood°
   And new-create this fault?
IAGO:                                    Alas, alas!
   It is not honesty in me to speak                          270
   What I have seen and known. You shall observe him,
   And his own courses will denote° him so
   That I may save my speech. Do but go after
   And mark how he continues.
LODOVICO:
   I am sorry that I am deceived in him.                    *Exeunt.*    275


## ACT 4, SCENE 2°

*Enter Othello and Emilia.*

OTHELLO:   You have seen nothing, then?
EMILIA:
   Nor ever heard, nor ever did suspect.
OTHELLO:
   Yes, you have seen Cassio and her together.
EMILIA:
   But then I saw no harm, and then I heard
   Each syllable that breath made up between them.          5
OTHELLO:   What, did they never whisper?
EMILIA:   Never, my lord.
OTHELLO:   Nor send you out o' th' way?
EMILIA:   Never.
OTHELLO:
   To fetch her fan, her gloves, her mask, nor nothing?    10
EMILIA:   Never, my lord.
OTHELLO:   That's strange.
EMILIA:
   I durst, my lord, to wager she is honest,
   Lay down my soul at stake.° If you think other,

---

267. **use:** custom.  268. **blood:** passions.  272. **courses will denote:** actions will reveal.
ACT 4, SCENE 2. Location: The citadel.  14. **at stake:** as the wager.

Remove your thought; it doth abuse your bosom.°          15
If any wretch have put this in your head,
Let heaven requite it with the serpent's curse!°
For if she be not honest, chaste, and true,
There's no man happy; the purest of their wives
Is foul as slander.

OTHELLO:          Bid her come hither. Go.         *Exit Emilia.*    20
   She says enough; yet she's a simple bawd
That cannot say as much.° This° is a subtle whore,
A closet lock and key° of villainous secrets.
And yet she'll kneel and pray; I have seen her do't.

*Enter Desdemona and Emilia.*

DESDEMONA:    My lord, what is your will?               25
OTHELLO:    Pray you, chuck, come hither.
DESDEMONA:
   What is your pleasure?
OTHELLO:           Let me see your eyes;
   Look in my face.
DESDEMONA:       What horrible fancy's this?
OTHELLO: [*to Emilia*]    Some of your function,° mistress.
   Leave procreants° alone and shut the door;          30
Cough or cry "hem" if anybody come.
Your mystery,° your mystery! Nay, dispatch.      *Exit Emilia.*
DESDEMONA: [*kneeling*]
   Upon my knees, what doth your speech import?
I understand a fury in your words.
But not the words.                               35
OTHELLO:
   Why, what art thou?
DESDEMONA:          Your wife, my lord, your true
   And loyal wife.
OTHELLO:       Come, swear it, damn thyself,
   Lest, being like one of heaven,° the devils themselves

---

15. **abuse your bosom:** deceive your breast, your heart.   17. **the serpent's curse:** the curse pronounced by God on the serpent for deceiving Eve, just as some man has done to Othello and Desdemona. (See Genesis 3:14.)   21–22. **she's . . . much:** i.e., any procuress or go-between who couldn't make up as plausible a story as Emilia's would have to be pretty stupid.   22. **This:** i.e., Desdemona.   23. **closet lock and key:** i.e., concealer.   29. **Some . . . function:** i.e., practice your chosen profession, that of bawd (by guarding the door).   30. **procreants:** mating couples. 32. **mystery:** trade, occupation.   38. **being . . . heaven:** looking like an angel.

Should fear to seize thee. Therefore be double damned:
Swear thou art honest.

DESDEMONA:                       Heaven doth truly know it.                    40

OTHELLO:
Heaven truly knows that thou art false as hell.

DESDEMONA:
To whom, my lord? With whom? How am I false?

OTHELLO: [*weeping*]
Ah! Desdemon! Away, away, away!

DESDEMONA:
Alas the heavy day! Why do you weep?
Am I the motive° of these tears, my lord?                                      45
If haply you my father do suspect
An instrument of this your calling back,
Lay not your blame on me. If you have lost him,
I have lost him too.

OTHELLO:                       Had it pleased heaven
To try me with affliction, had they° rained                                    50
All kinds of sores and shames on my bare head,
Steeped me in poverty to the very lips,
Given to captivity me and my utmost hopes,
I should have found in some place of my soul
A drop of patience. But, alas, to make me                                      55
A fixèd figure for the time of scorn
To point his slow and moving finger at!°
Yet could I bear that too, well, very well.
But there where I have garnered° up my heart,
Where either I must live or bear no life,
The fountain° from the which my current runs                                   60
Or else dries up — to be discarded thence!
Or keep it as a cistern° for foul toads
To knot and gender in!° Turn thy complexion there,
Patience, thou young and rose-lipped cherubin —                                65
Ay, there look grim as hell!°

---

45. **motive:** cause.   50. **they:** the heavenly powers.   56–57. **A fixèd . . . finger at:** a figure of ridicule to be pointed at scornfully for all of eternity by the slowly moving finger of Time.
59. **garnered:** stored.   61. **fountain:** spring.   63. **cistern:** cesspool.   64. **To . . . gender in:** to couple sexually and conceive in.   64–66. **Turn . . . hell!:** direct your gaze there, Patience, and your youthful and rosy cherubic countenance will turn grim and pale at this hellish spectacle!

DESDEMONA:
    I hope my noble lord esteems me honest.°
OTHELLO:
    Oh, ay; as summer flies are in the shambles,°
    That quicken even with blowing.° O thou weed,
    Who art so lovely fair and smell'st so sweet                    70
    That the sense aches at thee, would thou hadst ne'er been born!
DESDEMONA:
    Alas, what ignorant sin° have I committed?
OTHELLO:
    Was this fair paper, this most goodly book,
    Made to write "whore" upon? What committed?
    Committed? Oh, thou public commoner!°                          75
    I should make very forges of my cheeks,
    That would to cinders burn up modesty,
    Did I but speak thy deeds. What committed?
    Heaven stops the nose at it and the moon winks;°
    The bawdy° wind, that kisses all it meets                       80
    Is hushed within the hollow mine° of earth,
    And will not hear't. What committed?
    Impudent strumpet!
DESDEMONA:                    By heaven, you do me wrong.
OTHELLO:
    Are not you a strumpet?
DESDEMONA:    No, as I am a Christian.                             85
    If to preserve this vessel° for my lord
    From any other foul unlawful touch
    Be not to be a strumpet, I am none.
OTHELLO:    What, not a whore?
DESDEMONA:    No, as I shall be saved.                            90
OTHELLO:    Is't possible?
DESDEMONA:
    Oh, heaven forgive us!
OTHELLO:                    I cry you mercy,° then.
    I took you for that cunning whore of Venice

---

67. **honest:** chaste.    68. **shambles:** slaughterhouse.    69. **That . . . blowing:** that come to life
with the puffing up of the rotten meat on which the flies and their maggots are breeding.
72. **ignorant sin:** sin in ignorance.    75. **commoner:** prostitute.    79. **winks:** closes her eyes.
(The moon symbolizes chastity.)    80. **bawdy:** kissing one and all.    81. **mine:** cave (where the
winds were thought to dwell).    86. **vessel:** body.    92. **cry you mercy:** beg your pardon.
(Sarcastic.)

That married with Othello. [*Calling out*] You, mistress,
That have the office opposite to Saint Peter                    95
And keep the gate of hell!

*Enter Emilia.*

                                       You, you, ay, you!
We have done our course.° There's money for your pains. [*He gives money.*]
I pray you, turn the key and keep our counsel.                 *Exit.*
EMILIA:
Alas, what does this gentleman conceive?°
How do you, madam? How do you, my good lady?                   100
DESDEMONA:    Faith, half asleep.°
EMILIA:
Good madam, what's the matter with my lord?
DESDEMONA:    With who?
EMILIA:    Why, with my lord, madam.
DESDEMONA:    Who is thy lord?
EMILIA:                                He that is yours, sweet lady.      105
DESDEMONA:
I have none. Do not talk to me, Emilia.
I cannot weep, nor answers have I none,
But what should go by water.° Prithee, tonight
Lay on my bed my wedding sheets, remember;
And call thy husband hither.                                   110
EMILIA:    Here's a change indeed!                            *Exit.*
DESDEMONA:
'Tis meet I should be used so, very meet.°
How have I been behaved, that he might stick
The small'st opinion on my least misuse?°

*Enter Iago and Emilia.*

IAGO:
What is your pleasure, madam? How is't with you?              115
DESDEMONA:
I cannot tell. Those that do teach young babes

---

97. **course:** business. (With an indecent suggestion of "trick," turn at sex.)   99. **conceive:** suppose, think.   101. **half asleep:** i.e., dazed.   108. **go by water:** be conveyed by tears.   112. **'Tis . . . very meet:** i.e., it must be I somehow have deserved this.   113–14. **How . . . misuse?:** what have I done that prompts Othello to attach even the slightest censure to whatever little fault I may have committed?

Do it with gentle means and easy tasks.
He might have chid me so, for, in good faith,
I am a child to chiding.

IAGO:     What is the matter, lady?                                    120

EMILIA:
Alas, Iago, my lord hath so bewhored her,
Thrown such despite and heavy terms upon her,
As true hearts cannot bear it.

DESDEMONA:     Am I that name, Iago?

IAGO:     What name, fair lady?                                        125

DESDEMONA:
Such as she says my lord did say I was.

EMILIA:
He called her whore. A beggar in his drink
Could not have laid such terms upon his callet.°

IAGO:     Why did he so?

DESDEMONA: [*weeping*]
I do not know. I am sure I am none such.                              130

IAGO:     Do not weep, do not weep. Alas the day!

EMILIA:
Has she forsook so many noble matches,
Her father and her country and her friends,
To be called whore? Would it not make one weep?

DESDEMONA:
It is my wretched fortune.

IAGO:                              Beshrew° him for't!                 135
How comes this trick° upon him?

DESDEMONA:                              Nay, heaven doth know.

EMILIA:
I will be hanged if some eternal° villain,
Some busy and insinuating° rogue,
Some cogging, cozening° slave, to get some office,
Have not devised this slander. I'll be hanged else.                  140

IAGO:
Fie, there is no such man. It is impossible.

DESDEMONA:
If any such there be, heaven pardon him!

---

128. **callet:** whore.     135. **Beshrew:** may evil befall. (An oath.)     136. **trick:** strange behavior,
delusion.     137. **eternal:** inveterate.     138. **insinuating:** ingratiating, fawning, wheedling.
139. **cogging, cozening:** cheating, defrauding.

EMILIA:
A halter° pardon him! And hell gnaw his bones!
Why should he call her whore? Who keeps her company?
What place? What time? What form?° What likelihood?          145
The Moor's abused by some most villainous knave,
Some base notorious knave, some scurvy fellow.
Oh, heavens, that such companions thou'dst unfold,°
And put in every honest hand a whip
To lash the rascals naked through the world          150
Even from the east to th' west!

IAGO:                                        Speak within door.°

EMILIA:
Oh, fie upon them! Some such squire° he was
That turned your wit the seamy side without°
And made you to suspect me with the Moor.

IAGO:
You are a fool. Go to.°

DESDEMONA:                    O God, Iago,          155
What shall I do to win my lord again?
Good friend, go to him; for, by this light of heaven,
I know not how I lost him. Here I kneel.          [She kneels.]
If e'er my will did trespass 'gainst his love,
Either in discourse of thought° or actual deed,          160
Or that° mine eyes, mine ears, or any sense
Delighted them° in any other form;
Or that I do not yet,° and ever did,
And ever will — though he do shake me off
To beggarly divorcement — love him dearly,          165
Comfort forswear° me! Unkindness may do much,
And his unkindness may defeat° my life,
But never taint my love. I cannot say "whore."
It does abhor° me now I speak the word;
To do the act that might the addition° earn          170
Not the world's mass of vanity° could make me.          [She rises.]

---

143. halter: hangman's noose.  145. form: manner, circumstance.  148. that . . . unfold:
would that you would expose such fellows.  151. within door: i.e., not so loud.  152. squire:
fellow.  153. seamy side without: wrong side out.  155. Go to: i.e., that's enough.  160. discourse of thought: process of thinking.  161. that: if. (Also in line 163.)  162. Delighted
them: took delight.  163. yet: still.  166. Comfort forswear: may heavenly comfort forsake.
167. defeat: destroy.  169. abhor: (1) fill me with abhorrence (2) make me whorelike.  170. addition: title.  171. vanity: showy splendor.

IAGO:

I pray you, be content. 'Tis but his humor.°
The business of the state does him offense,
And he does chide with you.

DESDEMONA: If 'twere no other — 175

IAGO: It is but so, I warrant. [*Trumpets within.*]

Hark, how these instruments summon you to supper!
The messengers of Venice stays the meat.°
Go in, and weep not. All things shall be well.

[*Exeunt Desdemona and Emilia.*]

*Enter Roderigo.*

How now, Roderigo? 180

RODERIGO: I do not find that thou deal'st justly with me.

IAGO: What in the contrary?

RODERIGO: Every day thou daff'st me° with some device,° Iago, and rather,
as it seems to me now, keep'st from me all conveniency° than suppliest
me with the least advantage° of hope. I will indeed no longer endure it, 185
nor am I yet persuaded to put up° in peace what already I have foolishly
suffered.

IAGO: Will you hear me, Roderigo?

RODERIGO: Faith, I have heard too much, for your words and performances are no kin together. 190

IAGO: You charge me most unjustly.

RODERIGO: With naught but truth. I have wasted myself out of my means.
The jewels you have had from me to deliver° Desdemona would half
have corrupted a votarist.° You have told me she hath received them and
returned me expectations and comforts of sudden respect° and acquain- 195
tance, but I find none.

IAGO: Well, go to, very well.

RODERIGO: "Very well"! "Go to"! I cannot go to,° man, nor 'tis not very
well. By this hand, I think, it is scurvy, and begin to find myself fopped°
in it. 200

IAGO: Very well.

---

172. **humor:** mood.    178. **stays the meat:** are waiting to dine.    183. **thou daff'st me:** you put
me off.    **device:** excuse, trick.    184. **conveniency:** advantage, opportunity.    185. **advantage:**
increase.    186. **put up:** submit to, tolerate.    193. **deliver:** deliver to.    194. **votarist:** nun.
195. **sudden respect:** immediate consideration.    198. **I cannot go to:** (Roderigo changes Iago's
*go to,* an expression urging patience, to *I cannot go to,* "I have no opportunity for success in wooing.")    199. **fopped:** fooled, duped.

RODERIGO: I tell you 'tis not very well.° I will make myself known to Desdemona. If she will return me my jewels, I will give over my suit and repent my unlawful solicitation; if not, assure yourself I will seek satisfaction° of you.

IAGO: You have said now?°

RODERIGO: Ay, and said nothing but what I protest intendment° of doing.

IAGO: Why, now I see there's mettle in thee, and even from this instant do build on thee a better opinion than ever before. Give me thy hand, Roderigo. Thou hast taken against me a most just exception; but yet I protest I have dealt most directly in thy affair.

RODERIGO: It hath not appeared.

IAGO: I grant indeed it hath not appeared, and your suspicion is not without wit and judgment. But, Roderigo, if thou hast that in thee indeed which I have greater reason to believe now than ever — I mean purpose, courage, and valor — this night show it. If thou the next night following enjoy not Desdemona, take me from this world with treachery and devise engines° for my life.

RODERIGO: Well, what is it? Is it within reason and compass?

IAGO: Sir, there is especial commission come from Venice to depute Cassio in Othello's place.

RODERIGO: Is that true? Why, then Othello and Desdemona return again to Venice.

IAGO: Oh, no; he goes into Mauritania and takes away with him the fair Desdemona, unless his abode be lingered here by some accident; wherein none can be so determinate° as the removing of Cassio.

RODERIGO: How do you mean, removing of him?

IAGO: Why, by making him uncapable of Othello's place — knocking out his brains.

RODERIGO: And that you would have me do?

IAGO: Ay, if you dare do yourself a profit and a right. He sups tonight with a harlotry,° and thither will I go to him. He knows not yet of his honorable fortune. If you will watch his going thence, which I will fashion to fall out° between twelve and one, you may take him at your pleasure. I will be near to second your attempt, and he shall fall between us. Come, stand not amazed at it, but go along with me. I will show you such a

**202. not very well:** (Roderigo changes Iago's *very well,* "all right, then," to *not very well,* "not at all good.") **204–05. satisfaction:** repayment (The term normally means settling of accounts in a duel.) **206. You . . . now?:** have you finished? **207. protest intendment:** avow my intention. **218. engines:** plots, snares. **226. determinate:** conclusive, instrumental. **232. harlotry:** slut. **234. fall out:** occur.

necessity in his death that you shall think yourself bound to put it on
him. It is now high° suppertime, and the night grows to waste.° About it.

RODERIGO:    I will hear further reason for this.

IAGO:    And you shall be satisfied.                                    *Exeunt.*    240

## ACT 4, SCENE 3°

*Enter Othello, Lodovico, Desdemona, Emilia, and attendants.*

LODOVICO:
I do beseech you, sir, trouble yourself no further.

OTHELLO:
Oh, pardon me; 'twill do me good to walk.

LODOVICO:
Madam, good night. I humbly thank Your Ladyship.

DESDEMONA:
Your Honor is most welcome.

OTHELLO:                              Will you walk, sir?
Oh, Desdemona!                                                          5

DESDEMONA:    My lord?

OTHELLO:    Get you to bed on th'instant; I will be returned forthwith. Dismiss your attendant there. Look't be done.

DESDEMONA:    I will, my lord.        *Exit [Othello, with Lodovico and attendants].*

EMILIA:    How goes it now? He looks gentler than he did.               10

DESDEMONA:
He says he will return incontinent,°
And hath commanded me to go to bed,
And bade me to dismiss you.

EMILIA:    Dismiss me?

DESDEMONA:
It was his bidding. Therefore, good Emilia,                            15
Give me my nightly wearing, and adieu.
We must not now displease him.

EMILIA:    I would you had never seen him!

DESDEMONA:
So would not I. My love doth so approve him
That even his stubbornness,° his checks,° his frowns —                  20
Prithee, unpin me — have grace and favor in them.

                        *[Emilia prepares Desdemona for bed.]*

---

238. **high:** fully.  **grows to waste:** wastes away.  **ACT 4, SCENE 3. Location:** The citadel.
11. **incontinent:** immediately.  20. **stubbornness:** roughness.  **checks:** rebukes.

EMILIA:    I have laid those sheets you bade me on the bed.

DESDEMONA:

All's one.° Good faith, how foolish are our minds!
If I do die before thee, prithee, shroud me
In one of those same sheets.

EMILIA:                                    Come, come, you talk.°                    25

DESDEMONA:

My mother had a maid called Barbary.
She was in love, and he she loved proved mad°
And did forsake her. She had a song of "Willow."
An old thing 'twas, but it expressed her fortune,
And she died singing it. That song tonight                                30
Will not go from my mind; I have much to do
But to go hang° my head all at one side
And sing it like poor Barbary. Prithee, dispatch.

EMILIA:    Shall I go fetch your nightgown?°

DESDEMONA:    No, unpin me here.                                          35
This Lodovico is a proper° man.

EMILIA:    A very handsome man.

DESDEMONA:    He speaks well.

EMILIA:    I know a lady in Venice would have walked barefoot to Palestine
for a touch of his nether lip.                                            40

DESDEMONA: [singing]

    "The poor soul sat sighing by a sycamore tree,
        Sing all a green willow;°
    Her hand on her bosom, her head on her knee,
        Sing willow, willow, willow.
    The fresh streams ran by her and murmured her moans;                 45
        Sing willow, willow, willow;
    Her salt tears fell from her, and softened the stones —"
Lay by these.
[singing] "Sing willow, willow, willow —"
Prithee, hie thee.° He'll come anon.°                                     50
[singing] "Sing all a green willow must be my garland.
    Let nobody blame him, his scorn I approve —"

---

23. **All's one:** all right; it doesn't really matter.    25. **talk:** i.e., prattle.    27. **mad:** wild, lunatic.
31–32. **I . . . hang:** I can scarcely keep myself from hanging.    34. **nightgown:** dressing gown.
36. **proper:** handsome.    42. **willow:** (A conventional emblem of disappointed love.)    50. **hie thee:** hurry.    **anon:** right away.

Nay, that's not next. — Hark! who is't that knocks?

EMILIA:   It's the wind.

DESDEMONA: [*singing*]

　　　　"I called my love false love; but what said he then?　　　　　55
　　　　　Sing willow, willow, willow;
　　　　If I court more women, you'll couch with more men."

So, get thee gone; good-night. Mine eyes do itch;
Doth that bode weeping?

EMILIA:　　　　　　　　　　'Tis neither here nor there.

DESDEMONA:

I have heard it said so. Oh, these men, these men!　　　　　　60
Dost thou in conscience think — tell me — Emilia,
That there be women do abuse° their husbands
In such gross kind?

EMILIA:　　　　　　　There be some such, no question.

DESDEMONA:

Wouldst thou do such a deed for all the world?

EMILIA:

Why, would not you?

DESDEMONA:　　　　　No, by this heavenly light!　　　　　　65

EMILIA:

Nor I neither by this heavenly light;
I might do't as well i'th' dark.

DESDEMONA:

Wouldst thou do such a deed for all the world?

EMILIA:

The world's a huge thing. 'Tis a great price
For a small vice.　　　　　　　　　　　　　　　　　　　　70

DESDEMONA:

Good troth, I think thou wouldst not.

EMILIA:   By my troth, I think I should, and undo't when I had done.
Marry, I would not do such a thing for a joint ring,° nor for measures of
lawn,° nor for gowns, petticoats, nor caps, nor any petty exhibition.° But
for all the whole world! Uds° pity, who would not make her husband a　　75
cuckold to make him a monarch? I should venture purgatory for't.

---

62. **abuse:** deceive.   73. **joint ring:** a ring made in separate halves.   74. **lawn:** fine linen.
**exhibition:** gift.   75. **Uds:** God's.

DESDEMONA:
Beshrew me if I would do such a wrong
For the whole world.

EMILIA: Why, the wrong is but a wrong i'th' world, and having the world
for your labor, 'tis a wrong in your own world, and you might quickly 80
make it right.

DESDEMONA:
I do not think there is any such woman.

EMILIA: Yes, a dozen, and as many
To th' vantage as would store the world they played for.°
But I do think it is their husbands' faults 85
If wives do fall. Say that they° slack their duties°
And pour our treasures into foreign laps,°
Or else break out in peevish jealousies,
Throwing restraint upon us?° Or say they strike us,
Or scant our former having in despite?° 90
Why, we have galls,° and though we have some grace,°
Yet have we some revenge. Let husbands know
Their wives have sense° like them. They see, and smell,
And have their palates both for sweet and sour,
As husbands have. What is it that they° do 95
When they change° us for others? Is it sport?°
I think it is. And doth affection° breed it?
I think it doth. Is't frailty that thus errs?
It is so, too. And have not we affections,
Desires for sport, and frailty, as men have? 100
Then let them use us well; else let them know,
The ills we do, their ills instruct us so.

DESDEMONA:
Good night, good night. God me such uses° send
Not to pick bad from bad, but by bad mend!° *Exeunt.*

---

83–84. **and ... played for:** and enough additionally to stock the world men have gambled and
sported sexually for. **86. they:** our husbands. **duties:** marital duties. **87. pour ... laps:**
i.e., are unfaithful, give what is rightfully ours (semen) to other women. **89. Throwing ...
us:** jealously restricting our freedom. **90. Or ... despite:** or spitefully take away from us
whatever we enjoyed before. **91. have galls:** i.e., are capable of resenting injury and insult. **grace:** inclination to be merciful. **93. sense:** sensory perception and appetite.
**95. they:** husbands. **96. change:** exchange. **sport:** sexual pastime. **97. affection:** passion.
**103. uses:** habit, practice. **104. Not ... mend:** i.e., not to learn bad conduct from others'
badness (as Emilia has suggested women learn from men), but to mend my ways by perceiving
what badness is, making spiritual benefit out of evil and adversity.

# ACT 5, SCENE 1°

*Enter Iago and Roderigo.*

IAGO:
Here, stand behind this bulk.° Straight will he come.
Wear thy good rapier bare,° and put it home.°
Quick, quick! Fear nothing. I'll be at thy elbow.
It makes us or it mars us. Think on that,
And fix most firm thy resolution.                                                    5

RODERIGO:
Be near at hand. I may miscarry in't.

IAGO:
Here, at thy hand. Be bold, and take thy stand.
                        [*Iago stands aside, Roderigo conceals himself.*]

RODERIGO:
I have no great devotion to the deed;
And yet he hath given me satisfying reasons.
'Tis but a man gone. Forth, my sword! He dies.          [*He draws.*]  10

IAGO:
I have rubbed this young quat° almost to the sense,°
And he grows angry. Now, whether he kill Cassio
Or Cassio him, or each do kill the other,
Every way makes my gain. Live Roderigo,°
He calls me to a restitution large                                                   15
Of gold and jewels that I bobbed° from him
As gifts to Desdemona.
It must not be. If Cassio do remain,
He hath a daily beauty in his life
That makes me ugly; and besides, the Moor                             20
May unfold° me to him; there stand I in much peril.
No, he must die. Be't so. I hear him coming.

*Enter Cassio.*

RODERIGO: [*coming forth*]
I know his gait, 'tis he. — Villain, thou diest!          [*He attacks Cassio.*]

---

ACT 5, SCENE 1. **Location:** A street in Cyprus.  1. **bulk:** framework projecting from the front of a shop.  2. **bare:** unsheathed.  **home:** all the way into the target.  11. **quat:** pimple, pustule.  **to the sense:** to the quick.  14. **Live Roderigo:** if Roderigo lives.  16. **bobbed:** swindled.  21. **unfold:** expose.

CASSIO:
  That thrust had been mine enemy indeed,
  But that my coat° is better than thou know'st;                    25
  I will make proof° of thine.          [*He draws, and wounds Roderigo.*]
RODERIGO:                    Oh, I am slain!
              [*He falls. Iago, from behind, wounds Cassio in the leg, and exits.*]
CASSIO:
  I am maimed forever. Help, ho! Murder! Murder!

*Enter Othello.*

OTHELLO:   The voice of Cassio! Iago keeps his word.
RODERIGO:   Oh, villain that I am!
OTHELLO:   It is even so.
CASSIO:   Oh, help, ho! Light! A surgeon!                          30
OTHELLO:
  'Tis he: O brave Iago, honest and just,
  That hast such noble sense of thy friend's wrong!
  Thou teachest me. — Minion,° your dear lies dead,
  And your unblest fate hies.° Strumpet, I come!                   35
  Forth of° my heart those charms, thine eyes, are blotted;
  Thy bed, lust-stained, shall with lust's blood be spotted.    *Exit Othello.*

*Enter Lodovico and Gratiano.*

CASSIO:
  What ho! No watch? No passage?° Murder! Murder!
GRATIANO:
  'Tis some mischance. The cry is very direful.
CASSIO:   Oh, help!
LODOVICO:   Hark!                                                  40
RODERIGO:   Oh, wretched villain!
LODOVICO:
  Two or three groan. 'Tis heavy° night;
  These may be counterfeits. Let's think't unsafe
  To come in to° the cry without more help.   [*They remain near the entrance.*]   45
RODERIGO:
  Nobody come? Then shall I bleed to death.

---

25. **coat:** (Possibly a garment of mail under the outer clothing, or simply a tougher coat than Roderigo expected.)   26. **proof:** a test.   34. **Minion:** hussy (i.e., Desdemona).   35. **hies:** hastens on.   36. **Forth of:** from out.   38. **passage:** people passing by.   43. **heavy:** thick, dark.   45. **come in to:** approach.

*Enter Iago [in his shirtsleeves, with a light].*

LODOVICO:   Hark!

GRATIANO:
Here's one comes in his shirt, with light and weapons.

IAGO:
Who's there? Whose noise is this that cries° on murder?

LODOVICO:
We do not know.

IAGO:                    Did not you hear a cry?                    50

CASSIO:
Here, here! For heaven's sake, help me!

IAGO:                              What's the matter?

[*He moves toward Cassio.*]

GRATIANO: [*to Lodovico*]
This is Othello's ancient, as I take it.

LODOVICO: [*to Gratiano*]
The same indeed, a very valiant fellow.

IAGO: [*to Cassio*]
What° are you here that cry so grievously?

CASSIO:
Iago? Oh, I am spoiled,° undone by villains!                    55
Give me some help.

IAGO:
Oh, me, Lieutenant! What villains have done this?

CASSIO:
I think that one of them is hereabout,
And cannot make° away.

IAGO:                         Oh, treacherous villains! [*To Lodovico and Grati-*
*ano*] What are you there? Come in, and give some help.     [*They advance.*]   60

RODERIGO:   Oh, help me there!

CASSIO:
That's one of them.

IAGO:                    Oh, murderous slave! Oh, villain!   [*He stabs Roderigo.*]

RODERIGO:
Oh, damned Iago! Oh, inhuman dog!

IAGO:
Kill men i'th' dark? — Where be these bloody thieves? —

---

49. **cries:** cries out.   54. **What:** who. (Also at lines 60 and 66.)   55. **spoiled:** ruined, done for.   59. **make:** get.

How silent is this town! — Ho! Murder, murder! —                              65
[*To Lodovico and Gratiano*] What may you be? Are you of good or evil?
LODOVICO:    As you shall prove us,° praise° us.
IAGO:    Signor Lodovico?
LODOVICO:    He, sir.
IAGO:
    I cry you mercy.° Here's Cassio hurt by villains.                          70
GRATIANO:    Cassio?
IAGO:    How is't, brother?
CASSIO:    My leg is cut in two.
IAGO:    Marry, heaven forbid!
    Light, gentlemen! I'll bind it with my shirt.                             75

                            [*He hands them the light, and tends to Cassio's wound.*]

    *Enter Bianca.*

BIANCA:
    What is the matter, ho? Who is't that cried?
IAGO:    Who is't that cried?
BIANCA:                                Oh, my dear Cassio!
    My sweet Cassio! Oh, Cassio, Cassio, Cassio!
IAGO:
    Oh, notable strumpet! Cassio, may you suspect
    Who they should be that have thus mangled you?                            80
CASSIO:    No.
GRATIANO:
    I am sorry to find you thus. I have been to seek you.
IAGO:
    Lend me a garter. [*He applies a tourniquet.*] So. — Oh, for a chair,°
    To bear him easily hence!
BIANCA:
    Alas, he faints! O Cassio, Cassio, Cassio!                                85
IAGO:
    Gentlemen all, I do suspect this trash
    To be a party in this injury. —
    Patience awhile, good Cassio. — Come, come;
    Lend me a light. [*He shines the light on Roderigo.*] Know we this face or no?
    Alas, my friend and my dear countryman
    Roderigo! No. — Yes, sure. — Oh, heaven! Roderigo!                        90

---

67. **prove us:** prove us to be. **praise:** appraise.    70. **I cry you mercy:** I beg your pardon.
83. **chair:** litter.

GRATIANO:   What, of Venice?

IAGO:   Even he, sir. Did you know him?

GRATIANO:   Know him? Ay.

IAGO:

Signor Gratiano? I cry your gentle° pardon.                          95

These bloody accidents° must excuse my manners

That so neglected you.

GRATIANO:                    I am glad to see you.

IAGO:

How do you, Cassio? — Oh, a chair, a chair!

GRATIANO:   Roderigo!

IAGO:

He, he, 'tis he. [*A litter is brought in.*] Oh, that's well said;° the chair.    100

Some good man bear him carefully from hence;

I'll fetch the General's surgeon. [*To Bianca*] For° you, mistress,

Save you your labor.° — He that lies slain here, Cassio,

Was my dear friend. What malice° was between you?

CASSIO:

None in the world, nor do I know the man.                          105

IAGO: [*to Bianca*]

What, look you pale? — Oh, bear him out o' th' air.°

                    [*Cassio and Roderigo are borne off.*]

Stay you,° good gentlemen. — Look you pale, mistress? —

Do you perceive the gastness° of her eye? —

Nay, if you stare,° we shall hear more anon. —

Behold her well; I pray you, look upon her.                          110

Do you see, gentlemen? Nay, guiltiness

Will speak, though tongues were out of use.

[*Enter Emilia.*]

EMILIA:

'Las, what's the matter? What's the matter, husband?

IAGO:

Cassio hath here been set on in the dark

---

95. **gentle:** noble.   96. **accidents:** sudden events.   100. **well said:** well done.   102. **For:** as for.
103. **Save . . . labor:** i.e., never you mind tending Cassio.   104. **malice:** enmity.   106. **bear
. . . air:** (Fresh air was thought to be dangerous for a wound.)   107. **Stay you:** (Lodovico and
Gratiano are evidently about to leave.)   108. **gastness:** terror.   109. **stare:** (Iago pretends to
interpret Bianca's wild looks as an involuntary confession of guilt.)

By Roderigo and fellows that are scaped.                                115
He's almost slain, and Roderigo dead.

EMILIA:
Alas! good gentleman! Alas, good Cassio!

IAGO:
This is the fruits of whoring. Prithee, Emilia,
Go know° of Cassio where he supped tonight.
[*To Bianca*] What, do you shake at that?                               120

BIANCA:
He supped at my house, but I therefore shake not.

IAGO:
Oh, did he so? I charge you go with me.

EMILIA:    Oh, fie upon thee, strumpet!

BIANCA:
I am no strumpet, but of life as honest°
As you that thus abuse me.                                              125

EMILIA:    As I? Faugh! Fie upon thee!

IAGO:
Kind gentlemen, let's go see poor Cassio dressed.° —
Come, mistress, you must tell 's another tale. —
Emilia, run you to the citadel
And tell my lord and lady what hath happed. —                          130
Will you go on afore? [*Aside*] This is the night
That either makes me or fordoes° me quite.        *Exeunt.*

## Act 5, Scene 2°

*Enter Othello [with a light], and Desdemona in her bed.°*

OTHELLO:
It is the cause,° it is the cause, my soul.
Let me not name it to you, you chaste stars!
It is the cause. Yet I 'll not shed her blood,
Nor scar that whiter skin of hers than snow,
And smooth as monumental° alabaster.                                    5

---

119. **know:** learn.   124. **honest:** chaste.   127. **Cassio dressed:** Cassio's wounds dressed.
132. **fordoes:** undoes, ruins.   ACT 5, SCENE 2. Location: A bedchamber in the citadel.
s.d. *in her bed:* (Either the curtains are drawn back to reveal the bed in a recessed area back-
stage, or the bed is "thrust out" onstage as the scene begins.)   1. **cause:** i.e., cause of justice, the
offense itself, which must be corrected in the name of justice.   5. **monumental:** i.e., used in
making tombs and funeral monuments.

Yet she must die, else she'll betray more men.
Put out the light, and then put out the light.°
If I quench thee, thou flaming minister,°
I can again thy former light restore,
Should I repent me;° but once put out thy light,                    10
Thou cunning'st pattern° of excelling nature,
I know not where is that Promethean heat°
That can thy light relume.° When I have plucked thy rose,
I cannot give it vital growth again;
It needs must wither. I'll smell it on the tree.        [*He kisses her.*]  15
Oh, balmy breath, that dost almost persuade
Justice to break her sword! One more, one more.
Be thus when thou art dead, and I will kill thee,
And love thee after. One more, and this the last.       [*He kisses her.*]
So sweet was ne'er so fatal. I must weep,                            20
But they are cruel tears.° This sorrow's heavenly;
It strikes where it doth love.° She wakes.
DESDEMONA:   Who's there? Othello?
OTHELLO:   Ay, Desdemona.
DESDEMONA:   Will you come to bed, my lord?                          25
OTHELLO:   Have you prayed tonight, Desdemon?
DESDEMONA:   Ay, my lord.
OTHELLO:
    If you bethink yourself of any crime°
    Unreconciled as yet to heaven and grace,
    Solicit° for it straight.°                                       30
DESDEMONA:
    Alack, my lord, what may you mean by that?
OTHELLO:
    Well, do it, and be brief. I will walk by.
    I would not kill thy unprepared spirit.
    No, heaven forfend!° I would not kill thy soul.
DESDEMONA:
    Talk you of killing?

7. **the light . . . light:** the torch or lamp . . . Desdemona's life.   8. **minister:** servant (referring
to the torch that "serves" him. [Hall])   10. **repent me:** change my mind.   11. **Thou . . . pattern:** you skillfully wrought perfect example.   12. **Promethean heat:** (Alludes to two myths: that
of Prometheus stealing fire from heaven for humanity, and that of his creating humankind.)
13. **relume:** rekindle.   21. **they are cruel tears:** these tears betoken a sorrowful cruelty, regret-
table but just.   22. **It . . . love:** (Compare Hebrews 12:6: "For whom the Lord loveth he chas-
teneth.")   28. **crime:** sin.   30. **Solicit:** petition, pray.   **straight:** immediately.   34. **forfend:**
forbid.

OTHELLO:                    Ay, I do.
DESDEMONA:                          Then heaven                        35
   Have mercy on me!
OTHELLO:              Amen, with all my heart!
DESDEMONA:
   If you say so, I hope you will not kill me.
OTHELLO:   Humh!
DESDEMONA:
   And yet I fear you; for you're fatal then
   When your eyes roll so. Why I should fear I know not,   40
   Since guiltiness I know not; but yet I feel I fear.
OTHELLO:
   Think on thy sins.
DESDEMONA:              They are loves I bear to you.°
OTHELLO:   Ay, and for that thou diest.
DESDEMONA:
   That death's unnatural that kills for loving.
   Alas, why gnaw you so your nether lip?                  45
   Some bloody passion shakes your very frame.
   These are portents; but yet, I hope, I hope,
   They do not point on me.
OTHELLO:   Peace, and be still!
DESDEMONA:   I will so. What's the matter?                  50
OTHELLO:
   That handkerchief which I so loved and gave thee
   Thou gav'st to Cassio.
DESDEMONA:                    No, by my life and soul!
   Send for the man and ask him.
OTHELLO:
   Sweet soul, take heed, take heed of perjury.
   Thou art on thy deathbed.                               55
DESDEMONA:
   Ay, but not yet to die.
OTHELLO:                    Yes, presently.°
   Therefore confess thee freely of thy sin;
   For to deny each article with oath
   Cannot remove nor choke the strong conception°
   That I do groan withal.° Thou art to die.               60

**42. They . . . you:** i.e., my only sins are my idolatry of loving you too much.  **56. presently:** immediately.  **59. conception:** (1) belief in your guilt (2) plan in my mind.  **60. groan withal:** (1) groan at in sorrow (2) as in giving birth.

DESDEMONA:
Then Lord have mercy on me!
OTHELLO:                              I say, amen.
DESDEMONA:
And have you mercy too! I never did
Offend you in my life; never loved Cassio
But with such general warranty° of heaven
As I might love. I never gave him token.                              65
OTHELLO:
By heaven, I saw my handkerchief in 's hand.
Oh, perjured woman! Thou dost stone° my heart,
And makes me call what I intend to do
A murder, which I thought a sacrifice.
I saw the handkerchief.
DESDEMONA:                    He found it, then.                    70
I never gave it him. Send for him hither;
Let him confess a truth.
OTHELLO:                    He had confessed.
DESDEMONA:   What, my lord?
OTHELLO:
That he hath used thee.
DESDEMONA:                    How? Unlawfully?
OTHELLO:                                        Ay.
DESDEMONA:
He will not say so.
OTHELLO:              No, his mouth is stopped;                    75
Honest Iago hath ta'en order° for't.
DESDEMONA:
Oh, my fear interprets. What, is he dead?
OTHELLO:
Had all his hairs been lives, my great revenge
Had stomach for them all.
DESDEMONA:
Alas, he is betrayed and I undone!            [*She weeps.*]   80
OTHELLO:
Out, strumpet! Weep'st thou for him to my face?
DESDEMONA:
Oh, banish me, my lord, but kill me not!

64. **warranty:** sanction.   67. **stone:** turn to stone, harden.   76. **ta'en order:** taken measures.

OTHELLO: Down, strumpet!

DESDEMONA:

Kill me tomorrow; let me live tonight!

OTHELLO: Nay, if you strive —                                                    85

DESDEMONA:

But half an hour!

OTHELLO:                    Being done,° there is no pause.

DESDEMONA: But while I say one prayer!

OTHELLO:                                        It is too late.          *Smothers her.*

EMILIA: (*at the door*)

My lord, my lord! What, ho! my lord, my lord!

OTHELLO:

What noise is this? Not dead? Not yet quite dead?

I that am cruel am yet merciful;                                                        90

I would not have thee linger in thy pain.          [*He dispatches her.*]

So, so.

EMILIA: (*within*)    What, ho! My lord, my lord!

OTHELLO:                                        Who's there?

EMILIA: [*within*]

Oh, good my lord, I would speak a word with you!

OTHELLO:

Yes, 'tis Emilia. — By and by. — She's dead.

'Tis like° she comes to speak of Cassio's death. —                          95

The noise was here.° Ha! No more moving?

Still as the grave. Shall she come in? Were't good? —

I think she stirs again. No. What's best to do?

If she come in, she'll sure speak to my wife.

My wife! My wife! What wife? I have no wife.                              100

Oh, insupportable! Oh, heavy hour!

Methinks it should be now a huge eclipse

Of sun and moon, and that th'affrighted globe

Should yawn at alteration.°

EMILIA: [*within*]                    I do beseech you

That I may speak with you, oh, good my lord!                              105

---

86. **Being done:** i.e., since justice has begun its relentless course.    95. **like:** likely that.
96. **here:** (The Folio's "high" is possible, suggesting that the commotion of the attack on Cassio was loud.)    104. **Should . . . alteration:** should gape wide in an earthquake, as if expressing amazement at an eclipse. (According to Pliny, earthquakes often happen during eclipses. The cataclysmic event here is especially terrifying in that it imagines the impossible concurrence of a solar and lunar eclipse—an apocalyptic scenario befitting the horror of Desdemona's death.)

OTHELLO:
Ⅰ had forgot thee. Oh, come in, Emilia. —
Soft,° by and by. Let me the curtains draw. —

[*He closes the bedcurtains and opens the door.*]

Where art thou?

*Enter Emilia.*

What's the matter with thee now?

EMILIA:
Oh, my good lord, yonder's foul murders done!

OTHELLO:   What, now?                                                                    110

EMILIA:   But now, my lord.

OTHELLO:
It is the very error° of the moon;
She° comes more nearer earth than she was wont,
And makes men mad.°

EMILIA:
Cassio, my lord, hath killed a young Venetian                                          115
Called Roderigo.

OTHELLO:            Roderigo killed?
And Cassio killed?

EMILIA:                     No, Cassio is not killed.

OTHELLO:
Not Cassio killed? Then murder's out of tune,
And sweet revenge grows harsh.

DESDEMONA:   Oh, falsely, falsely murdered!                                            120

EMILIA:   Oh, Lord, what cry is that?

OTHELLO:   That? What?

EMILIA:
Out,° and alas, that was my lady's voice.          [*She opens the bedcurtains.*]
Help, help, ho, help! O lady, speak again!
Sweet Desdemona! O sweet mistress, speak!                                              125

DESDEMONA:   A guiltless death I die.

EMILIA:   Oh, who hath done this deed?

DESDEMONA:   Nobody; I myself. Farewell.
Commend me to my kind lord. Oh, farewell!          [*She dies.*]

OTHELLO:
Why, how should she be murdered?

---

107. **Soft:** wait a minute.   112. **error:** aberration, irregularity.   113. **She:** Luna, the moon
goddess.   114. **mad:** i.e., "lunatic."   123. **Out:** (A cry of dismay, intensifying *alas*.)

EMILIA:                                    Alas, who knows?                          130
OTHELLO:
  You heard her say herself it was not I.
EMILIA:
  She said so. I must needs report the truth.
OTHELLO:
  She's like a liar gone to burning hell!
  'Twas I that killed her.
EMILIA:                              Oh, the more angel she,
  And you the blacker devil!                                            135
OTHELLO:
  She turned to folly,° and she was a whore.
EMILIA:
  Thou dost belie° her, and thou art a devil.
OTHELLO:   She was false° as water.
EMILIA:   Thou art rash as fire to say
  That she was false. Oh, she was heavenly true!            140
OTHELLO:
  Cassio did top her. Ask thy husband else.°
  Oh, I were damned beneath all depth in hell
  But that I did proceed upon just grounds
  To this extremity. Thy husband knew it all.
EMILIA:   My husband?
OTHELLO:   Thy husband.                                                145
EMILIA:   That she was false to wedlock?
OTHELLO:
  Ay, with Cassio. Nay, had she been true,
  If heaven would make me such another world
  Of one entire and perfect chrysolite,°
  I'd not have sold her for it.                                        150
EMILIA:   My husband?
OTHELLO:
  Ay, 'twas he that told me on her first.
  An honest man he is, and hates the slime
  That sticks on filthy deeds.
EMILIA:   My husband?                                                  155

---

136. **folly:** i.e., wantonness, fleshly sin.   137. **belie:** slander.   138. **false:** unstable (proverbial).
[Hall]   141. **else:** i.e., if you don't believe me.   150. **chrysolite:** precious topaz.

OTHELLO:
What needs this iterance,° woman? I say thy husband.

EMILIA:
O mistress, villainy hath made mocks with° love!
My husband say she was false?

OTHELLO:                                        He, woman;
I say thy husband. Dost understand the word?                          160
My friend, thy husband, honest, honest Iago.

EMILIA:
If he say so, may his pernicious soul
Rot half a grain a day! he lies to th' heart.
She was too fond of her most filthy bargain.

OTHELLO:  Ha?                                            [*He draws.*]   165

EMILIA:  Do thy worst!
This deed of thine is no more worthy heaven
Than thou wast worthy her.

OTHELLO:                                Peace, you were best.°

EMILIA:
Thou hast not half that power to do me harm
As I have to be hurt.° O gull!° O dolt!                              170
As ignorant as dirt! Thou hast done a deed —
I care not for thy sword; I'll make thee known,
Though I lost twenty lives. — Help! Help, ho, help!
The Moor hath killed my mistress! Murder, murder!

*Enter Montano, Gratiano, and Iago.*

MONTANO:
What is the matter? How now, General?                                175

EMILIA:
Oh, are you come, Iago? You have done well,
That men must lay their murders on your neck.°

GRATIANO:   What is the matter?

EMILIA: [*to Iago*]
Disprove this villain, if thou be'st a man.
He says thou told'st him that his wife was false.                    180

---

157. **iterance:** iteration, repetition.   158. **made mocks with:** made a mockery of.   168. **Peace ... best:** you'd better be quiet.   170. **to be hurt:** i.e., to endure hurt.   **gull:** dupe.   177. **on your neck:** to your charge.

I know thou didst not; thou'rt not such a villain.°
Speak, for my heart is full.

IAGO:
I told him what I thought, and told no more
Than what he found himself was apt° and true.

EMILIA:
But did you ever tell him she was false? 185

IAGO: I did.

EMILIA:
You told a lie, an odious, damnèd lie!
Upon my soul, a lie, a wicked lie.
She false with Cassio? Did you say with Cassio?

IAGO:
With Cassio, mistress. Go to, charm° your tongue. 190

EMILIA:
I will not charm my tongue; I am bound to speak.
My mistress here lies murdered in her bed —

ALL: Oh, heavens forfend!

EMILIA:
And your reports have set the murder on.

OTHELLO:
Nay, stare not, masters. It is true indeed. 195

GRATIANO: 'Tis a strange truth.

MONTANO:
Oh, monstrous act!

EMILIA: Villainy, villainy, villainy!
I think upon't — I think, I smell't! O villainy!
I thought so then° — I'll kill myself for grief —
O! villainy, villainy! 200

IAGO:
What, are you mad? I charge you, get you home.

EMILIA:
Good gentlemen, let me have leave to speak.
'Tis proper I obey him, but not now.
Perchance, Iago, I will ne'er go home.

OTHELLO:
Oh! Oh! Oh! [Othello falls on the bed.]°

---

181. **such a villain:** such a villain as all that.   184. **apt:** plausible.   190. **charm:** control.
199. **then:** (Perhaps at 3.3.332–33 and 4.2.137–54.)   205. **s.d. Othello . . . bed:** (This direction is from the Quarto, as also *He kisses her* at line 19 and *She dies* at line 129.)

EMILIA:          Nay, lay thee down and roar,                                    205
For thou hast killed the sweetest innocent
That e'er did lift up eye.°
OTHELLO: [*rising*]          Oh, she was foul!
I scarce did know you, uncle. There lies your niece,
Whose breath indeed these hands have newly stopped.
I know this act shows° horrible and grim.                                        210

GRATIANO:
Poor Desdemon! I am glad thy father's dead.
Thy match was mortal to him, and pure grief
Shore his old thread° in twain. Did he live now,
This sight would make him do a desperate turn,°
Yea, curse his better angel from his side,                                       215
And fall to reprobance.°

OTHELLO:
'Tis pitiful. But yet Iago knows
That she with Cassio hath the act of shame
A thousand times committed. Cassio confessed it;
And she did gratify° his amorous works                                          220
With that recognizance° and pledge of love
Which I first gave her. I saw it in his hand;
It was a handkerchief, an antique token
My father gave my mother.
EMILIA:    Oh, God! Oh, heavenly God!                                           225

IAGO:
Zounds, hold your peace.
EMILIA:                    'Twill out, 'twill out! I peace?
No, I will speak as liberal as the north.°
Let heaven and men and devils, let them all,
All, all, cry shame against me, yet I'll speak.

IAGO:
Be wise, and get you home.
EMILIA:                    I will not.          [*Iago threatens Emilia.*]
GRATIANO:                    Fie,                                                230
Your sword upon a woman?

EMILIA:
Oh, thou dull Moor! That handkerchief thou speak'st of

207. **lift up eye:** i.e., lift her eyes to heaven.   210. **shows:** looks.   213. **Shore . . . thread:** sheared the thread of his old age (as Atropos, one of the three Fates, was thought to do). 214. **turn:** deed.   216. **reprobance:** damnation, i.e., suicide.   220. **gratify:** reward.   221. **recognizance:** token.   227. **liberal as the north:** freely as the north wind (blows).

I found by fortune and did give my husband;
For often, with a solemn earnestness,
More than indeed belonged° to such a trifle,                                235
He begged of me to steal't.

IAGO:                                          Villainous whore!

EMILIA:
She give it Cassio? No, alas! I found it,
And I did give't my husband.

IAGO:                                          Filth, thou liest!

EMILIA:
By heaven, I do not, I do not, gentlemen.
Oh, murderous coxcomb!° What should such a fool               240
Do with so good a wife?

OTHELLO:    Are there no stones° in heaven
But what serves for the thunder? — Precious° villain!

*[He runs at Iago; Montano disarms Othello. Iago, from behind, stabs Emilia.]*

GRATIANO:
The woman falls! Sure he hath killed his wife.

EMILIA:
Ay, ay. Oh, lay me by my mistress' side.                    *[Exit Iago.]*   245

GRATIANO:    He's gone, but his wife's killed.

MONTANO:
'Tis a notorious villain. Take you this weapon,
Which I have here recovered from the Moor.
Come, guard the door without. Let him not pass,
But kill him rather. I'll after that same villain,           250
For 'tis a damnèd slave.

*Exit [with all but Othello and Emilia, who has been laid by Desdemona's side].*

OTHELLO:    I am not valiant neither,
But every puny whipster gets my sword.°
But why should honor outlive honesty?°
Let it go all.

EMILIA:            What did thy song bode, lady?                     255
Hark, canst thou hear me? I will play the swan,
And die in music. *[She sings.]* "Willow, willow, willow."

---

235. **belonged:** was appropriate.    240. **coxcomb:** fool. (Addressed to Othello.)    242. **stones:** bolts, such as those used for thunderbolts.    243. **Precious:** i.e., arrant, utter.    243. **s.d. He . . . Emilia:** (The Quarto text reads, *"The Moore runnes at Iago. Iago kils his wife."* The Quarto also specifies the exit of Iago at line 245 and the death of Emilia at line 260.)    253. **every . . . sword:** every whipper-snapper can get the better of me and my sword.    254. **why . . . honesty?:** why should a soldier's reputation for bravery outlive true integrity?

Moor, she was chaste. She loved thee, cruel Moor.
So come my soul to bliss as I speak true.
So speaking as I think, alas, I die.                     [*She dies.*]  260

OTHELLO:
I have another weapon in this chamber;
It is a sword of Spain, the ice-brook's temper° —
Oh, here it is. [*He finds a sword.*] Uncle, I must come forth.

GRATIANO: [*within*]
If thou attempt it, it will cost thee dear.
Thou hast no weapon, and perforce must suffer.          265

OTHELLO:
Look in upon me then and speak with me,
Or, naked° as I am, I will assault thee.

[*Enter Gratiano.*]

GRATIANO:
What is the matter?

OTHELLO:                     Behold, I have a weapon;
A better never did itself sustain
Upon a soldier's thigh. I have seen the day             270
That, with this little arm, and this good sword,
I have made my way through more impediments
Than twenty times your stop.° But oh, vain boast!
Who can control his fate? 'Tis not so now.
Be not afraid, though you do see me weaponed;          275
Here is my journey's end, here is my butt°
And very seamark° of my utmost sail.        [*Gratiano steps back.*]
Do you go back dismayed? 'Tis a lost° fear;
Man but a rush° against Othello's breast
And he retires. Where should Othello go?     [*He turns to Desdemona.*]  280
Now, how dost thou look now? Oh, ill-starred wench!
Pale as thy smock! When we shall meet at compt,°
This look of thine will hurl my soul from heaven,
And fiends will snatch at it. Cold, cold, my girl?
Even like thy chastity. O! cursèd, cursèd slave!°       285
Whip me, ye devils,
From the possession of this heavenly sight!

---

262. **the ice-brook's temper:** tempered in ice-cold water.  267. **naked:** unarmed.  273. **your stop:** the obstruction you present.  276. **butt:** goal, limit. (An archery term.)  277. **seamark:** beacon (marking his destination or limit).  278. **lost:** groundless.  279. **Man . . . rush:** wield no more than a reed.  282. **compt:** account, judgment day.  285. **slave:** i.e., Othello himself.

Blow me about in winds! Roast me in sulfur!
Wash me in steep-down gulfs of liquid fire!
O Desdemon! Dead, Desdemon! Dead! Oh! Oh!                    290

*Enter Lodovico, Cassio [carried in a litter],° Montano, and Iago [ prisoner], with
officers.*

LODOVICO:
  Where is this rash and most unfortunate man?
OTHELLO:
  That's he that was Othello. Here I am.
LODOVICO:
  Where is that viper? Bring the villain forth.          *[ Iago is led forward.]*
OTHELLO:
  I look down towards his feet;° but that's a fable.
  If that thou be'st a devil, I cannot kill thee.        *[He wounds Iago.]*   295
LODOVICO:
  Wrench his sword from him.                             *[Othello is disarmed.]*
IAGO:                            I bleed, sir, but not killed.
OTHELLO:
  I am not sorry neither. I'd have thee live,
  For in my sense° 'tis happiness to die.
LODOVICO:
  O thou Othello, that was once so good,
  Fall'n in the practice° of a cursèd slave,°                    300
  What shall be said to thee?
OTHELLO:                            Why, anything.
  An honorable murderer, if you will,
  For naught did I in hate, but all in honor.
LODOVICO:
  This wretch hath part confessed his villainy.
  Did you and he consent° in Cassio's death?                    305
OTHELLO:   Ay.
CASSIO:
  Dear General, I never gave you cause.
OTHELLO:
  I do believe it, and I ask your pardon.
  Will you, I pray, demand that demi-devil

---

**290. s.d.** *in a litter:* (The Quarto specifies that Cassio is *"in a Chaire."*)   **294. towards his feet:**
i.e., to see if they are cloven, as the devil's are fabled to be.   **298. in my sense:** to one who feels
as I do.   **300. in the practice:** through the plotting, into the snare.   **slave:** villain.   **305. consent:** agree.

Why he hath thus ensnared my soul and body?                    310

IAGO:

  Demand me nothing. What you know, you know.

  From this time forth I never will speak word.

LODOVICO:     What, not to pray?

GRATIANO:     Torments° will ope your lips.

OTHELLO:     Well, thou dost best.°                             315

LODOVICO:

  Sir, you shall understand what hath befall'n,

  Which, as I think, you know not. Here is a letter

  Found in the pocket of the slain Roderigo;

  And here another. [ *He produces letters.* ] The one of them imports

  The death of Cassio, to be undertook                         320

  By Roderigo.

OTHELLO:

  O villain!

CASSIO:     Most heathenish and most gross!°

LODOVICO: [*showing another paper*]

  Now here's another discontented° paper

  Found in his pocket too. And this, it seems,

  Roderigo meant t'have sent this damnèd villain;              325

  But that belike° Iago in the interim

  Came in and satisfied him.°

OTHELLO: [*to Iago*]     O thou pernicious caitiff!

  How came you, Cassio, by that handkerchief

  That was my wife's?

CASSIO:                     I found it in my chamber;           330

  And he himself confessed but even now

  That there he dropped it for a special purpose

  Which wrought to his desire.°

OTHELLO:                     Oh, fool, fool, fool!

CASSIO:

  There is besides in Roderigo's letter

  How he upbraids Iago, that he made him                       335

  Brave° me upon the watch, whereon it came°

---

314. **Torments:** torture.   315. **thou dost best:** you (Iago) do best not to talk.   322. **gross:** monstrous.   323. **discontented:** full of discontent.   326. **belike:** most likely.   327. **Came . . . him:** interposed and gave him satisfactory explanation.   333. **wrought . . . desire:** worked out as he wished, fitted in with his plan.   336. **Brave:** defy.   **whereon it came:** wherefof it came about.

That I was cast;° and even but now he spake,
After long seeming dead, Iago hurt him,
Iago set him on.
LODOVICO: [*to Othello*]
   You must forsake this room and go with us.          340
   Your power and your command is taken off,°
   And Cassio rules in Cyprus. For this slave,
   If there be any cunning cruelty
   That can torment him much and hold him long,°
   It shall be his. You shall close prisoner rest°        345
   Till that the nature of your fault be known
   To the Venetian state. — Come, bring away.
OTHELLO:
   Soft you;° a word or two before you go.
   I have done the state some service, and they know't.
   No more of that. I pray you, in your letters,        350
   When you shall these unlucky° deeds relate,
   Speak of me as I am; nothing extenuate,
   Nor set down aught in malice. Then must you speak
   Of one that loved not wisely but too well;
   Of one not easily jealous but, being wrought,°      355
   Perplexed° in the extreme; of one whose hand,
   Like the base Indian,° threw a pearl away
   Richer than all his tribe; of one whose subdued° eyes,
   Albeit unusèd to the melting mood,
   Drop tears as fast as the Arabian trees        360
   Their medicinable gum.° Set you down this;
   And say besides that in Aleppo once,
   Where a malignant and a turbaned Turk
   Beat a Venetian and traduced the state,
   I took by th' throat the circumcisèd dog,        365
   And smote him, thus.             [*He stabs himself.*]°
LODOVICO:   Oh, bloody period!°

---

337. **cast:** dismissed.   341. **taken off:** taken away.   344. **hold him long:** keep him alive a long time (during his torture).   345. **rest:** remain.   348. **Soft you:** one moment.   351. **unlucky:** unfortunate.   355. **wrought:** worked upon, worked into a frenzy.   356. **Perplexed:** distraught.   357. **Indian:** (This reading from the Quarto pictures an ignorant savage who cannot recognize the value of a precious jewel. The Folio reading, "Iudean," i.e., infidel or disbeliever, may refer to Herod, who slew Miriamne in a fit of jealousy, or to Judas Iscariot, the betrayer of Christ.)   358. **subdued:** i.e., overcome by grief.   361. **gum:** i.e., myrrh.   366. **s.d.** *He stabs himself:* (This direction is in the Quarto text.)   367. **period:** termination, conclusion.

GRATIANO:    All that is spoke is marred.

OTHELLO:

I kissed thee ere I killed thee. No way but this,
Killing myself, to die upon a kiss.          [*He kisses Desdemona and*] *dies.*

CASSIO:

This did I fear, but thought he had no weapon;                    370
For he was great of heart.

LODOVICO: [*to Iago*]          O Spartan dog,°
More fell° than anguish, hunger, or the sea!
Look on the tragic loading of this bed.
This is thy work. The object poisons sight;                       375
Let it be hid.° Gratiano, keep° the house,          [*The bedcurtains are drawn.*]
And seize upon° the fortunes of the Moor,
For they succeed on° you. [*To Cassio*] To you, Lord Governor,
Remains the censure° of this hellish villain,
The time, the place, the torture. Oh, enforce it!                 380
Myself will straight aboard, and to the state
This heavy act with heavy heart relate.              *Exeunt.*

FINIS

---

372. **Spartan dog:** (Spartan dogs were noted for their savagery and silence.)   373. **fell:** cruel.
376. **Let it be hid:** i.e., draw the bedcurtains. (No stage direction specifies that the dead are to
be carried offstage at the end of the play.)   **keep:** guard.   377. **seize upon:** take legal possession of.   378. **succeed on:** pass as though by inheritance to.   379. **censure:** sentencing.

## OTHELLO

Copy text: the First Folio. The adopted readings are from the Quarto of 1622 [Q1], unless otherwise indicated; [eds.] means that the adopted reading was first proposed by some editor subsequent to the First Folio. Act and scene divisions are marked in the Folio with the exception of 2.3.

ACT 1, SCENE 1. 1. Tush, never: Neuer. 4. 'Sblood, but: But. 16. And, in conclusion: [Q1; not in F]. 26. togaed: Tongued. 30. other: others. 34. God bless: blesse. 68. full: fall. thick-lips: Thicks-lips. 74. changes: chances. 75. [and elsewhere] lose: [eds.] loose. 81. Thieves, thieves, thieves: Theeues, Theeues. 83. s.d. *Brabantio above:* [in F, printed as a speech prefix to line 84]. 88. Zounds, sir: Sir [also at line 111]. 103. bravery: knauerie. 119. are now: are. 156. pains: apines. 161. sign. That: [eds.] (signe) that. 184. night: might.

ACT 1, SCENE 2. 34. Duke: Dukes. 50. carrack: Carract. 64. her! [eds.] her. 69. darlings: Deareling. 89. I do: do.

ACT 1, SCENE 3. 1. There is: There's. these: this. 61. DUKE AND SENATORS: [*All* Q1] Sen. 101. maimed: main'd. 108. upon: vp on. DUKE: [Q1; not in F]. 109. overt: ouer. 112. [and elsewhere] FIRST SENATOR: *Sen.* 124. till: tell. 132. battles: Battaile. fortunes: Fortune. 141. travels': Trauellours. 143. rocks, and: Rocks. heads: head. 145. other: others. 146. Anthropophagi: *Antropophague.* 147. Do grow: Grew. 149. thence: hence. 157. intentively: instinctiuely. 161. sighs: kisses. 203. grece: grise. 204. Into your favor: [Q1; not in F]. 222. piercèd: pierc'd. ear: eares. 226–27. sovereign: more soueraigne. 231. couch: [eds.] Coach [F] Cooch [Q1]. 235. These: [eds.] This. 242. Nor I. I would not: Nor would I. 250. did love: loue. 266. me: [eds.] my. 272. instruments: Instrument. 280. DESDEMONA Tonight, my lord? DUKE This night: [Q1; not in F]. 284. With: And. 293. FIRST SENATOR: *Sen.* 295. s.d. *Exeunt: Exit.* 301. matters: matter. 302. the: the the. 324. beam: [eds.] braine [F] ballance [Q1]. 328. our unbitted: or vnbitted. scion: [eds.] Seyen [F] syen [Q1]. 342. error: errors. 342–43. She . . . she must: [Q1; not in F]. 346. a supersubtle: super-subtle. 361–64. What . . . purse: [Q1; not in F]. 368. a snipe: Snpe. 371. He's: [Ha's Q1] She ha's. 378. ear: eares.

ACT 2, SCENE 1. 35. prays: praye. 36. heaven: Heauens. 42. THIRD GENTLEMAN: *Gent.* 44. arrivance: Arriuancie. 45. this: the. 58. SECOND GENTLEMAN: *Gent.* [also at lines 61, 68, and 96]. 72. clog: enclogge. 84. And . . . comfort: [Q1; not in F]. 90. tell me: tell. 94. the sea: Sea. 96. their: this. 107. list: leaue. 111. doors: doore. 155. [and elsewhere] ne'er: *neu'r.* 157. such wight: *such wightes.* 167. gyve: [eds.] giue. 170. An: and. 171. courtesy: Curtsie. 172. clyster pipes: Cluster-pipes. 210. s.d. *Exeunt:* [eds.] *Exit.* 212. hither: thither. 222. again: a game. 229. fortune: Forune. 231. compassing: compasse. 232–33. finder out: finder. 233. occasions: occasion. has: he's. 247. mutualities: mutabilities. 279. for wife: for wift. 286. rank: right. 287. nightcap: Night-Cape.

ACT 2, SCENE 2. 4. addiction: [eds.] addition. 8. Heaven bless: Blesse.

ACT 2, SCENE 3. 24. stoup: [eds.] stope. 32. unfortunate: infortunate. 45. lads: else. 50. to put: put to. 54, 63. God: heauen. 67. Englishman: Englishmen. 80. Then . . . auld: [*Then . . . owd* Q1] *And take thy awl'd.* 82. 'Fore God: Why. 85. God's: heau'ns. 92–93. God forgive: Forgiue. 96. speak: I speake. 109. the: his. 123. s.d. *Cry within:* Help! Help!: [from Q1: "Helpe, helpe, within"]. 124. Zounds, you: You. 136. God's will: Alas. 137. Montano—sir: *Montano.* 140. God's will, Lieutenant, hold: Fie, fie Lieutenant. 142. Zounds, I: I. 145. sense of place: [eds.] place of sense. 168. wont be: wont to be. 185. Zounds, if I: If I once. 196. leagued: [eds.] league. 202. Thus: This. 211. the: then. 230. well now: well. 234. vile: vil'd. 239. God: Heauen. 243. thought: had thought. 261. Oh, God: Oh. 279. I'll: I. 282. denotement: [eds.] deuotement. 293. me here: me. 303. were't: were. 322. s.d. *Enter Roderigo:* [after line 356 in F]. 333. hast: hath. 336. By the Mass: Introth. 343. on: [on Q1] on. the while: [eds.] a while.

**ACT 3, SCENE 1. 1.** *Musicians:* [eds.] *Musicians, and Clowne.* **5.** [*and at lines* 7, 9, *and* 13].
**A MUSICIAN:** *Mus.* **18.** s.d. *Exeunt:* [eds.] *Exit.* **19.** hear: heare me. **22.** General's
wife: Generall. **27.** CASSIO Do, good my friend: [Q₁; not in F]. **38.** s.d. *Exit:* [at line 41
in F]. **48.** To . . . front: [Q₁; not in F].
**ACT 3, SCENE 3. 16.** circumstance: Circumstances. **41.** you: your. **55.** Yes, faith: I sooth.
**66.** or: on. **80.** By'r Lady: Trust me. **103.** you: he. **118.** By heaven: Alas. **124.** In:
Of. **148.** that all: that: All. free to: free. **152.** But some: Wherein. **160.** oft: of.
**161.** wisdom then: wisdome. **175.** By heaven, I'll: Ile. **184.** fondly: [eds.] soundly
[F] strongly [Q₁]. **189.** God: Heauen. **195.** Is once: Is. **197.** blown: blow'd.
**200.** dances well: Dances. **217.** God: Heauen. **219.** keep't: [eds.] keepe [Q₁] kept [F].
**226.** [and elsewhere] to: too. **231.** I'faith: Trust me. **233.** my: your. **250.** disproportion: disproportions. **265.** to hold: to. **276.** qualities: Quantities. **277.** human:
humane. **290.** of: to. **295.** oh, then heaven mocks: Heauen mock'd. **302.** Faith:
Why. **306.** s.d. *Exit:* [at line 304 in F]. **329.** faith: but. **346.** s.d. *Enter Othello:* [after
"I did say so" in F]. **355.** of her: in her. **386.** remorse: [remorce. Q₁] remorse. **408.**
see, sir: see. **412.** supervisor: super-vision. **440.** then laid: laid. **441.** Over: ore.
sighed: sigh. kissed: kisse. **442.** Cried: cry. **456.** any that was: [eds.] any, it was.
**469.** mind perhaps: minde. **472.** Ne'er feels: [eds.] Neu'r keepes.
**ACT 3, SCENE 4. 17.** that: the. **31.** It yet: It. **50.** faith: indeed. **71.** I'faith: Indeed.
**73.** God: Heauen. **77.** Heaven bless: Blesse. **82.** can, sir: can. **88.** DESDEMONA
I pray . . . Cassio. OTHELLO The handkerchief!: [Q₁; not in F]. **93.** I'faith: Insooth.
**94.** Zounds: Away. **136.** s.d. *Exit:* [after line 141 in F]. **158.** that: the. **163.** s.d. *Exit:*
[after line 168 in F]. **166.** I'faith: Indeed. **176.** friend.: [eds.] Friend. **177.** absence:
[eds.] absence, [Q₁] Absence: [F]. **182.** by my faith: in good troth.
**ACT 4, SCENE 1. 32.** Faith: Why. **36.** Zounds, that's: that's. **43.** work: workes. **50.** No,
forbear: [Q₁; not in F]. **70.** couch: [Coach Q₁] Cowch;. **77.** unsuiting: [Q₁ cor-
rected] vnfitting [Q₁ uncorrected] resulting [F]. **79.** 'scuse: scuses. **95.** clothes: Cloath.
**101.** conster: conserue. **103.** you now: you. **107.** power: dowre. **111.** a woman:
woman. **112.** i'faith: indeed. **119.** Do you triumph, Roman?: Do ye triumph,
Romaine?. **120.** marry her: marry. **122.** win: [eds.] winnes. **123.** Faith: Why. shall
marry: marry. **129.** beckons: becomes. **132.** by this hand, she: [Q₁; not in F].
**154.** Faith, I: I. **156.** Faith: Yes. **199.** s.d. [after line 212 in F]. **202.** God save: Saue.
**226.** By my troth: Trust me. **239.** Truly, an: Truely. **272.** denote: deonte [F uncor-
rected] deuote [F corrected].
**ACT 4, SCENE 2. 32.** Nay: May. **33.** knees: knee. **35.** But not the words: [Q₁; not in F].
**51.** kinds: kind. **56.** A: The. **66.** Ay, there: [eds.] I heere. **71.** ne'er: neuer.
**83.** Impudent strumpet: [Q₁; not in F]. **96.** keep: [eds.] keepes. s.d. *Enter Emilia:*
[after line 94 in F]. **155.** O God: Alas. **162.** them in: [eds.] them: or. **174.** And . . .
you: [Q₁; not in F]. **177.** you to: to. **189.** Faith, I: I. for: and. **199.** By this hand:
Nay. **224.** takes: taketh. **227.** of: [Q₁; not in F].
**ACT 4, SCENE 3. 9.** s.d. *Exit:* [after line 9 in F]. **21.** favor in them: fauour. **23.** faith:
Father. **24.** before thee: before. **33.** Barbary: *Braberie.* **41.** sighing: [eds.] *singing* [F
corrected] *sining* [F uncorrected]. **71.** Good troth: Introth. **72.** By my troth: Introth.
**75.** Uds pity: why. **103.** God: Heauen.
**ACT 5, SCENE 1. 1.** bulk: Barke. **22.** Be't: But. hear: heard. **36.** Forth: For. **50.** Did:
Do. **91.** Oh, heaven: Yes, 'tis. **106.** out th': o'. **113.** 'Las, what's . . . What's: Alas,
what is . . . What is. **116.** dead: quite dead. **126.** Faugh! Fie: Fie.
**ACT 5, SCENE 2. 34.** heaven: Heauens. **37.** say so: say. **56.** Yes, presently: Presently.
**61.** Then Lord: O Heauen. **96.** here: high. **104.** Should: Did. **108.** s.d. *Enter
Emilia:* [after line 108 in F]. **121.** Oh, Lord: Alas. **131.** heard: heare. **148.** Nay,
had: had. **225.** Oh, God! Oh, heavenly God: Oh Heauen! oh heauenly Powres.
**226.** Zounds: Come. **248.** have here: haue. **317.** not. Here: [not: here Q₁] not) heere.
**357.** Indian: Iudean.

# PART TWO

*Cultural Contexts*

# CHAPTER I

## *Race and Religion*

————————————————— ⟩⟨ —————————————————

Since the eighteenth century, race has dominated the Anglo-American world's thinking about human differences; however, for the early modern period, race was an emergent category, one with shifting and paradoxical contours. Conversely, even though religion remains an important means of negotiating the contemporary world, it was an even more pervasive system of thought for *Othello*'s Jacobean audience. Given the all-encompassing nature of early modern religious thought, many scholars argue that religion, rather than race, must assume primacy in studying this era. However, *Othello*'s recurring importance in the growth of modern race-thinking makes it critical to see the significance of race for *Othello*'s modern audiences while at same time understanding its roots in very different types of race-thinking. One way to do this is to consider race and religion simultaneously. Color, so crucial to understanding the play, binds the two realms, making them indispensable to each other.

A powerful cultural and political force, as well as a spiritual one, religion was the dominant means by which early moderns understood and ordered their world. Prayers, sermons heard during mandatory church attendance, and popular entertainments that educated laypeople in religious doctrine shaped their sense of family, community, nation, history, and politics. Religious solidarity, as well as history and commerce, affected both alliances and antagonisms between nations. This chapter is concerned less with theology (the preserve of a literate elite) than with the way religious habits of thought affected ordinary people. Such habits clearly show how early modern race-thinking is entangled with religious culture. If one thinks of "race as a concept which signifies and symbolizes social conflicts and interests by referring to different types of human bodies" (Omi and Winant 55) and understands how early moderns used sex, gender, color, and bodily differences to articulate religious being, the relation between race and religion — and their resonance for *Othello* — becomes amply clear. For example, the physical and cultural differences of people from different religious backgrounds, like "Turks" and "Moors," assume great importance in Jacobean writing about national identity, social struggle, and religious conflict. Race has a broad arsenal of effects but a curiously narrow repertoire in representation. Descriptions or drawings of other cultures are derived from similar narratives about difference; thus, depictions of groups that the English deemed "other" might have startling similarities. Moreover, alert observers will also see a superimposition of images; for example, a representation of an African or Moor might be similar to depictions of Native Americans. This is particularly true in visual representation, where the same image can appear across a range of contexts or cultures.

Although Shakespeare's black hero is unprecedented on the English stage, a long biblical tradition of the converted Moor precedes and shapes Othello. This figure, based on Jeremiah 13:23 (see p. 185), is particularly powerful: "Because it is extraordinary for Moors to be Christians, Christian Moors offer valuable testimony to the salvific powers of Christianity, testimony that confirms for the Christian audience the truths of the faith" (Barthelemy, *Black Face* 65). Religious iconography offers prominent examples of virtuous Moors or Ethiopians. In Acts 8, the Apostle Philip baptizes an Ethiopian eunuch. The Queen of Sheba, Zipporah (Moses's wife), Saint Maurice, and the black Magus at Christ's Nativity have all been used in different ways to testify to the power of Christianity.

The converted Moor in Rembrandt's striking painting *The Baptism of the Eunuch* shows one intersection of race-thinking and religion (see Figure 11). This vision of baptism and conversion involves a purification based on washing white the black man's soul, a process that, Peter Erickson notes, "generates tension between exterior blackness and inner whiteness because the latter tends to devalue the former" (136). Think of the many times *Othello* asks that one look beyond the skin to the soul beneath. However, the same verse that supports the ideal of the converted Moor, whose soul is washed white, also undermines it; the saying "washing the Ethiope white"

FIGURE 11 Baptism of the Eunuch, *by Rembrandt van Rijn (1626).*

(see p. 185) uses the seeming indelibility of blackness to create a popular image of impossibility. Peter Mark makes the important point that in the early Christian church black skin was relatively free of derogatory connotations, but that this situation was modified by subsequent commentators shortly after the deaths of the Church Fathers (*Africans* 11). Tellingly, in Rembrandt's painting it is a eunuch, a desexualized black man, who is rendered the converted ideal.

Erickson also draws attention to Rembrandt's portrayal of climate. Although the palm tree in the upper left corner implies a tropical or hot climate, the black eunuch wears a white ermine coat, externally registering his inner whiteness and identifying that purified whiteness with northern climes: "Becoming spiritually white is understood as the equivalent to location in the privileged space of Northern Europe; hence the need to be prepared for cold weather" (139–40). Erickson's observation brings us to another crucial facet of early modern race-thinking that permeates *Othello*: climate theory. This field of natural philosophy was the basis for most racial/ethnic distinctions of early modern Europe. As an environmental schema, it assumes that character, appearance, and temperament are all shaped by the individual's climate or region. Signified by terms like *temperament* and *complexion* as well as by concepts from humoral theory (see Chapter 5, Passions) such as *heat*, *cold*, and *humor*, it is a powerful way of organizing human differences. Even though exploration of the American continent significantly disrupted early modern geography, climate theory still adhered to a three-part division of the world with northern (cold), southern (hot), and middle (temperate) zones.

In appearance, Northerners were thought to be tall, white (or light tawny), and humorally cold and moist; they were reputedly big eaters and drinkers who could be dull, credulous, inconstant, warlike, and at times cruel and jealous. Southerners, by contrast, were portrayed as short, black, or tawny, with frizzled hair, and were often said to be cowardly, subtle, and wise as well as superstitious and jealous. Middle zones produced the temperate ideal; however, even in climates thought to produce an ideal balance, inhabitants tended toward characteristics from the nearest zone. Although many writers created elaborate accounts of climate's influence on the individual, in most works such divisions were relational or oppositional; one was a Northerner in comparison to Southerners, and so on. For example, traveler Henry Blount suggested that the Southeast (the land of the Ottomans) was the primary contrast to the Northwest (England) (80). More locally, continental Europe was also divided into three climatic zones, and many texts agree with *Othello* that Italians had characteristics associated with southern climes. Mary Floyd-Wilson cautions that "early modern geohumoralism contradicts many of the racial stereotypes concerning the behavior and capacities of non-English 'others' that began to emerge in the early modern period" (3). So too, complexion and climate theory do not immediately align nations according to modern racial schema. Complexion was considered the physical manifestation of temperament; since it was both relative and highly susceptible to change, complexion theory did not assign absolute and hierarchical difference along contemporary lines (for example, it denigrated whiteness). However, as the *The Baptism of the Eunuch* illustrates, the subtleties of complexion theory often collided with Christian notions of whiteness as evidence of purity and grace.

Climate theory frequently worried about geography's ability to change individuals physically and spiritually (Anderson 50–53; Floyd-Wilson 23–24). Hot climates were of particular concern when reading *Othello* because heat was seen as especially productive of lechery, unruly sexuality, and other types of disorder. African heat was a rich source of imagery for English writers (Eldred Jones 9): descriptions of the continent often claimed to find there misshapen humans, monstrous beasts, and transgressive cultural practices. However, the writings in Chapter 2, Cultural Geography, and Chapter 4, Masculinity and Military Life, reveal that the heat of southern climes within Europe also was thought to produce similar behaviors. For example, jealousy and credulity were said to be typical of both Italians and Moors, perhaps making both Roderigo and Othello susceptible to Iago's machinations. However, the effects of climate were uncertain and frequently debated: Cinthio's Disdemona tells her husband that Moors are "hot by nature" (see the selection from *Gli Hecatommithi*, p. 35), while Shakespeare's Desdemona alludes to a contravening theory when she claims that the sun takes away jealousy: "I think the sun where he was born / Drew all such humours from him" (3.4.24–25). Both climate theory and discussions of conversion speak to broader early modern anxieties about the mutability of identity. Writings on the passions (see Chapter 5) are filled with warnings against the dangerous power of emotions to alter the self. A similar fear haunts questions of conversion and climate in *Othello*.

Sexuality, as well as color, binds race-thinking and religious imagery in the play. Critic Ania Loomba argues that "sexual guilt . . . is rooted in and intensified by a colour consciousness" ("Sexuality" 181). Christianity's concerns with purity, sexual purity in particular, are most often located in the female; patriarchal order thus depends on surveillance and control of women. The English male deflected anxieties over sexuality onto his others: white women and foreign males. As does George Best (see p. 190), writers typically express concerns over race and purity by focusing on the vulnerability of the white woman to outsiders. She becomes a surrogate for threats to marriage or to the state. Note, for example, that the popular title for the ballad "The Lady and the Blackamoor" (p. 197) deflects attention from the central conflict between the husband and the Moorish servant to the vulnerability of the white woman. Physically and temperamentally, women are seen as particularly prone to lust (see Chapter 3, Marriage and the House-hold); they are also portrayed as tempters of men (an assumption that Emilia shockingly turns on its head: "But I do think it is their husbands' faults / If wives do fall" [4.3.85–86]). The need to secure social order through control of women means that the language of white purity and black damnation traps white women more frequently than white men. As his suspicions grow, Othello becomes increasingly enmeshed in this language: images of female frailty conjoin with his blackness (Loomba, "Sexuality" 180). His later condemnation of female wickedness reveals his own internalization of racial codes: "Was this fair paper, this most goodly book, / Made to write 'whore' upon?" (4.2.73–74). In this case, the image of Desdemona as unblemished white paper disfigured by black writing inevitably condemns Othello's own blackness and his marriage.

## Othello's Sword and English Sexuality

The English practice of projecting sexual unease onto distant lands often allowed gender and sexuality to be used to demonize racial and religious others (see K. Hall, *Things*, chapter 1; Hendricks and Parker; Korda, chapter 5; Loomba, *Race*; Traub, *Renaissance*, chapter 5). The reputed sexual license of African cultures was a source of fascination for readers and playgoers, and the subject of much comment in travel literature. For example, some writers suggest that the reputed sexual freedom of Islamic law made conversion to Islam attractive for Christians. Critic Nabil Matar argues that fears of the "sodomite" (a term that encompasses a range of transgressions) are fundamental to images of Turks and Moors: "By predicating the barbarous on the sodomite, English writers created the stereotype of the Turk and the Moor" (113).[1]

Circumcision, practiced in both Judaism and Islam, was a key signifier of difference that took on sexual overtones in English discourse (see Shapiro 113–30), paradoxically combining fears of castration with anxieties about the potency of hypersexual foreign others. Thus, castration and conversion were tightly joined in English representations of Turks. Given this conflation of sexual and religious fears, readers may want to consider what it means for Othello to refer to himself as both "circumcisèd dog" and "turbaned Turk" at

---

[1] Sodomy in the early modern period referred not simply to anal sex or sexual relations between men but to a broader "disorder in sexual relations," often spoken of as "unnatural" or demonic (Bray 25; Wiesner 261), which could encompass not only any form of nonprocreative sex but also transgressive sexual relations across barriers of class and culture.

his suicide. What does it say about his identity as a Christian? About Christian views of Muslims? These fears point to the prominence of the sword in Othello's suicide and in representations of Turks. In many illustrations of Othello, as in the George Noble engraving (Figure 12), his sword is often given a prominently phallic position that indicates the sexual danger of Turks and Moors. However, the sword is also figured as an instrument of conversion, as in the Sodoma rendition of St. Iago Matamoros (Figure 18, p. 204). Is Othello's "sword of Spain, the ice-brook's temper" (5.2.262) a sword of castration or of conversion? Or both?

## Blackness and Moors

The full title of the play, *Othello, the Moor of Venice*, immediately draws its central character and the audience into a host of stories about Moors. While Iago circulates the most explicit and negative visions of Moors as lascivious, duplicitous, vengeful, superstitious, and jealous, the audience might also have heard about noble Moors who were learned, trustworthy, and devout (Figure 13).[2] The next chapter, Cultural Geography (p. 228), will take a more detailed look into English views of Venice, but while reading this chapter, it is worth considering what it means for Othello to be a Moor *of* Venice. What possibilities of affinity and difference does the title suggest? How well, if at all, does the figure of Othello reconcile the many facets of his identity? Does the phrase "the Moor of Venice" speak to the possibility that Othello has an integrated "dual, rather than divided identity" (Bartels, *Othello* 62)? Or does it make him a "walking paradox, a contradiction in terms" (Vitkus, *Turning Turk* 161) who inhabits the "site of violent contradiction" (Neill, *Putting History* 271)?

The widespread use of *Moor* to refer to both religious and physical difference means that the word proves incredibly elastic, stretching to encompass a wide range of peoples and cultures. Nonetheless, the critical commentary on *Othello* is filled with rather notorious attempts to identify definitively Othello's race/ethnicity and geographic origins. Most of this commentary purports to identify what kind of "Moor" Othello is, asking whether he is a darker-skinned black African (Figure 14) or a lighter-skinned Arab (Figure 15, p. 184), but with a definite bias against seeing Othello as black (see K. Hall, "*Othello*"; Loomba, *Race*). However, it is simply impossible to know

---

[2] Eric Griffin makes a persuasive case for the influence of Spanish pastorals and romances, many of which sing the praises of chivalrous or learned Moors (69–72).

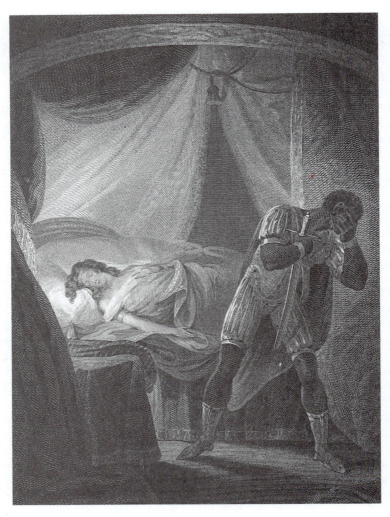

FIGURE 12 *Engraving of Act 5.2, by George Noble, collection of John and Josiah Boydell (1800). Publisher and engraver John Boydell almost bankrupted himself to create* The Shakespeare Gallery, *a collection of paintings commissioned from England's foremost artists. Thousands of visitors paid to enter the gallery and see scenes from Shakespeare's works, like this one by George Noble. Still more bought the engravings produced by Boydell and his nephew Joshua based on these works, and over the years these illustrations came to dominate public perceptions of the play as the engravings circulated individually and in editions of the plays. Notice the use of light and dark in the image. What is the source of light in the painting? Note the position of the sword — if the top looks like a cross, what does the bottom suggest?*

FIGURE 13  The Adoration of the Magi, *by Peter Paul Rubens. In the early Renaissance, the story of the Christ child being visited by kings from faraway lands was a popular vehicle for artists wishing to represent exotic peoples and objects. By the era of European discovery, it became common to represent one Magus as black, and Adoration paintings are one of the main sources for imagery of black African men (Blakely 84–92; Mark, Africans 44–53). The three Magi in Adoration paintings represent the tripartite division of the world into Africa, Asia, and Europe. These representations always portray a noble black Magus, but his gifts to Christ may suggest a larger colonial relation of subservience. How is the African Magus distinguished from the others?*

FIGURE 14 *The engraving from Cesare Vecellio's* Degli habiti antichi et moderni di diverse parti del mondo *offers yet another sense of the nobility of Moors. Compare this wealthy Moor with the portrait of the Moroccan ambassador on page 184 (Figure 15).*

for sure whether Othello came from anywhere except Shakespeare's imagination. While the word *Negro* in early modern texts almost always refers to African peoples, associating them with blackness and a certain physical type (see Bartels, "Making"), the word *Moor* in the Jacobean period referred to a profusion of identities and was shaped by individual concerns with language, nation, geography, color, and religion. Simply put, the meaning depended on the context and the speaker; it most often meant "non-black Muslim, black Christian or black Muslim" (Barthelemy, *Black Face* 7). Etymologically, its Greek and Latin origins suggest *Moor* as a synonym for *black*. In its most specific form, it referred to a person from an area of North Africa known variously as Morocco, Mauretania, or Barbary; however, its primal association with color meant that the term's reach frequently included inhabitants of the entire continent of Africa or, further afield, any dark-skinned person, even in the Americas. This racializing usage complemented the appearance of *Moor* as a religious designation; thus, Muslims in Africa, the Middle East, and Southeast Asia were also referred to as Moors.

As *the Moor of Venice*, Othello can be discussed in relation to the stories about Africans, Ethiopians, "Mahumetans" (Muslims), "Negros," and Indians that appear in travel accounts, biblical exegeses, classical lore, and plays. Since the term has such reach and overlap, my division of these documents into sections about Moors and those about Turks is artificial. Like many stereotypes, the image of the Moor is malleable, responsive to the different types of political, economic, and social transactions England was involved in at any given time, particularly in the seventeenth century, when England emerged into "nascent imperialism" (Neill, *Putting History* 248) even as it suffered the fear of being conquered itself by powerful Ottoman forces. For example, although North African and sub-Saharan Africans were all referred to as Moors, Nabil Matar cautions that "England's relations with sub-Saharan Africans were relations of power, domination and slavery, while relations with Muslims of North Africa and the Levant were of anxious equality and grudging admiration" (8). So, too, Emily Bartels notes the erasure of Moorish authority in English travel narratives, arguing that "what is sabotaged within representations of Moors is their ability to compete in religious and political arenas" ("Making" 439). Although it can become a general term of otherness and radical difference, in these documents *Moor* frequently is supplemented by color-laden terms — *blackamoore*, *black*, *tawny*, *white*, and *negro* — that narrow its range of meaning.

English travelers in the early modern era brought with them many preconceptions about darker-skinned peoples based on a wide-ranging language of blackness that permeated English culture (see K. Hall, *Things*).

The blackness associated with the Moor carried with it a rich and varied set of meanings that symbolically moved it beyond the naming of Muslims as Moors even as it fueled that connection. Arthur Little argues that Shakespeare's audiences both responded to and created blackness: "blackness is allegorical, it functions as Shakespeare's pre-text, what the audience knows before it comes to experience the play" (75). This language of blackness derives from a range of sources: from biblical and classical narrative as well as popular culture. Christian imagery in particular associated blackness with sin, damnation, and, eventually, sexual promiscuity. *Love's Labour's Lost* proposes that "Black is the badge of hell, / The hue of dungeons and the style of night" (4.3.253). Regional mystery plays showed black-painted demons springing from hell to torment (white) humans; so, too, the damned were at times represented by actors painted black or wearing black costumes (Barthelemy, *Black Face* 2–5). These negative meanings of blackness shaped the first encounters of the English with dark-skinned Africans and infused all subsequent representations of blacks and Moors: "the Christian tradition with remarkable economy attached to all people of African ancestry an irrevocable bond to a sinful past. In a theological system that believes that sinfulness is an inheritance of all . . . the mark of sin on blacks is uniquely severe because the sign of their sinfulness is indelible" (Barthelemy, *Black Face* 3). For example, Reginald Scot's *Discovery of Witchcraft* warns that "a damned soul may and doth take the shape of a black Moor" (535). Conversely, for the English, *white* and *fair* were synonymous with *beautiful* and associated with purity, virginity, and virtue. The terms *black* and *white* work reciprocally — "we can't see one without registering the other" (Erickson 134). Readers might want to consider carefully how Shakespeare mobilizes the connections between Moors and blackness: How does Othello's speech and behavior early in the play dislodge the seemingly indelible link between blackness, sin, and unlawful sexuality? Where in the play is this link reinstated? How else are *black* and *white* attached to Othello? To Desdemona and Bianca?

While Moors in travel accounts and other tales could be "characterized alternatively and sometimes simultaneously in contradictory extremes, as noble or monstrous, civil or savage" (Bartels, "Making" 434), Moors who frequented the Elizabethan stage and popular entertainment were overwhelmingly, stereotypically evil and male. Although a character in a ballad, the unnamed vengeful Moor in "The Lady and the Blackamoor" has much in common with the stage Moor. Their appearance solidified the links among blackness, evil, and Moors. If Venetian rulers are examples of virtuous rule, Moorish kings are barbarous tyrants, "despots who know no limits"

(D'Amico, *Moor* 79–81). If travelers like Leo Africanus testify to the coura- geousness and wisdom of Moors, the stage shows Moors as cruel, vengeful, emotional, oversexed, and treacherous. The evil of the stage Moor was so assumed that one who "was other than Muslim or black . . . had to identify himself as such by denying his kinship with his kind" (Barthelemy, *Black Face* 17). Aaron, Othello's stage cousin from Shakespeare's *Titus Andronicus*, is typical of such figures who gloat in their villainy: "Aaron will have his soul black like his face" (3.2.204). Aaron also speaks self-consciously about the meanings of his own blackness. Othello is notable as an exception in this stage history; he seems to have made possible a new English tradition of the "noble Moor" (drawn from classical tradition and the religious trope of the converted Moor), which would become popular in the seventeenth century.

There are few detailed records of how black or African Moors were por- trayed onstage. It does seem clear that performers used either cloth, vizards (masks), or paint with black wigs. Theater records show payments for black velvet: Eldred Jones notes payments for "Corled hed sculles of black laune [Curled headpieces of black lawn fabric]" (123). Those who painted used a mixture of soot, lampblack, and water to paint faces and hands. The use of black cloth and paint indicates how absolutely *black* was interpreted in rela- tion to Africans as well as how potent its symbolic contrast was with white (Barthelemy, *Black Face* 1–17; Eldred Jones 41). Although evidence of makeup on the Elizabethan stage is scant (Gurr and Ichikawa 56), one might also do well to remember that aristocratic ladies (and possibly the men who emulated them onstage) wore extremely heavy makeup that exag- gerated the whiteness of their skin. Notably, James I's court witnessed a sig- nificant performance in blackface shortly after *Othello* was first performed. Ben Jonson's *The Masque of Blackness* (1605) featured Queen Anne and her court ladies painted as "black-moors," at the queen's request. There was con- sternation at her use of black paint, which some contemporary scholars have interpreted to mean that painting was a new practice; however, it seems more likely that the practice was new only for aristocratic women. Nonethe- less, it is clear that by the end of the seventeenth century, painting was the norm; this laborious and time-consuming process continued well into the twentieth century. The audience created the meanings of Moors and black- ness out of the endless narratives circulating in English culture; however, the play uses these associations in its own image-making. How many different views of blackness and of Moors can you identify in *Othello*? In the contex- tual materials in this volume?

## AN AMBASSADOR'S VISIT

Diplomatically, Queen Elizabeth's reign was characterized by cautious cooperation "with both Turks of the Ottoman empire and Moors of the Kingdom of Morocco" (Matar 9). The queen's commercial and political overtures were conducted through correspondence and in person. The triangle of Protestant England, Catholic Europe, and Muslim states (Moroccan and Ottoman) framed political and diplomatic ties. While Elizabeth I and King Ahmed el-Mansour found common cause in their enmity with Spain, James I's antipathy to Islam was compatible with attempts to reach peace with Spain; hence, the Spanish name Iago might conflate pro-Spanish with anti-Muslim sentiment. Several ambassadors or emissaries came to London during Elizabeth's reign; the most documented visit occurred a few years before *Othello* appeared onstage and surely influenced audiences' thinking about the play. The Moroccan ambassador, Abd el-Ouahed ben Messaoud ben Mohammed Anoun (known as Hamet Xarife in English), spent six months in England beginning in the fall of 1600, staying with a company of fifteen in the Royal Exchange. Unlike Moors or Muslims who came as refugees or prisoners, the Moorish ambassadors visited on their own terms and thus gave the English a taste of how elite Muslims worshipped and lived. A conspicuous presence in London, they went out "looking at and being looked at by Londoners," but their foreign attire and seemingly strange ways alienated many Elizabethans, who complained of duplicity and selfishness (see B. Harris; Matar 33–35). An anonymous 1600 portrait (Figure 15) commemorated Ambassador Abd el-Ouahed's visit. Compare the realistic rendering of the Ambassador with other representations in this volume. How do you interpret the Ambassador's expression? The portrait contains items — a turban and sword — that loom large in depictions of Ottoman forces. Swords are ambivalent indications of masculinity: often positioned and sized to suggest military and phallic might, they also at times signify castration.

FIGURE 15 *Portrait of Abd el-Ouahed ben Messaoud ben Mohammed Anoun (1600), Ambassador to Queen Elizabeth I.*

## TO WASH AN ETHIOPE WHITE

In early modern Europe *Ethiopian* frequently referred to black peoples in general and "the Ethiope" was often used to represent Christianity's powers of salvation. Emblem books, which combined poetic and artistic expression, circulated widely in the Renaissance. This emblem, *"Aethiopem lavare,"* from Geffrey Whitney's *A Choice of Emblems* (1586), illustrates the proverb for impossibility: "to wash an Ethiope white." The popular proverb is based on a verse from Jeremiah: "Can the black Moor change his skin? Or the leopard his spots? Then may ye also do good, that are accustomed to do evil" (*Geneva Bible*, Jeremiah 13:23). While the original seems to suggest the possibility of transformation through faith, the proverb's many forms ("you wash an Ethiope," "you labor in vain as to scrub an Ethiope," "you wash a blackmoor white," "my labor in vain") jokingly maintained just the opposite and remained in popular use until the nineteenth century (Blakely 92–95; Newman; Praeger). Interestingly, the expression seems to have first appeared in Thomas Elyot's 1548 dictionary *Biblioteca Eliotae*, which was published just before England made its first inroads into the African slave trade. He identifies *Aethiopem lavas* as "a proverb applied to him that praiseth a thing that is naught, or teacheth a fool wisdom" (C5$_v$). How does the emblem's verse align blackness with virtue? What does it suggest about humankind's relation to nature?

*Leave off with pain, the blackamore to scour,*
*With washing oft, and wiping more than due:*
*For thou shalt find, that Nature is of power,*
*Do what thou canst, to keep his former hue.*
*Though with a fork, we Nature thrust away,*
*She turns again, if we withdraw our hand.*
*And though, we oft to conquer her assay [trial or test]*
*Yet all in vain, she turns if still we stand:*
   *Then evermore, in what thou dost assay,*
   *Let reason rule, and do the things thou may.*

FIGURE 16 "Aethiopem lavare," *by Geffrey Whitney,* A Choice of Emblems *(1586).*

→ PETER MARTYR

# *From* The Decades of the New World or West India

*1555*

*Translated by Richard Eden*

*The Decades of the New World or West India* — Richard Eden's translation/adaptation of Peter Martyr's (Pietro Martire d'Anghiera's) *De Orbo Novo Decades cum Legatione* — appeared early in the literature of English travel. Such texts were meant to convey new maritime information and to fuel English interest in travel to other lands. Although the original was an Italian text, its immense interest for England lay in the fact that Eden published with the translation the first two accounts of English travel to Africa, Thomas Wyndham's voyage to Guinea in 1553 and John Lok's voyage to Mina (Ghana) in 1554–55. These accounts are typical of the genre in that they intersperse actual observation with fantastic myths and images gleaned from Scripture and classical works that had already filtered into popular lore. Europe's earliest African and Indian exploration was energized by the hope that travelers would encounter the mythical Prester John (described in Martyr), a Christian black African king said to live in the unexplored interior of the continent.

Although Prester John was at times thought to reside in other areas of the world also relatively unexplored by the English, the African location coincided with Europeans' already existing desires to convert Muslims to Christianity, and readers might wish to pay careful attention to the narrator's use of the Bible. Prester John, with his fabulous wealth, power, and Christian devotion, was hoped to be Christian Europe's much-needed ally against the Ottomans. So, too, colonial exploration fueled the religious imagery of the black Magus, another figure glorifying conversion to Christianity and augmenting Christian might. Readers might wish to compare Martyr's perspective with that of Leo Africanus (see p. 195). What does this text say about how Africans and Europeans appreciate valuable items? About their honesty and the value of their promises?

## A BRIEF DESCRIPTION OF AFRICA

*A*frica the great, is one of the three parts of the world, known in old time, and severed from *Asia*, on the East by the river *Nile*, on the West, from Europe by the pillars of Hercules. The hither part is now called Barbary, and the people Moors. The inner part is called *Libya* and *Ethiopia*. . . .

Peter Martyr, *The Decades of the New World or West India*, trans. Richard Eden (London 1555), 337Yy1v–338Yy2v, 419Hhh3r, 420Hhh4r–420Hhh4v

In the East side of *Africa*, beneath the Red Sea, dwelleth the great and mighty Emperor and Christian king Prester John, well known to the Portugals in their voyages to *Calicut*. His dominions reach very far on every side: and hath under him many other kings both Christian and heathen that pay him tribute. This mighty prince is called David the emperor of Ethiopia. Some write that the king of Portugal sendeth him yearly eight ships laden with merchandise. His kingdom confineth with the Red Sea, and reacheth far into Africa toward Egypt and Barbary. Southward it confineth with the sea toward the *Cape de Buona Speranza* [Cape of Good Hope] and on the other side with the Sea of Sand, called *Mare de Sabione*, a very dangerous sea, lying between the great city of . . . *Cairo* in Egypt, and the country of Ethiopia: In the which way are many uninhabitable deserts, continuing for the space of five days' journey. And they affirm, that if the said Christian Emperor were not hindered by those deserts (in the which is great lack of victuals, and especially of water) he would ere now have invaded the kingdom of Egypt, and the city of *Cairo*. The chief city of Ethiopia, where this great Emperor is resident, is called *Amacaiz*, being a fair city, whose inhabitants are of the color of an Olive. There are also many other cities, as the city of *Saua* upon the river of *Niles*, where the emperor is accustomed to remain in the summer season. There is likewise a great city named *Barbaregaf*, and *Ascon*, from whence it is said that the Queen of *Sheba* came to Jerusalem to hear the wisdom of Solomon. This city is but little, yet very fair, and one of the chief cities in *Ethiopia*. In the said kingdom is a province called *Manicongni*, whose king is a Moor and tributary to the emperor of *Ethiopia*. In this province are many exceeding high mountains, upon the which is said to be the earthly Paradise: and some say that there are the trees of the Sun and Moon, whereof the antiquity maketh mention: yet that none can pass thither, by reason of great deserts of a hundred days' journey. Also beyond these mountains is the cape of *Buona Speranza*. And to have said thus much of *Africa* it may suffice.

## OF THE ISLAND OF *MOZAMBIQUE* AND THE INHABITANTS THEREOF

The island is not big, and is inhabited with black Mahumetans,[1] living in manner in necessity of all things, yet hath it a commodious port. They have no corn but that is brought from the continent, where also we went aland to see the country, where we saw nothing but a vagabond and rascal kind of

---

[1] **Mahumetans:** a derogatory term for Muslims.

black men, covering only their privates with leaves of trees, and are besides naked, and the women in like manner. Their lips are two fingers thick, their foreheads very large, their teeth great and as white as snow. They are fearful at the sight of everything, and especially when they see armed men. Therefore seeing their fearfulness, and knowing them to be without weapons that can do any great hurt, only five of us well armed, bearing also with us Arquebuses,[2] and having in our company a black slave that somewhat knew the country, we began to enter further into the land; and when we had gone forward one day's journey, we found many herds of Elephants. Here the slave that was our guide gave us counsel to take firebrands[3] in our hands, because these beasts fear fire above all things. But we once chanced to find three Female Elephants, which had very lately brought forth their Calves, and therefore feared not the fire: but without all fear, followed us so far that we were fain to flee to a mountain to save us from the beasts.

When we had entered about ten miles into the land, we found a certain den on the side of a mountain, where some of the black inhabitants lurked. These spoke so confoundedly and chatteringly like Apes, that I am not able to express their manner of speech. Yet to go the nearest thereto that I can, their speech is likest to the evil favored voice which the Muleteers of *Sicilia* use when they drive their Mules: and such manner of blabbering use these people in their speech. Here the Pilot of the Ship asked us if we would buy any kine,[4] saying that here we should have them good cheap. But we, thinking that either he had mocked us, or that agreeing with the inhabitants (whom he knew before) he would have deceived us of our money and wares, said that we had no money. Then said he unto us, "These people desire nothing less than money, having much more plenty of gold than we have, which is found not far hence." Then said we to him, "What desire they then?" "They love (said he) despicable things, and of small value: as pins, knives, scissors, looking Glasses, Hawks' bells, bags or boxes, to keep their gold in, Copper Rings, Jangelinges to hang at their Timberelles,[5] bosses,[6] laces, broaches, copper chains, carkenettes,[7] bracelets, and such other trifles to trim their wives and children." We answered that we were content to give them such wares for their kine, if they would bring them to the next mountain. Then said our Pilot again, "They will bring them with us to the mountain: but no further in any condition: Therefore speak what you will give." Then one of our companions said that he had a boss of green copper and also a little bell. But I, because I had no such merchandise, yet being

---

[2] **Arquebuses:** an early type of portable gun.   [3] **firebrands:** a piece of wood lit at a fire.   [4] **kine:** cows.   [5] **Timberelles:** timbrels; bells to hang on tamborines.   [6] **bosses:** the projection at the center of a shield or buckler.   [7] **carkenettes:** carcenets; ornamental collars or necklaces.

desirous to eat flesh, said that I would sell one of my shirts for kine. Then said the Pilot, "Let me alone with the matter." Then calling unto him five or six of the Inhabitants, he showed them our goodly Jewels, and demanded for them three hundred kine. But the inhabitants, not much differing from beasts, made signs that they would give only fifteen. In sign, we agreed yet suspecting some deceit, nevertheless they kept their promise, and sent us fifteen kine by two of their companions.

We were scarcely departed, but we heard a noise and tumult in their dens, and were partly afraid lest these Troglodites would follow us, and therefore leaving our kine, we took us to our weapons. But they made signs unto us to fear nothing. Then our pilot told us that their tumult was only which of them should have the boss of copper. Then recovering our kine, we drove them forward to the top of the mountain, and there dismissed the two black slaves that came with them. While we were thus driving our kine by the side of a little wood, we met again with the Elephants, whereof being in great fear, we forsook our kine, and trusted to our feet. Therefore departing from hence, we returned to the Island, where making provision for our voyage, we sailed toward the Cape, called *Caput Bona Spei*, passing the Island of Saint Lawrence (otherwise named *Madagascar*) being four score leagues distant from the nearest continent or firm land. I suppose that in short time the king of Portugal will be Lord of this Island: For having now burned and destroyed many villages and towns of the Island, his name is fearful among them. And as far as I can conjecture by my peregrinations of the world (especially of *India* and *Ethiopia*) I think that the king of Portugal, if he continue as he hath begun, is like to be the richest king in the world, and doubtless not unworthily for the dignity and godly zeal of so noble a prince, as by whose means the Christian faith is daily greatly increased. For it is certain that in *India*, and especially in the city of *Cucin*, where the Viceroy remaineth, every holy day, ten or twelve Idolaters or Mahumetans are professed to our religion, whereby we may conceive good hope, that in time our faith shall there be greatly enlarged by the grace of God, who hath there given such supernatural victories to the Christians, and therefore all professors of Christ's holy name ought to pray to almighty God to assist him in so godly an enterprise.

→ GEORGE BEST

# *From* A True Discourse of the Late Voyages of Discovery

*1578*

The body's "exquisite sensitivity to atmospheric change" (Paster, *Body* 10) was a source of increasing concern to the English as they began moving out of their isolation in the early modern period; thus, George Best's discussion of a black English child's complexion begins with the question of whether white travelers in tropical climes would change in "complexion" and temperament. Investigations into the meanings and origins of blackness accelerated as Europeans increased their engagements in Africa. It is important to remember that these investigations were not neutral since "whiteness functions as the originary truth and . . . blackness signifies a later horror" (Little 308). Three explanations were given for blackness: climate, infection, and sin.

George Best published his account of Martin Frobisher's attempts to find a northwest passage to Asia after the third voyage in 1578. This excerpt explains differences in human complexion, particularly the origins of black skin color. Whereas earlier Christian writers such as Jerome and Augustine took for granted the assumption that Africans were descended from Ham's sons, who were cursed by his father, Noah (Jordan 18; Barthelemy, *Black Face* 3), in the early modern period blackness became central to the story. Best and others attached blackness and national origin to sin, disobedience, and errant sexuality (see Braude; K. Hall, *Things*; Newman 128). How does Ham challenge the social order in Best's version? Where do economic concerns shape the story of Ham and Queen Elizabeth's order of expulsion (see p. 194)? What conflicts over "place" or service shape the actions of Ham and those of the Moor in "The Lady and the Blackamoor" (see p. 197)?

Also the Englishmen made another voyage very prosperous and gainful, Anno 1554, to the coasts of *Benin*, lying East from *Guinea*, being within three degrees of the Equinoctial. And yet it is reported of a truth, . . . all the whole Bay is more subject to many blooming and smothering heats, with infectious and contagious airs, than any other place in all *Torrida Zone*:[1] and the cause thereof is some accidents in the land. For it is most certain, that mountains, seas, woods, and lakes, etc. may cause through their sundry kind of situation sundry strange and extraordinary effects, which the reason of the clime otherwise would not give. I mention these voyages of our English-

---

[1] *Torrida Zone*: region of the earth between the tropics.

---

George Best, *A True Discourse of the Late Voyages of Discovery for the Finding of a Passage to Cathaya by the Northwest* . . . (London 1578), 19–21, 28–32.

men not so much to prove that *Torrida Zone* may be, and is inhabited, as to show their readiness in attempting long and dangerous Navigations. We also among us in England, have black Moors, Ethiopians, out of all parts of Torrida Zone, which after a small continuance, can well endure the cold of our Country, and why should not we as well abide the heat of their Country? But what should I name any more experiences, seeing that all the coasts of Guinea and Benin are inhabited of Portugals, Spaniards, French, and some Englishmen, and there have built Castles and Towns. Only this I will say to the Merchants of London that trade yearly to Marochus,[2] it is very certain that the greatest part of the burning Zone is far more temperate and cool than the Country of Marochus, as shall appear by these reasons and experiences following. . . .

And first by the experience of sundry men, yea thousands, Travelers and Merchants, to the East and West *Indies* in many places both directly under and hard by the Equinoctial, they with one consent affirm that it aboundeth in the middle of *Torrida Zone* with all manner of grain, herbs, grass, fruit, wood, and cattle that we have here, and thousands other sorts, far more wholesome, delectable, and precious than any we have in these Northern climates, as very well shall appear to him that will read the Histories and Navigations of such as have traveled *Arabia*, *India*, . . . the Islands *Molucca*, *America*, etc., which all lie about the middle of the burning Zone, where it is truly reported that the great herbs, . . . do wax ripe, greater, more savory and delectable in taste than ours, within sixteen days after the seed is sown. . . .

Others again imagine the middle Zone to be extreme hot, because the people of *Africa*, especially the Ethiopians, are so coal black, and their hair like wool curled short, which blackness and crooked hair they suppose to come only by the parching heat of the Sun, which how it should be possible, I cannot see. For even under the Equinoctial in America, and in the East Indies, and in the Islands Malucca, the people are not black, but white, with long hair uncurled as we have, so that if the Ethiopians' blackness came by the heat of the Sun, why should not those Americans and Indians also be as black as they, seeing the Sun is equally distant from them both, they abiding in one Parallel . . . ?

. . . Therefore, to return again to the black Moors, I myself have seen an Ethiopian as black as a coal brought into England, who, taking a fair English woman to Wife, begat a son in all respects as black as the father was, although England were his native Country, and an English woman his Mother: whereby it seemeth this blackness proceedeth rather of some natural infection of that man, which was so strong that neither the nature of the

[2] **Marochus:** Morocco.

Clime, neither the good complexion of the Mother concurring, could anything alter, and therefore we cannot impute it to the nature of the Clime. And for a more fresh example, our people of Meta Incognita[3] (of whom and for whom this discourse is taken in hand) that were brought this last year into England, were all generally of the same color that many Nations be, lying in the middle of the middle Zone. And this their color was not only in the face, which was subject to Sun and Air, but also in their bodies, which were still covered with garments, as ours are: yea, the very sucking child, of twelve months' age, had his skin of the very same color that most have under the Equinoctial, which thing cannot proceed by reason of the clime, for that they are at least ten degrees more toward the North than we in England are . . . whereby it followeth that there is some other cause than the Climate, or the Sun's perpendicular reflection, that should cause the Ethiopians' great blackness. And the most probable cause to my judgment is that this blackness proceedeth of some natural infection of the first inhabitants of that Country, and so all the whole progeny of them descended are still polluted with the same blot of infection.

Therefore, it shall not be far from our purpose to examine the first original of these black men and how by lineal descent they have hitherto continued thus black. It manifestly and plainly appeareth by holy Scripture that after the general inundation and overflowing of the Earth,[4] there remained no more men alive, but Noah and his three sons, Shem, Ham, and Japheth, who only were left to possess and inhabit the whole face of the earth: therefore, all the land that until this day hath been inhabited by sundry descents must needs come of the offspring either of Shem, Ham, and Japheth, as the only sons of Noah, who, all three being white, and their wives also, by course of nature should have begotten and brought forth white children. But the envy of our great and continual enemy the wicked Spirit is such that, as he could not suffer our old Father Adam to live in the felicity and Angelic state wherein he was first created, but tempting him, sought and procured his ruin and fall. So again, finding at this flood none but a father and three sons living, he so caused one of them to transgress and disobey his father's commandment, that after him, all his posterity should be accursed.

The fact of disobedience was this: When Noah at the commandment of God had made and entered the Ark and the floodgates of Heaven were

---

[3] **our people of Meta Incognita**: Meta Incognita means "Of Limits unknown." Best is referring to the three Inuit captives Frobisher brought to England after his second voyage to the Artic. They died within one month of their arrival in England.    [4] **inundation and overflowing of the Earth**: the biblical flood.

opened so that the whole face of the earth, every tree and mountain, was covered with abundance of water, he straightly commanded his sons and their wives that they should with reverence and fear behold the justice and mighty power of God, and that during the time of the flood, while they remained in the Ark, they should use continency and abstain from carnal copulation with their wives: and many other precepts he gave unto them, and admonitions, touching the justice of God in revenging sin and his mercy in delivering them, who nothing deserved it. Which good instructions and exhortations notwithstanding, his wicked son Ham disobeyed, and being persuaded that the first child born after the flood (by right and law of nature) should inherit and possess all the dominion of the earth, he, contrary to his father's commandment, while they were yet in the Ark, used company with his wife, and craftily went about, thereby to disinherit the offspring of his other two brethren. For the which wicked and detestable fact, as an example for contempt of Almighty God and disobedience of parents, God would a son should be born whose name was Chus, who, not only itself but all his posterity after him, should be so black and loathsome that it might remain a spectacle of disobedience to all the World.

And of this black and cursed Chus came all these black Moors which are in Africa, for after the water was banished from off the face of the earth, and that the land was dry, Shem chose that part of the land to inhabit in which now is called Asia, and Japheth had that which now is called Europe, wherein we dwell, and Africa remained for Cham [Ham], and his black son Chus, and was called Chamesis, after the father's name, being perhaps a cursed, dry, sandy, and unfruitful ground, fit for such a generation to inhabit in. Thus, you see that the cause of the Ethiopians' blackness is the curse and natural infection of blood, and not the distemperature of the climate, which also may be proved by this example: that these black men are found in all parts of Africa, as well without the Tropics, as within, even unto Capo d'buona Speranza Southward, where, by reason of the Sphere, should be the same temperature as is in Spain, Laddigna, and Sicilia, where all be of very good complexions. Wherefore I conclude that the blackness proceedeth not of the hotness of the Clime but, as I said, of the infection of blood, and therefore this their argument gathered of the Africans' blackness is not able to destroy the temperature of the middle Zone.

# Licensing Casper van Senden to Deport Negroes    *1601*

Jack D'Amico notes that early modern views of Moors are rooted in "close inter-action between inherited preconceptions and experience" (*Moor* 1). The many images of and stories about Moors adhered not only to Othello, but also to the black Africans and many Moors who lived, visited, and conducted business in England, particularly London. Individually, travelers and traders abroad brought people (mostly men, both slave and free) from different parts of Africa as translators, prisoners, servants, and seamen (Fryer 4–19; Eldred Jones 16–18; Walvin 12–19). Some Moors came as merchants; others were brought as refu-gees or prisoners captured in pirate raids throughout the Mediterranean. Queen Elizabeth's order of expulsion and George Best's *Discourse* (p. 190) both give evi-dence of the presence of blacks in England and suggest the terms on which black people lived and settled there. In 1596 Queen Elizabeth issued a procla-mation licensing Dutch captain Casper van Senden to transport "Negars and blackamoors" from England in exchange for English prisoners he delivered from Spain. Evidently this first edict was not successful. Van Senden com-plained that citizens refused to give up their slaves and in 1601 Elizabeth wrote this warrant requiring the transportation of "Negars and blackamoors" out of the realm. Although the document reproduced here is used to suggest that there were large numbers of Black people in England at the time, it seems instead that these black people were used as repayment for van Senden's services (Fryer 10–12; Hall, *Reading*; Newman). Why does Elizabeth suggest that the expulsion of "Blackamoors" is in the interest of "the good and welfare of her own natural subjects"?

Whereas the Queen's majesty, tendering the good and welfare of her own natural subjects, greatly distressed in these hard times of dearth, is highly discontented to understand the great numbers of [Negars] and blackamoors which (as she is informed) are carried into this realm since the troubles between her highness and the King of Spain; who are fostered and powered here, to the great annoyance of her own liege people that which co[vet?] the relief which these people consume, as also for that the most of them are infi-dels having no understanding of Christ or his Gospel: hath given a special commandment that the said kind of people shall be with all speed avoided

Queen Elizabeth I, "Licensing Casper van Senden to Deport Negroes," *Tudor Royal Proclama-tions*, vol. 3, ed. Paul L. Hughes and James F. Larkin (New Haven: Yale University Press, 1964–69), 221–22.

and discharged out of this her majesty's realms; and to that end and purpose hath appointed Casper van Senden, merchant of Lubeck, for their speedy transportation, a man that hath somewhat deserved of this realm in respect that by his own labor and charge he hath relieved and brought from Spain divers of our English nation who otherwise would have perished there.

These shall therefore be to will and require you and every of you to aid and assist the said Casper van Senden or his assignees to taking such [Negars] and blackamoors to be transported as aforesaid as he shall find within the realm of England; and if there shall be any person or persons which be possessed of any such blackamoors that refuse to deliver them in sort aforesaid, then we require you to call them before you and to advise and persuade them by all good means to satisfy her majesty's pleasure therein; which if they shall eftsoons willfully and obstinately refuse, we pray you to certify their names to us, to the end her majesty may take such further course therein as it shall seem best in her princely wisdom.

→ JOHN LEO AFRICANUS

## *From* A Geographical History of Africa  *1600*

Hasan ibn Muhammad al-Wazzan, known in England as John Leo Africanus (1485?–1554), was an almost revered authority on African travel: his description of Africa, first published in Italian in 1550, was for centuries the most authoritative source of information about North and West Africa. Considered by many scholars a model for the converted Othello, Hasan was captured in the Mediterranean by pirates and taken to Rome, where he was given to Pope Leo X and christened Johannes Leo de Medicis. He subsequently became known throughout Europe when texts in Latin, French, and Italian circulated under the name Johannes Leo Africanus, given Hasan by the first editor of his work. Part of a diasporic community of Andalusian Muslims who lived in Fez, the young Hasan had traveled through northern Africa, sub-Saharan Africa, and the Arabian peninsula. As John Pory's 1600 English translation was eagerly consumed by English readers, Leo Africanus was widely cited on many aspects of Africa until the more extensive colonial exploration of the continent in the nineteenth century, even though much of his writing was shaped and directed by European editors like Ramusio and Pory (see Andrea, "Assimilation"; Zhiri). Consider why Leo Africanus includes jealousy in a discussion of virtues.

John Leo Africanus, *A Geographical History of Africa*, trans. John Pory (London, 1600), 182–85. For more about Leo Africanus, see Chapter 2, p. 260.

# From *A Geographical History of Africa*

## THE COMMENDABLE ACTIONS AND VIRTUES OF THE AFRICANS

Those Arabians which inhabit in Barbary or upon the coast of the Mediterranean sea, are greatly addicted unto the study of good arts and sciences: and those things which concern their law and religion are esteemed by them in the first place. Moreover they have been heretofore most studious of the Mathematics, of Philosophy, and of Astrology: but these arts (as it is aforesaid) were four hundred years ago, utterly destroyed and taken away by the chief professors of their law. The inhabitants of cities do most religiously observe and reverence those things which appertain unto their religion; yea they honor those doctors and priests, of whom they learn their law, as if they were petty-gods. Their Churches they frequent very diligently, to the end they may repeat certain prescript and formal prayers; most superstitiously persuading themselves that the same day wherein they make their prayers, it is not lawful for them to wash certain of their members, when as at other times they will wash their whole bodies. . . .

Moreover, those which inhabit Barbary are of great cunning and dexterity for building and for mathematical inventions, which a man may easily conjecture by their artificial works. Most honest people they are, and destitute of all fraud and guile; not only embracing all simplicity and truth, but also practicing the same throughout the whole course of their lives: albeit certain Latin authors, which have written of the same regions, are far otherwise of opinion. Likewise they are most strong and valiant people, especially those which dwell upon the mountains. They keep their covenant most faithfully; insomuch that they had rather die than break promise. No nation in the world is so subject unto jealousy; for they will rather lose their lives, than put up any disgrace in the behalf of their women. So desirous they are of riches and honor, that therein no other people can go beyond them. They travel in a manner over the whole world to exercise traffic. . . . They have always been much delighted with all kind of civility and modest behavior: and it is accounted heinous among them for any man to utter in company, any bawdy or unseemly word. . . . These are the things which we thought most worthy of relation as concerning the civility, humanity, and upright dealing of the Barbarians.

→ # The Lady and the Blackamoor *1660?*

Although the earliest printed editions of "The Lady and the Blackamoor" date from the 1660s, this sensational ballad in which a black servant takes revenge for his master's harsh punishment seems to have been popular much earlier and remained in print into the nineteenth century. Tales of vengeful Moors are often set in classical Rome (even though the accompanying image, Figure 17, is thoroughly English). Since this is also a tale of "service," readers might want to consider the Moor's position in the household and ideas of service embedded in the text. It is also worth comparing both the Moor's justification for revenge and his ending with those of Iago. What relationship between the household and the larger world does the physical setting of the ballad (the moated castle surrounded by forest) suggest?

THE TUNE IS, *THE LADY'S FALL.*

In Rome a noble man did wed
   a virgin of great fame,
A fairer creature never did
   Dame Nature ever frame;
By whom he had two children fair,           5
   whose beauty did excel:
They were their parents' only joy,
   they loved them both so well.

The lord he loved to hunt the buck,
   the tiger, and the boar:              10
And still for swiftness always took
   with him a Blackamoor;
Which Blackamoor, within the wood,
   his lord he did offend,
For which he did him then correct,         15
   in hopes he would amend.

The day it grew unto an end,
   then homewards he did haste,
Where with his lady he did rest
   until the night was past.             20

---

"A Lamentable Ballad of the Tragical End of a Gallant Lord and a Virtuous Lady, with the Untimely End of Their Two Children, Wickedly Performed by a Heathenish Blackamoor Their Servant; The Like Never Heard Of" (1660?), *The Roxburghe Ballads*, vol. 2, ed. William Chappell (1869; New York: AMS Press, 1966), 48–55.

FIGURE 17 *Woodcut illustrating the ballad "The Lady and the Blackamoor," from* The Roxburghe Ballads.

Then in the morning he did rise,
   and did his servants call;
A hunting he provides to go:
   straight they were ready all.

To cause the toil[1] the lady did
   entreat him not to go;         25
"Alas, good lady," then quoth he,
   "why art thou grievèd so?
Content thyself: I will return
   with speed to thee again."        30
"Good father," (quoth the little babes)
   "with us here still remain."

"Farewell, dear children, I will go
   a fine thing for to buy."
But they therewith, nothing content,     35
   aloud began to cry.
The mother takes them by the hand,

[1] The meaning here is unclear; it is possible the line should read "to save the toil." [Hall]

saying, "Come, go with me
  Unto the highest tower, where
    your father you shall see." 40

The Blackamoor, perceiving now
    (who then did stay behind)
His lord to be a hunting gone,
    began to call to mind:
"My master he did me correct, 45
    my fault not being great;
Now of his wife I'll be reveng'd,
    she shall not me entreat."

The place was moted round about;
    the bridge he up did draw; 50
The gates he bolted very fast:
    of none he stood in awe.
He up into the tower went,
    the lady being there,
Who, when she saw his countenance grim, 55
    she straight began to fear.

But now my trembling heart it quakes
    to think what I must write;
My senses all begin to fail,
    my soul it doth affright: 60
Yet I must make an end of this,
    which here I have begun,
Which will make sad the hardest heart,
    before that I have done.

This wretch unto the Lady went, 65
    and her with speed did will
His lust forthwith to satisfy,
    his mind for to fulfill.
The lady she amazèd was
    to hear the villain speak, 70
"Alas!" (quoth she) "what shall I do?
    with grief my heart will break."

With that he took her in his arms;
    she straight for help did cry.
"Content yourself, lady," (he said) 75

"your husband is not nigh.
The bridge is drawn, the gates are shut,
   therefore come lie with me,
Or else I do protest and vow
   thy butcher I will be."            80

The crystal tears ran down her face;
   her children cried amain,[2]
And sought to help their mother dear,
   but all it was in vain:
For that outrageous filthy rogue,         85
   her hands behind her bound,
And then perforce with all his might
   he threw her on the ground.

With that she shrieked, her children cried,
   and such a noise did make,         90
That towns-folks, hearing her lament,
   did seek their parts to take;
But all in vain! no way was found
   to help the lady's need,
Who cried to them most piteously,        95
   "Oh help, oh help with speed."

Some run into the forest wide,
   her lord home for to call;
And they that stood still did lament
   this gallant lady's fall.         100
With speed her love came posting home,
   he could not enter in,
His lady's cries did pierce his heart,
   to call he did begin.

"O hold thy hand, thou savage Moor,      105
   to hurt her do forbear,
Or else be sure if I do live,
   wild horses shall thee tear."
With that the rogue ran to the wall,
   he having had his will,        110

---

[2] **amain:** with all their might, exceedingly. [Hall]

And brought one child under his arm,
   his dearest blood to spill.

The child, seeing his father there,
   to him for help did call:
"O, father, help my mother dear,            115
   we shall be killèd all."
Then fell the lord upon his knee,
   and did the Moor entreat
To save the life of his poor child,
   whose fear as then was great.          120

But this vile wretch the little child
   by both the heels did take,
And dashed his brains against the wall,
   whilst parents' hearts did ache.
That being done, straightway he ran       125
   the other child to fetch,
And plucked it from the mother's breast,
   most like a cruel wretch.

Within one hand a knife he brought,
   the child within the other;         130
And holding it over the wall,
   saying, "Thus die shall thy mother."
With that he cut the throat of it;
   then to the father he did call,
To look how he the head had cut,        135
   and down the head did fall.

This done he threw it down the wall,
   into the mote so deep.
Which made the father wring his hands,
   and grievously to weep.          140
Then to the lady went this rogue,
   who was near dead with fear;
Yet this vile wretch most cruelly
   did drag her by the hair;

And drew her to the very wall,         145
   which when the lord did see,
Then presently he cried out,

and fell upon his knee:
Quoth he, "If thou wilt save her life,
   whom I do love so dear,                150
I will forgive thee all is past,
   though they concern me near.

"O save her life, I thee beseech;
   O save her, I thee pray,
And I will grant thee what thou wilt      155
   demand of me this day."
"Well," quoth the Moor, "I do regard
   the moan that thou dost make;
If thou wilt grant me what I ask,
   I'll save her for thy sake."            160

"O save her life, and then demand
   of me what thing thou wilt."
"Cut off thy nose, and not one drop
   of her blood shall be spilt."
With that the lord presently took        165
   a knife within his hand,
And then his nose he quite cut off,
   in place where he did stand.

"Now I have bought the lady's life,"
   [he] to the Moor did call.         170
"Then take her," quoth this wicked rogue,
   and down he let her fall:
Which when her gallant lord did see,
   his senses all did fail;
Yet many sought to save his life,        175
   yet nothing could prevail.

When as the Moor did see him dead,
   then did he laugh amain
At them who for their gallant lord
   and lady did complain.         180
Quoth he, "I know you'll torture me,
   if that you can me get;
But all your threats I do not fear,
   nor yet regard one whit.

"Wild horses shall my body tear" —     185

"I know it to be true;
But I'll prevent you of that pain,"
    and down himself he threw —
Too good a death for such a wretch,
    a villain void of fear;                                    190
And thus doth end as sad a tale,
    as ever man did hear.

## The Ottoman Empire and "Turning Turk"

Never seen, the "Turk" nonetheless menaces *Othello*, particularly in its opening scenes. As the Duke and the Senate worry over the looming Ottoman
threat to the island of Cyprus (1.3.1–51), audience members would have been
well aware that the Muslim Ottoman empire, which Richard Knolles
famously called "the present terror of the world," had long been in control of
Cyprus. Throughout the sixteenth century, London would hum with
reports of Ottoman successes in Mediterranean and Balkan battles as well
as reports of Christians captured through war or piracy who were made
slaves or forcibly converted to Islam. The Ottoman empire initially grew
largely through the conquest of formerly Christian territories in the Eastern
Mediterranean. Ruling over the same territory that had once belonged to
the legendary emperor Constantine, "the Ottoman polity seemed to have
arisen like a monster out of the Byzantine ashes" (Goffman 12). In the
English mind, each Mediterranean battle held out the possibility of the
advancement of Islam and the extinction of Christianity, and therefore the
damnation of each Christian.

The empire's expansion coincided with the spread of print technology, and
a vast body of literature appeared concerning the Ottoman empire and Islam.
Works like Baudier's *Inventory of the General History of the Turks* (see Figure 19
on p. 206) kept concern over Ottoman might in the air; news of military
battles — at Malta, Lepanto, Cyprus, and elsewhere — spread throughout
Europe. Iago offers his participation in such battles as proof that he deserves
promotion: "And I, of whom his eyes had seen the proof / At Rhodes, at Cyprus, and on other grounds / Christened and heathen" (1.1.29–31). The prayer
from Elizabeth I's reign (see p. 216), along with ballads and broadsides about
renegados (Christian converts to Islam) or sea battles, shows how news about
Ottoman actions would have spread through all levels of society. For early
modern Europe, one could say, Islam was "a lasting trauma" (Said 60).

English fears of Ottoman religious and political domination in the early
modern period coalesced in the figure of the Turk. Like *Moor*, *Turk* was a

## ST. IAGO MATAMOROS

In giving the name Iago to Cinthio's unnamed conniving ensign, Shakespeare evokes cultural and political associations with Spain, which Barbara Everett notes "was the leading power of Europe, and as such, played a huge part in the Elizabethan consciousness" (68). Spain's seven-century history of Islamic occupation and vexed diplomatic relations with England during Shakespeare's time subtly animates many aspects of the play (see Everett; Griffin; Orlin, *Private Matters* 202–07). Associated with the third Apostle James and known throughout Europe as the "Slayer of Moors," St. James or Saint Iago is the patron saint of Spain; his divine presence is credited with triumph in battle and he becomes the embodiment of militant Christian resistance to Islam. This fresco is one of many images that circulated in Europe depicting St. James bringing down Islamic forces in the ninth century Battle of Clavijo; it offers a powerful image of Christian superiority which allayed fears of Islamic might that gripped sixteenth-century Europe. Likewise, Roderigo, who has no equivalent in Cinthio, may be named for Don Rodrigo, El Cid or "the Challenger," a legendary fighter against Moors. Lena Orlin demon-

FIGURE 18 Fresco of St. James Riding over the Corpses of Saracens, *from Il Sodoma (Giovanni Antonio Bazzi, Il Sodoma), Spanish Chapel, S. Spirito, Siena, Italy.*

strates that ideas of sexual appropriation and violence surface throughout Spanish legends of Islamic conquest (*Private Matters* 202–05), and readers might wish to think about what it meant for Shakespeare to give Iago and Roderigo names so durably linked to the Spanish occupation by and conquest of Moors.

Although Christian triumph in Spain was admired, the country's polyglot, multiethnic character and fervent Catholicism made it a foil for England in the English imagination. The storm that defeats the Ottoman forces in *Othello* may very well allude to the storm that helped the English defeat the Spanish Armada in 1588 and became a defining moment of English nationalism. Like the Lepanto (see p. 251), this victory had religious overtones; read as a sign of God's favor against a Catholic enemy, it fed England's nationalist Protestant fervor. Spain also loomed large in England's conceptions of race: Spain's history of conquest by the Moors and its practices of cultural mixture in exploitation of the Americas made Spain the embodiment of mixed or impure blood.

St. James of course also refers to England's monarch, James I. One of James I's most controversial acts was to make peace with Spain despite popular English enmity. In fact, Barbara Everett suggests that his overtures to Spain took place at the same time that the government debated sending aid to Moorish rebels in Valencia (68). These multiple references to Spain raise several questions about naming in *Othello*: What's the political significance of naming the play's villain after the ruling monarch and a legendary killer of Moors? What does it mean that Brabantio may be named after the Netherlands' Brabant, at the time ruled by Spain? This fresco of Saint Giacomo defeating Islamic forces shares much with the rich iconography of Saint Iago. How does Sodoma make use of dark and light? Does Saint Iago resemble any other religious figure?

---

generic term with a wide range of references: it conflated Turkish people, Muslims, and the Ottoman state in almost entirely disparaging ways. During most of the Renaissance, writers used the derogatory term *Mahumetan* to refer to Muslims; the word *Muslim* itself was first coined in the early seventeenth century. Nabil Matar warns that "simplification and stereotyping were the rules by which Britons represented Muslims" (116). Nicholas Nicolay's lurid description is typical of descriptions of Muslim piracy: "The most part of the Turks of Alger . . . are Christians reined, or Mahumetised, of all Nations, but most of them Spaniards, Italians, and of Provence, of the Islands and Coasts of the Sea Mediterane, given all to whoredom, sodomy, theft, and all other detestable vices, living only of rovings, spoils and pilling [pillaging] at the Seas" (B4$^r$).

FIGURE 19 *Michel Baudier,* Inventaire de l'histoire generalle des Turcz *(1631).* *This frontispiece from* The Inventory of the General History of the Turks *vividly evokes the desire for advantage against the Ottoman empire. The top panel indicates that Ottoman defeat assumes Muslim conversion to Christianity. Notice how this image of defeat undoes the idea of Islamic might seen in writings about Islam and images such as the portrait of the Moroccan ambassador in Figure 15, page 184. Compare the confident Christian warrior on the left with the enchained and defeated Turk on the right. Compare both images with that of St. James in Figure 18, page 204.*

English writings on the Turk, particularly for the stage, demonized Islam and the Ottomans, rendering them cruel, barbarous, bloody, corrupt, militaristic, and sexually promiscuous. Christian misreadings of the Koran and Muslim practice heavily associate Islam with unruly sexuality, including sodomy (Matar 109–27; Vitkus, *Turning* 86–90). Muslims "were represented as a people who defied God, nature and English law, and therefore deserved punishment" (Matar 112); the Ottoman empire in particular was seen as brutal and tyrannical, even if at times unmanly. Fascinated by Ottoman dynastic politics, observers circulated numerous stories of Ottoman rulers as despots who dispensed a rather arbitrary justice. For Richard Knolles (see p. 210), the empire was a politically absolutist state whose tyranny reached into every facet of Ottoman life. As the Nicolay quote in the preceding paragraph suggests, conversion to Islam was not uncommon in Muslim states. The popular phrase "to turn Turk" entered the language about the time of *Othello* and referred to the English citizen's deepest fear: conversion to Islam and thus damnation. The association of Islam with hypersexuality also gave the phrase sexual connotations including the secondary meaning "to become a whore" or "to commit adultery" (Vitkus, *Turning* 88). Moreover, religious conversion was described in erotic terms: "converts to Catholicism were accused of sleeping with the papal 'whore of Babylon' and spiritually fornicating with the Devil's minions" (Vitkus, *Turning* 84). How does a discourse of conversion frame Othello's suspicions in the following lines: "Sir, she can turn, and turn, and yet go on / And turn again; and she can weep, sir, weep" (4.1.246–47)? What other characters are said to "turn" in the play? What values are placed on "turning"? Several characters move or "return" from one space or psychological state to another; thus, readers might consider mental "turning" in the context of other movement in the play.

According to English writers, Englishmen were "turned Turk" either through forced conversion after they were captured and enslaved or through the thinly understood Ottoman practice of *devşirme*. In this practice, described by Knolles in this section, the sultanate captured, enslaved, and converted non-Muslim boys to supply the empire's need for warriors and statesmen. Torn from family and community, these "tribute children," as Knolles calls them, were converted to Islam, taught Turkish, and made to affirm loyalty to the sultan. Some would grow into prominent men, particularly in the famed janissary corps. Several modern historians suggest that the wholly negative view of this practice given in European sources be read with other evidence that some families saw it as a way out of stagnating poverty: it is possible that men taken through this system were not as utterly alienated from family and community as Knolles and many modern historians insist (Goffman 68). Nonetheless, the practice intensified the shame of

Christian defeat and added to fears of Ottoman cruelty. Perhaps even greater than the fear that one might be forced to "turn Turk" was the (largely unspoken) horror that a Christian might convert voluntarily to Islam. Christian adventurers, pirates, and mercenaries worked for Ottoman forces: the Ottomans' notable acceptance of diverse religions within the empire made it easy for merchants, statesmen, and others doing business to settle comfortably in their lands (see Goffman 139), a practice at times misread by many English. Moreover, the borderlands of the Ottoman empire may have seemed a haven for those escaping the religious tyranny of some Christian states. In contrast, England maintained a strong separation between Christians and other religious groups.

Indeed, the Ottoman empire's greater accommodation of individual cultures and religions, with the blurring of distinctions it allowed, may have been the greatest threat it posed. Several men who were captured and served under Ottoman rule returned to England and wrote of their experiences. Nabil Matar astutely notes that the interest in these returned captives suggests a deeper insecurity in Christian identity. So, too, the tales of *devşirme* show a similar vulnerability under which the attributes of English identity — family loyalty, local origins, religion, loyalty to the monarch — could mutate through Ottoman influence. The fear of enslavement was the obverse of a deeper fear that Christians might willingly seek out the freedom of Ottoman religious toleration or pursue possibilities for advancement not available in less mobile Christian Europe.

While the popular image of Islam and of the Turks as a monstrous, invading evil suffused the English imagination, individual English travelers and politicians were capable of much more subtle views. There was an impressive amount of cross-cultural contact between the Ottoman court and Christian states. In the 1580s, England began commercial and diplomatic relations with the empire to an extent that the "the Pope viewed Elizabeth as 'confederate' with the Turk" (quoted in Matar 20; see also Burton 58–68). Literate English people would have had quite a bit of information about Turkish customs as well as Ottoman social, judicial, and political institutions. A few writers showed evidence of Turkish courtesy, courage, discipline, and humor, but many more were fascinated by Ottoman dynastic politics and offered grudging admiration for Ottoman military prowess. One of the Venetian senators in *Othello* cautions: "We must not think the Turk is so unskillful / To leave that latest which concerns him first" (1.3.29–30). England, struggling into a new era of militarism (see Chapter 4), feared and marveled at the empire's ability to manage a huge standing army without bankrupting the state. *Othello* economically combines the negative and positive: acknowledgment of Ottoman discipline merges with the image of "turning Turk" as a descent into barbarity: "Are we turned Turks, and to ourselves do that / Which heaven hath forbid the Ottomites?" (2.3.148–49).

→ RICHARD KNOLLES

## *From* The General History of the Turks     *1603*

Schoolteacher and historian Richard Knolles (late 1540s–1610) wrote the first major book on the Ottoman empire in English. His *General History of the Turks* "launched Ottoman studies in Britain" (Andrea, "Pamphilia's" 349). Primarily a compilation of previous writings about the Ottoman empire from a range of continental sources, it achieved great popularity and was reprinted and amended for over one hundred years. Where does Knolles find vulnerability at the same time that he represents Ottoman might? Why are the fates of "tribute children" of such concern?

### A Brief Discourse of the Greatness of the Turkish Empire

The History of the Turks (being indeed nothing else but the true record of the woeful ruins of the greatest part of the Christian commonweal) thus as before passed through, and at length brought to end; and their empire (of all others now upon earth far the greatest) as a proud champion still standing up as it were in defiance of the whole world. I thought it good for the conclusion of this my labor, to propose unto the view of the zealous Christian, the greatness thereof and so near as I could to set down the bounds and limits within the which it is (by the goodness of God) as yet contained, together with the strength and power thereof. . . .

The Othoman government in this his so great empire is altogether like the government of the master over the slave, and indeed more tyranical. For the great Sultan is so absolute a lord of all things within the compass of his empire, that all his subjects and people be they never so great, do call themselves his slaves and not his subjects: neither hath any man power over himself, much less is he lord of the house wherein he dwelleth, or of the land which he tilleth, except some few families in Constantinople, unto whom

Richard Knolles, *The General History of the Turks from the first beginning of that Nation to the rising of the Ottoman family: with all the notable expeditions of the Christian princes against them* (London, 1603), Fffff–Fffffii; Ggggg–Gggggii.

FIGURE 20 *Frontispiece, from Richard Knolles,* The General History of the Turks *(1603).*

some few such things were by way of reward and upon special favor given by *Mahomet* the second, at such time as he won the same. . . . In which is so absolute a sovereignty (by any free born people not to be endured) the tyrant preserveth himself by two most especial means: first by taking of all arms from his natural subjects; and then by putting the same and all things else concerning the state and the government thereof into the hands of the Apostata or renegade Christians,[1] whom for most part every third, fourth, or fifth year (or oftener if his need so require) be taken in their childhood from their miserable parents, as his tenths or tribute children. Whereby he gaineth two great commodities: first for that in so doing he spoileth the provinces he most feareth of the flower, sinews, and strength of the people, choice being still made of the strongest youths and fittest for war: then, for that with these as with his own creatures he armeth himself, and by them assureth his state. For they in their childhood taken from their parents' laps and delivered in charge to one or other appointed to that purpose, quickly and before they be aware become Mahometanes; and so no more acknowledging father or mother, depend wholly of the great Sultan, who to make use of them, both feeds them and fosters them, at whose hands only they look for all things, and whom they thank for all. Of which fry[2] so taken from their Christian parents (the only seminary[3] of his wars) some become horsemen, some footmen, and so in time the greatest commanders of his state and empire next unto himself, the natural Turks in the mean time giving themselves wholly unto the trade of merchandise and other their mechanical occupations: or else unto the feeding of cattle, their most ancient and natural vocation, not intermeddling at all with matters of government or state. . . .

So that by this we have already said is easily to be gathered how much the Turk is too strong for any one of the neighbor princes, either Mahometanes or Christians, bordering upon him, and therefore to be of them the more feared. Yet least some mistaking me, might think, What, is then the Turk invincible? Far be that thought from me, to think any enemy of Christ Jesu (be his arm never so strong) to be able to withstand his power, either quite to devour his little flock, rage he never so much about it. As for the Turk, the most dangerous and professed enemy of the Christian commonweal, be his strength so great, yea and happily greater too than is before declared (the greatness of his dominions and empire considered) yet is he not to be thought therefore invincible, or his power indeed so great as it in show seemeth for to be. . . . It is not otherwise to be thought, but that he bringeth

---

[1] **Apostata or renegade Christians:** apostate or deserter, one who renounces religious faith.
[2] **fry:** children, offspring.   [3] **seminary:** place of origin and early development.

FIGURE 21 *Osman, from Philip Lonicer,* Chronicorum Turcicorum *(1578). This engraving of the Osman, the founder of the Ottoman empire, stresses the ferocity Europeans thought key to Ottoman military might. Compare this figure with the defeated soldiers in the Sodoma fresco on page 204.*

into the field far more men than good soldiers, more bravery than true valor, more show than worth, his multitude being his chiefest strength, his supposed greatness the terror of his neighbor princes, and both together the very majesty of his Empire. Which although it be indeed very strong (for the reasons before alleged) yet is it by many probably thought to be now upon the declining hand, their late emperors in their own persons far degenerating from their warlike progenitors, their soldiers generally giving themselves to unwonted pleasures, their ancient discipline of war neglected, their superstition not with so much zeal as of old regarded, and rebellions in divers parts of his Empire of late strangely raised, and mightily supported: all of the signs of a declining state. Which were they not at all to be seen, as indeed they be very pregnant, yet the greatness of this Empire being such as that it laboreth with nothing more than the weightiness of itself, it must needs (after the manner of worldly things) of itself fall, and again come to nought, no man knowing when or how so great a work shall be brought to pass, but he in whose deep counsels all these great revolutions of empires and kingdoms are from eternity shut up: who at his pleasure shall in due time by such means as he seeth best accomplish the same, to the unspeakable comfort of his poor afflicted flock, in one place or other still in danger to be by this roaring lion devoured. Which work of so great wonder, he for his son our Savior Christ his sake, the glory of his name, and comfort of many thousand oppressed Christians fed with the bread of carefulness amidst the furnace of tribulation, in mercy hasten, that we with them, and they with us, all as members of one body, may continually sing, Unto him be all honor and praise world without end.

→ GILES FLETCHER THE ELDER

## *From* Policy of the Turkish Empire                            *1597*

This anonymously published treatise was one of several that purported to explain why the Ottoman empire dominated Christian forces. Its chapter 5 discusses conversion to Islam from Christianity, popularly known as "turning Turk." The word *policy* is highly ambiguous; readers might compare its use here with the excerpt from Nicholas Udall's *Respublica* (pp. 222–23).

### To the Reader

Many men do wonder at the great power and puissance of the Turks: and they think it is strange, how this nation (being a people most rude and barbarous, and their beginning most base, vile, and ignominious) could attain within the compass of so few years, to the excessive height of their present

Giles Fletcher the Elder, *Policy of the Turkish Empire* (London, 1597), A3r–A3v, F2r–F4v.

greatness. Which their admiration (as it seemeth) proceedeth only of ignorance: Because they know not the manner nor the means, by which they have so suddenly prevailed in their Conquests. For such as are acquainted with the Histories of the Turkish affairs, and do advisedly look into the order and course of their proceedings do well perceive, that the chiefest cause of their sudden and fearful puissance, hath been the excellency of their Martial discipline joined with a singular desire and resolution to advance and enlarge both the bounds of their Empire and the profession of their Religion. The which was always accompanied with such notable Policy[1] and prudence, that the singularity of their virtue and good government hath made their Arms always fearful and fortunate, and consequently hath caused the greatness of their estate.

And yet, as their virtue hath made them way to their excessive fortune: so is this one thing worthy to be wondered at: how so rare virtue could be found in so brutish and barbarous a nation, rather than how they could attain to so great conquests and dominions. Considering therefore both the wonderful puissance of their Empire: and conferring it with the baseness and obscurity of their beginning, as also with the barbarousness of their disposition. To the intent this strange union and conjunction of so rare virtues with so notable Barbarism might be the better discovered, I supposed it would be a matter neither unpleasing nor unprofitable in some sort to make known that order of Policy, Discipline, and government, by which the Turks have purchased so goodly and glorious Empire: making themselves Lord and masters of a great part of the world: in so much as the fury of their Arms hath not only by this means swallowed up infinite, and those most mighty nations in the East. But the terror of their name doth even now make the kings and Princes of West, with the weak and dismembered relics of their kingdoms and estates, to tremble and quake through the fear of their victorious forces. . . .

## CHAPTER 5

And notwithstanding the equality which they acknowledge in these three Prophets[2]: yet they do hold that Mahomet is to be loved, honored and reverenced in the highest and chiefest place next to God himself. Because he is the last Prophet that God will send into the world: And because the law which God hath revealed by him, is now only in force, and so ought to continue, and to be observed unto the end of the world. And this is the cause,

---

[1] **Policy:** statecraft or diplomacy; also political cunning or dissimulation.  [2] **three Prophets:** Muhammed, Moses, and Jesus, said to be descendants of the sons of Abraham.

why they are taught and enjoined out of this commandment, not only to love and honor God, but also to reverence and love his Prophet Mahomet before all other things whatsoever. Whereunto the Turks do accordingly with notable vehemency intend all their thoughts and endeavors, using all possible reverence and devotion both in naming and speaking of him. In so much that if there be any one that blasphemeth God, and another do blaspheme Mahomet, the former shall be punished only with a hundreth stripes and blows of the Bastinado,[3] but the latter is sure to lose his life for it.

And they yield this reason for it. Because God, being omnipotent, can and will plague the blasphemers of his holy name with any plagues whatsoever, as it shall seem good unto him: but Mahomet being no God but a poor Prophet cannot revenge that injury done unto him. For which cause they say, that they (who profess and are to observe the law given by Mahomet) are bound to see it most severely punished. Besides, they do think by virtue of this commandment, in regard of their love, devotion, and duty to Mahomet, that they are bound by all means as in them lieth, to amplify and increase their Religion in all parts of the world, both arms and otherwise: and that it is lawful for them to enforce and compel to allure, to seduce, and to persuade all men to embracing of their sect and superstitions: and to prosecute all such with fire and sword, as shall either oppose themselves against their Religion, or shall refuse to conform and submit themselves to their Ceremonies and traditions. And this they do to the intent [that] the name and doctrine of their Prophet Mahomet may be everywhere, and of all nations reverenced and embraced. Hence it is that the Turks do desire nothing more than to draw both Christians and others to embrace their Religion and to turn Turk. And they do hold that in so doing they do God good service, be it by any means good or bad, right or wrong.

For this cause they do plot and devise sundry ways how to gain them to their faith. And many times when they see that no other means will prevail, they will frame false accusations against them; saying, that either they did blaspheme the name of Mahomet or some of their Prophets: or that they did argue and dispute of their law and religion, or some such like matter: which being strictly forbidden by their laws, is punishable by death. And to prove them guilty they will find many, sometimes forty or fifty false witnesses to testify and aver the accusation. For there be certain of their Priests (of whom we shall speak hereafter) who for a Ducat[4] or some such small reward, will swear a thousand untruths, especially if it be to condemn a Christian: against whom they think it a great honor to forswear themselves: because it may be an occasion to make him forsake Christianity and to turn

---

[3] **Bastinado:** stick, staff, or rod.    [4] **Ducat:** gold coin.

Turk. For being thus convicted by the testimony of those false wretches, they have judgment presently given either to suffer death by being burnt or else to abjure their religion, and to embrace the law and profession of Mahometism: whereof it ensueth that there scant passeth any one year, but there is some one or other which doeth suffer martyrdom for the faith of Christ, but many more for fear of death do change their religion, and deny their faith. Of whom they do afterwards make so great reckoning and account, that they are not only rewarded with store of money, livings and other necessaries for their maintenance: but commonly they are preferred and advance to great offices, dignities and honors. All which showeth most apparently, how reverently and devoutly they do esteem of their Prophet, and how vehemently they are addicted to the maintenance of his superstitions: seeing they make no conscience of such wicked and detestable practices to gain men to their sect and religion, and to procure them to be circumcised: which is the proper mark and (as it were) the badge and cognizance of a professed Turk or Musulman.[5] For that they think not any man to be rightly religious as a true Mahometist, unless he takes upon him this mark of Circumcision.

[5] **Musulman**: Muslim.

→ CHURCH OF ENGLAND

# Prayer for the Preservation of Those Christians and Their Countries That Are Now Invaded by the Turk    *1566*

It was not uncommon for the monarch to order special prayers in times of national crisis. While several prayers were issued during Elizabeth I's reign that called on God to protect Christians subject to Ottoman invasion, the text printed here responds to a battle over Malta and was written "to excite all godly people to pray unto God for the delivery of those Christians that are now invaded by the Turk." Church attendance was mandatory on Sundays and des-

---

Church of England, "A Form to be used in Common Prayer, every Sunday, Wednesday, and Friday, through the Whole Realm: To Excite and Stir all godly people to pray unto God for the Preservation of those Christians and their Countries, that are now invaded by the Turk in Hungary, or elsewhere," *Liturgical services: Liturgies and Occasional Forms of Prayer set forth in the Reign of Queen Elizabeth*, ed. William Keatinge Clay (Cambridge: Cambridge University Press, 1847), 527–35.

ignated holy days, but here all ministers are told to urge parishioners to come to the church on Wednesdays and Fridays "with as many of their family as may be spared from their necessary business." The prayer also gives a plan for a service that includes a reading from Psalms.

## THE PREFACE

Where as the Turks the last year most fiercely assailing the Isle of *Malta*, with a great army and navy, by the grace and assistance of Almighty God (for the which we with other Christians at that time by our hearty prayers made most humble suit) were from thence repelled and driven, with their great loss, shame and confusion; they, being inflamed with malice and desire of vengeance, do now by land invade the kingdom of Hungary (which hath of long time been as a most strong wall and defence to all Christendom) far more terribly and dreadfully, and with greater force and violence, than they did either the last year, or at any time within the remembrance of man: It is our parts, which for distance of place cannot succour them with temporal aid of men, to assist them at the least with spiritual aid, that is to say, with earnest, hearty, and fervent prayer to Almighty God for them, desiring him, after the examples of Moses, Josaphat, Ezechias, and other godly men, in his great mercy to defend, preserve, and deliver Christians, professing his holy name, and to give sufficient might and power to the Emperor's excellent Majesty, as God's principal minister, to repress the rage and violence of these Infidels, who by all tyranny and cruelty labor utterly to root out not only true religion, but also the very name and memory of Christ our only Savior, and all Christianity. And forsomuch as if the Infidels, who have already a great part of that most goodly and strong kingdom in their possession, should prevail wholly against the same (which God forbid) all the rest of Christendom should lie as it were naked and open to the incursions and invasions of the said savage and most cruel enemies the Turks, to the most dreadful danger of whole Christendom; all diligence, heartiness, and fervency is so much the more now to be used in our prayers for God's aid, how far greater the danger and peril is now, than before it was. And although it is every Christian man's duty, of his own devotion to pray at all times: yet for that the corrupt nature of man is so slothful and negligent in this his duty, he hath need by often and sundry means to be stirred up, and put in remembrance of his duty. For the effectual accomplishment whereof, it is ordered and appointed as followeth.

First, that all Parsons and Curates shall exhort their parishioners to endeavor themselves to come unto the Church, with as many of their family, as may be spared from their necessary business: And they to resort thither, not only upon Sundays and holidays, but also upon Wednesdays and Fridays, during this dangerous and perilous time: exhorting them there reverently and godly to behave themselves, and with penitent minds, kneeling on their knees, to lift up their hearts, and pray to the merciful God to turn from us, and all Christendom, those plagues and punishments, which we and they through our unthankfulness and sinful lives have deserved.

Secondly, that the said Parsons and Curates shall then distinctly and plainly read the general confession appointed in the book of Service, with the residue of the Morning prayer, unto the first lesson. . . .

## THE PRAYER

Almighty and everliving God, our heavenly Father, we thy disobedient and rebellious children, now by thy just judgment sore afflicted, and in great danger to be oppressed, by thine and our sworn and most deadly enemies, the Turks, Infidels, and miscreants, do make humble suit to the throne of thy grace, for thy mercy and aid against the same our mortal enemies. For though we do profess the name of thy only Son Christ our Savior, yet through our manifold sins and wickedness we have most justly deserved so much of thy wrath and indignation, that we can not but say: O Lord, correct us in thy mercy, and not in thy fury. And better it is for us to fall into thy hands, than into the hands of men, and especially into the hands of Turks and Infidels, thy professed enemies, who now invade thine inheritance. Against thee (O Lord) have we sinned, and transgressed thy command-ments: Against Turks, Infidels, and other enemies of the Gospel of thy dear Son Jesus Christ have we not offended, but only in this, that we acknowl-edge thee, the eternal Father, and thy only Son our redeemer, with the Holy Ghost, the comforter, to be one only true, almighty, and everliving God. For if we would deny and blaspheme thy most holy name, forsake the Gospel of thy dear Son, embrace false religion, commit horrible Idolatries, and give ourselves to all impure, wicked, and abominable life, as they do; the devil, the world, the Turk, and all other thine enemies would be at peace with us, according to the saying of thy Son Christ: If you were of the world, the world would love his own. But therefore hate they us, because we love thee; therefore persecute they us, because we acknowledge thee God the Father, and Jesus Christ thy Son, whom thou hast sent. The Turk goeth about to set up, to extol, and to magnify that wicked monster and damned soul Mahumet, above thy dearly beloved Son Jesus Christ, whom we in heart believe, and with mouth confess to be our only savior and redeemer. Wherefore awake, O Lord our God and heavenly Father, and with thy fatherly and merciful countenance look upon us thy children, and all such Christians, as are now by those most cruel enemies invaded and assaulted: overthrow and destroy thine and our enemies, sanctify thy blessed name among us, which they blaspheme, establish thy kingdom, which they labor to overthrow: suffer not thine enemies to prevail against those that now call upon thy name and put their trust in thee, lest the Heathen and Infidels say: Where is now their GOD? But in thy great mercy save, defend, and deliver all thy afflicted Christians, in this and all other invasions of these infidels, and give to the Emperor[1] thy servant, and all the Christian army now assembled with him, thy comfortable might and courage, that we and they that delight to be named Christians, may enjoy both outward peace, and inwardly laud, praise, and magnify thy holy name for ever, with thy only Son Jesus Christ, and the Holy Ghost, to whom be all laud, praise, glory and empire for ever and ever. Amen.

## Christianity

England's break with Catholicism, although a momentous event, turned out to be less a total rejection of the Catholic church and the authority of Rome than a series of skirmishes over the establishment of the "true" religion. In the memorable words of John Foxe in 1578: "Christian divinity is tossed and turmoiled to and fro, with innumerable, intricated, entangled, and wandering questions" (quoted in Shapiro 141) as citizens experienced religious changes imposed by each successive ruler: the country was Protestant under Henry VIII, Catholic under Mary Tudor, and then Protestant again under Elizabeth I. Reconciling these "intricated, entangled, and wandering questions," occupied much of Elizabeth's reign and shaped attitudes toward her successor, James I. Much effort went into resolving the "crisis of religious identity produced by England's break with Catholicism" (Shapiro 134). Elizabeth I faced the complex problem of creating a unifying church that did not alienate otherwise loyal subjects who held on to time-honored beliefs and practices. The *Book of Common Prayer*, published in 1549, had begun to create a national church by setting forth uniform liturgies in a common language. Elizabeth ratified other policies that continued this sense of commonality.

However, England, particularly London, was a place of legal uniformity yet religious diversity. Even with her attempts at moderation, Elizabeth's later reign was in many ways shaped by the rise of a radical Protestantism

---

[1] Maximilian II lay then encamped in the vicinity of Raab, with the main body of his army, to watch the motions of the Turks, who, under Süleyman, again entered Hungary in the spring of 1566. Coxe's *House of Austria*, Vol. II. p. 322.

that some of the most important writers of the age — Sir Philip Sidney and Edmund Spenser, among others — supported in political action and literature. A sense of England as the keeper of a "true" religion was shored up by cultural and legal means. In addition to making Protestantism the only legal religion, treatises and books debating the nature of the true church circulated widely among the educated, often containing stridently anti-Catholic imagery that shored up England's image of itself as a righteous nation. Catholicism became not simply a doctrinal difference, but a possible treason and source of damnation. Protestant rhetoric heatedly linked Catholicism, Islam, and Judaism as powerful threats to true Christianity.

The most salient aspect of English religious belief, both Catholic and Protestant, was its materiality. As you will see throughout this volume, English texts of all genres are embedded with a sense of a world of temptation in which people must daily struggle against the devices of evil. Spiritual struggles that are in modern times represented as internal debate took place for early moderns in the physical world ruled by a Manichaean struggle between good and evil. While this is clearer in the more ardent Protestant writers, the spiritual was understood and felt tangibly by all Christians. For believers of all stripes, the fear of damnation was palpable; thus, when Othello asks, "Have you prayed tonight, Desdemon?" (5.2.26), and inquires about the state of his wife's soul, the audience might feel the very real sense of a soul put in peril, perhaps by the very infidel/devil they so feared.

Satan loomed large within the early moderns' highly visible, very tangible cosmography — as he does in *Othello*. The word *devil* appears more often in *Othello* than in almost any other Shakespeare play. Critic S. L. Bethell calls the play "a solemn game of hunt the devil" (72). Leah Scragg notes, "The word 'devil' is passed constantly from mouth to mouth. Much of the action of the play seems to take place in the darkness and horror of hell itself" (62).

Early modern depictions of the devil may have been as influenced by assumptions rooted in folk culture and folkways as by the Bible (Oldridge 61). The devil was not an abstraction or a distanced threat from the afterlife, but a very real entity who could destroy sinners in this world and after. Letting one's guard down in any way (with drunkenness or lust, for example) made one susceptible to the devil's wiles. The devil and his minions appeared often in popular culture: contemporary crime pamphlets often "identified Satan as the originator of murderous thoughts" (Oldridge 82). Morality plays, folktales, and ballads all made the devil a living being with a desire to destroy human souls; they stressed physical attacks by the devil over spiritual torment (Oldridge 58). In them, the devil appears as a supernatural avenger, yet with a very human personality. As in medieval literature, he is playful and humorous, a seducer of mankind.

Thus, medieval religious performances provided England with one of the most dramatically compelling figures to hit the stage: the villain (also called the vice). *Othello's dramatis personae*[1] identifies Iago as a villain, thereby locating him within a tradition familiar to his audience (Barthelemy, *Black Face* 72–80; Scragg; Spivak). Rather than showing Satan or his lesser minions, as often happened in the mystery cycles, the morality plays put Satan's energy into the figure of the vice or villain and, although he was an allegorical representation of evil and mankind's frailty, his dramatic vitality was such that he survived the decline of the morality play to influence later drama. Richard III, Aaron in *Titus Andronicus*, and Iago are all the dramatic successors to the vice and share his most vivid qualities: seductive duplicity, mocking irreverence, histrionic style, challenge to accepted morality, and intimacy with the audience. Emilia's ironic description of the person who has caused Othello's jealousy evokes the stage villain: "I will be hanged if some eternal villain, / Some busy and insinuating rogue, / Some cogging, cozening slave, to get some office, / Have not devised this slander" (4.2.137–40).

Iago specifically reminds the audience of his own kinship with this figure: "And what's he then that says I play the villain, / When this advice is free I give, and honest" (2.3.296–97). He further enacts the tradition by pointing out the duplicity of his actions and his use of honesty for dishonest ends. Iago continually lets us in on his plans, and it is this intimacy that is one of the most commented-on characteristics of the vice and the vice-inspired villain. Such familiarity is most often achieved through soliloquies, monologues, or mocking asides; the audience is in on the game from the beginning and shares the villain's superior knowledge. Indeed, one of the horrors of watching *Othello* is that peculiar sense of being involved in the action, of knowing too much and not being able to stop the tragic unfolding of events. Since Iago is also the spokesman of the most overt racism and sexism in the play, this raises the question of whether his asides make us complicit in these positions, if not in the action. The Tudor play *Respublica* (see p. 222) opens with the vice, Avarice, introducing himself to the audience, and it may be useful to compare his view of his own deception with Iago's. How do they both attach themselves to the audience?

Iago's roots in the vice tradition also speak to one of the most vexing issues of his character: the problem of motive. He gives the audience three reasons for executing his plans, and most critics agree that none of them sufficiently accounts for the devastation he wreaks. Critics disagree vehemently about which of his motives are most credible or, if indeed, he really means any of them at all. The poet Coleridge famously called him "motiveless

[1] Literally, "the persons of the drama," a list of characters who will appear onstage.

malignity." Critic Bernard Spivack argues that the multiple attributions of motives without emotional attachment to them indicate Iago's relationship to the vice: "They express themselves as moved by resentment, ambition, hatred, professional and sexual jealousy, but they do not behave as if they were so moved" (35). Instead, they revel in their own machinations, in their ability to make mischief and lead others astray. In contrast, Leah Scragg sees Iago more as a stage devil who is "a jealous outsider to the world of virtue. . . . Hence the 'daily beauty' of the lives of Othello, Cassio, and Desdemona is a constant affront to him" (64).

→ NICHOLAS UDALL

## *From* Respublica

1553

An overarching sense of tangible spiritual conflict complements efforts by the church to make doctrinal and ethical problems come alive for the layperson. Early liturgical drama made the scripture that was heard rather abstractly in church sermons more concrete and meaningful to the lay audience. Mystery cycles and morality plays evolved from such church performances and were popular from the thirteenth century well into the sixteenth. The mystery cycles, initially sponsored by medieval guilds, would display a biblical history of the world for an entire town. Morality plays, often performed in churches or guildhalls, took on more abstract ethical or religious principles. Titles like *Everyman* or *Mankind* reveal the plays' focus on a single character representing all humanity. Through dissimulation and persuasion, a vice or villain leads a soul to damnation, as in *Respublica*. Elizabethans (including Shakespeare) were shown the soul's struggle for salvation through actors who embodied and portrayed these cosmic conflicts between the forces of good and the forces of evil. Every townsperson would see his or her stage double literally talk with and be tempted by Avarice, Lust, Pride, and other deadly sins, and be brought to temptation or salvation by the agents of God or the devil.

AVARICE:    Ye must pardon my wits, for I tell you plain
     I have a hive of humble bees swarming in my brain
     And he that hath the compass to fetch[1] that[2]
          I must fetch,

---

[1] **fetch:** reach.    [2] **that:** that which.

---

Nicholas Udall, *Respublica. Recently Recovered "Lost" Tudor Plays with Some Others*, ed. John S. Farmer (New York: Barnes and Noble, 1966), 239–40.

I may say in Council, had need his wits to stretch. 5
But now what my name is and what is my purpose,
Taking you all for friends I fear not to disclose.
My very true unchristian name is Avarice,
Which I may not have openly known in no wise,
For though to most men I am found commodious, 10
Yet to those that use me my name is Odious,
For who is so foolish that the evil he hath wrought
For his own behoof he would to light should be brought,
Or who had not rather his ill doings to hide
Than to have the same bruited on every side? 15
Therefore to work my feat I will my name disguise,
And call my name Policy instead of Covetise.
The name of Policy is praised of each one
But to rake[3] gromwell seed Avarice is alone.
The name of Policy is of none suspected, 20
Policy is ne'er of any crime detected,
So that under the name and cloak of Policy
Avarice may work facts and 'scape all jealousy.

[3] **rake:** rake in money.

## The White Devil

Although his actions and language proclaim his stage lineage, Iago is not the only character associated with diabolic imagery. The previous section outlined the early modern link between Moors and the devil, but Othello, at the height of his rage, calls Desdemona a "fair devil." As you can see from the verses included in this section, a "white devil" is a particular kind of hypocrite, one who deceives using the pretense of goodness. Othello draws on a popular pattern of imagery that depicts women as natural hypocrites — having a fair outside that masks a poison and degeneration within. The image, which appears in New Testament warnings against false apostles, is a paradox rooted in the typical associations of the devil with blackness. This biblical image is elaborated on at some length by Martin Luther: "for the devil will not be ugly and black in his ministers, but fair and white; and to the end that he may appear to be such one, he setteth forth and decketh all his words and works with the color of truth, and with the name of God" (33). Notice how closely Luther's words fit Iago's revelation of his method:

"When devils will the blackest sins put on, / They do suggest at first with heavenly shows, / As I do now" (2.3.311–13)

In popular culture, women most often are white devils. This image of deceit is part of the arsenal of misogynist rhetoric that positions all women as ultimately untrustworthy (Loomba, "Sexuality" 181). Othello's lack of faith in Desdemona's chastity is provoked not simply by sexual jealousy: he is susceptible to Iago's wiles (as is Roderigo) because Iago contains Desdemona in a story about women's inherent deception that blinds others to her virtue. Within this rhetoric women are thought to disguise their true selves through figural whiteness — cosmetics — and with the show of goodness. An excerpt from Henry Chettle's *The Tragedy of Hoffman* (1603) offers a potent image of the white devil when the main character's sister-in-law is suspected of adultery:

> She is as harlots, faire, like guilded tombs
> Goodly without; within all rottenness:
> she's like a painted fire upon a hill,
> set to allure the frost-nipped passengers,
> And starve them after hope: she is indeed
> As all such trumpets are, Angel in show,
> Devil in heart . . .   (II.ii.826–30)

When attached to women, this image is part of a constellation of attacks that associate face-painting, hypocrisy, and whoredom. Shakespeare offers another sly example of how easy it is to be misled by appearances. The most visibly virtuous character's name — "Des*demon*a" — speaks of the diabolic, while the most transgressive woman bears a name that suggests fairness and virtue: Bianca, Italian for "white."

→ GENEVA BIBLE

# Verses on the White Devil

The Geneva Bible was the most influential Bible of Shakespeare's time. To make the word of God more accessible to a lay reader, the Geneva Bible was portable; it divided scripture into verses and offered commentary "upon all the hard places." The following New Testament verses — from Jesus' warning against hypocrites in Matthew and Paul's attack on the false apostle in 2

---

Geneva Bible (London, 1603), 531r, 584r.

Corinthians — provide the biblical basis for depictions of the white devil. Jesus stresses the corruption and putrefaction underneath the righteous (and white) disguise, while Paul focuses on the potency of the disguise, its beauty and ability to deceive.

### FROM MATTHEW 23:26–28

Thou blind Pharisee, cleanse first the inside of the cup and platter, that the outside of them may be clean also.

Woe *be* to you, Scribes, and Pharisees, hypocrites: for ye are like unto whited tombs, which appear beautiful outward, but are within full of dead men's bones, and all filthiness.

So are ye also: for outward ye appear righteous unto men, but within ye are full of hypocrisy and iniquity.

### 2 CORINTHIANS 11:13–15

For such false apostles[1] are deceitful workers, and transform themselves into the Apostles of Christ.

And no marvel: for Satan himself is transformed in an Angel of light.

Therefore it is no great thing, though his ministers transform themselves, as though *they were* the ministers of righteousness, whose end shall be according to their works.

[1] **false apostles:** here is not meant such as teach false doctrine (which doubtless they would have grown into) but such as were vainglorious, and did not do their duty sincerely.

→ MARTIN LUTHER

## *From* A Commentary upon the Epistle of St. Paul to the Galatians
*1575*

Martin Luther's (1483–1546) widely circulated commentary on Paul's letter to the Galatians was one of the texts used to "prove" the righteousness of Protestantism. He urges that Protestants actively defend the faith, imagining a world of Christian engagement: "when thou must dispute with Jews, Turks, Papists, Heretics, & etc. concerning the power, wisdom, and majesty of God, then

Martin Luther, *A Commentary of M. Doctor Martin Luther upon the Epistle of S. Paul to the Galatians* (London, 1575), C4v–D1r.

employ all thy wit and industry to that end, and be as profound and as subtle a disputer as thou canst" (15r). What role does the devil play in the affairs of humans, according to Luther? How does the devil deceive?

# From *A Commentary upon the Epistle of St. Paul to the Galatians*

Here again you see that no man is able by his own works or his own strength to put away sin, because this present world is evil, and as Saint John saith, "is set upon mischief" (1 John 5:19). As many therefore, as are in the world, are the bond slaves of the devil, constrained to serve him, and to do all things at his pleasure. What availed it then to set up so many orders of religions for the putting away of sins: to devise so many great and exceeding painful works, to wear hairy coats, to beat the body with whips till the blood followed, to go on pilgrimage to *Saint James* in harness[1] and such other like? Be it so that thou doest all these things, yet nevertheless doth this determinate sentence remain still, *that thou are in this present evil world, and not in the kingdom of Christ*. And if thou be not in the kingdom of Christ, it is certain that thou doest belong unto the kingdom of Satan which is this evil world. Therefore all gifts either of the body or of the mind which thou possessest, as wisdom, righteousness, holiness, eloquence, power, beauty, riches, are but the slavish instruments of the hellish tyranny, and with all these thou are compelled to serve the devil, and to promote and enlarge his kingdom.

First with thy wisdom thou doth darken the wisdom and knowledge of Christ, and by thy wicked doctrine leadest men out of the way, so that they cannot come to the grace and knowledge of Christ. . . . I overpass those gross vices which are against the second table,[2] as disobedience to parents, to magistrates, adulteries, whoredoms, covetousness, thefts, murders, and maliciousness, wherein the world is altogether drowned, which notwithstanding are light faults if ye compare them with the wisdom and righteousness of the wicked, wherewith they fight against the first table. This white Devil which forceth men to commit spiritual sins, that they may sell them for righteousness, is far more dangerous than the black devil, which only enforceth them to commit fleshly sins which the world acknowledgeth to be sins. . . .

---

[1] in harness: in armor.   [2] First . . . second table: the two divisions of the Decalogue, relating to religious and moral duties, respectively.

## Verse 6, Unto Another Gospel

Here we may learn to espy the crafty sleights and subtleties of the Devil. No heretic commeth under the title of errors and of the Devil, neither doth the Devil himself come as a Devil in his own likeness, especially that white Devil which we spoke of before. Yea even the black devil, which forceth men to manifest wickedness, maketh a cloak for them to cover that sin which they commit or purpose to commit. The murderer in his rage seeth not that murder is so great and horrible a sin as it is in deed, for that he hath a cloak to cover the same. Whoremasters, thieves, covetous persons, drunkards and such others, have wherewith to flatter themselves and cover their sins. So the black devil also commeth out disguised and counterfeit in all his works and devices. But in spiritual matters, where Satan commeth forth, not black, but white in the likeness of an Angel or of God himself, there he passeth himself with most crafty dissimulation and wonderful sleights, and is wont to set forth to sale[3] his most deadly poison for the doctrine of grace, for the word of God, for the Gospel of Christ.

[3] **sale:** sell.

# CHAPTER 2

## *Cultural Geography*

————————————————— →← —————————————————

Fittingly, the first identified illustration of *Othello* (see Figure 22, p. 229) was initially known as *The Geography Lesson* (P. Kaplan). This 1776 Capella painting portrays an intimate conversation between a young white woman and an older black man. To the left of the scene lie a globe, a map, and a compass/divider, indicators of Othello's "traveller's history" in act 1, scene 2, as well as of the distance between the homebound Venetian girl and the traveling soldier-convert. Conveying both intimacy and distance, the image suggests the primacy of travel and geography in the couple's developing relationship. While Desdemona is more obviously linked with the instruments of geography (the intellectual arm of travel), Othello seems to embody the mysteries of travel itself. Like Desdemona, many early moderns were deeply interested in "antres vast and deserts idle" (1.3.142). Globes and maps, the symbols of that interest, were purchased by armchair travelers as well as by actual explorers: they also appeared as stage props, signaling new spatial understandings of the world, property interests, colonial desires, and the more scholarly geographic interests of the age. In naming its theater the Globe, Shakespeare's company held out the promise of seeing the world through "play," advertising its ability to make the audience travel beyond the self while remaining securely at home.

FIGURE 22 *Detail from* The Geography Lesson, *by Andreas Capella (1776).*

The early modern period was the great era of geography. The globalism and intercultural exchange that constitutes the contemporary world was inaugurated in fifteenth-century overseas expansion. For England, geographic movement was also an imaginative and ideological expansion; pilgrims, merchants, pirates, and adventurers explored and reinvented the world — often in their own image. Their travels and the changing image of the world provoked a broader "transformation in the texture of everyday life" (Brotton 172). While writers like Marco Polo and Ibn-Battuta in the medieval era wrote accounts of actual individual travel, it was in the sixteenth century that collectors attempted to write the world by compiling and classifying accounts of European travelers from across the globe, and that mapmaking became both art and science (Brotton 154–83; Gillies; K. Hall, *Things* 44–48; Kamps and Singh 4–7). Richard Hakluyt, editor of England's great epic *Principal Navigations, Voyages, Traffiques and Discoveries of the English Nation* (1599), invokes geography as the new optic through which one understood the world when claiming that he compiled the work "by the help of Geography and Chronology (which I may call the Sun and the Moon, the right eye and the left of all history)."

In this age of movement, travelers, always powerful figures in literature, become even more evocative. They offer routes to self-discovery, giving readers both the opportunity to experience foreign places and cultures vicariously and a different vantage point from which to view their own lives. For example, Venice as represented in *Othello* and in travelers' accounts, is a combination of Venetian myth and English self-examination, both itself and a metaphor for England (Hoenselaars 30). Early modern travelers, both actual and literary, were also viewed with caution, however, because they transgressed (and therefore marked) the borders of the community. Jean Howard notes that, in having an outsider come to Venice and be undone by the experience, *Othello* actually reverses a common pattern for the adventure hero, who is more typically put "on the front line of contact with an array of stigmatized, exoticized, and slenderly understood peoples: the Irish, the Spanish, the Moors, the Turks, and the Jews" (356, 359). Such travelers and heroes can easily become wanderers, dangerously displaced figures unconstrained by cultural codes and laws. *Wander* and *error* are etymologically related, an association Roderigo exploits when calling Othello an "erring barbarian," and "an extravagant and wheeling stranger / Of here and everywhere" (1.1.137–38) — that is, a wandering outsider with no home or community (Gillies 3).

In Europe, this suspicion of "wandering" often sprang from ideas about private property and kinship and became a way of judging others — women and foreigners — as well. For example, nomadic peoples with different conceptions of property and land were frequently judged negatively, as if without a culture. Thus, Richard Knolles's *General History of the Turks* calls the original Turks (the progenitors of the Ottoman rulers) "a wandring and unregarded people" (3). Given this bias, one wonders how an English reader would respond to John Leo Africanus's assertion that barbarism literally has its origins in wandering exile. Interestingly, the divide between wandering and traveling seems thinner for women than for men; the ideals for women — "chastity, silence and obedience" (see Chapter 3) — often demanded stillness, and closeness to home. Women who wandered or traveled were often seen as sexually promiscuous, a connection Paula Vogel's *Desdemona; a Play about a Handkerchief* (see Chapter 6, p. 353) disturbingly exploits. What does an implicit injunction against female wandering mean for women in *Othello*? Particularly, what does it mean for Desdemona who moves between her "domestical duties" and her rapt attention to Othello's tales and who openly expresses a desire to travel with her husband?

The early modern interest in geography stimulated the publication of numerous travel accounts as well as the first compilations of travel narratives. Actual travelers' histories, the stories of travels into distant lands, were an increasingly popular genre in the early modern period: such accounts made available stories of exotic people and locales that were used by other writers. Othello's account of his past in act 1, scene 3, seems to be woven from several different kinds of travel writing: captivity narratives, tales of the marvelous, and ethnography/history. Travelers' quasi-ethnographic musings reveal much about their own culture. In many cases the traveler brings with him strong preconceived notions of how societies should operate that may obscure his ability to understand the practices of other peoples; consequently, his written observations may distort and disfigure the foreign culture while glorifying his own (Fanon 210).

While some accounts — like the medieval text *The Travels of Sir John Mandeville*, which was still wildly popular in Shakespeare's day (and from which Shakespeare likely drew part of Othello's life story) — were more compilations of known myths and legends than records of actual travel, all early modern travel writing was to some degree animated by an interest in "wonders" or "marvels"; often, the works tack between reality, desire, and fantasy (Walvin 19–20). The terms *marvels* and *wonders* referred to "things or events that were unusual, unexpected, exotic, extraordinary or rare" (Kenseth 25; see also Gillies 33–34; Greenblatt, *Marvelous* 16–25; Platt, *Reason* esp. 10–18; Yachnin). The age's eagerness for wonders led readers back to ancient writers for insights into the marvelous and, although later travelers' accounts may be seen as more authoritative because based on experience rather than legend, the modern reader would do well to remember how often ancient legend and cultural myths shaped how the traveler understood his experience. For example, travelers familiar with Herodotus's mythical races of flesh-eating men, the anthropophagi (which Othello mentions — see 1.3.146), often superimposed those images on the actual tribes who practiced ritual eating of flesh; thus, Herodotus's mythical races became as real as the peoples met by Columbus and other travelers.

The wonder evoked by foreign objects or events (or people) was thought to stimulate the imagination, to offer new ways of understanding everyday experience, or to secure religious belief by offering proof of God's power. We might consider the marvelous qualities of Othello's handkerchief and join other critics in asking if Desdemona sees Othello as more of a "marvel" than a person.[1] As you read the selections included in this chapter, ask yourself: Do the travelers draw their conclusions from observation, custom, legend, the Bible, or some combination of these? Remembering, as Mary Campbell does, that wonders are often projections of European cultural fantasy (8), what do you think these writers' conclusions say about their own culture?

---

[1] For a discussion of the handkerchief as both ordinary and a wonder, see Yachnin. For Desdemona's attraction to the exotic, see Cowhig, "Actors"; Gillies 3.

Early modern atlases and travel accounts — as well as the literary works that draw from them for inspiration — see geography as a potent factor in shaping individual and national character. In some cases this may contribute to an early form of stereotyping, a flattening out of individual characteristics in the face of assumptions about the influence of geography on character. Climate theory, the most popular schema of difference of the time, proposed that geography shapes both physiology and psychology. Thus, to identify Cassio as a "Florentine" and Desdemona as a "super-subtle" Venetian links them to two-dimensional views of national character. You might compare the characterizations of different national types in this chapter's reading selections with those in Chapters 4 and 5. How, for example, do writers view Moors or Italians in different contexts? How do judgments about other cultures reveal English values or articulate a sense of English identity? How conscious are writers of internal differences within a country or continent?

Although the Capella painting (p. 229) is unusual in depicting a woman's interest in geography and in associating women with the instruments of travel, Desdemona's primacy in the painting helps us focus on actual and symbolic connections between women, gender, and geography. In the early modern period, marriages of ruling and elite women often cemented diplomatic and trade bonds between countries; even today, child rearing is said to make women the main agents for reproducing ethnic or cultural identity. More pervasive than such familial arrangements, however, are the ways in which assumptions about gender infiltrate representations of culture and race. Women are "a focus and symbol . . . in the construction, reproduction and transformation of ethnic/national categories" (Anthias and Yuval-Davis 313); therefore, the idea of woman plays an important symbolic role in representing countries or nations — think of popular images of nations as women. You might also note how generalizations about women (or about gender relations) are also seen to reflect the character of a country. What does it mean to give a country female (or male) attributes? Or to think of a country as a "virgin" (see, e.g., p. 238)?

## The Early Modern Mediterranean

*Othello* is profoundly shaped by its movement through the imagined and real spaces of the Mediterranean; its settings evoke particular stories about place and about the hopes and dreams of its English audience. Jean Howard contends that the Mediterranean was on the "periphery of actual and imagined experience" (345). Although English trade in the Mediterranean world would later be superceded by Atlantic trade, in the early seventeenth century the Mediterranean was still Europe's dominant nexus of trade and travel — a space with multiple frontiers where powerful forces struggled, often brutally, for dominance. Historian Andrew Hess calls it "a long frontier between two civilizations, a zone of division determined not solely by battles, but by where Muslim and Western European states could and could not impose their institutions" (73; see also Braudel; Vitkus, *Turning* 13–16).

Tellingly, most of the Mediterranean spaces in *Othello* can be considered "contact zones" in which cultures meet or collide over asymmetrical power relations (Pratt), or "borderlands," which Gloria Anzaldúa defines as places where "two or more cultures edge each other, where people of different cultures occupy the same territory . . . where the space between two individuals shrinks with intimacy" (Preface). Venice, Cyprus, Aleppo, and the Barbary Coast were all sites of enormous cultural contact (mostly sparked by international trade) that were animated both by tension between "indigenous and alien subjectivity" (Oz 188) and by an equally thrilling and troubling intimacy with strangers. Cyprus and Aleppo, in particular, were spaces of ongoing religious-based conflict. As you will see, Cyprus was a battleground in the struggle between Ottoman and Venetian/Christian forces, while Aleppo was beset by internal conflict sparked by indigenous struggle against Ottoman imperial rule. The actual diversity of these spaces made them rich with possibility for Europeans grappling with such oppositions as East/West, Muslim/Christian, and civilization/barbarism.

While popular views of Venice and Cyprus are woven into *Othello*'s action, allusions to other geographical spaces like Barbary, Aleppo, Africa, and Florence deepen the texture of the play. Florence was an intellectual and cultural center on the forefront of the rebirth known as the Renaissance. The new military theory discussed in Chapter 4 was among its many intellectual developments, and Florentines like Machiavelli became noted military theorists (Draper 291). It seems fitting, then, that the "proper" gentleman and new ensign Cassio is a Florentine. However, by the time of *Othello*, Florence was also a financial center whose bankers were based throughout Europe and whose values centered on that commercial economy: "Credit, sacrifice, shame and honor . . . are important aspects of the cultural frame through which Florentines discoursed about their social structures" (Trexler 8). One might see elements of this history in Iago's slurs against Cassio as a "countercaster" (1.1.32) who is concerned with "bookish theoric" (1.1.25). It might also lie behind Cassio's immense concern with his reputation, which, we will see in Chapter 3, has moral, social, and economic overtones.

Another facet of Florentine identity is less obvious: "Along with Greeks [and] Italians . . . Florentines were reckoned as notorious practitioners of sodomy" (A. Smith 90; see also Trexler 14). Ian Smith notes the tendency in criticism either to overlook the question of sodomy (which generally refers to nonprocreative sexual practices deemed "unnatural" by early moderns) or to locate questions of homoerotic (same-sex) and sodomitical desire solely in Iago ("Queer").[2] What attention is paid to homoeroticism in the play concentrates primarily on "Cassio's dream," discussed in Chapter 4 (see Goldberg; Hammill 251 n16; Little 84–86). Smith, however, reminds readers that Cyprus is "the place where different economies of sex meet, converge and transform each other ("Queer Moor" 16), and it is important not to rest on simplistic notions of latent homosexuality in Iago. Rather, one can question the convergence of sexual and racial difference in Cyprus. How does the appearance of figures like Turks and Florentines who are associated with sodomy transform a drama of sexual jealousy seemingly rooted in heterosexual desire? Why is so much illicit sexuality concentrated on Cyprus?

## The Myth of Venice

Shakespeare's Venice was both a city-state and an idea, distant and near; it was a place with specific geographic coordinates and trade relations in addition to cultural space on which hung English hopes and ideals and which England imaginatively enlisted to fight its fears and prejudices. Venice was also a major site of East–West exchange. Jerry Brotton highlights the influence of Eastern cultures on Venice, noting that it "was a quintessential Renaissance city, not just for its combination of commerce and aesthetic luxury, but for its admiration and emulation of the east" (40). English relations with Venice were poor under Elizabeth (fractured mostly over issues of piracy), but James established formal relations soon after taking the throne. Two of Shakespeare's major Italian plays, *Othello* and *The Merchant of Venice*, were performed for the court during these first years of diplomatic harmony. It is possible that the Venetian ambassadors might have seen them, although, as Virginia Vaughan notes, they would have found Shakespeare's representation of the Venetian state and the council "strangely ambivalent, particularly in its depiction of vulnerability underlying the state's apparent strength" (21).

---

[2] For a concise discussion of the meanings of sodomy, see Bray; see also DiGangi 6–10ff.; Goldberg. For this volume, *homoerotic* refers to same-sex desire and *sodomitical* retains the early modern sense of a nonprocreative or otherwise transgressive sexual practice.

Albeit in different ways, all of Europe ascribed to a myth of Venice that elevated this principality above other Italian city-states. Critic David McPherson outlines four components to this myth: Venice the Rich, Venice the Wise, Venice the Just, and *Venezia Citta galante* (Venice the Galant City) (see also Logan 1–19). Writers envision Venice as wealthy and cosmopolitan, "a heady mix of political order, mercantile success and sexual glamour" (Mulryne 87). Brabantio alludes to another aspect of Venice — its sophisticated urbanity — when chastising Roderigo: "This is Venice; / My house is not a grange" (1.1.108–9). Allied with this cosmopolitanism are a reputation for tolerance and an ability to maintain political supremacy in the Mediterranean while keeping a well-regulated and successful trade with multitudes of strangers at home. Venetian writer Gaspar Contarini gushes: "Others exceedingly admired the wonderful concourse of strange and foreign people, yea, of the farthest and remotest nations, as though the City of *Venice* were a common and general market to the whole world" (1). Both Venice's laws and its openness to strangers were part of the same marvel: the ability to maintain social order and free trade in a diverse and competitively capitalist society. Venice's putative openness to strangers seemed particularly intriguing: Shakespeare positions both Shylock from *The Merchant of Venice* and Othello to challenge "the commodity that strangers have" (*The Merchant of Venice* 3.3.27) in Venice.

As with many myths, Venice's had a troubling nether side, hinted at by all of the authors in this chapter. Although it was a bulwark of Christian and mercantile strength in the early sixteenth century, by the time of *Othello* Venice had suffered the devastating loss of Cyprus, and formerly preeminent Venetian traders were losing their hold on Mediterranean trade, in some cases to English traders. Writers at times spoke of Venice as a once-great power in sad decline. In this view, the Venetian commitment to peace was a form of cowardice; its strict laws and ruling elite evidence of tyranny; its success in trade the product of rapacious guile ("super-subtle" Venetians); its cosmopolitanism a corrupting susceptibility to outsiders; and, most important, its sophistication a kind of licentiousness. How well does the Venetian Senate in *Othello* represent the mythical political order of Venice? Othello relies on his "parts, . . . title, and . . . perfect soul" (1.2.31) for success in Venice, but how do we understand Roderigo, the Venetian rival for Desdemona? How might Roderigo's attempts to undermine Othello and Desdemona's marriage embody negative ideas of Venetian character?

The ambivalence in the myth of Venice was often projected onto the city's geography. The Bertelli map in Figure 23 shows that Venice is topographically liminal, a city-state composed of both land and water. While it is heavily fortified, its "in-betweenness" also renders it vulnerable. This spatial

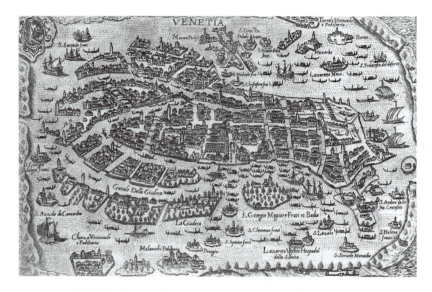

FIGURE 23  *The City-State of Venice, from Pietro Bertelli,* Theatrum Urbium Italicarum *(1599).*

liminality and the ingenuity it demands become potent metaphors for the writers in this section. The openness in trade that was Venice's great commercial strength was also seen as its greatest potential weakness. You might pay attention to other ways in which descriptions of land imply moral or political comments. How might the idea of Venice as a city of artifice and of liminality reflect on the Venetian characters in *Othello*?

Venetian art and architecture bear witness to a long-standing black presence in the city. Figure 24, a detail from Vittore Carpaccio's *The Healing of a Madman* (1496), shows a black gondolier working in the canals of Venice. If the Bertelli map emphasizes a Venice fortified to withstand the potential vulnerability of its geography, the Carpaccio painting shows the Venetian waterways as emblematic of the city's cosmopolitan urbanity. In the opening scene of *Othello*, Roderigo, tellingly, encourages Brabantio to see his now unstable household in the image of Desdemona being "Transported with no worse nor better guard / But with a knave of common hire, a gondolier" (1.1.125–26). How might the story of Othello and Desdemona's elopement represent a domestic version of Venice's vulnerability?

FIGURE 24  *Detail from* The Healing of a Madman, *by Vittorio Carpaccio (1496).*

⇥ DEDICATORY POEMS

## *From* The Commonwealth and Government of Venice

*1599*

*Translated by Lewes Lewkenor*

Lewes Lewkenor (d. 1626) was largely responsible for spreading the myth of Venice in England. His translation of Gaspar Contarini's *De Magistratibus et Republica Venetorum* was the first of several accounts that extolled the many glories of Venice. England had a particular investment in this myth; even during political disputes, many writers saw a special relationship with Venice, a belief that Venice was a cousin to England, the ultimate in rational government and good order (D'Amico, *Shakespeare*; McPherson; Vaughan 14–17). Venice's extensive sea trade and commanding navy surely would have been coveted by an England rapidly building up its naval power. The four poems that follow preface Lewkenor's volume: they combine images of Venice itself with praise for Lewkenor's translations of Contarini's representations of the city (Platt, "Mervailouse" 134–37). How do the comparisons of the city with the book affect our sense of Venice? How should we interpret the comparisons of Venice to Babel and Rome? How does the image of Venice as a woman compare with Thomas Coryate's description of the city (p. 244)?

### EDMUND SPENSER

The antique *Babel*, Empress of the East,
  Upreared her buildings to the threatened sky:
  And Second *Babel* tyrant of the West,[1]
  Her airy Towers upraised much more high.
But with the weight of their own surquedry,[2]                                    5
  They both are fallen, that all the earth did fear,
  And buried now in their own ashes lie,
  Yet showing by their heaps how great they were.
But in their place doth now a third appear,
  Fair *Venice*, flower of the last world's delight,                            10
  And next to them in beauty draweth near,
  But far exceeds in policy of right.
Yet not so fair her buildings to behold
  As *Lewkenor's* style that hath her beauty told.

---

[1] **tyrant of the West:** Rome.   [2] **surquedry:** arrogance; haughty pride.

---

Gaspar Contarini, *The Commonwealth and Government of Venice*, trans. Lewis Lewkenor. (London, 1599), 3v–4r.

## I. Ashley

Fair maiden town that in rich *Thetis*'[3] arms,
   Hath still been fostered since thy first foundation.
   Whose glorious beauty calls unnumbered swarms
   Of rarest spirits from each foreign nation,
And yet (sole wonder to all *Europe's* ears,             5
   Most lovely Nymph, that ever *Neptune* got)
   In all this space of thirteen hundred years,
   Thy virgin's state ambition ne'er could blot.
Now I prognosticate thy ruinous case,
   When thou shalt from thy Adriatic seas,            10
   View in this Ocean Isle thy painted face,
   In these pure colors coyest eyes to please,
Then gazing in thy shadow's peerless eye,
   Enamored like *Narcissus* thou shalt die.

## Maurice Kissen

*Venice* invincible, the Adriatic wonder,
     Admired of all the world for power and glory,
     Whom no ambitious force could yet bring under,
Is here presented in her State's rare story,
Where all corrupt means to aspire are curbed,         5
And Officers for virtue's worth elected.
The contrary wherof hath much disturbed
All states, where the like cause is unrespected,
A document that Justice fortifies
Each government (although in some things faulty)     10
And makes it dreadful to the envying eyes
Of ill-affecting foes and tyrants haughty.
*Lewkenor*, whom arms and letters have made known,
In this work hath the fruits of either shown.

## Henry Elmes

'Tis not affected grace or mock disguise
Assures a true return from foreign parts.
Travel confounds the vain, confirms the wise,

---

[3] **Thetis:** Mother of Achilles; she created the armor that made Achilles almost invincible.

*Lewkenor* live thou esteemed for thy deserts,
While thy last travels do thy first commend,                    5
To strangers proved in them a grateful friend,
And for thy absence to thy native clime,
A welcome Venturer of rich prized time.


→ FYNES MORYSON

## *From* An Itinerary                                          *1617*

After four years traveling and studying in Europe as a young man, Fynes
Moryson (1566–1630) fulfilled his desire to see Jerusalem and Constantinople in
1595 with an arduous journey across the Alps to Venice, and from there to
Cyprus and Jerusalem. Like many English travelers, Moryson kept his Protestant faith secret and often disguised himself in order to blend in with his sur-
roundings. He spent years writing and revising an enormous account of his
travels, and published a short version in 1617. This selection is from a longer
fourth part that was not published in his lifetime.

Moryson's *Itinerary* covers the national character, politics, law, economy, and
religion of each country he visited. Like other philosophers and political
observers, Moryson nods to the virtues of the Venetian Senate, which was said
to guarantee rational and wise decision making in government and virtue in the
citizenry. Although he opens by praising the "gray heads" of the Senate,
Moryson suggests that much of their efforts are put into controlling the rampant violence of the city and identifies adultery as a particular problem. How
does Moryson's description of Venetian reactions to adultery compare with
Othello's reaction to Desdemona's perceived infidelity? Moryson also assesses
Venice's military organization. How does he link Venice's military practices,
particularly the hiring of foreign mercenaries, to the city's powerful economic
position?


## OF THE POWER OF ITALY IN WAR GENERALLY

The Princes of Italy placing all the hope of preserving their States in the
greatness of their treasure, not in the love of their subjects, which they lose
by the foresaid cruel exactions (under which they groan as under the

---

Charles Hughes, ed., *Shakespeare's Europe, A Survey of the Condition of Europe at the end of the
16th century, being unpublished chapters of Fynes Moryson's Itinerary* (1617), 2nd ed. (New York:
B. Blom, 1967), 132, 163–65.

bondage of Egypt) and so hold their faithfulness suspected, for that cause keep them from any the least experience in military service, or so much as the use of the wearing of the sword desiring to have them as base & fearful as men may be. And for this Cause in their wars, they use auxiliary soldiers, and especially Generals of other Nations. Yet I confess that the State of Venice being a free State, under the which the people are not so much oppressed as under other Princes of Italy, raise part of their foote[1] of their own Peasants, but the strength thereof is in strangers, as likewise they employ some gentlemen of the Cities subject to the State to command some troops of men at Arms or Armed horses. But howsoever they make gentlemen of Venice Governors and Generals of their Navy, yet they never employ them to command their Land forces, having always a Stranger to their General. But this they do, not that they suspect their faith, but lest any gentleman gaining great reputation in Arms, and the love of the soldiers, should have power at any time to usurp upon the Freedom of their State. . . .

## The Justice, Laws, and Judgments in the State of Venice

The Senate of Venice is most reverent for the gray heads, gravity and Comeliness of their persons, and their stately habits but for nothing more than their strict observing of Justice. They have a law that in time of Carnival or Shrovetide, no man that is masked may wear a sword, because being unknown, he might thereby have means to kill his enemy on the sudden. . . . But since the City of Venice lies open without any walls, so as malefactors may easily escape, and the City lies upon Lombardie where murders are frequent, this City especially in the time of Carnival is much subject to murders, and like outrages. And so is the next City Padua, upon priviledges of the university, whereby murder in scholars is punished only by banishment. And that the rather, because in the State of Venice (for the great Confluence of strangers) it is free for all men to wear Arms by the day, excepting Pistols, which no man may have without the Locks taken off, and also because they who have ill purposes, will adventure and use to wear these Arms by night also, I say for these reasons, murders (especially in the libertine time of Carnival) are frequent in this City, from which also the lesser Cities of that State are not free. Murder was punished by hanging till death, till Duke Michaele Morosino created in the year 1381, made a law that murderers should be beheaded. But most commonly they escape by flight, and so are

---

[1] **foote:** infantry or foot soldiers.

banished till they can make peace with the friends of the murdered, and so obtain liberty to return into their Country. Adulterers are punished (as other like Crimes) according to the Civil and Canon laws, but the Italians impatient to bring their honor under public trials dispatch the punishment of all Jealousies by private revenge, killing not only the men so provoking them, but their wives, sisters, or daughters dishonoring themselves in those kinds. Yea brothers knowing their sisters to be unchaste when they are married, and out of their own house, yet will make this offense known to their husbands, that they may kill them. Whereof Examples are frequent, as namely of a Florentine gentleman, who understanding from his wife's brother that she had dishonored them by adultery, took her forth in a Coach having only a Priest with them, and when they came to a fit place gave her a short time to confess her sins to the Priest, and then killed her with his own hands. And howsoever in this Case, it is like she Confessed the Crime, yet in this and like Cases the Magistrate useth not to inquire after these revenges, which the Italians' nature hath drawn into Custom, besides that many are done secretly without danger to be revealed.

## Venice: The Virgin/Whore

England's desired and actual affinity with Venice can be seen in representations of Venice as a virgin city (see, for example Ashley's verse on p. 239). Such representations established England, once ruled by a virgin queen, as a rationally ordered state that shared civic values with the city-state of Venice. Unlike Elizabeth, whose virginity often represented a homogenous insularity that would protect the English, the virgin Venice was often depicted as a prostitute, constantly open to strangers. The imaginative discourse of Venice as virgin meshed with two actual Venetian practices: strict control of marriage among elites and state regulation of prostitution. Like Thomas Coryate, visitors described Venetian women as sophisticated, beautiful, and fashionable yet excessively confined by jealous husbands or overprotective fathers; such writers often drew a causal link between the confinement of wives and daughters and the city's open prostitution said to be carried on by thousands of women (see M. Kaplan 126).

→ THOMAS CORYATE

## *From* Coryats Crudities *1611*

Thomas Coryate (1577–1617) lived as a hanger-on and a licensed fool at court until his father's death, after which he embarked on a grand tour of Europe; by his own account, his writings covered the greater part of his 1,975-mile trip. Upon his return, he ran an ambitious campaign to find a publisher for his travelogue by having a number of famous people compose commendatory verses praising his efforts. The resulting 800-page volume, *Coryats Crudities* (1611), contained 150 pages of often scurrilous verse and was quite popular. Although elite men in the early seventeenth century frequently took a continental trip as part of their upbringing, *Coryats Crudities* was the only handbook on continental travel to date, seemingly enjoyed as much for Coryate's witty style and often imprudent comments as for his detailed observation and practical information. As you compare Coryate's description with the verses praising Venice (pp. 238–39), try to discern what emotions Coryate's descriptions of Venice are meant to evoke in the reader.

Although not literally in Venice, the ironically named Bianca would surely have reminded audiences that Venice was "famoused over all Christendom" for its courtesans (see p. 245). More important, Othello's violent outburst, "I took you for that cunning whore of Venice" (4.2.93), moves from common sexual slander to a very specific indictment of "super-subtle" Venetian women. English merchant Laurence Aldersey shows the negative side of the Venetian myth in his disdain for fashionable Venetian women not subject to England's strict sumptuary laws: "As for the women of Venice, they be rather monsters, than women. Every Shoemaker's or Taylor's wife will have a gown of silk, and one to carry up her train, wearing their shoes very near half a yard high from the ground; if a stranger meet one of them, he will surely think by the state that she goeth with, that he meeteth a Lady" (Hakluyt ii.I.151). How might these views of Venetian women have helped fuel Othello's suspicion of Desdemona? How does Shakespeare, particularly in the characters of Bianca and Desdemona, develop the literal virgin/whore binary that suffuses descriptions of Venice? In the coupling of Cassio (whom the play most associates with courtesy) and Bianca, Shakespeare might be playing with the same connection Coryate makes between the words *courtesan* and *courtesy* (see p. 245).

---

Thomas Coryate, *Coryats Crudities: Hastily Gobbled Up in Five Months Travels in France, Savoy, Italy, . . . Switzerland &c.* (London, 1611), 159–61, 263–65, 267.

## My Observations of the Most Glorious, Peerless, and Maiden City of Venice

Though the incomparable and most decantated[1] majesty of this city doth deserve a far more elegant and curious pencil to paint her out in her colors than mine. For I ingenuously confess mine own insufficiency and unworthiness, as being the unworthiest of ten thousand to describe so beautiful, so renowned, so glorious a Virgin (for by that title doth the world most deservedly style her) because my rude and unpolished pen may rather stain and eclipse the resplendent rays of her unparalleled beauty, than add any luster unto it: yet since I have hitherto continued this slender and naked narration of my observations of five months' travels in foreign countries; this noble city doth in a manner challenge this at my hands, that I should describe her also as well as the other cities I saw in my journey, partly because she gave me most loving and kind entertainment for the space of six weeks, which was the sweetest time (I must needs confess) for so much that ever I spent in my life; and partly for that she ministered unto me more variety of remarkable and delicious objects than mine eyes ever surveyed in any city before, or ever shall, if I should with famous Sir *John Mandeville*[2] our English *Ulysses* spend thirty whole years together in traveling over most places of the Christian and Ethnic[3] world. Therefore omitting tedious introductions, I will descend to the description of this thrice worthy city: the fairest Lady, yea the richest Paragon and *Queen of Christendom.

Such is the rareness of the situation of Venice, that it doth even amaze and drive into admiration all strangers that upon their first arrival behold the same. For it is built altogether upon the water in the innermost gulf of the Adriatic Sea which is commonly called the *Gulfo di Venetia*, and is distant from the main sea about the space of three miles. From the which it is divided by a certain great bank called *litto maggior*, which is at the least fifty miles in length. This bank is so necessary a defense for the City, that it serveth instead of a strong wall to repulse and reverberate the violence of the furious waves of the sea.

*I call her not thus [Queen] in respect of any sovereignty that she hath over other nations, in which sense Rome was in former times called Queen of the world, but in regard of her incomparable situation, surpassing wealth and most magnificent buildings.

---

[1] **decantated:** sung or said over and over again; repeated often.   [2] **Sir *John Mandeville*:** author of famous medieval travel narrative *The Travels of Sir John Mandeville*, now presumed to be a compilation of legends rather than an actual account of travel.   [3] **Ethnic:** pertaining to nations not Christian or Jewish; gentile, heathen, pagan.

For were not this bank interposed like a bulwark betwixt the City and the Sea, the waves would utterly overwhelm and deface the City in a moment. The form of this foresaid bank is very strange to behold. For nature herself the most cunning mistress and architect of all things hath framed it crooked in the form of a bow, and by the Art of man there are five Ostia, that is mouths, or gaps made therein, whereof each maketh a haven, and yieldeth passage to the ships to sail forth and back to Venice . . . Others do show like fair little green Islands, which are the very places that yielded harbor to diverse companies of people, that in the time of the Huns, Goths, and Vandals devastation and depopulation of Italy repaired thither with their whole families as to a safe refuge and Sanctuary for the better security of their lives, the greatest part of them that made their habitation in these Isles being the bordering people that dwelt partly in the towns and villages by the seashore, and partly in the inland cities. . . .

## [ON THE COURTESANS OF VENICE]

But since I have taken occasion to mention some notable particulars of their women, I will insist further upon that matter, and make relation of their Courtesans also, as being a thing incident and very proper to this discourse, especially because the name of a courtesan of Venice is famoused over all Christendom. And I have here inserted a picture of one of their nobler Courtesans, according to her Venetian habits, with my own near unto her, made in that form as we saluted each other (see Figure 25, p. 246). Surely by so much the more willing I am to treat something of them, because I perceive it is so rare a matter to find a description of the Venetian Courtesans in any Author, that all the writers that I could ever see, which have described the city, have altogether excluded them out of their writings . . . Only I fear lest I shall expose myself to the severe censure and scandalous imputations of many carping Critics, who I think will tax me for luxury and wantonness to infer so lascivious a matter into this Treatise of Venice. Wherefore at the end of this discourse of the courtesans I will add some Apology for myself, which I hope will in some sort satisfy them, if they are not too captious.[4]

The woman that professeth this trade is called in the Italian tongue *Cortezana*, which word is derived from the Italian word *cortesia* that signifieth courtesy. Because these kind of women are said to receive courtesies of their favorites. Which word hath some kind of *affinity* with the Greek word *hetaira* which signifieth properly a sociable woman, and is by *Demosthenes*,

---

[4] **captious:** fault-finding.

FIGURE 25 *Thomas Coryate with courtesan Margarita Emiliana. This engraving of Coryate offering "courtesy" to a Venetian prostitute suggests a powerful link between displays of courtesy and the selling of the self. Earlier in his book, Coryate claims that this rich courtesan built a monastery for Augustinian monks (249). Why does Coryate include this image if he thinks readers might find it unseemly (see p. 245)?*

*Atheneus*, and diverse other prose writers often taken for a woman of a dissolute conversation. As for the number of these Venetian Courtesans it is very great. For it is thought there are of them in the whole city and other adjacent places, as Murano, Malomocco,[5] &c. at the least twenty thousand, whereof many are esteemed so loose, that they are said to open their quivers to every arrow. A most ungodly thing without doubt that there should be a toleration of such licentious wantons in so glorious, so potent, so renowned a City. For methinks that the Venetians should be daily afraid lest their winking at such uncleanness should be an occasion to draw down upon them God's curses and vengeance from heaven, and to consume their city with fire and brimstone, as in times past he did Sodom and Gomorrah. But they not fearing any such thing do grant large dispensation and indulgence unto them, and that for these two causes. First *ad vitandi maior a mala*.[6] For they think that the chastity of their wives would be the sooner assaulted, and so consequently they should be *capricornified*[7] (which of all the indignities in the world the Venetian cannot patiently endure) were it not for these places of evacuation. But I marvel how that should be true though these Courtesans were utterly rooted out of the City. For the Gentlemen do even coop up their wives always within the walls of their houses for fear of these inconveniences, as much as if there were no Courtesans at all in the City.

. . . Moreover she will endeavor to enchant thee partly with her melodious notes that she warbles out upon her lute, which she fingers with as laudable a stroke as many men that are excellent professors in the noble science of Music; and partly with that heart-tempting harmony of her voice. Also thou wilt find the Venetian Courtesan (if she be a selected woman indeed) a good Rhetorician, and a most elegant discourser, so that if she cannot move thee with all these foresaid delights, she will assay thy constancy with her Rhetorical tongue. And to the end she may minister unto thee the stronger temptations to come to her lure, she will show thee her chamber of recreation, where thou will see all manner of pleasing objects. . . . But beware notwithstanding all these *illecebrae and lenocinia amoris*,[8] that thou enter not into terms of private conversation with her. For then thou shalt find her such a one as *Lipsius*[9] truly calls her . . . the crafty and hot daughter of the Sun.

---

[5] **Murano, Malomocco:** Murano is a Venetian island, and Malomocco an area on the periphery of Venice.  [6] *ad vitandi maior a mala*: escaping from bad to better.  [7] *capricornified*: literally, "goat-horned"; to have an adulterous wife (See *The Cuckhold's Haven* in Chapter 3, p. 285).  [8] *illecebrae and lenocinia amoris*: the enticements and the allurement of love.  [9] **Lipsius:** a Belgian Stoic philosopher.

## Cyprus: The Birthplace of Love

If Venice and Florence were sophisticated urban centers, Cyprus could be called the Wild West of the Mediterranean. A violent borderland, it was a politically volatile outpost during the Crusades and later became a source of constant battle and friction between Venice, which held it from 1517, and Ottoman forces (see Figure 26). As in *Othello*, Cyprus was for Europe the "stage" on which the "bloody tragedy" of Ottoman-Venetian enmity was

FIGURE 26 *Flemish mapmaker and collector Abraham Ortelius helped Europeans leave behind classical models of the world by Pliny and Ptolemy in favor of a more scientifically and experientially based cartography. Ortelius traveled extensively and consulted with geographers and travelers across Europe to publish his* Theatrum Orbis Terrarum *(Epitome of the Theater of the World) in 1570. Considered the first modern atlas because of its uniformity and scrupulous attribution of sources, this collection of over seventy maps was revised frequently over Ortelius's lifetime to reflect the latest information. Each map is accompanied by description and commentary. With the map shown here, Ortelius notes the extensive Ottoman holdings and laments that the empire "threatens to do worse if God inspires not the hearts of Christian princes unitedly to resist him" (102). Note how the borders of the Ottoman empire seem to encircle Cyprus. What does this suggest about European views of Cyprus and of Ottoman power? What visual similarities do you see between Venice and Cyprus?*

played out (see the selection by Richard Knolles, p. 250). Early in the six-teenth century, Venice's easternmost colony was a heavily fortified outpost that brutally subjected indigenous Cypriots to its will. The closest island to the heart of the Ottoman empire and strategically located on the paths to markets in Syria, Egypt, and Istanbul, Cyprus was a haven for pirates and thus "simultaneously vulnerable to attack from without and subversion from within" (Vaughan 22). You might examine moments in *Othello* that refer to the potential for violence in Cyprus (see, e.g., 2.3.45–51). How is the threat of violence read against actual violence in the play?

The move to Cyprus in act 2 of *Othello* connects the action to the general sense of Ottoman threat in English culture, thus providing a spatial under-pinning to the themes of the play. Cyprus, however, resonates far beyond its geopolitical significance: classical tradition identified Cyprus as the birth-place of Venus (Aphrodite). Many Western observers spoke of the island as ruled by the goddess of love and held "romantic presuppositions about the island of Venus" (Jennings 15; see also Andrea, "Pamphilia's" 348–51). How might the location of Cyprus help intertwine ideas of love and violence in *Othello*? Cyprus was for Europe a place of hope and fear, and Othello's jeal-ousy mirrors English associations of Cyprus with passionate love and uncontrolled violence. Although for most of the sixteenth century, Cyprus was Venice's wealthiest possession as well as its most important naval base, when the Venetian Senate sends Othello to protect Cyprus from the Turks, Shakespeare's audience would have been keenly aware that Cyprus had been an Ottoman stronghold for over thirty years, the result of a great Ottoman victory that ended with Venice paying substantial tribute to Sultan Selim II. Battles over such outposts were pan-Christian and thus helped form a sense of European identity, albeit a fragile one. However, even when in Christian hands, Cyprus was imagined as irredeemably "oriental" and irrational.

→ RICHARD KNOLLES

## *From* The General History of the Turks

*1603*

### CYPRUS DESCRIBED

But for as much as the island of Cyprus was the prey whereafter the greedy tyrant so much gaped, and for which the bloody wars betwixt the Turk and Venetians, with their Christian confederates, presently ensued; it shall not be from our purpose to spend a few words in the describing thereof, as the stage whereon the bloody tragedy following was as it were acted: as also how it came first into the hands of the Venetians, and by what right of them so long possessed (although it be in some part before declared) until it was now by *Selymus* the great Turk against all right injuriously demanded, and at length by strong hand by him wrested from them. . . . It is worthily accounted amongst the greatest islands of the Mediterranean, containing in circuit 427 miles, and is in length (after the description of *Strabo*) 175 miles, and in breadth not above 65. It aboundeth with corn, wine, oil, cotton wool, saffron, honey, rosin, turpentine, sugar canes, and whatsoever else is needful for the sustentation[1] of man, whereof it sendeth forth great abundance to other countries, of whom it craveth no help again. It was in ancient time called *Macaria*, that is to say, Blessed. The people therein generally lived so at ease and pleasure, that thereof the island was dedicated to *Venus*, who was there especially worshipped and thereof called Cypria. *Marcellinus* to show the fertility thereof, saith, that Cyprus aboundeth with such plenty of all things, that without the help of any other foreign country, it is of itself able to build a tall ship, from the keel to the top sail, and so put it to sea furnished of all things needful. And *Sextus Rufus* writing thereof, saith: . . . Cyprus famous for wealth, allured the poverty of the people of Rome[2] to lay hold upon it, so that we have rather covetously than justly got the rule thereof. In the heart of the island standeth Nicosia, sometime the regal and late metropolitical[3] city thereof. And in the East end thereof Famagusta, sometime called Tamassus, a famous rich city, the chief and only port of all that most pleasant island.

---

[1] **sustentation:** maintenance; preservation. [2] **allured the poverty of the people of Rome:** the wealth of Cyprus enticed an impoverished Rome. [3] **metropolitical:** designating a metropolitan see or bishop, a possible indication that the city was once under Catholic control.

Richard Knolles, *The General History of the Turks from the first beginning of that Nation to the rising of the Ottoman family: with all the notable expeditions of the Christian princes against them* (London, 1603), 843. For biographical information on Knolles, see Chapter 1, page 210.

→ JAMES VI AND I

## *From* The Lepanto  *1603*

Christian Europe imaginatively compensated for the devastating defeat at Cyprus in 1571 by celebrating the Holy Christian League's proximate victory later that year in the battle of Lepanto, a historic battle that, along with the English victory over the Spanish Armada, may underlie the rout of Ottomans in *Othello*. Although less strategically significant than the loss of Cyprus, the victory at Lepanto was of huge symbolic importance to European Christians, sparking the great, if unfulfilled, hope of Christian ascendancy in the Mediterranean. This was the first major Ottoman defeat in battle. It revealed a chink in the armor of Muslim invincibility and gave rise to an expectation that a Christian alliance would beat back the Ottoman empire (Figure 27). For years afterward, the 1571 battle of Lepanto was commemorated and propagandized in European art, music, and literature. King James's celebration of Christian victory over Ottoman forces, *The Lepanto,* was first published in 1591 while he was King James VI of Scotland. This epic poem was published again in 1603 when he became James I of England. How does this poem envision Christian forces? Ottoman strength? What is Venice's place in James's conception of Christendom? What does James mean when he refers to Venice as "this artificial town"?

The first section tells of the archangel Gabriel's visit to Venice at God's behest to call together Christian forces; the second describes Christian and then Ottoman leaders stirring up their forces for the upcoming battle. What attributes does James give each nation?

This God began, from thundering throat,
    Grave words of weight to bring:
"All Christians serves [*sic*] my Son, though not
    Aright in every thing.                    80
No more shall now these Christians be
    With infidels oppressed,
So of my holy hallowed name
    The force is great and blessed.
Desist, ô tempter. Gabriel, come
    O thou Archangel true,
Whom I have oft in message sent
    To realms and towns anew.

James VI and I, *The Lepanto,* in *Reading Monarchs' Writing: The Poetry of Henry VII, Mary Stuart, Elizabeth I and James VI/I*, ed. Peter C. Herman (Tempe: Arizona Center for Medieval and Renaissance Studies, 2002), 295–96; 307–9.

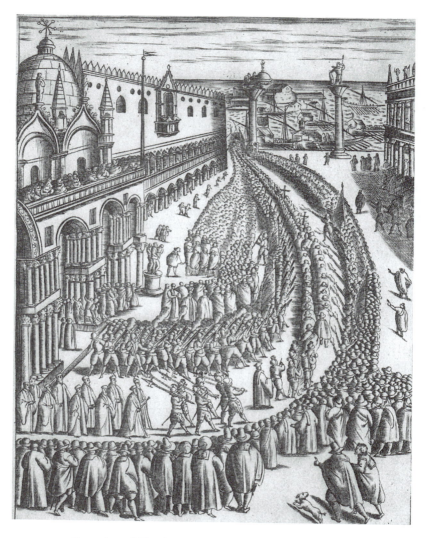

FIGURE 27 *Procession of Venetian troops joining the Holy League from Giacomo Franco* Habiti d'huomeni et donne venetiane, *Plate 33 (Venice 1609). Otherwise hostile and competitive European countries buried their differences to form a unified Christian army known as the Holy League. This illustration is one of many portraying the processions, masques, and other celebrations that took place across Europe when Holy League forces prepared for the Battle of Lepanto.*

Go quickly hence to Venice town,
   And put into their minds                                    90
To take revenge of wrongs the Turks
   Have done in sundry kinds."
No whistling wind with such a speed,
   From hills can hurl o'er heugh[1]
As he whose thought doth furnish speed,
   His thought was speed aneugh[2]
This town it stands with the sea,
   Five miles or thereabout,
Upon no isle nor ground, the sea
   Runs all the streets throughout.                           100
Who stood upon the steeplehead
   Should see a wondrous sight,
A town to stand without a ground,
   Her ground is made by slight:
Strong timber props dug in the sea
   Do bear her up by art,
An isle is all her marketplace,
   A large and spacious part,
A duke with senate joined doth rule,
   Saint Mark is patron chief,                                 110
Ilk[3] year they wed the sea with rings
   To be their sure relief.
The angel then arrived into
   This artificial town,[4]
And changed in likeness of a man,
   He walks both up and down,
While time he met some man of spright,[5]
   And then began to say,
"What do we all? Methink we sleep!
   Are we not day by day                                       120
By cruel Turks and infidels
   Most spitefully oppressed?
They kill our knights, they brash[6] our forts,
   They let us never rest!
Go to, go to, once make a proof:
   No more let us desist,

Notes to this selection are reprinted from the Herman edition of James's writings.
[1] Valley.   [2] Enough.   [3] Each.   [4] Venice exists through art, through human intervention, not naturally.   [5] Spirit.   [6] Attack. [Hall]

To bold attempts God gives success,
  If once assay we list."[7]

. . . . . . . . . . . . . . . . .

There came eight thousand Spaniards brave,
  From hot and barren Spain,
Good order keepers, cold in fight,
  With proud disdainful brain.
From pleasant fertile Italy,
  There came twelve thousand als,[8]
With subtle sprights bent to revenge,
  By crafty means and false.
Three thousand Almans also came,
  From countries cold and wide,
These money men with awful cheer
  The choke will dourly bide.[9]
From divers parts did also come,
  Three thousand venturers brave,
All voluntaries of conscience moved,
  And would no wages have.

. . . . . . . . . .

the Spanish prince
  did row about them all,
And on the names of special men
  With loving speech did call,
Remembering them how righteous was
  Their quarrel, and how good,
Immortal praise, and infinite gains,
  To conquer with their blood,
And that the glory of God in earth,
  Into their manhead[10] stands,
Through just relief of Christian souls
  From cruel Pagans' hands.
But if the enemy triumphed
  Of them and of their fame,
In millions men to bondage would
  Professing Jesus' name.
The Spanish prince, exhorting thus,
  With glad and smiling cheer,

270

280

490

[7] If once we try.  [8] In addition. [Hall]  [9] Will boldly withstand the attack. [Hall]  [10] Humanity. [Hall]

With sugared words, and gesture good,
   So pleased both eye and ear             500
That every man cried victory.
   This word abroad they blew,
A good presage that victory
   Thereafter should ensue.
The Turkish host in manner like
   Themselves they did array,
The which two Bashas did command
   And order every way.
For Portav Basha[11] had in charge
   To govern all by land,               510
And Ali Basha[12] had by sea,
   The only chief command,
These Bashas in the battle were,
   With mo[13] than I can tell
And Mahomet Bey[14] the right wing had,
   The left Ochiali fell.[15]
Then Ali Basha visied[16] all
   With bold and manly face,
Whose tongue did utter courage more
   Than had alluring grace.           520
He did recount amongst the rest
   What victory Turks obtained
On caitif[17] Christians, and how long
   The Ottoman's race had reigned.
He told them als,[18] "how long themselves
   Had victors ever been,
Even of these same three Princes small,
   That now durst so convene,
And would ye then give such a lie
   Unto your glories past           530
As let your selves be overthrown
   By losers at the last?
This victory shall Europe make

---

[11] Pertew Mehemet Pasha, commander of the center of the Turkish fleet, and not the land forces. [12] Kapudan Ali Pasha, admiral of the Turkish fleet. [13] More. [14] Viceroy of Alexandria. [15] "Fell," meaning evil. Ochialli, or "Aluch Ali," Pasha, commander of the left-wing squadron of the Turkish fleet, earned this sobriquet because he was a renegade Christian originally from Calabria who rose to be viceroy of Algiers. [16] Viewed. [17] Base, despicable. [18] As well. [Hall]

To be your conquest prey,
And all the rare things thereintill,
    Ye shall carry away.
But if ye leese,[19] remember well
    How ye have made them thrall,
This samin[20] way, or worse shall they
    Demaine[21] you one and all,
And then shall all your honors past       540
    In smoke evanish quite,
And all your pleasures turn in pain
    In dolor your delight.
Take courage then, and boldly to it,
    Our Mahomet will aid,
Conducting all your shots, and strokes,
    Of arrow, dart, and blade.
For nothing care but only one
    Which only doth me fray,[22]           550
That ere with them we ever meet
    For fear they flee away."

[19] Lose.   [20] Same. [Hall]   [21] Demean.   [22] Make me afraid.


## Aleppo

Strategically located at an intersection of the Christian and Muslim worlds and equidistant between the Euphrates and the Mediterranean, Syrian Aleppo was a thriving international center of commerce. This fabled stop along the silk route became in the sixteenth century a key Ottoman capital that solidified Ottoman control in the Mediterranean, although early in the seventeenth century it became a center of unrest when local tribal forces battled Ottoman-installed rulers. During Elizabeth's reign, the Levant Company initiated long-lasting trading partnerships with Aleppo, placing its headquarters there and sending English merchants to learn the intricacies of foreign trade despite the high death rate (Davis 126). Investors and traders interested in assessing potential avenues of trade and the perils of travel might have carefully scrutinized the story of John Newberry and merchant Ralph Fitch that follows.

## *From* His Discourse of Voyages into the East and West Indies

*1598*

First published by Flemish traveler Jan Huyghen van Linschoten (1563–1611), his *Itinerario, Voyage or Passage of Jan Huyghen van Linschoten to East or Portugal's India* (1596) was written specifically to encourage Dutch exploration of the East Indies. While Linschoten depicted the perils of foreign trade in telling the story of John Newberry, Englishman Richard Hakluyt also reprinted Newberry's story as a model of English fortitude and perseverance.

John Newberry traveled more widely in the Arabian peninsula than any other Englishman of his era. He became conversant in Arabic and in cultures of the Middle East through study with the noted geographers of the day and multiple trips into the Levant. In two separate trips, Newberry aroused the ire of Venetian traders who feared competition. During this second trip in 1583, the Venetians spread word of English "heresy" and poisoned their relationships with the Portuguese. Newberry and his fellow merchants were imprisoned in both Aleppo and Goa, where they were eventually released. What is the English traders' position in Aleppo? What does Linschoten reveal about Christian-Muslim relations? About relations between Christians of different nationalities? In *Othello*, why does Othello project his own self-destruction into Aleppo?

In the month of December, *Anno* 1583, there arrived in the town and island of Ormuz four Englishmen, which came from *Aleppo* in the country of *Syria*, having sailed out of *England*, and passed through the straights of *Gibraltar* to *Tripoli*, a town and haven lying on the coast of *Syria*, where all the ships discharge their wares and merchandises, and from thence are carried by land unto *Aleppo*, which is nine days' journey. In *Aleppo* there are resident, diverse merchants and factors[1] of all nations, as Italians, French men, Englishmen, Armenians, Turks and Moores, every man having his religion apart, paying tribute unto the great Turk. In that town there is great traffic, for that from thence every year twice, there travel two Cafilas,[2] that is, companies of people and camels, which travel unto India, Persia, Arabia, and all the countries bordering on the same, and deal in all sorts of merchandise, both to and from those countries, as I in another place have already declared. Three of the said Englishmen aforesaid, were sent by the

---

[1] **Factors:** agents or representatives.    [2] **Cafilas:** caravans.

Jan Huyghen van Linschoten, *His Discourse of Voyages into the East and West Indies Divided into Four Books* (London, 1598), 140–41.

company of Englishmen that are resident in *Aleppo*, to see if in *Ormuz* they might keep any factors, and so traffic in that place, like as also the Italians do, that is to say, the Venetians which in *Ormuz*, *Goa*, and *Malacca*[3] have their factors and traffic there, as well for stones and pearls, as for other wares and spices of those countries, which from thence are carried over land into *Venice*. One of these Englishmen had been once before in the said town of *Ormuz*, and there had taken good information of the trade, and upon his advice and advertisement, the other were as then come thither with him, bringing great store of merchandises with them, as Clothes, Saffron, all kinds of drinking glasses, and Haberdasher's wares, as looking glasses, knives, and such like stuff. And to conclude, brought with them all kind of small wares that may be devised. And although those wares amounted unto great sums of money, notwithstanding it was but only a shadow or color, thereby to give no occasion to be mistrusted, or seen into: for that their principal intent was to buy great quantities of precious stones as Diamonds, Pearl, Rubies, etc. to which end they brought with them a great sum of money and gold, and that very secretly, not to be deceived or robbed thereof, or to run into any danger for the same. They being thus arrived in *Ormuz*, hired a shop, and began to sell their wares: which the Italians perceiving, whose factors continue there (as I said before) and fearing that those Englishmen, finding good vent for their commodities in that place, would be resident therein, and so daily increase, which would be no small loss and hindrance unto them, did presently invent all the subtle means they could to hinder them. And to that end they went unto the Captain of *Ormuz*, as then called *Don Gonsalo de Menses*, telling him that there were certain Englishmen come unto *Ormuz*, that were sent only to spy the country; and said further, that they were heretics: and therefore they said it was convenient they should not be suffered so to depart, without being examined, and punished as enemies, to the example of others.

## Africa and Barbary

In addition to specific places like Venice, Cyprus, and Aleppo, which were sites of international trade, politics, and intrigue, *Othello* is haunted by the less detailed ideas of Africa that occupied important mythic as well as geographic space. The marvels of the "Cannibals" and "Anthropophagi" that Othello recounts for Desdemona (1.3.145, 146); the handkerchief made by the Egyptian "charmer" (3.4.53); and the maid, Barbary (4.3.26), remem-

---

[3] **Malacca**: Malaysia.

bered in the "Willow" scene, all draw on an early modern sense of Africa as a place not only of wonder and magic but also of disorder and unruly sexuality (K. Hall, *Things* 25). John Gillies notes the links among "monstrosity, margins and sexual 'promiscuity'" (13), which do not apply solely to invocations of Africa, but are certainly central to English imaginings of the continent. Before the early modern period, there was only sporadic contact between Europe and Africa, but heavy taxes imposed by the Ottoman empire stimulated the discovery of new trade routes around the African coastline (Brotton 54–61).

As indicated in Chapter 1, the Moor was a complex figure that was both demonized and praised; images of the virtuous or noble Moor are intricately connected to place. One of many reasons John Leo Africanus's *Geographical History of Africa* remained so popular in the early modern period was that it offered firsthand accounts of regions little known to Europeans then. While many travelers explored and were familiar with the northern part of the continent, fewer had explored sub-Saharan Africa; the interior was still a mystery to most Europeans, making the continent a place ripe for the projection of racialist fantasies. Often, Africa was seen as a place of sexual and political disorder, and thus served as a repository of English anxieties about race, sexuality, and religion. In the excerpt from Leo Africanus's *Geographical History* (p. 260), readers will see the author address some of the more potent myths about African origins, including its link to "Barbary." The term *Barbary*, which was at times used to refer to the whole of Africa, more often indistinctly referred to the geographical region encompassing portions of the North African states of Libya, Tunisia, Algeria, and Morocco. Despite a period of Portuguese dominion, a large portion of this area "lay outside the European system of international law and conduct" (quoted in Willan 93). Piracy was endemic in the region, and European travelers could find themselves unusually vulnerable. Although the English had been trading in the area for decades, relations in the area, particularly with Morocco, accelerated and became institutionalized under Elizabeth (the Barbary Company was given its monopoly in 1585). However, trade relations were shaken with allegations of Moorish treachery and guile. England's dealings with Barbary/Morocco had larger political overtones since in exchange for sugar, saltpeter, and coveted Barbary horses, the Barbary Company would trade guns that then might be used against other Christian countries.

The term *barbarian* literally refers to those whose language marks them as outsiders. Leo Africanus's etymology of the word *Barbary* (pp. 260–61) locates travel and language in the very origins of Africa (I. Smith, "Barbarian" 172) and thus links Africa with more general judgments about barbarian

outsiders (Gillies 14–19). All of the usual associations with Barbary — trade
(Barbary horse), incivility, and language *(barbarous)* — appear in *Othello*,
but the most powerful link is clearly the maid Barbary, whose song Desdemona sings at the height of tension and danger in her marriage. It
also presages a particularly female moment in the play, in which she and
Emilia engage in a frank conversation about adultery. This ultimate scene
of domestic privacy, a woman and maid in a bedchamber, is set far from
home and is distinctly associated with foreign difference. Given the English
habit of naming black servants after geographical regions, it would not be
far-fetched to think of Barbary as African. What does mentioning a maid
named after an African region bring to the scene? What does it mean to
have Desdemona sing a song associated with both her absent mother and
Africa?

→ JOHN LEO AFRICANUS

## *From* A Geographical History of Africa  *1600*

Like Othello, Leo Africanus was a traveler and a hybrid figure who seemed to
move easily between disparate cultures. What places claim his allegiance and
affinity? What places claim Othello's? When he says "our," whom does he
mean? The opening chapters of Leo Africanus's history give stories of origin.
For example, the story of Bar-Bar places African origins within ideas of wandering and expulsion. What are the origins of "Negroes" and "tawny moors,"
according to Leo Africanus? Compare this origin story with Othello's story
of his younger days, with his story of the handkerchief, and with other legends of origin in the contextual materials (like that of George Best, p. 190). How
do these tales of beginnings serve to shape our understanding of culture and
character?

### OF THE INHABITANTS OF AFRICA, AND OF THE SIGNIFICATION OF THIS WORD *BARBAR*

Our Cosmographers and historiographers affirm that in times past Africa
was altogether disinhabited, except that part which is now called the land of
Negroes: And most certain it is that Barbary and Numidia were for many
ages destitute of inhabitants. The tawny people of the said region were

John Leo Africanus, *A Geographical History of Africa*, trans. John Pory (London, 1600), 5–6. For
biographical information on Leo Africanus, see Chapter 1, page 195.

called by the name of *Barbar*, being derived of the verb *Barbara*, which in their tongue signifieth to murmur: because the African tongue soundeth in the ears of the Arabians no otherwise than the voice of beasts which utter their sounds without any accents. Others will have *Barbar* to be one word twice repeated, for so much as *Bar* in the Arabian tongue signifieth a desert. For (say they) when king *Iphricus*, being by the Assyrians or Ethiopians driven out of his own kingdom, traveled toward Egypt, and seeing himself so oppressed with his enemies that he knew not what should become of him and his followers, he asked his people how or which way it was possible to escape, who answered him, *Bar-Bar*, that is, to the desert. Giving him to understand by this speech that he could have no safer refuge than to cross over Nilus and to flee unto the desert of Africa. And this reason seemth to agree with them, which affirm the Africans to be descended from the people of Arabia felix.[1]

## THE ORIGINAL OF THE PEOPLE OF AFRICA

About the original of the Africans, our historiographers do much disagree. For some will have them to be derived from the inhabitants of Palestine; because (as they say), being expelled out of their own country by the Assyrians, they came at length into Africa and seeing the fruitfulness of the soil, chose it to be their place of habitation. Others are of opinion, that they took their original from the Sabeans a people of Arabia felix, and that, before such time as they were put to flight by the Assyrians or Ethiopians as hath been aforesaid. . . . All which opinions and reports are to be understood only of the original of the tawny people, that is to say, of the Numidians and Barbarians. For all the Negroes or black Moors take their descent from *Cush* the son of *Ham*, who was the son of *Noah*. But whatsoever difference there be between the Negroes and the tawny Moors, certain it is they had all one beginning. For the Negroes are descended of the Philistines, and the Philistines of *Mesraim* the son of *Cush*.[2] But the tawny Moors fetch their pedigree from the Sabeans, and it is evident that *Saba* was begotten of *Rama*, which was the eldest son of *Cush*. Divers other opinions there be as touching this matter: which because they seem not so necessary, we have purposely omitted.

---

[1] **felix:** i.e., happy.    [2] **Cush:** the eldest son of Ham, who was cursed by his grandfather, Noah.

# CHAPTER 3

## *Marriage and the Household*

—————————————————— >‹ ——————————————————

If women in *Othello* seem carefully positioned according to their relationship to men and marriage (Desdemona, the newly married woman; Emilia, the long-suffering wife; Bianca, the prostitute), it is because early modern women were largely defined by their relationship to family, particularly to fathers and husbands. The household was not only the primary social unit in the early modern era but also the dominant model for a range of political and social arrangements, as well as the core institution that defined women's roles. Defined primarily in relation to marriage, early modern women were seen as highly visible social subjects, always the objects of surveillance, correction, and comment. A woman alone was the subject of jest or horror; single young women were more subject to arrest than married women simply because they lived beyond male authority (Capp 121). A woman was expected to make a seamless transition from dutiful daughter to obedient wife; in each case, her behavior affected not only her reputation but her husband's and father's reputations as well. It is important that *Othello* presents Desdemona at that moment of transition: because it is transgressive, her move from daughter to wife without her father's permission casts a broad net of suspicion that ultimately traps her within beliefs about women's unfaithfulness.

The Renaissance was an unprecedented era of intellectual openness and artistic growth given momentum by European exploration of the physical, natural, and social world; however, feminist historians and critics remind us that women of the Renaissance at times experienced diminishing social, legal, and economic independence (Kelly-Gadol; see also Henderson and McManus). While humanist writers brought new attention to the importance of women's education, the ideal of the educated, refined noblewoman was often at odds with general expectations of feminine passivity. Suzanne Hull's survey of conduct books demonstrates that "chastity, silence, and obedience" formed a tripod of patriarchal order on which balanced the early modern ideal of woman. Readers might pay particular attention to how Baldassare Castiglione's *The Book of the Courtier* (p. 268) and Juan Luis Vives's *Instruction of a Christian Woman* (p. 271) negotiate codes of silence and obedience.

Women who transgressed these codes — particularly those who did so openly and consciously — were seen as *disorderly*, a term that in the Renaissance suggested a more cataclysmic destruction of divinely inspired social order than it does to modern readers. Their real and perceived transgressions were often marked by sexual slander: *whore* was a particularly potent term of abuse with class connotations that took away a woman's place in society (Dusinberre 52). Philosophical, religious, and medical treatises frequently depicted women as naturally disorderly, provoked to misbehavior by their inferior female bodies, and made proper subjects only through the loving control of fathers and husbands. *Othello*'s women would have been primarily understood through the heated argument and voluminous literature (written mostly by men) on the nature of women and the ideal of marriage.

English civil law adhered to the principle of coverture, in which women were legally the property of men; a married woman had no independent legal or economic status since she was considered "covered" by her husband's or father's legal status as head of house. Ann McLaren astutely observes, "nor did women actually have to be married to experience this loss of personhood" (451–52). Although in practice some women achieved more power than the law offered, in theory women could own neither property nor themselves. Within this context, Brabantio's insistence in the opening that Desdemona has been "stol'n" from him (1.3.62) makes literal sense, as does Desdemona's remarkable self-possession both in choosing to give herself away by eloping and in eloquently defending that act before the Senate. Many critics have noted how her violation of patriarchal norms becomes the grounds for other characters (and even some critics) to doubt her later behavior. Natasha Korda and Lena Orlin have both argued powerfully that the circulation of household objects and ideas of women as property are linked to ideologies of possession represented in household goods. Orlin specifically argues that the play homes in on a key point of anxiety within patriarchy as it "asserts possession and finds possession always uncertain" (*Private* 226). Critics have also observed that the patriarchal prerogatives offered European men might not be as secure for an outsider like Othello, rendering him doubtful of his wife. Notice how often men in the play question the legitimacy of Othello's "possession" of Desdemona (Korda 144).

Although Iago mocks reputation as "an idle and most false imposition" (2.3.245), loss of reputation had profound consequences for early moderns, particularly women. Craig Muldrew notes, "Accusations of misconduct and insults were taken very seriously; they could lead to shame, possible isolation, and finally economic damage within a community," and any number of people spent large amounts of money defending themselves in court (*Economy* 53). Just as concepts of honesty are gendered, so, too, is reputation. For men, a good reputation meant being known for honesty (Muldrew, *Economy* 53); in contrast, chastity defined a woman's reputation (Gowing 129). Moreover, the woman was largely responsible for the reputation of the entire household: the honor of the family depended on her piety and chastity. An Englishman's identity and reputation rested in large part on having a wife who conspicuously adhered to patriarchal norms. Being called a whore could have profound consequences, and women took sexual insult and slander seriously. Thus, the conversation between Iago and Othello that conflates Desdemona's honor with the handkerchief (4.1.9–22) might also be read within the economic value of reputation and ideologies of male possession.

The continual emphasis on containing women's sexuality (both to protect the man's security that his offspring were actually his and to "order" the woman's body, seen as naturally prone to sin) and on possession of women meant that worries about adultery primarily focused on the wife's infidelity. Female adultery was more than a betrayal of a spouse: it was considered a crime against God and the state. This double standard was given the force of law when England's Adultery Act (1650) made adultery by a married woman a capital offense, while married men convicted of adultery were to be given only three months in prison (Wiesner 297) — a fact that demonstrates both the increasing circumscription of women's lives in the period as well as great anxiety over women's behavior. Many early modern texts (and modern critics) attribute Othello's over-the-top jealousy to his Moorish background; however, the image of the jealous Moor should not obscure rampant English fears of female sexuality.

Susan Amussen and David Underdown argue that early modern England experienced a crisis in gender relations: early modern texts worried over the roles of men and women and the desirability of love in marriage. Although the extent of change in actual married life is unclear, scholars generally agree that this period's analyses of marriage focus more directly on the emotional content of family life than did any in earlier periods. Historian Martha Howell summarizes: "European marriages were being more explicitly defined as voluntary bonds between spouses who regarded their unions not just as vehicles for full membership in the community but as the principal site of their emotional lives and the exclusive domains of their sexual lives" (236). An earlier, more Catholic, view that marriage was a necessary evil that kept men and women from sin and ensured orderly propagation and property was contested by a developing Protestant ideal of "holy matrimony" that celebrated conjugal love, including a new emphasis on the primacy of the family in the emotional lives of individuals and more attention to parental duties. This struggle over the meaning of marriage was carried out across a range of genres, but it found its fullest expression in the proliferation of domestic manuals and conduct books. Most often written by men to women, these manuals represented a patriarchal ideal of marriage. The relation of the emphasis on "companionate" or "affective" marriage in the written texts to the actual emotional lives of married people remains unclear. Do these texts reflect a true shift in belief (Stone), or are they insistent precisely because the "marriage pact had come to seem insecure, fragile and uneasy" (Howell 237)?

The drive to contain women's sexuality also shaped early modern attitudes toward love. Mistrust of romantic love was not limited to suspicious fathers like Brabantio. Even when the companionate ideal of marriage between people united by love became more prevalent, there was no celebration of unchecked mutual desire. Writers who championed companionate marriage were still uneasy about the powers of romantic love, and in the readings given here any emphasis on conjugal love is tempered by a deep-seated fear of excess emotion and unchecked sexuality. Texts on the passions make clear that surrendering to any powerful emotion threatens to dismantle the individual self. Women in particular were viewed as having a "powerful, potentially disruptive sexuality" (Henderson and McManus 55) that could ensnare the married man; for men, any surrender to passion, even within marriage, violated the masculine ideal of temperance and restraint: "male heterosexual desire could entail a loss of masculinity" (Shannon 66; see also Bach). If male identity is formed primarily by bonds with men, "heterosexual passion, rather than serving as an identity, instead threatens the gendered self" (Shannon 66). For example, we can see in *Romeo and Juliet* that Romeo's desire for Juliet threatens his bonds with his male mates. In *Othello*, such fears seem intensified, since husbands who overindulge their love for their wives are specifically seen as effeminate. Where does the play mark this fear of effeminization, or of subordination to a woman? How might the military setting heighten such fears?

Celebrations of conjugal love and concerns with women's sexuality were reconciled through the seemingly contradictory early modern notion of married chastity. Texts of this time reveal an almost obsessive concern with women's chastity, defining women's honor almost entirely in sexual terms. Even as they held up fidelity as an ideal for both partners, books and broadsides overwhelmingly focused on women's chastity as the cornerstone of marriage. Perhaps influenced by Puritan thought, over time Protestant marriage manuals come to emphasize an ideal of wifely obedience slightly more than the need for female chastity. For example, *Counsel to the Husband* (p. 278) in particular addresses the proper balance of authority and obedience. Insisting that the wife is a partner, "a helpmeet" who manages the household, diluted a rigorous insistence on absolute obedience. As domestic managers, wives had responsibilities for maintaining household order, including correction of servants. The wife was, in effect, "a subordinate magistrate within the miniature commonwealth of the family" (Capp 127). However, it is unclear how her responsibility translated into power and autonomy. For instance, *Counsel to the Husband* struggles to define the notion of the wife's absolute obedience against her power in the household and her position as a moral being.

You will see in the documents included here that notions of hierarchy, obligation, and affection are more complexly layered than sole attention to the husband's authority over the wife would suggest. Multiple layers of obedience and obligation animate *Othello*, but the specific problem of female obedience drives the plot. Tension rises with Desdemona's disregard of her father's authority, and Iago's perfidy is made "public" only when Emilia dares to reveal her guilty knowledge. Critics debate how English culture would have understood these behaviors and how they jibe with actual women's lives, but many agree that accusations (jesting or otherwise) of female disobedience in the play focus on three topics: speech, movement, and sexuality. Conduct books offered the wife no right to defy the husband (only pleading was allowed), even in cases of domestic abuse. While in extreme cases a woman might have resorted to the law, she would have been subject to harsh scrutiny, and would have had to make sure that her "own behavior had been modest and dutiful" (Capp 133), lest she be judged as harshly as the man. Prescriptive literature offers few examples of power struggles in the household; however, breakdowns in authority and family order (with the resulting family friction) provided fodder for ballads, which were quick to point out the consequences of poor matches or misbehavior.

As I noted in the introduction to this volume, the many possibilities of female disobedience or disorderliness were in early modern England resolutely linked to sexual disorder. Readers might note the unruly behaviors *The Cuckold's Haven* (p. 285) associates with infidelity as well as behaviors Iago uses to upbraid women in his jesting with Desdemona. In what ways does Martin Parker's *The Married Man's Lesson* (p. 283) differ from *The Cuckold's Haven* in locating the causes of wifely misbehavior? A more subtle reading of prescriptive literature reveals multiple possibilities for praise and blame within the marriage. Not knowing the tragic outcome, might a viewer share Brabantio's outrage, judging Desdemona by Vives's insistence on the importance of following parental wisdom in choosing a mate? Or might Desdemona's actions be compared with Castiglione's catalogue of the many ways women are seduced into love? Has Desdemona, who "shunned / The wealthy curlèd darlings of our nation" (1.2.68–69) and saw Othello's "visage in his mind" (1.3.254), in fact demonstrated a wise choice based on virtue (rather than on riches and looks), as advocated by Vives and other writers of conduct books? Although Emilia is conscious of her vow of marital obedience, critics are still vexed by the timing and nature of her revelation of Iago's betrayal. Does her outburst show the chinks in patriarchal armor, or does the extremity of the situation demonstrate just how restrictive these codes are (see Dash 101)?

If loquacity, wantonness, and public movement (and you might compare Bianca's and Desdemona's behaviors on these fronts) all define women's disorderly conduct, then a wife's physical and verbal stillness best protected her honor. Clergyman Henry Smith, writing in 1591, directly associated chastity with stillness: "Paul biddeth Titus to exhort women that they be chaste, and keeping at home; presently after chaste, he sayeth, keeping at home, as though home were chastity's keeper" (62). Such injunctions suggest that readers might pay particular attention to women's movement in the play. Increasingly, private space comes to define marriage and the early modern elite household. These architectural arrangements were preceded by a history that represented chaste women as an enclosed land or vessel (Stallybrass 127–30). Most early moderns postponed marriage until they could afford to set up a separate household (Wiesner 57; Ziegler). In fact, Lena Orlin suggests that Othello's marrying without an established home might have already alerted viewers to the vulnerability of the marriage, as would its beginnings under the sign of the Sagittary (1.1.160), an inn whose name evokes the centaur, a hybrid being known for raping human women. The mythological and astrological associations with Sagittary mean that the inn serves as "a focal element in a nexus of images for unquiet relationships, violent sexuality, and murderous jealousy" (*Private* 206).

One of the most potent critiques of early modern attitudes toward women takes place in the bedchamber. Emilia and Desdemona's frank discussion of marital sex and fidelity in act 4, scene 3 (the "Willow" scene), certainly defies the norms of female behavior outlined in the prescriptive literature: gossiping and faulting husbands for sexual transgressions were a species of female insubordination. This scene, frequently cut from productions of *Othello,* offers tantalizing perspectives on loyalty. It establishes affection between mistress and servant, a relationship in this instance defined against the demands of loyalty and rules made by men. Readers might compare the women's behavior there with the impressions made earlier in the play. How does it alter the play to omit this scene?

The fact of Desdemona's innocence is often drowned in the sea of patriarchal discourse in the play (and in much criticism) that judges all women. Critics struggle to read Desdemona against the ideal of womanhood revealed in writings on marriage, either finding in her a paragon of obedience and passivity or seeing her death as punishment for her violation of the structures of patriarchal life (see Jardine and see Neely 105–8 for critiques of these views). More recently, feminist critics have warned against identifying Desdemona with images in marriage texts, suggesting that critics too readily use the same patriarchal logic found within the texts to make Desdemona complicit in her own murder (Dash). If anything, the "Willow" scene suggests that, even within early modern culture, individuals were capable of thinking outside of patriarchal restrictions despite the enormous penalties for doing so.

## BALDASSARE CASTIGLIONE

## *From* The Book of the Courtier                    1636

Marriage and the nature of women were frequent topics of often heated disputation in the Renaissance. In what is known as the controversy over women, women spoke up in their own defense against misogynist commonplaces, a practice that some critics suggest was one of the earliest forms of feminism (see Woodbridge, *Women* 2–3). On one side, misogynist writers mobilized historical

Baldassare Castiglione, *The Book of the Courtier,* trans. Thomas Hoby (London, 1636), Book III C3r–C4r, 231–34.

examples of and commonplaces about women to attack women as scolds, temp-tresses, and spendthrifts: they bemoaned the miseries these women brought to men. Women and their defenders, in turn, attacked the sexual double standard, characterizing men as cravens who seduce women and then abandon them. Pro-woman forces condemned custom's role in male domination over women while rarely challenging biblical injunctions to female subordination. They relied instead on a female ideal, demanding praise and gratitude for the female sex's innate chastity and piety. Esther Sowernam's *Esther Hath Hang'd Haman* (1617) suggests that debating the nature of woman was a popular pastime: "as nothing is more usual for table-talk there fell out a discourse concerning women, some defending, others objecting against our Sex" (A2r). The "old paradoxes" Iago repeats on the quay in act 2, scene 1, are the residue of this practice. So, too, Bal-dassare Castiglione (1478–1529) shaped his *Book of the Courtier* according to this type of entertainment.

Castiglione's belief that manners and attitudes were as important as high birth in fashioning a gentleman made *The Book of the Courtier* a favorite text for discerning elite social codes. Structured as a series of dialogues purportedly tak-ing place at the Duke of Urbino's court in 1507, actual historical personages take up a challenge "to fashion in words a perfect courtier." Despite the assertion that the ideal gentlewoman shares the same traits as the ideal gentleman, the prob-lem of female modesty complicates the necessity of performing "courtesy" at court. How does Castiglione's description of the ideal gentlewoman compare with women's behaviors in *Othello*? How does women's speech define them in this document and in other documents in this section?

# From *The Book of the Courtier*

Leaving therefore apart the virtues of the mind that ought to be common to her [as] with the Courtier, as wisdom, nobleness of courage, staidness,[1] and many more, and likewise the conditions that are meet for all women, as to be good and discreet, to have the understanding to order her husband's goods and her house and children when she is married, and all those parts that belong to a good housewife. I say that for her that liveth in Court, me think there belongeth unto her above all other things, a certain sweetness in language that may delight, whereby she may gently entertain all kind of men with talk worth the hearing, and honest, and applied to the time and place, and to the degree of the person she communeth withal. Accompanying with sober and quiet manners and with the honesty that must always be a stay to her deeds, a ready liveliness of wit, whereby she may declare herself far wide from all dullness: but with such a kind of goodness, that she may be

---

[1] **staidness:** constancy, sobriety of conduct or character.

esteemed no less chaste, wise, and courteous than pleasant, feat conceited,[2] and sober: and therefore must she keep a certain mean,[3] very hard and (in a manner) derived of contrary matters, and most just to certain limits, but not pass them. This woman ought not therefore (to make herself good and honest) be so squeamish and make wise to abhor both the company and the talk (though somewhat of the wantonest) if she be present, to get her thence by and by, for a man may lightly guess that she feigned to be so coy to hide that in herself, which she doubted others might come to the knowledge of: and such nice fashions[4] are always hateful. Neither ought she again (to show herself free and pleasant) speak words of dishonesty, nor use a certain familiarity without measure and bridle, and fashions to make men believe that of her, that perhaps is not: but being present at such kind of talk, she ought to give the hearing with a little blushing and shamefastness. . . . Wherefore it is seen that one word, a laughter or a gesture of good will (how little soever it be) of an honest woman, is more set by of every man, than all the toys and wanton gestures of them that so lavishly show small shamefastness. And where they lead not indeed an unclean life, yet with those wanton countenances, babbling, scornfulness, and such scoffing conditions they make men to think they do. . . . Let her not go mingle with pleasant and laughing talk, matters of gravity: nor yet with grave Jests any feat conceits. Let her not foolishly take upon her to know that she knoweth not, but soberly seek to be esteemed for that she knoweth not, avoiding (as is said) curiosity in all things. . . .

Then said the Lord Caesar: Truth it is that these so great effects and rare virtues are seen in few women. Yet are they also that resist the battles of love, all to be wondered at, and such as otherwhile[5] be overcome deserve much compassion. For surely the provocations of lovers, the crafts that they use, the snares that they lay in wait are such and so applied, that it is too great a wonder, that a tender girl should escape them. What day, what hour passeth at any time that the young woman thus layed at[6] is not tempted by her lover with money, tokens, and all things that he can imagine may please her? . . . I omit his preciseness in sundry things, inventions, merry conceits, undertaking enterprises, sports, dances, games, masques, jousts, tournaments, the which things she knoweth all to be taken in hand for her sake. Again, in the night time she can never awake, but she heareth music, or at the least that unquiet spirit about the walls of her house casting forth sighs and lamentable voices. If by a hap she talketh with one of her waiting women about her, she (being already corrupted with money) hath straight way in a readiness

---

[2] **feat conceited:** suitably witty or expressive.   [3] **mean:** moderation.   [4] **fashions:** appearances.   [5] **otherwhile:** occasionally.   [6] **layed at:** assailed, assaulted.

some pretty token, a Letter, a rhyme, or some such matter to present her in the Lover's behalf: and here entering to purpose, maketh her to understand how this silly soul burneth, how he setteth little by his own life, to do her service, and how he seeketh nothing of her but honesty, and that only his desire is to speak with her. . . .

Others seek by Enchantments, and Witchcrafts to take from them the liberty that God hath granted to souls, wherin are seen wonderful conclusions.[7] But in a thousand years I could not repeat all the crafts that men use to frame women to their wills, which be infinite. . . . Now judge you how from so many nets these simple doves can be safe, tempted with so sweet a bait. And what great matter is it then, in case a woman knowing her self so much beloved and worshipped many years together, of a noble and fair conditioned young man, which a thousand times a day hazardeth his life to serve her, and never thinketh upon other but to please her with the continual beating which the water maketh when it pierceth the most hard marble stone, at length is brought to love him? Is this (think you) so heinous a trespass that the silly poor creature taken with so many enticements, deserveth not, if the worst should fall, the pardon that many times murderers, thieves, felons, and traitors have? Will you have this vice so uncomparable great, that because one woman is found to run into it, all womenkind should be clean despised for it, and generally counted void of continency? Not regarding that many are found most invincible, that against the continual flickering provocations of love are made of Diamonds, and stiff in their infinite steadiness, more than the rocks against the surges of the sea.

[7] **wonderful conclusions:** astonishing outcomes.

→ JUAN LUIS VIVES

## *From* Instruction of a Christian Woman                                    *1557*

Even though the choice of spouse was often negotiated among competing economic and familial interests in the early modern period, it would not have been unusual for women to have some degree of say (and in general women of lower classes had greater choice than those of higher classes did). The documents excerpted in this volume idealize marriage between social equals, but matching couples was a complicated matter. Although the prescriptive literature proclaimed

Juan Luis Vives, *A Very Fruitful and Pleasant Book Called the Instruction of a Christian Woman* (1524), trans. Richard Hyde (London, 1557), 52–55, 58–60.

the steadfastness of the grounding categories of early modern life — gender and rank or class — actual life was rather more complex since people's positions in the social order did not necessarily align within marriage. For example, books and illustrations affirmed the wife's inferiority to the husband and a chain of command in which the wife had control over children and servants while the husband had dominion over all. However, men did on occasion marry their social superiors, women who by rank, experience, or wealth brought their own power to the household. Such misalliances were often seen as sources of potential conflict and provocative of larger social disruption. In *The Taming of the Shrew,* for instance, Gremio, who marries a rich older widow, is the object of scorn when his wife refuses to obey him. In *Othello,* the question of a fitting match fuels Brabantio's anger, Othello's anxiety, and Roderigo's foolish hope; it may be that Shakespeare was aware that Venetian elites tightly controlled marriage in order to maintain pure bloodlines (Vaughan 28, 29). In what ways besides color are Desdemona and Othello said to be mismatched?

Juan Luis Vives (1492–1540) was a Spanish humanist who came to England in 1523; his *Instruction of a Christian Woman,* the single most influential text to define the roles and educational possibilities for early modern women, is structured around women's three life stages — maid, wife, and widow. Vives was a Spanish converso (Jewish convert to Christianity) who wrote *Instruction* in England in 1523 during his family's persecution under the Inquisition. The text is dedicated to Catherine of Aragon and is written as a guide for the education of her daughter, Mary, although much of its content seems aimed at a middle-class readership. While humanists like Vives and Castiglione brought new attention to the importance of women's education, the ideal of the educated, refined noblewoman could be at odds with general expectations of feminine passivity.

# From *Instruction of a Christian Woman*

## HOW THE MAID SHALL SEEK A HUSBAND

The wise poet Virgil, where he doth bring in king Latinus, and his wife Amata, talking together with Turnus, which should be their daughter's husband, their daughter also present, he maketh the maid to do no more but weep and blush, without speaking of words: whereby he signifieth, that it becometh not a maid to talk, where her father and mother be in communication about her marriage: but to leave all that care and charge wholly unto them which love her as well as her self doth. And let her think that her father and mother will provide no less diligently for her, than she would for herself: but much better, by the reason they have more experience and wisdom. Moreover it is not comely for a maid to desire marriage, and much less to show herself to long therefore. . . .

It is a great charge for a man to seek a husband for his daughter, neither it ought not to be gone about negligently. It is a knot that cannot be lightly loosed, only death undoeth it. Wherefore the fathers and mothers procure unto their daughters, either perpetual felicity, if they marry them to good men, or perpetual misery, marrying them unto ill. Here is much to be studied, and great deliberation to be taken, with good advisement and counsel, afore a man determine ought. For there is much weariness in marriage, and many pains must be suffered. There is nothing but one, that shall cause marriage to be easy unto a woman: that is, if she chance on a good and a wise husband. . . .

I thought it had been but a fable, that men tell, how Pasiphae[1] the queen of Candy,[2] did lie with a Bull: and other as ungracious deeds as that: which I have heard say, other women have done: but now me thinketh them all likely enough to be true, when I see women can find in their hearts, to tumble and lie with vicious and filthy men, and drunkards, and brawlers, and dawish,[3] and brainless, cruel and murderers. For what difference is between them and asses, swine, boars, bulls, or bears? What madness is it to have delight in such men, and to flee and eschew wise men, as Plutarch the Philosopher saith, and flee honest men and good men, as warily as they would flee from venomous beasts? Wherefore it was well and aptly spoken, that a countryman of mine said, that the nature of women was in choosing men, like to the female wolves: which among a great sort of males, take the foulest and worst favored. But men never cast any favor to a woman, but for some good property, either of substance, person, or wit. And women many times love some men, because there is nothing in them worthy to be beloved. Whereby they declare the more plainly, that they go without reason. Which things I say by some, that have nothing a do with their reason, but all given and applied unto their body. . . .

Now afore I make an end of this book, I will answer unto a mad and a frantic opinion, which both maidens and wives have, and all the common people in general, that think it is expedient for maids, that are come to lawful age of marriage, to be seen oft abroad among people, goodly and pickedly[4] arrayed, and to keep company and communication with men, to be eloquent in speech, and cunning in dancing and singing: yea and to love him aforehand, whom they intend to marry. For so (they say), they shall the

---

[1] **Pasiphae:** mother of the Minotaur.   [2] **Candy:** Crete (by way of "Candia").   [3] **dawish:** silly, sluttish.   [4] **pickedly:** fastidously, elegantly.

more lightly meet with a bargain. . . . What wise man, I pray you, would ever counsel this thing, knowing, that ill is not to be done, that good may come thereof? And specially where the ill is evident enough, and the good neither certain nor customed to follow commonly upon the deed. Wherefore if the maid can get no marriage, except she infect her mind, and jeopardize her honesty on this fashion, it were better never to marry: or else to marry only Christ, than to marry first unto the devil, that she may be married to a man afterward.

Now two things there be, the most precious that a woman can bring with her to a man, honesty of body, and good fame. Nor there is no man so foolish and mad, neither so set upon beauty and covetous of goods, neither so ungracious and so unthrifty of living, but he will be content with any wife, having these two: which if she lack, how can he be content? Then would I wit, whether maid is the more likely to be of good fame and behavior, whether she that bideth most at home, or she that walketh much abroad? At home there is none occasion of evil, and forth abroad every place is full. And of her that tarrieth at home, no man maketh question or argument: but of her that walketh much about, every man will say his opinion. Where among so diverse sentences a maid shall soon catch a blot, which will stick in no place more sooner than on a maid, neither worse to get out. . . .

And as for those that keep much company with men, what man is there, that will not suspect ill by them? Or what husband shall she find so patient, that will be content to have his wife to company still and common with men? Or would not rather have such a one, as would more gladly company with her husband alone, than with a great multitude of men? Where one shall tempt her mind with eloquence, another with comeliness of person, some with beauty, some with liberty, and some with nobleness. For as for maids to be eloquent of speech, that is to say great babblers, is a token of a light mind and shrewd conditions. In so much that he that shall marry her, shall think he hath a serpent and no wife. For young men will praise her unto her face, that is full of talk, and a jolly dancer, and full of merry conceits, and play, and pleasant, and call her well mannered, and well brought up, all to have her at their pleasure, but none to marry her: and all believe that they may quickly obtain their purpose of such one. But never a one will be glad to have such one to his wife, that he seeth is applying[5] unto every man's will. They praise for the time all that she doth, because they have delight therein. But and[6] the foolish maids could hear what men speak afterwards among themself one unto another, without dissimulation: then,

---

[5] **applying:** assiduous practice or attention; that is, working for the attentions of every man.
[6] **and:** if.

should they know indeed how heartily they praised them and liked them. They should understand then, that when the men called her merry conceited, they meant they were babblers, and chatters: and when they called them lusty stirers[7] they meant they were light minded: and where they called them well nurtured, they meant they were wanton. . . .

Now will I speak a few words of love, the which doteth all maids for the most part, and deceiveth them greatly, and bringeth to much mischief. For it doth not become a maid to make any sign, that she would fain be married, or that she love any young man to wed. For if she love him afore she have him, that it be known, what shall he think, but that she will as lightly love another as she hath done him, whom as yet she ought to show no love unto. Neither he will believe that she loveth him alone, seeing there is as great cause to love other. And if he should marry her, he will think she will have as good mind to other as himself, when she is so light of love.

Let everybody excuse the matter as they will, but in very deed every woman, that loveth any man beside her husband, is accursed, if she have ado with him: and though she have not, yet is she an harlot in mind. And there hath been many that have loved so outrageously, that they have been obedient unto the pleasure of those men, whom they hoped should be their husbands. And afterwards these men have despised and cast them up which in my mind was well and wisely done. For they be unworthy to be married, that dare show an example unto those men, whom they should have, how well they can find in their heart to lie with a man that is not their husband. For by likelihood they will both do that same with other men afore their marriage, and in their marriage with their adulterers. . . . And so it chanceth unto such women, even by the punishment of God, that all the love, which they ought to keep in their marriage, they spend it out afore. . . . Wherefore it is not expedient to make marriages by love aforehand, neither to couple and bind that most holy charity with so filthy and brittle bands. And yet much worse is it to make them to marry by striving, and hate, threatening, and suit,[8] as when they go to law together, the man for the woman, bearing her in hand, that she is his wife: and the woman in like manner for the man.

---

[7] **stirers:** stirrers; active people.    [8] **suit:** to sue for in a court of law.

## *From* A Bride-bush: Or, A Wedding Sermon      *1617*

Puritan divine William Whately (1583–1639) was a popular Oxfordshire preacher whose sermon *A Bride-bush* provoked great controversy in the church. He was brought before a church commission to answer for his assertion that adultery and desertion are grounds for divorce, and he retracted this opinion in the 1623 edition of the text. There was disagreement in the early modern period about the meaning of marriage, and some writers may have idealized the institution to compensate for potential fissures within it. Readers need to pay particular attention to contradictions or tonal shifts between and within texts from this time. For example, how does a prescriptive writer like Whately change his tone or language as he moves from describing the marital ideal to discussing its possible problems?

No one place of Scripture doth either directly contain, or plainly express, the full duty of the married couple: which yet from many places may well be collected into the body of one discourse. But lest I should seem to affect novelty, in recalling the long disused practice of antiquity, I will make the ground of all my speech, those words of the Apostle *Paul*, Ephesians 5:23, where he saith, "The husband is the wife's head."

The comparison which the Holy Ghost here useth, affords this general point, that there is a mutual bond of duty standing betwixt man and wife. They are indebted each to other in a reciprocal debt. The parcels and specials of which debt, I am at this time to declare unto you for the direction of all such as either are or shall be entered into this estate. . . .

3. These main duties are two. The first is, the chaste keeping of each one's body each for other. The Husband must not dare to give himself to any woman in this world but to his wife; nor the wife to company with any under heaven besides her own husband. Against which duty if either of them shall offend, the party so transgressing hath committed adultery, broken the covenant of God, removed the yoke from the yoke fellow's neck, and laid himself open (if the Magistrate did as God's law commands) to the bloody stroke of a violent death.

But if it be demanded, whether the party wronged may lawfully admit the other party again, after the offense known: I answer, that in case the man or woman have offended once or so, through infirmity, and yet being convicted, shall by manifest outward tokens, testify his or her repentance, and

---

William Whately, *A Bride-bush: Or, A Wedding Sermon* (London, 1617), 1–3.

sure desire of amendment, then it is meet and convenient that this offense be by the yoke-fellow passed by for the love of the married couple should be very fervent and abundant, and therefore able to pass by great, yea the greatest wrongs, so far as it may with safe conscience be done. And we read not of any express commandment which enjoins a final separation. But again I say, that in case the party transgressing shall continue in the begun fault, and declare himself irreformable,[1] the party thus injured is bound in conscience both to complain of the sin, and separate himself utterly: for no man must make himself a member of an harlot, nor woman of a whore-master. The chief thing therefore that married people must take heed of, is this, lest by any means they should so far offend God, neglect their public covenant, wrong their yoke-fellow, scandalize the Church, pollute their bodies, and adventure their souls to damnation, as to follow strange flesh, and receive unto the use of their bodies any besides themselves, whom God hath coupled together, and sanctified one for another. Yet not alone the gross act of adultery, but all such over-familiar and light behaviors, as may give either occasion or suspicion of an evil meaning, must be by them forborne[2] and shunned: always bearing in mind the grave speech of wise Solomon: "Whosoever toucheth her (speaking of his neighbor's wife) shall not be innocent" (Proverbs 6:29). Let no man, therefore, let no woman take this burning fire into their bosoms, or walk upon these scorching coals. . . .

4. The next is cohabitation or dwelling together, enjoined in express terms to the husband by the Apostle *Peter* (who bids him, *Dwell with his Wife* [1 Peter 3:7]) and therefore by good consequent extending to her also: for who can dwell with a woman that will run from him? And the Apostle *Paul* commands the husband to give unto the wife due benevolence, and the wife to give the same to the husband, which cannot be without this cohabitation; yea, he especially forbids them to "defraud each the other, unless it be by consent, and afterwards to come together again" (1 Corinthians. 7:3–5) which doth necessarily import the abode in one home. So that the married man or woman may not abide or dwell where each of them pleaseth, but they must have the same habitation as one body. I deny not, that the service of the country, and needful private affairs, may cause a just departure for (even) a long time.

---

[1] **irreformable:** incapable of being reformed.   [2] **forborne:** past tense of forbear.

→ STE. B

## *From* Counsel to the Husband: To the Wife Instruction

1608

The household was not simply a social institution; it was a very powerful metaphor for interpreting other hierarchal social arrangements. In general, relations between the sexes are the model for many relationships that depend on notions of inferiority/superiority (Scott 45; Wiesner 252–55); however, marriage metaphors speak to a carefully observed balance of obligation, hierarchy, love, and loyalty. Some texts, like the anonymous[1] *Counsel to the Husband*, directly describe the household as a commonwealth; other texts throughout this edition compare the relationship between husband and wife to the relationship between the king and his subjects or between Christ and the church. Marriage frequently symbolized idealized political arrangements as well. James I represented himself to Parliament as the head of a national "family": "I am the Husband, and the whole Isle is my lawful Wife" (James VI/I 272).

Analogies between the family and the commonwealth depend on the idea that "order in the family was both necessary for, and parallel to, order in the state" (Amussen 35). Conversely, disorder in one realm was thought to lead to disorder in another. For example, Juan Luis Vives, in arguing for the importance of love and companionship, claims that, "the household when their master and their mistress are at debate can no otherwise be in quiet and at rest than a city whose rulers agree not" (quoted in Klein 135). In a like manner, *Othello*'s Brabantio sees the disruption of his parental rights as emblematic of larger disorder: "So let the Turk of Cyprus us beguile, / We lose it not, so long as we can smile" (1.3.213–14). Metaphors associating the family with an absolutist state had profound implications for women's status within the household. Laurie Shannon notes, "The duty of obedience, loyalty, and love to someone who held absolute legal sway . . . placed wives in the same position with respect to husbands that citizens occupied with respect to tyrants or absolutists" (63–64). Notice, for example, how the very title *Counsel to the Husband: To the Wife Instruction* positions each partner in the marriage.

A family may be compared unto a commonwealth: wherein, there are diverse societies and degrees, reciprocally relating, and mutually depending one upon another. The highest degree of society is between the husband and the wife; and this is as the first wheel of a clock, that turneth about all the rest in order. The next society is between the Parents and the children. The

---

[1] No author appears on the title page; however, the book's dedicatory letter is signed "Ste. B."

Ste. B, *Counsel to the Husband: To the Wife Instruction* . . . (London, 1608), 40–43, 48–51.

third between the servants one with another, and toward all other superiors in the family. Into these three societies may a family be disposed. As touching the first and principle society (wherein also principally I purpose to insist) which is between yourself and your loving *Hind* or *Roe*, whom many a time I have blessed and shall bless (by God's grace) unto your use and comfort give me leave, (as one that can speak by the surest learning) to pour forth my mind mutually to you both; who can tell you, that the Canker unto happiness, and danger of confusion to a family, is the contention and disagreement of man and wife.

You will say, how may this be avoided? I answer, very easily, if in time true regard be had unto mutual duty, without which there can be no comfort, nor that blessing of happiness which before we spoke of. Nay, (which is more) to have the blessing of God, which is the foundation and cause of all happiness. It standeth not in what man and wife shall conclude upon, that there may be peace and quietness, but what order God hath prescribed them, to be obeyed in their places: so that they must look unto God's wisdom, order, and polity for economical government, and not what may seem right and good in their own eyes. And that, if the man may not wear woman's apparel, nor the woman man's, how much less may the one usurp the other's dignity, or the other (to wit the husband) resign or give over his sovereignty unto his wife? But each must keep their place, their order, and heavenly polity,[1] whereto God hath called them. The husband is made the head, and the wife resembled to the body: may the head of a body (natural) be turned downward? Can the whole person so continue, and live well in that state? How unseemly is it? No more can the body politic be in peaceable or blessed condition, if order be inverted. A most monstrous thing it was that the Prophet *Isaiah* complained of when he said, "Children are extortioners of my people, and women rule over them" (Isaiah 3:12). You will say the Prophet speaketh of another case: I know it well: yet doth it (and very well may it) serve, in any case that is contrary to God's word to show deformity; but in his right case most notoriously. . . .

So that it was not for naught, that before I said it might be a glorious spectacle, to see the wife sustain the household government and to manage the affairs pertaining thereunto. Where I meant not every wife, the foolish and unprofitable wife, the corruption of her husband's bones and dishonor of his life, which becometh an heifer for his adversaries and the vile to plough withal (Judges 14:18);[2] but (as I said) with respect of these cautions: 1. That the wife be fit for the government she undertaketh. 2. Being never so

---

[1] **polity:** organized society or community; a form of government.   [2] **Judges 14:18:** a reference to Samson.

fit, with the consent and reverence of her husband's will, taking all her light (as the Moon is said from the Sun), so she from her husband, for government and authority, as his Lieutenant under him; and so wisely disposing all to his honor accordingly. In such a case, how great an honor is the wife's godly government unto the husband? Whiles he as king to command, yet with love as a husband, shall go in and out, in the midst of his family? Not fearing spoil, whether he be at home or abroad; nor needing unlawful spoils to maintain his state. As also, how honorable a service is it in the wife, to depend upon his beck?[3] To advise with her head? To lean upon his breast? And yet have the authority to do what she will? That is, whilst her will is honest, lawful, and to her husband's good, as hath been spoken of.

Can this be counted slavery, or servile subjection? Must there not be some subjection? Can all in a nation be kings? Can all in a family be fathers? Can all be wives? Can all be everything? "If the whole body (saith the Apostle) were an eye, where were the hearing? Or if all were the ear, where were the smelling?" (1 Corinthians 12:17). If therefore in a kingdom, or family, there must of necessity be these degrees, and that we see men so subject to Princes, that they contentedly delight therein, and neither count it slavishness, nor affect above their state (though some wicked do otherwise) should not the wife look unto the hand of God, which made her the wife, and not the husband, the weaker vessel, and not the stronger? The body, and not the head? To obey, and not to rule? That is, not to rule without obedience. To grudge hereat,[4] is not against the husband, but against God withal: to govern otherwise, is not to rule, but to usurp. Therefore, the Apostle said not, the wife shall not rule, but he said: "I permit not a woman to teach, nor to usurp authority over the man" (1 Timothy 2:12). That is (as under correction I take it) without the husband's content, will, and approbation; neither constrained by her shrewdness, but referred for cause (voluntarily) to exercise the rule and government of the family.

---

[3] **beck:** a commanding or controlling gesture.   [4] **hereat:** here.

⇥ HANNAH WOOLLEY

## *From* The Gentlewoman's Companion: Or, A Guide to the Female Sex   *1675*

An early modern household was a social and economic unit consisting of extended family, servants (who may or may not have been relations), and possibly apprentices: "Servants were perhaps the most distinctive socio-economic feature of sixteenth and seventeenth century society" (Burnett 1). "Service," a key life stage for most early moderns, was not limited to the working poor; even in the upper classes, adolescent men and women would be sent to other elite households to serve the master or mistress and learn household management. For those who did not learn from living in another home, there were domestic manuals, like those written by Hannah Woolley (1622?–1675), that taught the housekeeping practices of elite households. Although the duties differed, the ideal of loyal service and reciprocal obligation obtains as powerfully in the military as in the household. When Iago complains about being overlooked for promotion, he uses the term *service* ("'Tis the curse of service"), which places military advancement within the larger realm of domestic relations (Burnett 1; see also Neill, "His Master's" 214–22).

Strikingly, Othello and Desdemona are paralleled with a married couple in service to them. While much of the available evidence on master-servant relations focuses on the tension between unequals, there is some evidence of strong emotional ties between masters and servants. Servants were known to leave bequests to masters and other household members, while masters frequently left cash or clothing to servants (McIntosh 19). Woolley, the first woman to write a domestic manual in England, carefully delineates the duties of the waiting-woman and chambermaid. Which of these roles does Emilia perform? Compare Woolley's descriptions of the reciprocal obligations of mistress and servant with the articulations of other ties of loyalty in marriage texts and in the military manuals. How does it enrich *Othello*'s gendered perspectives on loyalty, affection, and obedience to have each of the principals intimately tied to an underling?

Hannah Woolley, *The Gentlewoman's Companion: Or, A Guide to the Female Sex . . .* (London, 1675), 109–10, 205–7.

# From *The Gentlewoman's Companion; Or, A Guide to the Female Sex*

## OF WOMEN'S BEHAVIOR TO THEIR SERVANTS, AND WHAT IS TO BE REQUIRED OF THEM IN THE HOUSE, OR WHAT THEREUNTO APPERTAINS.

If by a thorough inspection and experience, you find you have a faithful Servant, give her to understand you are not insensible thereof by your loving carriage, and kind acknowledgment of her fidelity, and frequently find out some occasions to give her some little encouragements to engage her continuance therein; do not dishearten her in her duty, by often finding fault where there is little or none committed, yet be not remiss in reproving where she doth amiss. . . .

Be not too passionate with your Servants; and look narrowly to them, that they waste or lavish nothing, lest thereby you impair your estate, and so purchase the repute of a careless and indiscreet Woman.

## AND FIRST TO ALL GENTLEWOMEN, WHO THOUGH WELL BORN ARE NOT WITHSTANDING BY INDIGENCY NECESSITATED TO SERVE SOME PERSON OF QUALITY.

. . . If you desire to be a Waiting-Gentlewoman, it will be expected that you can Dress well; Preserve well; and Write well in a legible hand, good language, and good *English*; have some skill in Arithmetic; Carve well, and let your behavior be modest and courteous to all persons according to their degree; humble and submissive to your Lord and Lady or Master and Mistress; neat in your habit; loving to Servants; sober in your Countenance and Discourse; not using any wanton gesture, which may give Gentlemen occasion to suspect your levity, and so court you to Debauchery, and lose a reputation irrecoverable.

## TO ALL MAIDENS, WHO DESIRE TO BE CHAMBER-MAIDS TO PERSONS OF QUALITY.

It will be required of you, that you Dress well that you may be able to supply the place of the Waiting-woman, should she chance to fall sick, or be absent from your Lady; you must wash fine Linen well and starch Tiffanies, Lawns, Points, and Laces, mend them neatly; and wash white Sarcenets,[1] with such like things.

---

[1] **Sarcenets:** very fine silks and the dresses made from them.

You must make your Lady's bed; lay up, and lay out her Night-clothes; see that her Chamber be kept clean, and nothing wanting which she desires or requires to be done. Be modest in your deportment, ready at her call, always diligent, answering not again when reproved, but with pacifying words, loving and courteous to your fellow-servants not giggling or idling out your time, nor wantoning in the society of men. You will find the benefit thereof; for an honest and sober man will sooner make that woman his Wife whom he seeth continually employed about her business, than one who makes it her business to trifle away her own and others' time.

→ **MARTIN PARKER**

## *From* The Married Man's Lesson: Or, A Dissuasion from Jealousy

*1624*

Desdemona sings a popular ballad, "The Willow Song," in her private bed-chamber, but ballads were a resolutely public form. They often circulated on large sheets of paper printed on one side, known as broadsides, which were used as decorations in alehouses, peddled in rural areas, and read on street corners and at fairs. Broadsides and the ballads printed on them were one of the earliest forms of mass media and they covered a huge variety of popular and topical subjects, including stories of grisly crimes, war news, and folktales. The ballads' communal origins call for modern readers to pay careful attention to their representations of community life, as well as to their sense of public and private behavior. Obviously, ballads printed on broadsides were read, but one might think of them as prompting an interactive public performance accompanied by suitable gestures, facial expressions, music, and audience reaction (Wiltenberg 27). In comparing Emilia's views on adultery with those given in the ballads included here, also compare the circumstances of both types of performance.

Many English ballads focused on battles between the sexes; thus, they frequently represented disorderly or insubordinate women. Although it was men who primarily sold and sang ballads (some women did, too, but it is unclear how many), women would certainly have been a significant part of the audience, and many critics wonder if ballads intentionally provoked or catered to women's tastes. Most ballads, like "The Cuckold's Haven" (p. 285), were written anonymously; however, Martin Parker (d. 1656?), author of "The Married Man's Lesson," was one of the few to achieve fame writing ballads and broadsides on a range of topical and popular subjects. His acclaim was such that his signature, "M.P.," continued to be used on ballads for years after his death.

Martin Parker, *The Married Man's Lesson: Or, A Dissuasion from Jealousy* (London, 1624).

# From *The Married Man's Lesson: Or, A Dissuasion from Jealousy*

TO THE TUNE OF *ALL YOU THAT WILL WOO A WENCH.*

You men who are married come hearken to me,
    I'll teach you a Lesson if wise you will be,
Then take my advice that's intended for good,
    and so 'tis if it be but well understood:
'Twill cause you to shun all contention and spleen,          5
    that daily betwixt man and woman are seen,
I speak against jealousy that monster fierce,
    and wish I could conquer the Fiend with my verse,
*O be not thou jealous I prithee[1] dear Lad,*
    *For jealousy makes many good women bad.*          10

If thou have a good wife then I thee advise,
    to cherish her well for she is a rare prize,
If she be indifferent between good and bad,
    good means to reform her may easily be had:
If she be so evil that there is few worse,          15
    imagine thy sins have deserved that curse,
*Then bear with true patience thy cross as 'tis fit,*
    *and thou to a blessing thereby may'st turn it.*
*But be not, &c.*

Between these three winds the good, bad, and the mean,          20
    I ground the whole argument of this my Theme,
For in them a man's human bliss, or his woe,
    doth chiefly consist as experience doth show:
Thus is it not counsel that's worthy regard,
    which teacheth to soften a thing that is hard,          25
*And what I intend is in every man's will,*
    *to turn to a virtue what seemeth most ill.*
*Then be, &c.*

A wife that is good being beautiful may
    Perhaps raise suspicion that she'll go astray,          30
O note the fond humors that most men possess,
    they're neither content with the more nor the less,

---

[1] **prithee:** archaic colloquialism for "(I) pray thee."

For if she be homely, then her he will slight,
    to such neither fair, nor foul, can yield delight,
*If once he'll be jealous the other he scorns,*                    35
    *there's no greater plagues than imagined horns.*
*Then be not, &c.*

A wife that's indifferent between good and ill,
    is she that in housewifery shows her good will,
Yet sometimes her voice she too much elevates,                    40
    is that the occasion for which her he hates:
A sovereign remedy for this disease,
    is to hold thy tongue let her say what she please:
Judge, is not this better than to fight and scratch,
    for silence will soonest a Shrew overmatch,                    45
*However I pray thee shun jealousy Lad,*
    *for jealousy makes many good women bad.*

A wife that's all bad if thy luck be to have,
    seek not to reclaim her by making her slave,
If she be as bad as ever trod on ground,                          50
    not fighting nor jealousy will heal that wound:
For mark when a River is stopped in its course,
    it overflows the banks: then the danger is worse,
*Thy own good example and patience withal,*
    *may her from her vices much rather recall.*                   55
*Then be not, &c.*

## ⤳ *From* The Cuckhold's Haven                              *1638*

Given the number of ballads, broadsides, and jesting asides on the subject, one could understandably conclude that female adultery was a constant preoccupation of the early modern man. Adultery was not simply a rejection of the husband, but a challenge to the entire social order. It threw into doubt the husband's authority in the household, his ownership of his children, and thus his masculine honor. With its potential to disrupt bloodlines and inheritance, women's adultery was more harshly judged and punished than men's; women higher on the social scale were also more scrutinized than those further down. Almost all facets of women's behavior, honorable or disorderly, were ultimately

---

*The Cuckold's Haven* (London, 1638), 46–47

linked to their sexuality. The chief sins attributed to women — "gadding" (wandering outside of the household, particularly for gossip or out of curiosity), "Frowardness" (disobedience), and adultery — were inextricably linked in the Renaissance mind. Guilt in one arena provoked suspicions in the other: the woman who was "free of speech" may also have been free with her body. In his 1416 tract *Of Wifely Duties,* Francesco Barbaro warned: "Not only arms but indeed also the speech of women can never be made public; for the speech of a noble woman can be no less dangerous than the nakedness of her limbs" (205).

Male anxiety about female fidelity and disobedience in early modern England is articulated primarily through two superimposed images: the cuckold and the "horned" man. *Cuckold* was a term alluding to the cuckoo's habit of leaving eggs in another bird's nest; thus, the cuckold was a popular figure of jest and the word was a common insult, "a slur on both [a husband's] virility and his capacity to rule his own household" (Stone 316–17). To be cuckolded was to have paternity — and the orderly transfer of property — thrown into doubt; hence, the disorder jokingly implied in the idea of a cuckold's "haven." As in this ballad, the cuckold was at times intertwined with the image of the horned man, a figure that referred to a shaming ritual in which a man with an adulterous wife was ridden through town wearing a cap with animal horns. Although the deeper associations of horns with adultery are unclear, both the word *cuckold* and the symbol of horns suggest that the woman's behavior (and the man's lack of control over it) animalized the man — a connection noted by Othello: "A hornèd man's a monster and a beast" (4.1.60). Although the idea of "cuckoldry" speaks to great anxieties over patriarchal control, as Laura Gowing notes, *cuckold* did not have the material effect on men that *whore* and other sexual slanders had on women (112–13; see also Stanton). Gowing further points out that charges of adultery relied on interpreting evidence of "suspicious familiarity" (184) such as private conversations between women and men not their husbands. Consider the way Iago uses Desdemona's conversation with Cassio to inflame Othello's suspicions (3.3.39–41). Since legal charges of adultery required proof, such charges would have pulled the household further into the public eye, increasing the community's scrutiny of the wife's behavior. In the play, the suspicion of adultery increases Othello's scrutiny and opens Desdemona's actions to interpretation.

# *From* The Cuckold's Haven

*OR,*

The married man's misery, who must abide
The penalty of being hornified
He unto his neighbors doth make his case known,
And tells them all plainly, "The case[1] is their own."
(To the tune of *The Spanish Gypsy*)


Come, neighbors, follow me,
    that cuckolized be,
That all the Town may see
    our slavish misery:
*Let every man who keeps a bride,*         5
    *take heed he not be hornify'd.*


Though narrowly I do watch,
    and use Lock, Bolt, and Latch,
My wife will me o'ermatch,
    my forehead I may scratch:         10
*For though I wait both time and tide,*
    *I oftentimes am hornify'd.*


For now the time's so grown,
    men cannot keep their own,
But every slave unknown,         15
    will reap what we have sown:
*Yea, though we keep them by our side,*
    *we now and then are hornify'd*


They have so many ways,
    by nights or else by days,         20
That though our wealth decays,
    yet they our horns will raise:
*And many of them take a pride*
    *to keep their Husbands hornify'd.*

---

[1] **case:** a procedure in common law; slang for female genitalia.

O what a case this is,                                                    25
    O what a grief this is,
My wife hath learned to kiss,
    and thinks 'tis not amiss:
*She oftentimes doth me deride,*
    *and tells me I am hornify'd.*                                        30


What ever I do say,
    she will have her own way,
She scorneth to obey;
    She'll take time while she may:
*And if I beat her back and side,*                                        35
    *In spite I shall be hornify'd.*


Nay, you would little think,
    how they will friendly link,
And how they'll sit and drink,
    Till they begin to wink:
*And then if Vulcan*[2] *will but ride,*                                  40
    *Some Cuckold shall be hornify'd.*


A woman that will be drunk,
    will easily play the Punk;[3]
For when her wits are sunk,
    all keys will fit her Trunk:                                          45
*Then by experience oft is tried,*
    *poor men that way are hornify'd.*


Thus honest men must bear,
    and 'tis in vain to fear,
For we are ne're the near                                                 50
    our hearts with grief to tear:
*For while we mourn it is their pride,*
    *the more to keep us hornify'd.*


---

[2] **Vulcan:** God of fire who caught his wife Venus in an affair with the god Mars.  [3] **Punk:** a prostitute, strumpet, harlot.

And be we great or small,                                          55
  we must be at their call,
How e're the Cards do fall,
  we men must suffer all:
*Do what we can we must abide*
  *the pain of being hornify'd.*                          60

## The Second Part, to the Same Tune.

If they once bid us go,
  we dare not twice say no,
Although too well we know
  'Tis to our grief and woe:
*Nay, we are glad their faults to hide,*                           65
  *though often we are hornify'd.*

If I my wife provoke,
  with words in anger spoke,
She swears she'll make all smoke,
  and I must be her Cloak:                                 70
*Her baseness and my wrongs I hide,*
  *and patiently am hornify'd.*

When these good Gossips meet,
  In Alley, Lane, or Street,
Poor men we do not see't,                                          75
  with Wine and Sugar sweet,
*They arm themselves, and then beside*
  *their husbands must be hornify'd.*

Not your Italian locks,[4]
  which seems a Paradox,                                  80
Can keep these Hens from Cocks,
  till they are paid with a *P——:*[5]

---

[4] **Italian locks:** lock and key types were known for being both well-made and elegant; what the author suggests here is that not even the most well-made locks can keep women from leaving to commit adultery; that such locks are Italian refers to the reputed licentiousness of Italian men and the confinement of Italian women (see Coryate on courtesans of Venice, p. 243).

[5] *P——*: pox, venereal disease.

*So long as they can go or ride,*
    *They'll have their husbands hornify'd.*


The more you have intent,                                            85
    the business to prevent,
The more her mind is bent
    your will to circumvent:
*Such secret means they can provide*
    *to get their husbands hornify'd.*                               90


For if we them do blame,
    or tell them of their shame;
Although the men we name,
    with whom they did the same:
*They'll swear who ever spoke it lied,*                              95
    *Thus still poor men are hornify'd.*


All you that single be,
    avoid this slavery,
Much danger is, you see,
    in women's company:                                             100
*For he who to a Wife is tied,*
    *May look still to be hornify'd.*


Yet must I needs confess,
    (though many do transgress)
A number, numberless,                                               105
    Which virtue do possess,
*And to their Husbands are a guide:*
    *By such no man is hornify'd.*


They who are of that race,
    this Ditty in any case                                          110
Is not to their disgrace,
    They are not for this place:
*To such this only is applied,*
    *By whom good men are hornify'd.*

# CHAPTER 4

# *Masculinity and Military Life*

>‹

Although driven by domestic conflict, *Othello* is also a theater of war. The erupting passion and domestic distrust in the play are intricately connected to its representation of a military culture similarly caught in a net of distrust and disorder. Although it lacks the stirring prebattle speeches of *Henry V* or the stridently masculinist rhetoric of *Troilus and Cressida*, *Othello* is just as much shaped by a male social order and the field of battle. Othello reminds his soldiers that Cyprus is "a town of war": the Venetians are an occupying force whose behavior potentially provokes the very violence and disorder an occupation is meant to prevent. Military strife shapes *Othello* just as it shaped an early modern Europe developing a "modern" military machine. The documents included in this chapter share with the play an interest in negotiating older and more modern military forms and structures, an emphasis on rank and loyalty, and a heavily gendered language of military discipline needed to address fears of social disorder and uncontained sexuality. As you will see, the marital and the martial mirror each other through shared understandings of loyalty, obedience, subordination, and order.

The early modern period witnessed what scholars call a military revolution or a new militarism, during which armies assumed a recognizably modern shape. The nature of war changed dramatically: infantry forces came to dominate over cavalry; muskets and pikes began to replace the longbow and the sword, and short battles in the countryside turned into extensive sieges in towns. Despite this new sense of a military order, in the early stages of the change there were not clear lines between the army and society, "a blurring attested by the lack of clear distinction between military and civilian costume" (Hacker 646). Thus, the army was initially distinguished more by its behavior and rituals than by its dress and insignia. Even though they had no sense that these military developments would survive for centuries, most early modern Europeans were keenly aware that their world was being altered substantially by them. They engaged in lively debate over the nature of the military and its relation to society, a discussion energized by ongoing fear of Ottoman supremacy. The Ottoman empire had an enormous military machine whose structure and manpower made it a dominant force in the region (see Figure 28). Even as strategists examined the intricacies of Ottoman methods, accounts of Ottoman battles with Christendom alerted citizens at home to military innovation and technique in far-flung territories.

In earlier eras, the dominant figure of war was the heavily armed horseman, usually an aristocratic knight who carried a lance or a sword and was backed by anonymous villagers forced into battle. Battle stories mostly told of individual courage and of the opportunity war offered to win personal glory and reputation. However, by Shakespeare's time, men on foot — infantry from the lower classes — had come to dominate, and the professional soldier acting in concert with others became the new image of war. War became more professional as armies gradually developed more specialist troops with highly elaborated roles. Historical accounts of wars, once focusing on the achievements of individuals, began to focus on the place of the army and the ability of soldiers with different functions to act as a unit. One can see this in King James's *Lepanto* (Chapter 2, p. 251), which focuses on the coming together of Christian forces rather than on the single Christian knight.

Othello is not a citizen-soldier, but rather a foreign mercenary hired by the Venetians. The eloquent descriptions of military experiences with which he woos Desdemona carry traces of the old horseman-knight (note that he calls his life a "pilgrimage" [1.3.155]), for whom war was a noble calling and a religious duty rather than a profession. In contrast, the play opens with Iago's obsession over rank and professional advancement (Genster 797–98; Neill, "His Master's" 222–26), concerns that speak to the increasing importance of clearly delineated hierarchy and the interests of the professional soldier. You will notice that Iago's complaints over lack of advancement are intertwined with concerns about money ("And I, of whom his eyes had seen the proof / . . . must be beleed and calmed / By debitor and creditor"

FIGURE 28 Battle of the Mohacs, *from* The Book of Suleyman. *The Ottoman empire was the only power in Europe that had a state-operated standing military. The prowess of Turkish soldiers and their innovative methods of combat were widely known in Europe and discussed in military texts (see the excerpt from King James VI & I's* Lepanto *in Chapter 2). English traveler Fynes Moryson notes that, "the Turks both adventure their persons and carefully perform all duties in war" (38). This sixteenth-century miniature by an artist of Suleyman's court depicts the two-hour Battle of Mohacs in which mobile Ottoman troops defeated heavily armored Hungarian troops.*

[1.1.29–32]. Although this may simply be the prelude to wheedling money out of Roderigo, it might have resonated with English officers dependent on an underfinanced army for their welfare. More important, Iago's resentment of his position is at odds with the culture's prevailing belief in the virtue and necessity of "service" (Neill, *Putting* 33–48).

Most European countries still operated on a semifeudal model of combat in which individual rulers maintained limited standing militia for home defense; when a monarch needed to send troops overseas, he or she instructed local princes and nobles to raise an army. Officials raised troops (at times by force) for battle as needed from the available adult males. All able-bodied men between sixteen and sixty were liable for service; however, those with means hired substitutes or bribed officials, thus leaving armies to consist of impoverished men, troublemakers, and volunteers eager to escape problems at home. (In *2 Henry IV*, 2.1, Shakespeare shows "the muster" with men begging and bribing their way out of service.) These men would be trained on the field of battle, and their pay was often poor, if they were paid at all; not surprisingly, death and desertion rates were high.

In England, the new militarism occurred comparatively late (around mid-sixteenth century) and took the form of an elaborate war machine — the formation of which left almost no member of society unaffected. As an island, England was spared many of the town-based battles that profoundly affected the rest of Europe, but entire societies experienced and suffered from war. Apart from the marginal men who comprised the bulk of the military, "citizens were assessed military taxes; merchants made loans to the government and contracted to supply soldiers with food, clothing, and equipment; and both men and women found work . . . in military camps" (Cahill 8). The very people who comprised Shakespeare's audiences were likely to have been touched in some way by England's expanding military.

In the 1580s a new literature sprang up with an interest in military procedure, histories of ancient and modern battles, and the new sciences of war. This vast military literature took up the moral and physical qualities of officers and soldiers, effective battle training and tactics, methods for instilling discipline, and the best organization for different types of warfare. Thomas Proctor's *Of the Knowledge and Conduct of Wars* (1578; p. 305) represents war as the proving ground of masculinity and discipline; like many of the texts in this chapter, it generated a sense of pride in national character based on specific ideas of manhood.

Since the army came increasingly to depend on men from the lower classes to fill the swelling infantry, many of the military manuals seem to be written for the middling sort of men who would compose these new armies (and who would patronize theater). J. R. Hale argues: "The extent of military interests . . . meant that war, its techniques and its issues, penetrated the imaginative life of people more deeply than at any previous time, and the proliferation of books ensured that this penetration was not restricted to places where wars were actually being fought" (3). War, an ongoing interest and concern of rulers, became the subject of discussion and debate for the common people as well. Nor was soldiery a temporary concern; Virginia Vaughan argues that military issues were particularly pressing during the Restoration, when former army officers performed *Othello* and the public at large was concerned about the maintenance of a peacetime garrison (Vaughan 104ff.).[1]

English military treatises, particularly the ones selected here, are greatly concerned with the soldier's place, or "office," and stress the dangers in relying on inexperienced and ignorant officers. These concerns may have been motivated by the increased class mobility offered in the new militarism. As rank became attached to certain skills rather than social status, men beyond the gentry had opportunities for advancement. Outsiders to the previously closed circles of the military elite could adapt to and perform the virtues of the gentry by following the guidelines of such volumes. The discipline and training of the professional soldier seemed at times indistinguishable from immersion in class codes and lingered in these treatises' recurring interest (shared with Cassio) in the importance of reputation in military life. How do these works address the issue of reputation?

Modernization of the English army increasingly relied on principles of hierarchical subordination, discipline, and social obligation. As armies became more stratified, the independent knight gave way to the soldier, who subordinated his will to the dictates of his superior. Robert Barret, for example, reminds his reader that there is no honor in "singular combat . . . without his General's license, (for he is not now his own man, but the Prince's, who doth give him pay)" (p. 302). Thus, one of the greatest "modern" military innovations was the codification of military hierarchy through scrupulous articulation of rank. While titles such as lieutenant, ensign, and general existed long before the military revolution, they tended to be more generic terms of leadership than precise indications of rank. Military texts played a large role in codifying the responsibilities of officers, making them closer to modern designations. However, the process of codification was not centralized, leading to some confusion over the responsibilities of rank, a confusion exacerbated by the complete overhaul of the officer corps during the Elizabethan era.

---

[1] The pamphlet *Iago Display'd*, which rewrites the story of *Othello* wholly as a tale of military intrigue and malfeasance, testifies to the resonance of the play's military setting.

Iago's eyes are on the lieutenancy, but the ensign's rank carries powerful symbolic weight. Images of battle formation from Thomas Styward's *The Pathway to Martial Discipline* always place the ensign in the center. Figure 29 demonstrates the new emphasis on battle formation, subordination, and units of soldiers rather than individual combatants. Styward recommends the sudden formation of a "D" or "Snail" in combat, which protects the ensign and intersperses "shot" or gunners with the officers. This formation relies on footmen for its speed and mobility, thus demonstrating Styward's argument that battle plans should rely on infantry. Each letter represents a different type of soldier with a separate function.

If the lieutenant could represent the general by wielding his power, we see in Barret (p. 299) that the ensign literally represented the company by carrying its "colors" — its standard or flag — and its reputation. Iago may in some ways be an anti-ensign, a soldier who treats his compatriots as enemies, who uses the "colors" of rhetoric to mislead the soldiers, who makes them misread signs such as Desdemona's handkerchief, and who destroys rather than saves reputations.

The documents included here demonstrate that military rank is not simply a chain of command; it is a carefully coded way of organizing relations between men who often lived far away from the customs that govern civilian society. In most of these texts, rank or office is not simply a function or list of responsibilities — it marks a series of relationships. As you read, note where these texts articulate how soldiers should behave toward each other. Look for concepts such as loyalty, honor, and service as well as practices that define and limit relationships, such as vows. For example, critic Julie Genster suggests that the office of "lieutenant," which so ignites Iago's jealousy in *Othello*, is a potent emblem of the anxiety over absence and substitution in the play. Barret's description of the lieutenant is typical in its reminder that the lieutenant's command is always temporary, meant to be relinquished immediately. The lieutenant is both the symbol and conduit of the general's power; however, as the one who stands in for the general in times of need, he is also a potential substitute and therefore a reminder of the general's absence. Anxiety over absence and transfers of power may magnify Othello's jealous concerns over being cuckolded, a term that, as discussed in Chapter 3, refers to a substitution of the husband by another man. In addition, the lieutenant also can function as an intercessor for the general; in pleading for leniency for Cassio, Desdemona may be assuming his function.

Military treatises strive for an ideal; nonetheless, they are equally clear that even a "valiant" (1.3.50) soldier like Othello obtains the military ideal with difficulty and easily reverts to flawed humanity. The fear of human-

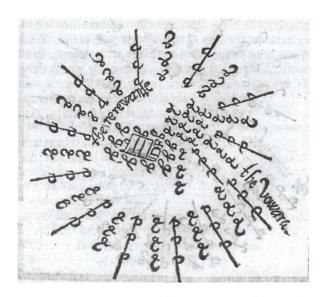

FIGURE 29 *"Snail" battle formation from* The Pathway to Martial Discipline *by Thomas Styward (1581).*

kind's instability, evident in texts on passions, runs throughout military texts as well. Almost every treatise represents the soldier as much at war with his own base nature as with an external enemy. Even Thomas Proctor, whose *Of the Knowledge and Conduct of Wars* lauds the appropriateness of the English character for war, also warns the reader to guard against the English habit of "mutability and variable changing of mind" (p. 306). As Chapter 5 indicates, Renaissance thinkers believed that hypersexuality and excess emotion could literally change a person. The changing of mind feared by Proctor is a total transformation of self, a movement from a rational being to a beast mired in gross materiality. A similar fear surrounds *Othello* — note how often the men are said to "change" to something less than men (which would include women, who were considered lesser beings), as when Iago warns Othello: "patience! / Or I shall say you're all-in-all in spleen, / And nothing of a man" (4.1.87–89). The bestial language that runs through the play often signals degeneration. So, too, these texts' reiteration of punishments for and warnings about drunkenness, brawling, and sensual indulgence suggests that this "changing of mind" can be brought about by overindulgence in the "grosser" side of humanity; thus, the texts share with the play fears of degeneration into grossness (see K. Hall, *Othello* 368–70).

A marginal note in Thomas and Leonard Digges's *Stratioticos* reads "rest effeminates / training makes soldiers," summing up important concerns about masculinity in military life. The fear of "effeminization" — of men succumbing to uncontrolled and "womanish" sexual excess — undergirds the inculcation of military discipline. In the early modern era, a man who lost control of his sexual desires for women, was thought to become "womanish." As Mario DiGangi notes, such "male effeminacy was understood to cause heteroerotic or homoerotic disorder," which then caused larger social disorder (5). One imagines that, as war evolved into ever-longer sieges with long periods of inaction for soldiers waiting for combat, the problem of an effeminizing rest, of giving into disorderly impulses — both sexual and social — became particularly acute.

As *Othello* forces the military and domestic worlds into collision, it reveals a primal fear of effeminacy, of the overweening power of both women's appetites and men's uncontrolled desires for women. Desdemona's request to accompany Othello to Cyprus raises both fears, which Othello attempts to allay by rejecting the possibility of lust ("I therefor beg it not / To please the palate of my appetite" [1.3.263–64]) and insisting on his own incorruptibility. He articulates his martial single-mindedness in terms that remind the reader that women and desire are inimical to a soldier's life:

> No, when light-winged toys
> Of feathered Cupid seel with wanton dullness
> My speculative and officed instruments,
> That my disports corrupt and taint my business,
> Let huswives make a skillet of my helm,
> And all indign and base adversities
> Make head against my estimation!    (1.3.270–76)

The punishment he imagines for sexual license is conquest by women — the very image of effeminacy. One might compare this metaphor with a typical Renaissance figure for effeminacy: Hercules' excessive love for Omphale, which forces the hero to dress as a woman and spin yarn. Even though Othello's rather odd and much reviled image of housewives cooking with his helmet argues for a complete containment of women's sexuality and gendered duties from the military sphere, a careful reading of the play and the treatises in this chapter reveals this as a fiction of military masculinity. Readers might consider what space military texts make for women. How do these texts compare with the involvement of *Othello*'s women in Cyprus? How are domestic or sexual metaphors and images mobilized to imagine military life?

The frequent use of erotic or sexual metaphors to articulate multiple power relations means that the erotic, the marital, and the military frequently converge. As Michael Neill argues, "The same language of authority and subordination that characterizes relationships in what we might think of as the 'public' world of state affairs and soldiership, governs the domestic world of husbands and wives, fathers and children" ("His Master's" 220). These analogical discourses increasingly parallel and overlap as the play's action accelerates. Cassio humorously refers to Desdemona as "our great captain's captain" (2.1.76), while Iago mockingly reminds him that "Our general's wife is now the general" (2.3.280); both suggest domination by women and the possibility of Othello's losing his military might in his newfound love. However, this splitting and melding of erotic and military "office" is most potently rendered in "Cassio's dream" (Neill, "His Master's" 220). Instead of "ocular proof," Iago produces an optical illusion: he makes the audience "see" a simultaneously homoerotic and heteroerotic image. The dueling homosocial bonds of the military (particularly between Iago and Othello) and the heterosexual bonds of marriage reach their crescendo in the "monstrous" image, in which Iago takes the place of Desdemona in Cassio's arms: "laid his leg / Over my thigh, and sighed, and kissed, and then / Cried, 'Cursèd fate that gave thee to the Moor!'" (3.3.440–42). Iago's imaginative substitution of himself for Desdemona provokes a professional and emotional substitution. Iago and Othello's "sacred vow" (3.3.478) replaces Othello's marriage vow to Desdemona, just as it replaces Cassio with Iago in rank.


ROBERT BARRET

## *From* The Theory and Practice of Modern Wars     *1598*

→ Technology, most notably the triumph of firearms over armor, brought about most of the major changes in military life during this period. Moreover, with the increased production of guns as well as bullets that could pierce armor, hand-to-hand or closely waged combat became more dangerous than effective. The use of newly developing weapons necessitated innovations in military strategies; as a result, war increasingly became perceived as a science. For example, as war moved from remote fields to towns, military treatises increasingly came to advocate a science of fortification and tactics heavily dependent on mathematics.

    Robert Barret (1586?–1607) opens his treatise with a debate between a "Captain" and a "Gentleman" over the changing nature of war. The Gentleman

Robert Barret, *The Theory and Practice of Modern Wars* (London, 1598), 8–11, 19–22.

praises England's historical success with the longbow. To this defense of the "old archery of England" (2), the Captain responds that times have changed: "Sir that was then, and now is now; the wars are much altered since the fiery weapons first came up: the Cannon, the Musket, the Caliver an[d] Pistol" (2). Barret reveals the link between changing military practice and class status as he shows a debate between an ordinary man well versed in the newest forms of military practice and a gentleman nostalgic for an older order in which successful wars depended on elite warriors. Like Barret's "Gentleman" and "Captain," Iago and Cassio embody competing models of military leadership that are vigorously debated in the texts in this section. Iago's condemnation of Cassio as a "great arithmetician" who has more book-based knowledge than experience represents an older view that sneeringly underplays the significant role of mathematics in fortification and arms. Barret, who spent most of his life in the military before turning to writing, challenges books by learned men, "politicians, geometricians and mathematicians which never saw any wars" (5). Why is Barret, like Cassio, so concerned about reputation? How does a soldier lose his reputation?

# From *The Theory and Practice of Modern Wars*

THE FIRST BOOK OF WAR, DISCOURSES AND MARTIAL
DISCIPLINE
THE SECOND DIALOGUE, WHEREIN IS DECLARED THE
GENERAL PARTS OF A SOLDIER.

Well now, I pray you declare the general parts of a Soldier.

CAPTAIN: It is necessary that he which enters into this action, that he ground his valorous determination upon four principles. First, upon defense of true Religion; secondly, the honor of his Prince; thirdly, the safety of his country; fourthly, diligently to learn the Art he professeth, which is war, whereby many men of low degree and base lineage have attained unto great dignity, credit, and fame: . . . Many others might be remembered, both English, French, Italian, and Spanish, born of low degree, which by their value, virtue, prudence, and conduction mounted to such high Types of honor.

Now he that taketh this resolution, ought to be diligent, careful, vigilant, and obedient, and above all, to have the fear of God. To choose to his Comrades and companions men well acquainted, and of honest conditions; no factioners nor mutineers,[1] whose company is more dangerous than the devil himself. With his Comrades, he is to demean himself,

---

[1] **factioners nor mutineers:** partisans, rebellious or mutinous persons.

sober, quiet, and friendly: rather severe than lavish in speeches, for licentious talkers do easily lose their friends, their estimation, and own quietness. . . .

Let him be no blasphemer, nor swearer: for besides that such a one is infamous to the world, he is assured to be punished by God's divine justice, whereof many examples have been seen.

Let him abstain from dice, cards, and idle games; for common gamesters, although they have many other good parts in them, yet are they not esteemed according to their better parts, but rather discredited, getting enemies, questions, and brawls, with many other inconveniences that follow.

Let him not be over-curious in his fare and diet, but content himself with such provisions as be provided in the camp.

In any wise let him eschew the beastly vice of drunkenness; for crammed paunches and drunken nowls[2] are apt to nothing but to be sluggish, slothful, and drowsy, and in their drunken pangs to have their throats cut. Examples whereof there are too many extant, as of *Tomyris*,[3] Queen of the *Scythians*, who overthrew *Cyrus*, with his three hundred thousand *Persians*, in their beastly drunkenness. . . . Besides, the Soldier given to this vice of gluttony and drunkenness doth disturb all towns, villages, and all lodgments wheresoever he cometh with his unruly hurly burly and robberies, never contenting himself with the ability of his poor host; whereby great scandals do arise, causing many times many Towns, Cities, and whole provinces to revolt from their Princes, caused by the disorder of such insatiable drunkards and gluttons. The which insolencies are carefully to be prevented, and severely punished. . . . On the contrary, the virtue of abstinence and temperance hath been such, and so great in some, as it hath rested a perpetual fame and praise to their names; and have thereby achieved great and honorable enterprises.

Moreover, let our soldier be chaste and honest in his living, refraining [from] sensuality with all possible instancy,[4] avoiding all occasions which might move him to that vice: for those that do give themselves thereunto, do commonly become cowards in their determinations, with little felicity, or good hap[5] in their attempts. For they become lazy, sickly, and feeble, and chiefly, such as do carry women with them, having most ordinarily their ends accompanied with dishonor and shame, and their effeminacy many times the hindrance of great actions: . . . The which vice ought with all rigor to be chastened.

---

[2] **nowls:** dull, drunken persons.   [3] *Tomyris:* widowed Scythian queen who went to battle against the Persian invader Cyrus, who captured her son.   [4] **instancy:** the quality of being instant; urgency, earnestness, solicitation, pressure, pressing nature.   [5] **hap:** luck or fortune.

He ought to be very moderate, and not over garish in his apparel and garments: for it is a principle, found true by experience, that he that is curious in his gait and attire is never like to prove a perfect soldier: for they require different humors, to the deep skill in war, and the dainty curiosity of Carpet knights.[6] Examples of garish camps, easily defeated, many might be produced, but time permitteth me not: but the beauty and bravery of a soldier is his bright and glittering armor, not gaudy attire and peacocks' plumes. . . .

He shall bear a great love and true affection unto his Captain, and obey him, and the other officers of the camp, with great respect; for the very day that he first entreth to be a soldier, he doth secretly swear and promise to serve his Prince, by obeying his officers; for the true order of war is a very resemblance of true religion, ordained of God, which bindeth the soldier to observe Justice, Loyalty, constancy, patience, and silence, and above all, obedience, through the which is easily attained the perfection in arms, and means to achieve great enterprises, though never so difficult. As *Plato* sayeth very well, that love and obedience is sign of a generous mind, not subject unto passions and unruly fits; for he that wanteth the virtue of obedience and patience, though otherwise never so valiant a soldier, is unworthy the name. For no greater mischief can befall a camp than disobedience, nor from whence greater damages do proceed: too many examples thereof do abound. Therefore, a good soldier ought not go against the determinations of his General, no nor to pass out of the trenches, although it were with intent to show his valor in some singular combat, or in any particular challenge, without his General's license (for he is not now his own man, but the Prince's, who doth give him pay). . . .

## THE SECOND BOOK OF WAR, DISCOURSES AND MARTIAL DISCIPLINE
## THE ENSIGN-BEARER ALFERES,[7] HIS ELECTION AND OFFICE.

In the choice of Ensign-bearer, the Captain is to have many and great considerations, for that it is not only enough for such a one to be a good Soldier, bold and valiant, but to be his equal (if it may be) in valor, discretion, and counsel, because many times, in his and his Lieutenant's absence, the government of the Company doth belong to this Officer. And for as much as

---

[6] **Carpet knights:** derogatory term for soldiers who exercised their might in a woman's bedroom rather than on the battlefield.   [7] **Alferes:** another term for ensign.

the Ensign is the very foundation of the Company, and therein consisteth the honor, and his and his soldiers' reputation, it is necessary that he unto whom this office is incommended[8] and committed have in him the parts of a perfect *Castellano*, or Captain of a castle, in nobleness and estimation of honor, to know how to keep it, and die in the defense thereof, never abandoning the same, as many valiant and honorable Ensign-bearers have done, to their immortal praise and fame. . . .

GENTLEMAN: Why are they called Ensigns, and from whence came that name?

CAPTAIN: The ancient *Romans* reparted[9] the people of their Armies into Legions, Cohorts, Centuries, and Maniples: and to be several known, they carried upon spears or pikes' ends the figures of eagles, dragons, and such like; and some the pictures of their Emperor, and called the same *Signa*: whereupon the *Italian* and *French* calleth them *Insignes*: but the Spaniard nameth them *Vanderas*, from the *Almaine*[10] word *Vanderen*: and we Englishmen do call them of late "Colors," by reason of the variety of colors they be made of; whereby they be the better noted and known to the Company.

Now, the Ensign made and finished and fastened unto a spear-headed staff, sharp-pointed with iron, the Captain with his own hands delivereth it unto his Ensign-bearer, encharging him the custody and defense thereof, with a solemn oath, to be true to his Prince and Captain. Accompanied with many honorable words, the which he is bound to return to the Captain, if the Company be dissolved or cashed,[11] before any notable piece of service performed, either at breach, battery, encounter, or battle, wherein he hath valiantly fought, and honorably defended the same. For from thence forward it is the Alferes' due, as deserved for his manhood and valor, but yet to receive the same from the Captain as an honorable gift.

GENTLEMAN: If in fight the Ensign be broken, and the Enemy do carry away a part thereof, doth the Ensign-bearer lose thereby his reputation?

CAPTAIN: No, not a jot: so that he keepeth the very trunk of the staff in his hand.

When the Company doth march, the Ensign-bearer may carry his Colors resting upon his shoulder, either open or folded up: but making a stand or *Alto*, he is bound by duty to advance the Ensign, and not to campear[12] it, or pitch it on the ground; for that is the trick of a *Bisognio*,[13] and doth repugne[14] the authority and gravity of his office. . . .

---

[8] **incommended:** entrusted.  [9] **reparted:** divided.  [10] *Almaine*: German.  [11] **cashed:** dismissed.  [12] **campear:** flourish.  [13] *Bisognio*: a raw, inexperienced soldier.  [14] **repugne:** oppose, stand contrary to.

In the lodging the Ensign should be accompanied with a Corps de garde,[15] although it be in place of quiet, and out of all suspicion, as well for the authority and reputation of the same, as to avoid many inconveniences which happen to succeed through mutinies, brawls, and frays. It is also convenient that the Ensign-bearer have always with him a Drum, to call his Company together, and for such occasions as shall be offered; for the Ensigns should be of such veneration, and have been so respected of the Soldiers, that there hath seldom been seen anyone flying to the sanctuary thereof (avoiding the Soldiers' fury) to be pursued or hurt, esteeming their Ensign a thing inviolable. . . .

## The Lieutenant, His Office and Duty.

He therefore that is chosen to this office ought to be a man of great experience, fidelity, and valor, who in the absence of his Captain, carrieth his room, charge, and command; unto whom the soldiers and under-officers are to obey, for the time, as unto the Captain himself. Notwithstanding, he must use it with such discretion and moderation that he arrogate not too much unto himself, but at his Captain's return he shall, with all love, truth, and duty, inform him of all things and matters passed.

If any questions and civil debates do arise amongst the soldiers of his band, he is to pacify, judge, and determine the same with gravity and good speeches: whereby he shall bind them more firmly unto him in obedience and love. And when as he cannot concert and agree them, he is to refer them over unto his Captain; but the most faulty and offenders he may cause to be apprehended, and send them to the Colonel or Marshal.

It is his charge and office to see that the Company be provided of all necessaries, advertising the Corporals to see well to their charges, and advising the Sergeant to be diligent, careful, and ready in his office, wherein he shall aid, help, and assist him, both in ordering the Company, and in setting the watch, the which he is precisely bound to perform himself, in the Sergeant's absence or time of infirmity.

He is to pass with the Company unto the Corps de garde, to see the watch and Sentinels set, and oftentimes to visit and revisit the same; and to persuade the soldiers to respect, with obedience, their Sergeant and Corporals: wherefore it importeth him to be well spoken, discreet and wise, to move and persuade them with sound reasons, to the observation and obedience of military discipline, disburdening thereby his Captain of many and sundry toils.

---

[15] **Corps de garde:** guard soldiers or sentinels.

It toucheth him also to see the soldiers appointed to their lodgings, giving order for the same unto the Harbinger,[16] and how he shall distribute the baggage and carriage amongst the particular soldiers, and the sick men carefully to be looked unto, not suffering these Harbingers or Furriers to rob, purloin, and filch as they are wont to do, whereby great scandals do arise, as at the rising of the *Vlishingers*,[17] and in sundry other places hath appeared.

[16] **Harbinger:** a quartermaster; one who goes in advance of the army to procure accommodations and so on. [17] *Vlishingers*: those who come from Vlishing, a province in the Netherlands once held by the British.

⤳ THOMAS PROCTOR

## *From* Of the Knowledge and Conduct of Wars      *1578*

Like many military writers who debated which nations produced the best warriors in terms of climate and humor, Thomas Proctor (fl. 1578–1584?) begins his treatise with a humoral approach to war: notice how this excerpt from *Of the Knowledge and Conduct of Wars* delineates national characters and their fitness for war. Proctor is not alone in arguing that England's temperate Northern climate produces the best soldiers. Readers might compare his view of climate's effects on Moors with the linking of Moorish temperament with climate in *Othello*. What characteristics does Proctor attribute to other nations, and on what basis? What, according to him, prevented the English from attaining full military glory? You might compare Proctor's thoughts on "mutability" or changing of mind with the writings on the passions in Chapter 5. Where does Proctor stand on the relative importance of experience or training?

### THE PREFACE

The Climate or Region of the firmament, under which every Country is planted and settled, hath great force and influence for the temperature and complexion of men's bodies, which also worketh sundry effects and motions in the minds and dispositions of them. . . . Experience showeth, that the Italian and Frenchman commonly, is more inclined to be court-like, prompt, and quick of spirit, than the Dutchman or Fleming, and the Spaniard, the Moor, or Libyan, more nimble, more politic, and more subject to choler, envy, and pride than the man of Sweden, or the Muscovite[1] being

[1] **Muscovite:** an inhabitant of Muscovy or Moscow; a Russian.

Thomas Proctor, *Of the Knowledge and Conduct of Wars* (London, 1578), ¶3r–¶5r.

more of phlegmatic constitution of body. The Greeks also, for this purpose, have been noted of learned men, to be by disposition and motion of nature exquisite searchers of cunning in manual crafts, and very studious in the liberal Sciences. The Egyptians and Jews (by observation of wise men) are found more given to superstitions and idolatry, than other nations. The Scythian,[2] the Turk, and Tartarian[3] addicted to cruelty, and the Persian to delicate[4] life.

But to draw nearer unto our scope, and mark, the Englishman (for whom this travail is taken), living in a fertile country and under a temperate Climate, and thereby endowed with the more excellent disposition of mind and body, being by the great bounty and blessing of God not unfurnished of any virtue that other people have. So is there principally seen in him, that yet remains of the right stamp or race undegenerate, an honorable desire to the exercise of arms, having by the prick of Magnanimity, a victorious mind, affecting fame, sovereignty, and honor above other nations. But lest I flatter him whom I love, and would to be warned, Two only points of imperfection, though not yet, now, notably exceeding to any great vice, (howbeit some defects) are noted to be in a great part of Englishmen, which may well be reformed. The one is, negligence or security. The other is mutability, and variable changing of mind, principally showed in delectable things, not of the greatest importance, as in dainty fare of sundry delicate meats, diverse curious buildings, and most of all in many almost infinite guises, sorts, and fashions of habit, yea, and disguised attire, wherein oftentimes is planted and bestowed so much care and study, that, there is the less employed on virtuous and needful exercises. . . .

For what is in want or lett[5] that the Englishman, having a strong body, goodwill enough, and a fertile country sufficient to supply the provision and maintenance of a mighty army, should not excel other nations in deeds and exploits of Arms, and extend the victorious forces of this Realm, by renowned conquests far? Surely the defects are, lack of endeavor, and discipline. By these the City of Rome from extreme poverty (having most bare and slender beginnings, their territories being as short, as the content or bounds of the smallest shire within this land) in short time advanced her Empire over the whole world. . . . By this exercise partly, though principally by the huge monstrous multitudes of barbarous Scythians, the Turks in no long time have subdued so many kings and countries, and extended their

---

[2] **Scythian:** an inhabitant of an ancient region extending over a large part of Russia.   [3] **Tartarian:** an inhabitant of the region of Central Asia extending eastward from the Caspian Sea.   [4] **delicate:** indolent, self-indulgent.   [5] **lett:** hindrance or obstruction.

Empire so far into all the three parts of the world,[6] and yet prosecuteth and thrusteth the same further daily.

Now it is to be remembered that the knowledge, and practice of the acts and feats of arms, principally and properly are of the profession of noblemen, and gentlemen of great revenues, For and by which, they were first ordained and preferred into that place to be a wall and defense for their country. . . . Security and long peace breedeth idleness, which sucketh the valor out of noble minds. . . . Thus seeing the causes of these defects in Englishmen discovered, the cure is the more plain and easy, and the rather, if the remedy unto the other impediment be applied, that is want of skill or discipline, which proceeding and growing partly upon the other cause, viz.,[7] lack of practice, the rest is also to be sought for and supplied. For as use and exercise, maketh [one] prompt, ready, and skillful in many things: So by most just and sure argument, the contrary, which is the privation, or lack thereof, worketh and causeth contrary effects: And yet not always in all things doth exercise and labor bring knowledge and perfection, but there must be skill withal, which in this matter, is for the more part to be obtained by collection and judgment of the reports, histories, and Chronicles written of wars. . . .

Besides that, reason will easily discuss that the knowledge of the ancient orders and government of war . . . be requisite and needful unto a good Captain: for what is the experience or opinion of one man to the practice and judgment of a great number of such as have conquered in all Countries, vanquished great armies, overthrown many mighty battles, and honorably passed all dangers of war: [and] whose doings [are] judicially and perfectly noted of most learned and wise men, in sundry great volumes and writings, for example and profit of the posterity, which the unlearned cannot taste or attain, without some preparative by plain plot drawn, or introduction in apt order made, to lead them into the knowledge thereof.

For the accomplishing whereof, though, through the grossness of my style, lack of experience, and sundry kinds of knowledge, wherewith a writer of so weighty a matter ought to be furnished, together with my study of brevity herein and little leisure, which from mine other affairs I had, one time long after another, to accomplish this same, I shall not sufficiently in all points content the exquisite judgments which are to deem hereof: Yet for the necessity and scarcity of writing in this matter (A willing mind, and faithful affection to profit my Country, thrusting me forth to bear a burden too big for my shoulders). This labor of mine, may be a beginning to

---

[6] **the three parts of the world:** Asia, Africa, and Europe.   [7] **viz.:** that is to say; namely.

encourage some other of their greatest experience to make larger addition or supply herein. For yet now I find Vegetius[8] only, an ancient writer, and Machiavelli, of these affairs, well translated into English, which authors being both expert in wars and also very learned, their industry herein is of so much the more commendation, as those two qualities are rare, and seldom meet together. For such a one as hath knowledge, joined with courage & experience, is a man worth men & may avail more than a number.

[8] **Vegetius:** Flavius Vegetius Renatus, a fourth-century Roman military expert.

→ THOMAS AND LEONARD DIGGES

## *From* An Arithmetical Military Treatise, Named Stratioticos
*1579*

Thomas Digges comes down firmly on the side of theory in the ongoing debate over the importance of scholarship versus experience in battle. His *Stratioticos* claims to "arithmetically resolve" questions of military organization, combining descriptions of officers' duties with "The Art of Algebra as I find necessary for a Soldier" (a.ij) and ending his treatise with sections on "great ordinance." Eager to prove the applicability of advanced mathematics in military action, Digges twice served in the military and attempted to prove his theories on navigation and fortification to experienced soldiers and sailors.

*Stratioticos* draws on the early work of Thomas Digges's father, Leonard: it offers training in practical mathematics in addition to discriminating between the different army ranks. What is Digges's image of a soldier, and how does it match ideas of soldiery in *Othello*? How does a general establish control over his men? What are some of the chief threats to military discipline? This "arithmetical" view of the military privileges numbers and volume, leading to a view of "men as interchangeable units in a larger machine" (Cahill 59). One could consider whether this idea of interchangeability might shape Othello's suspicions of Desdemona's loyalty as well as the play's many instances of substitution. Characters frequently covet or step into each other's "places" both structurally and thematically.

Thomas and Leonard Digges, *An Arithmetical Military Treatise, Named Stratioticos* (London, 1579), A4v, a1r, 146–47.

## To the Reader

... And *Reason* teacheth me, how barbarous that common opinion is, that an *Englishman* will be trained in a few weeks to be a perfect Soldier. For if a Mason, a Painter, or other *Mechanical Artificer* be scarcely able in seven years to learn the perfection of his *Science*, that we think the *Art* of a *Soldier* so base and abject, that it is to be attained in a few Weeks or Months? But such is the *Vanity* of the common sort, that if they have carried arms, and been in a few services, they presently think themselves worthy the name of perfect Soldiers. ...

But seeing it would require at the least an whole age, and the direction of some rare *Prince* to reduce *Soldiery* to the antique perfection, and therefore in vain for any private man to intermeddle therewithal: yet somewhat to discover that gross *Error*, that *Soldiery* may so soon be learned, and that we may have some taste and feeling at least of our own ignorance and imperfection, and to awake our *Nation* out of that secure Dream, having partly by experience myself seen, what extreme disorders grow, and dishonors are received for want of *Military Discipline*: I have therefore thought good, according to the best observations of our *Modern* Wars, and *Service* of this *Time*, to set down the *Office* and duty of each person and calling, passing from a *Private Soldier*, to a *General*, with certain *Military* Laws to be observed in every well governed *Army*.

## from Chapter 15, Of the General

... *The General* should not so much seek to place his *Camp* in seats strong by *Nature*, as to *Fortify* them by *Art*, as well to keep his Soldiers in *Action*, and from idleness (the only ruin of *Armies*), as also that due order in *Camps* may be maintained: And therefore let him imitate the ancient *Romans*, the very Masters of the Art of War, who never coveted other than the *plain* to encamp upon: *Entrenching* themselves nightly in no less strong and sure manner, than if the Enemy had encamped by them, and that even in places utterly void of all suspicion, to make these *Military Travels* familiar to them, and to avoid those idle, or rather dissolute *Effeminate* Pastimes that our *Christian Camps* are bewitched withal, to the utter ruin of all good *Military* Discipline, and confusion of our *Armies*.

*The General* ought for avoiding of *Mutinies* and all disorders within his *Camp*, to have his *Statutes* and Laws openly *Proclaimed* and set up publicly for every man to read, with the pain to every offense assigned, and the same severely to be put in execution on all offenders without any respect of *Persons*. ...

*He* should see his Soldiers kept in continual *Military Exercise*, and by feigned *Alarms* to see in what readiness his *Bands* would be if necessity required: To show them all manner ways how the *Enemy* may attempt them discovering also to them the remedy, and how they are to answer those *Attempts*. For no man is born a *Soldier*, but by Exercise and Training it is attained: and by discontinuance again it is lost, as all other *Arts* and *Sciences*. Neither is there any *Nation* for *Military* Actions so Honorable, as by Rest and Discontinuance will not grow *Effeminate* and Reproachful. Nor any *Nation* by nature so abject and base, that by a worthy *General* with Training will not produce good *Soldiery*; As by infinite examples of *Antiquity* may be approved. And in these days we have seen the *Flemings*, a people by reason of their Rest, Riches, and Delicate Life, condemned, and no valor for *Armies* supposed in them.

→ THOMAS STYWARD

## *From* The Pathway to Martial Discipline           *1581*

Thomas Styward lists the six principles of a soldier "in order" as "silence, obedience, secretness, sobriety, hardiness, truth" (46–47). Interestingly, silence and obedience lead this list rather than the perhaps more obvious virtues of hardiness and sobriety; Styward's ordering of virtues reflects a growing emphasis on (and nervousness over) an order based on subordination of the will to the commands of a superior. One can deduce from the many punishments outlined in this and other such texts that the ideal qualities of temperance and obedience were often more admired than followed. Why is the penalty for envy (Item 26) and revenge (Items 15 and 54) more severe than the penalty for conspiracy (Item 13)? Note in particular Item 75, which requires that every soldier wear a "special sign or token." How might a system that assumes a clear, knowable line between friend and enemy be particularly vulnerable to treachery and disloyalty? How, in *Othello*, might the handkerchief (also called a "token") function as a sign of affinity or loyalty?

## THE LAWS AND CONSTITUTIONS OF THE FIELD

*Here begin the Articles where*unto all soldiers which serve under Emperor, or any other King or Prince, ought to be sworn unto, and them to keep and maintain inviolated at all times, and in all places, upon such pains as follow.

---

Thomas Styward, *The Pathway to Martial Discipline* (London, 1581), 51–55, 58–62.

First, ye shall be sworn to be true, just, and dutiful to his Lord and sovereign and his grand General or chief Captain of the field, to be tractable and obedient unto every officer placed and appointed to rule over him, and to be ready both day and night to serve, whether it be by land or by water, as occasion of service shall fall out and require. And whosoever doth repine[1] or showeth disobedience herein, of what degree or condition so ever he be, he must be duly punished by the judgment of the superiors appointed for that purpose. . . .

11. Item, it standeth with the law of arms that each common soldier shall be sworn that they will not have amongst themselves any private counsels, assemblies, or conventicles,[2] upon pain of the loss of their lives.

12. Item, there shall no soldier neither in time of marching, nor during the time of their encamping, hold or keep any whispering or talk, or secretly convey any letters unto their adversaries, without license from the chief Captain upon pain of the loss of his life.

13. Item, if there be any one or a more number that shall go about any treason or any other conspiracy to be committed against the camp or garrison, such a traitor or conspirator shall be accused unto the Knight marshal, and he that bewrayeth[3] and accuseth such an offender shall have for his reward a month's wages or more: as the fact is heinous, so the reward is to be increased unto the party that revealeth the same, and the offender to receive the reward of a false traitor.

14. Item, that no soldier shall be suffered to be of a ruffian like behavior, either to provoke or to give any blow or thrust, or otherwise willfully strike with his dagger, to injure any his fellow soldiers with any weapon, whereby mutinies many times ensueth, upon pain of the loss of his life.

15. Item, if any one beareth hatred or malice, or any evil will for any occasion done unto him, and so striketh him, he loseth his hand; if otherwise he seeketh revenge, then by law he loseth his life.

16. Item, if any soldier be warned to watch or ward and he do not come, he shall be punished at the discretion of the Captain; but if any soldier be summoned to watch, and he appear, and after the watch word given and the watch set, he departeth and leaveth the watch, such a one shall without mercy be punished with the loss of his life, neither shall any man let another to watch in his place without the leave of the Captain upon pain of his life.

17. Item, that no soldier or soldiers draw his or their sword or swords, or use any other kind of weapon with violence to do hurt within or without the camp, during the time of the wars, upon pain of death. It hath lately been

---

[1] **repine:** to feel discontent or to complain.   [2] **conventicles:** clandestine or illegal meetings.
[3] **bewrayeth:** expose, accuse.

used with more favor of life as such an offender to lose his hand, but it is the discretion of the Lord Chief General, in whose hands lieth both life and death of offenders, after their arraignment and just condemnation. . . .

19. Item, that no person or persons presume to be mustered or to take wages before he be sworn to be faithful, and truly to serve his Prince in those wars present, upon pain of death. . . .

25. Item, if there be any found, that hath entered his name under two Captains and hath taken wages, armor, and weapons beforehand, such a person shall be taken for a perjured man and shall by the law of arms for the same lose his life.

26. Item, if any that hath a place appointed him by the harbinger[4] or officers for his tent or lodging, he must hold himself content withal, neither shall he molest any man lodging within his tent, or other lodging at any time for any occasion upon pain of the chief Captain's displeasure, and such punishment as he shall think most fit for the offense. . . .

35. Item, that no man, of what degree so ever he be of, shall commit adultery with married wives, nor force widows, maids, or virgins, and by violence defile them, shall without mercy be punished with death. . . .

54. Item, he that should be revenged of any injury received, either newly or before time done, by any indirect way that is, traitorously, and not by way of reason, or by way of combat body to body, by the license of his General shall suffer death.

55. Item, he that should be so bold as to play with false cards and dice or should dare to use in play any privy falsehood, theft, or deceit in any wise, shall be punished. . . .

65. Item, if at any time any man shall in the time of his drunkenness quarrel and fight with his fellow, and in so doing chance to kill him, he shall in so doing receive as great punishment by death as if he had been sober. . . .

75. Item, that every soldier shall have upon his outermost garment some special sign or token whereby he may be known, such a one as the higher Captains shall agree upon. As, for example, he shall have on his garment a red cross, and upon his armor a red lace or such like, whereby he may the better be known of his fellows, and if there shall be any found without the said signs and tokens, he shall be used as an adversary or enemy.

---

[4] **harbinger:** one sent ahead to arrange lodgings for the army.

→ JOHN TAYLOR

## From A Valorous and Perilous Sea-fight
## Fought with Three Turkish Ships          *1640*

Interest in new methods of warfare was not limited to the literate elite: early moderns of all classes learned both of war and foreign cultures through tales of skirmishes and major battles abroad. Broadside accounts of battles offered insight into military strategy as well as the dangers and horrors of war, while ballads offered popular accounts of the fates of soldiers abroad. John Taylor (1578–1653) concludes his account of a battle on the ship *Elizabeth* with a short treatise on the importance of navigation, which calls Noah the first pilot and ships "the impregnable Wooden walls of great Brittaine and Ireland" (Cv). Just as *The Lepanto* (p. 251) offers a glorified image of united Christian forces that may eventually prevail over Ottoman might, John Taylor's *A Valorous and Perilous Sea-fight* uses local skirmishes to argue for the possibility of success against Turks. The men of the ship *Elizabeth* showed an ideal of English masculine courage when they encountered three Turkish ships off the coast of Cornwall in the summer of 1640. The account makes it clear that the Englishmen were outgunned and outmanned.

The fight continued about the time between seven and eight hours, and though the English Ship had but three Pieces of ordinance (that could be used) yet by God's Assistance the Master Gunner (being a skillful valiant and experienced man), he so plied and played upon the miscreants, that he killed many of them.

The Gunner of the Ship's name is John *Whidon.* And all the while that the Master of the Ship (Master *Doves*) most manfully and courageously, did labor and bestir himself and by his Valorous example gave encouragement to all the rest of his Company that were in the Ship, amongst whom the three Passengers which were with us, did most worthy deserving service. The Master still cheered them up, and told them, that (by God's Grace) he would not give away his ship and himself to those accursed misbelievers, but that he was resolved with Christian courage to fight it out so long as his life lasted. . . .

In this terrible turmoil, there were two of the Turks had got themselves up into the Top and one of the three passengers (with a Musket) shot at them, and killed them both: one of those slain Pirates, was a man of an extraordinary great stature, and for his Corpulency, not to be equaled amongst them all; he being killed, the *English* did cleave his head, and then they divided it from his carcass, they showed the head and the corpse to the Turks, and with renewed courage and unwearied Valor they hailed to the enemy, and in braving manner said, "Come aboard you Dogs if you dare, and fetch your country-man." But the *Turks* finding the business so hot, and the men so resolute, that their damnable courages were quelled, than they had no more mind to assault the *English* Ship any more. So they in deriding and shouting to the *Turks*, cast the dead body overboard, on the one side of the Ship, and the Cloven head into the sea, on the other. . . .

The Master Gunner, being the Chief Commander left alive in the Ship, did hail to the *Turks* again, and dared them to come on again and try the other boat. But they had such proof of his courage and knowledge before in the fight, being so shattered, torn, and gauled;[1] that they could neither boast of Victory, nor durst they venture any more to gain it, for they perceived the Gunners resolution was never to yield, and so they fell to their sails, and tackling, and very much discontented, slunk away, making their moans to *Mahomet*.

There were certain *Hogs* and *Poultry*, in the *Elizabeth*; and in the heat of the fight, (the Ship being much rent and torn with the Shot of the enemy) the poor Swine and Pullen[2] were killed, partly with the Bullets, but most with the shatters and splinters of shivered Planks, and timber of the Ship. Wherefore (in derision and scorn of the *Turks*, who do abhor and hold all manner of Swines' flesh in abomination) the *English* mariners lifted up the Hogs, and shoed them to the *Turk*, as it were in a merry or jeering way, to invite them to come aboard the Ship to eat some Pork. Thus, (by the merciful assistance of God) this one poor Ship, so weekly manned, and so meanly furnished with Artillery or Ordinance, against so many, and so great a multitude, (as were three Ships, 500 Men, and 56 Pieces), maintain a fight almost eight hours, and (with the loss of three Men) not only kill and spoil a great number of their enemies, but also to escape them, and come off with reputation, (as it were with Conquest, Triumph, and Victory). It is almost to be thought miraculous and beyond belief, but that the truth of the matter is so plainly manifested that all opposing unbelief is vain and frivolous.

---

[1] **gauled:** galled; harassed or annoyed, particularly with arrows or gunfire.   [2] **Pullen:** plural for poultry.

# CHAPTER 5

## *Passions*

—————————————————— ⇥⇤ ——————————————————

After seeing Othello strike Desdemona in act 4, scene 1, Lodovico exclaims, "Is this the nature / Whom passion could not shake?" (4.1.258–59). His question echoes the wonder of early modern commentators at the ability of what they called the passions to bring about extreme transformations in individuals. Lodovico also expresses an ideal: a proper man will endure and resist an almost constant onslaught of feeling. Early moderns gave new significance to reason's ability to control passion, and such interest in controlling the passions accompanied a larger internalizing of Christian discipline and codes of cultural civility in the period (Gaukroger 4–5).

Readers should note the many ways the authors whose works appear in this chapter imagine the individual's relation to her or his desires and passions. In the hope that an accurate theory of passions would have a palliative effect on various "perturbations" of the mind, most of these texts revisit and reorganize classical models of human psychology. Discussions of passions by moral and political philosophers like Francis Bacon and Thomas Wright tended to focus on those passions subject to self-control, whereas medical and philosophical writers like Robert Burton seemed concerned with more unruly passions that defy restraint (Gaukroger 2). Regardless of their approach, many early moderns interested in the emotions shared in a broader concern with problems of knowledge and self-discipline. In addition to promoting the exercise of self-restraint, they also explored how one might command or move others (see pp. 322–24). In that regard, medical and philosophical treatises might be aligned with texts on rhetoric. Unsurprisingly, many of these texts address themselves to ruling elites. As Susan James notes, "Therapy, self-control and power over others are blended to produce an image of healthy dominion" (3).

While classical authors offered a range of ways to rank and understand the passions, most natural philosophers in England followed a Ciceronian schema that identified four basic emotions: pleasure, lust/desire, fear/dread, and sadness/grief. The frontispiece to Henry, Earl of Monmouth's translation of Senault's very popular French work *De l'usage des passions* (see Figure 30) relies on St. Thomas Aquinas's identification of eleven passions. The image trumpets the sovereignty of Reason and clearly depicts the early modern view that passions were powerful and unruly facets of life that needed to be subdued and properly directed. How does the engraver represent Reason's control over passion? Readers might also note how spatial relations suggest conceptual relations in the image.

The authors of the documents in this chapter see passion as an overwhelmingly powerful and inescapable part of human nature, one that often conspires with the body to overturn reason. The ideal body is one that has achieved temperance or humoral balance; passions threaten that balance, making the individual uncertain and vulnerable. This fear of total transformation underlies the language of "turning" in the play (discussed in Chapter 1). While the word *perturbations* frequently acts as a synonym for *passions*, writers struggle for other ways to convey the power and movement of emotions. One might profitably examine the metaphors these writers use to represent both disorder and the desired control of reason over passion. Just as the drama of *Othello* depends on an audience seeing the external manifestation of internal states, many of these texts offer a tangible, visible sense of the passions, and readers will want to pay attention to how writers anthropomorphize or endow passions with human or living qualities.

As Senault's inclusion of "eschewing" in Figure 30 indicates, passions (and the entire range of human feeling) are generally understood as states of inclination or aversion, which may be why Thomas Buoni (see p. 329) joins so many other authors in considering the effects of love tokens that may sway a person to love or desire. Many of these works locate the passions somewhere between the immaterial and the material self; there is, nonetheless, an overwhelming emphasis on the materiality of affections and their location in the body. Medical texts often identify a specific part of the body as the seat of individual humoral or emotional states and suggest that other

FIGURE 30 *Title page, from Jean François Senault,* The Use of the Passions, *translated by Henry, Earl of Monmouth (London, 1649). In this image, what is Reason's relationship to Divine Grace? Which passions are arranged as opposites? Which appear similar?*

parts have particularly regulative functions. For example, most writers considered the palm the most temperate part of the body. Dialogue in *Othello* frequently refers to the body's ability to assign and convey feelings. Even though Brabantio rejects the power of language, his lament "I never yet did hear / That the bruised heart was piercèd through the ear" (1.3.221–22) is consistent with attempts to theorize the relation between the immaterial functions of the brain and heart and the workings of eyes and ears. One might consider where other characters in *Othello* locate the source of passion. Bacon's "Of Envy" (p. 338) is likewise fascinated with this relation. Where do all of our authors locate passions in relation to the body, soul, and imagination? How do words act on emotions in the play?

All discussions of passion are rooted in humoral and complexion theory, systems of conceptualizing the human body that dominated Western thought until the nineteenth century when they came to be replaced by more rigid and explicitly racializing classifications (see Floyd-Wilson, and see Paster, *Humoring*). Historian Nancy Siraisi notes, "Complexion theory usefully accounted for psychological and social as well as physiological characteristics and stereotype" (103). While referred to as separate schema, systems based on complexion and those based on humors are quite interrelated since humors are the "vehicle of complexion" (Siraisi 106). Early moderns often read a person's inner state through physical characteristics, a practice derived from both humoral theory and Neoplatonic schema that associated physical appearances with spiritual states (Tokson 37–38).

The articulation of complexion and humoral theory is thoroughly intertwined with ideas of gender, nation, and ethnicity. As Gail Kern Paster notes, "humoral theory was instrumental in the production and maintenance of gender and class difference" (*Body* 7). Women were understood as moister and colder by nature and therefore inferior to men, who were generally seen as hot and dry. This physiological theory underlies the gendering of early modern emotions as feminine, "with reason and intellect deemed masculine"; thus, losing control to passion was "a sign of weakness or degeneration" for men (Kennedy 5). Such ideas spread from elite texts into the common culture. Iago's banter on the Cyprus quay echoes popular (and often misogynist) verse like that included in Benedetto Varchi's *Blazon of Jealousy* (see p. 330). Besides gender, nationality looms large in early modern psychology: groups who lived in different climates were said to have specific humoral constitutions and complexions. Thus, Thomas Wright (see p. 320) suggests that to move passion in others, one must first know their country of origin. While the health and balance of an individual within an ethnic group would be assessed in relation to others (a Scythian might be seen as "hot" in relation to other Scythians, who were generally thought to be of a cold complexion), nations were judged by how far they strayed from the ideal of temperate balance. Compare, for example, the discussions of Italians, Turks, and Africans in this chapter's texts and the military texts in Chapter 4. How are their allegedly characteristic complexions represented in *Othello*? Most writings on passions assume that "passions are quintessentially feminine" (Kennedy 5) and that women are more mutable and susceptible to passion. However, it might be worth noting the many examples of men's vulnerability in these texts along with the possibility that elite men project their perceived vulnerability onto women and foreigners.

The bodily basis for psychological and physiological states means that emotions are profoundly physical and material: both emotional and physical health existed in a precarious balance: "besides being open and fungible in its internal workings, the humoral body was also porous and thus able to be influenced by the immediate environment" (Paster, *Body* 9). While modern readers are used to emotions having immediate but short-term physical effects (the flush of anger, for example), early modern texts worry about emotion's domination of the body. In the opening to *The Passions of the Mind in General*, Thomas Wright claims that "spirits and humors wait upon the Passions as their Lords and Masters" (Bk. 1: 91). Thus every powerful emotion alters the humoral balance of the body.

The earliest surviving comment on *Othello* reacts to the play's intense emotions: actors in an Oxford performance were said to draw "tears not only by their speech, but also by their action" and Desdemona's face "itself implored the pity of the audience" (quoted in Rosenburg 5). The play's own discourse of passions, with its almost unparalleled level of emotional intensity, has been a constant focus for critics over the centuries; indeed, one can assess a period's views of emotion through such criticism. For example, Henry James, writing at a time when Shakespeare was beginning to be seen as the epitome of high art and pure thought, hinted that Italian actor Tomasso Salvini's notoriously passionate performance was somehow not quite Shakespearean: "it is a study of pure feeling — of passion, with as little as possible of that intellectual iridescence which . . . is the sign of Shakespeare's hand" (189). Although such commentary mostly focuses on Othello, the treatises included here suggest that we would do well to examine the passions of all the characters as well as the possible effect of passions on the audience.

→ THOMAS WRIGHT

## *From* The Passions of the Mind in General      *1604*

Many investigations of passion address the individual's negotiation of external stimulation. In *The Passions of the Mind in General*, theologian and ex-Jesuit Thomas Wright (c. 1561–1623) notes that passions are "certain internal acts or operations of the soul, bordering upon reason and sense, prosecuting some good thing or flying some ill thing, causing therewithal some alteration in the body" (p. 321). His vision of passions moving toward or away from external objects is foundational for early modern psychology. Our modern use of the word *affections* (often a synonym for passion in these texts) contains the residue of this idea. For contemporary readers, *affection* refers to a specific kind of loving attachment; for early moderns, it referred broadly to emotions in the sense of a force that inclines a person toward one object or another. Thus, "Passion for a beloved object arouses the fear of losing it, also producing jealousy" (Gundersheimer 324). Wright's definition rests on an inextricable link between body and soul, specifically the ability of passions and the soul to act on and transform the body. Theories of the passions are deeply concerned with coupling and uncoupling of soul and spirit, body and mind, also the concerns of *Othello*.

Despite their extreme caution about passion's power to overwhelm sense and reason, philosophers and theologians also tried to discern the more benign role passions play in human life. Since they are part of a divine order, such writers reasoned, passions must play some role in preserving well-being (James 10). Wright was one of the first to systematically emphasize passion's "potential for good or evil" (Newbold 24). What metaphors does Wright use to describe the relation between passion, sense, and reason? How do his ideas of dominion or mastery mirror problems of control (over self and others) in *Othello*?

### FROM BOOK I

*What we understand by Passions and Affections*

Three sorts of actions proceed from men's souls: some are internal and immaterial, as the acts of our wits and wills; others be mere external and material, as the acts of our senses (seeing, hearing, moving, etc.); others stand betwixt these two extremes and border upon them both; the which we may best discover in children, because they lack the use of reason and are guided by an internal imagination, following nothing else but that pleaseth their senses, even after the same manner as brute beasts do. . . . Those

Thomas Wright, *The Passions of the Mind in General*, ed. William Webster Newbold (New York: Garland, 1986), 94–96, 283–86.

actions then which are common with us and beasts we call Passions and Affections, or perturbations, of the mind. . . . "The motions of the soul, called of the Greeks *pathe,* some Latins, as Cicero, called them perturbations, others affections, others affects, others more expressly name them Passions."[1] They are called Passions (although indeed they be acts of the sensitive power or faculty of our soul, and are defined of Damascene . . . "a sensual motion of our appetitive faculty through imagination of some good or ill thing")[2] because when these affections are stirring in our minds they alter the humors of our bodies, causing some passion or alteration in them. They are called perturbations for that (as afterward shall be declared) they trouble wonderfully the soul,[3] corrupting the judgment and seducing the will, inducing, for the most part, to vice, and commonly withdrawing from virtue; and therefore some call them maladies or sores of the soul. They be also named affections, because the soul by them either affecteth some good or, for the affection of some good, detesteth some ill. [4]These passions then be certain internal acts or operations of the soul, bordering upon reason and sense, prosecuting some good thing or flying some ill thing, causing therewithal some alteration in the body.

[5]Here must be noted that albeit these passions inhabit the confines both of sense and reason, yet they keep not equal friendship with both; for passions and sense are like two naughty servants who ofttimes bear more love one to [a]nother than they are obedient to their Master. And the reason of this amity betwixt the passions and sense I take to be the greater conformity and likeness betwixt them than there is between passions and reason. For passions are drowned in corporal organs and instruments, as well as sense; reason dependeth of no corporal subject, but as a Princess in her throne considereth the state of her kingdom. Passions and sense are determined to one thing, and as soon as they perceive their object sense presently receives it and the passions love or hate it; but reason, after she perceiveth her object, she stands in deliberation whether it be convenient she should accept it or refuse it. Besides, sense and passions, as they have had a leagure the longer, so their friendship is stronger; for all the time of our infancy and childhood our senses were joint friends in such sort with passions, that whatsoever delighted sense pleased the passions, and whatsoever was hurtful to the one was an enemy to the other.[6] And so by long agreement and familiarity the passions had so engaged themselves to sense, and with such bonds and seals of sensual habits confirmed their friendship, that as soon as reason came to

---

[1] Augustine, lib.9 *De civitate dei*, cap. 4. [*A; not in B*]   [2] Damascene, 2 *De fide orthodoxa*, cap. 22.
[3] Cicero in 3 *Tusc.*   [4] The definition of Passions.   [5] Why passions follow rather Sense than Reason.   [6] Aristotle insinuates, 3 *Eth.*, cap. 2.

possession of her kingdom they began presently to make rebellion; for right reason oftentimes deprived sense of those pleasures he had of so long time enjoyed, as by commanding continency and fasting, which sense most abhorred. Then passions repugned, and very often haled her by force to condescend to that they demanded. . . .

Moreover, after that men by reason take possession over their souls and bodies, feeling this war so mighty, so continual, so near, so domestical that either they must consent to do their enemy's will, or still be in conflict; and withal foreseeing by making peace with them they were to receive great pleasures and delights, the most part of men resolve themselves never to displease their sense or passions, but to grant them whatsoever they demand. . . . Yet if the matter here were ended, and reason yielded but only to the suits of sensuality, it were without doubt a great disorder to see the Lord attend so basely upon his servants. But reason, once being entered into league with passions and sense, becometh a better friend to sensuality than the passions were before; for reason straightways inventeth ten thousand sorts of new delights which the passions never could have imagined. . . . By this we may gather how passions stand so confined with sense and reason that for the friendship they bear to the one they draw the other to be their mate and companion.

## FROM Book V

*Means to Move Flight and Fear*

If an Orator would by the passion of fear move the Italians, Almains, and Spaniards to join in league and war upon the Turk, he might urge them in this manner:

[7]The Romans in past ages, who with most careful eye did foresee and prevent the dangers of their Empire, thought not themselves secure in Italy except the Carthaginians were vanquished; but how much more near are the Turkish cities to Spain, Germany, and Italy than Carthage was to Rome! [8]What a swift Navy of Galleys hath he always prepared by Sea, and therefore in one night may enter either the coasts of Italy or Spain! What an infinite Army as well of horsemen as footmen hath he always in a readiness to invade, offend, and ruin whom he will almost at unawares, at least them that border upon him, ere they can be half prepared! Of what force is this tyrant! . . . What fortresses hath he won from Christians! What Cities sacked! What Provinces vanquished! What Kingdoms subdued! What

---

[7] Danger imminent.   [8] The Turk's forces.

Empires spoiled, enjoyed, possessed! Who ruleth now Afric? The Turk, either all or most. Who signorizeth over Asia? The Turk. Who doth domineer over the greatest part of Europe? The Turk. His treasures are infinite, his victuals abundant, his people innumerable and so subject and obedient that they repute it a favor to be bereaved of their lives at their Emperor's pleasure. Are all Princes Christian able to levy and maintain an army of 300,000 fighting men? Soliman brought so many before Vienna in Austria. What will such a world of combatants do? Nay, what will they not do! Cover the fields like Locusts in expugnation of cities, rear up mountains of earth in a moment, fill up ditches with dead corpse of their own men to scale the walls, with the very sight of such an invincible multitude strike terror and amazement in the hearts of all them that shall see them or hear of them.

[9]His malice is no less than his might. . . . Did he ever yet overslip opportunity when Christians were at civil brawls among themselves, or that he perceived any little advantage ready to further his plots? Let Rhodes, Cyprus, Buda, and the best part of Hungary witness his vigilant malice and malicious intent. Whom hateth he more than Christians, who hold him for an usurper, who of right should possess and inherit all he hath? Whose religion hath he extinguished in all those worthy kingdoms he now enjoyeth, but Christianity? Whom calleth he dogs, but Christians? But the Persian as yet holdeth him play, as potent as he, thirsty of his blood as the Turk of Christians'. If that were not, truly (except miraculously God preserved Christianity) we should have seen all Europe overrun. But why may we not suppose that at last they will come to some truce or cessation from wars for a long time, as awearied with so much warring and bloodshed, or finally conclude a peace; and what then is like to befall us? Why rather were it not better now for all Christians to be at peace among themselves and assault and invade him upon this side while we have the Persian to encounter him on the other? O blindness! O proud ambition of Christian Princes, who seek rather to spoil their brethren of their own with injury than they will war against their common Adversary to recover their own right!

[10]Put case the Turks break over their banks, and make a general inundation over all Europe; what great harm might we expect? What harm! God avert us from proving the Turkish tyranny! What man is secure of his life in their Invasion who hath either strength, wisdom, wealth, or nobility, whereby he may seem either to have opposed, or hereafter oppose himself against them! What Matron, what Virgin, what Lady shall be free from their beastly violence! Who shall keep lands or livings under the clutches of

[9] The Turk's hatred against Christians.    [10] The greatness of the evil feared.

such ravenous Kites and devouring Cormorants! Whatsoever a man getteth with his sweat and industry, when he dieth the great Turkish Tyrant must inherit, and what he deemeth or pleaseth shall be allowed the wife and children. The Galleys shall then want no Slaves to lead a hellish thralldom when they have vanquished so many as they may use in all drudgery and slavery at their pleasure. The children who are warlike in their infancy perforce shall be taken from their parents and sent into a far country from them, and there trained up in martial prowess and Turcism, and forget both father and mother, country and kindred, and neither yield comfort ever to progenitors nor receive any comfort from them. Many more such tyrannical vexations and barbarous cruelties I could recount, but he that will not be moved with these I hold him neither a wise moral man nor any way touched with one spark of Christian zeal.

→ PIERRE DE LA PRIMAUDAYE

## *From* The French Academy

*1586*

*Translated by Thomas Bowe*

English translations of Pierre de La Primaudaye's (1545–?) *L'Académie Françoise* were widely read; Thomas Bowe's (fl. 1579–89) translation went through five editions in fifteen years. The work is a conversation with four participants: Aser (Felicity), Amana (Truth), Aram (Highness or Sublimity), Achitob (Goodness). Although the chapter excerpted here purports to focus on "diseases of the body and soul," readers might consider why La Primaudaye does not actually focus on the body. What is the source of bodily infirmity?

### CHAPTER 3

*Of the diseases and passions of the body and soul, and of the tranquilities thereof.*

*A*ram. One of the ancient philosophers used to say that no living creature was worse to man than man himself, because, albeit he hath dominion over all things, yet he cannot rule himself, nor his desires. Experience causeth us but too much to know the truth of this saying. . . . So undoubtedly we have

Pierre de La Primaudaye, *The French Academy*, trans. Thomas Bowe (London, 1586), 27–30.

both body and soul compassed about with so many pernicious passions that it is very hard, yea altogether impossible, that what good thing soever is in us should not faint and sink under their heavy weight without a special and divine grace.

*Achitob.* Truly this is no vain speculation, nor unprofitable to man: as also for a man to know that he is, as it were, tied in this world to all uncertain things, which he, being mortal by nature, cannot any way shun and avoid without the help of God. He which is in health expecteth sickness; he that is sick, health. Doth anyone desire in his mind anything? Before he enjoyeth it, his desire is often changed into another. In a word, no man abideth still in one and the same estate. And therefore *Plato* calleth man a mutable creature, as if he meant to say that he is easily altered and changed.

*Aser.* The change which this divine philosopher meant (if I be not deceived) hath relation principally to the conditions of the soul, which, being filled with infinite perturbations, fastened in the midst of it with the nail of pleasure and grief, is carried away with inconstancy and uncertainty into a stream of troublesome passions, which, if they be not cut off and mastered by reason, draw a man into utter destruction. But give us to understand, Amana, more at large of these passions of the soul and of the way to remedy them: and if you think good, you may speak somewhat of those of the body.

*Amana.* Among the innumerable evils which the desire of pleasure and fear of grief, engraven in the most secret parts of our soul by our first corruption, bring to man, this is the greatest and most pernicious: that they make sensible things more evident and plain unto him than things intelligible,[1] and constrain the understanding to judge more by passion than by reason. For using, through the sense of pleasure or travel, to attend to the erroneous, uncertain, and mutable nature of the body, as to that which is subsisting and subject to sight, he remaineth blind and loseth all knowledge of that which truly is and subsisteth, namely, of the light of the soul, which is divine and immortal. Moreover, applying himself wholly to the sensual and unreasonable will, which is that part of the soul that proceedeth of the corruption thereof, he laboreth with all his might to quench and choke that weak instinct of the soul which aspireth unto the true Good, from whence she perceiveth herself to have fallen. And this he doth with such force and power, that if God strengthen not the soul, and reason, the divine guide, accompany her not, without doubt she yieldeth to such mighty enemies: and

---

[1] **sensible things more evident and plain unto him than things intelligible:** things pertaining to the senses become more evident than things derived from understanding or intelligence.

then (as we have said), staying himself wholly in things subject to sight, he appeareth too careful and curious in seeking to deck[2] that which belongeth to the body: but as for the soul (whereof all human felicity dependeth) because she is invisible, and not seen of him, it is the least of his cares to furnish her with that which she seeketh and desireth, and which is necessary for her. Whereupon in the end it cometh to pass that the least overthwarts[3] and discommodities of his flesh seem very grievous and burdensome to a man, but as for the incurable diseases which overwhelm his soul, he doth not so much as feel them. . . .

And first we will speak a word of the diseases of the body, next of the natural and necessary passions thereof, albeit we will entreat of the passions of the soul as of our chief matter subject. Concerning the maladies and evil dispositions of the body, one *Hippocrates*, one *Galen*,[4] nay, infinite others skillful in physic, are not able to describe them exactly, much less prescribe certain and sure remedies. . . . I will content myself to speak these few words by the way, that we ought to take every bodily infirmity as a fatherly chastisement of our sins and as a necessary mean to awaken us, to warn us of our duty, and to keep us in awe. Besides, one principal cause of all bodily diseases proceedeth ordinarily from vices, which are the proper inheritance of man, and with which we defile ourselves continually. Therefore, if we heal our souls, we may cure ourselves of the most of them: and as for others, which come by defect of nature, or by some other hidden cause, we have the counsel and help of physicians, whom willingly and diligently we seek after.

There are besides these, certain natural and necessary passions in the body, properly belonging unto it, even from the first creation thereof, which are not to be condemned, neither can be taken away but with the abolishing man's nature: as the desire of drinking, eating, sleeping, and such like, which only by the direction of reason are to be freed from all superfluity. But it standeth otherwise with the diseases and passions of the soul, derived from our first corruption and driven forward by sin, being plentiful and rich, which without comparison are far more dangerous than those of the body, more hard to be perceived and known, more headstrong and uneasy to cure, and which is worse, man is very slothful in seeking out a remedy for them.

---

[2] **deck:** to cover, beautify.   [3] **overthwarts:** adversities.   [4] *Galen:* classical author who popularized humoral theory.

## Love and Jealousy

The English philosopher Francis Bacon, a contemporary of Shakespeare's, begins his essay "On Love" by disparaging romantic love, proclaiming, "The Stage is more beholding to Love, than the life of man. . . . In life it doth much mischief: sometimes like a Siren; sometimes like a Fury" (50). This essay, which appears in the same volume as his "Of Envy" reprinted in this chapter (p. 338), encapsulates a curious phenomenon of reading early modern literature in the context of philosophical writings on the passions: literature takes delight in the nature and mishaps of love, while most philosophical texts share Bacon's view of love as a kind of disturbance or illness. The relation between literary idealizations of love (such as Petrarchism), theories of love, and actual emotional experiences seems murky indeed. Most commentators agree that love is a species of attraction that is primary among the states of inclination that constitute passion. Many writers draw from Aristotle in emphasizing love's relationship to resemblance or similitude; not only is like attracted to like but the attraction of love makes one person desire to conform his or her feelings and actions to the other person's. In its highest form, love is an inclination toward or affection for the good or sublimely beautiful. The model for this idealized state is the soul's love for God. However, writers show less agreement when considering human affections' capacity for elevation or degradation. Even those advocating companionate marriages, in which affection and companionship play a large role, caution against love's excess. Disconcertingly for modern readers raised on a diet of romance, most early moderns would agree that love based on sexual attraction or romantic inclination would be less likely to lead to happier marriages even as they enjoyed seeing the vagaries of romantic love onstage and in verse.

One might see Othello and Desdemona's defense of their elopement as an extended dialogue on virtuous love, as the couple responds to at times unspoken concerns about the proper boundaries on romantic love, particularly across differences. Against Brabantio's accusation that Desdemona has fallen under the dangerous spell of romantic attraction caused by witchcraft, the couple insist on the virtue of their choice and take care to de-emphasize erotic desire. Desdemona stresses the role of "duty" in her actions; her insistence on seeing Othello's "visage in his mind" then becomes not simply about looking past his blackness but also about being drawn to the noble inner qualities that characterize a virtuous love. So, too, Othello reassures the Senators that the request to have Desdemona accompany him has nothing to do with a dangerous desire, but rather "to be free and bounteous to her mind" (1.3.267).

The attraction of love is, unfortunately, unstable: honorable love can lead one to virtue and God, while sexual desire or possessive love may put one under the spell of lesser and degrading passions, such as jealousy. In "On Love," Bacon reminds his readers that "It is impossible to love, and to be wise" (52) and urges men to make love "keep quarter [i.e., maintain good order] and sever it wholly from their serious affairs and actions of life" (53). Even as Othello and Desdemona proclaim the exalted nature of their love, Iago emphasizes the bestial and degrading nature of sexual desire and pushes Othello into a more dangerously impassioned state. The dangers of excessive love for men were well catalogued in the period: uxoriousness, effeminacy, jealousy, envy, and even madness. When Othello asks that onlookers speak of him as "one that loved not wisely but too well" (5.2.354), is he still holding out a place for romantic love even as he acknowledges its fatal effects in him?

The precise nature of extreme passions related to love were subject to special scrutiny in the early modern period. Is jealousy a form of love, or does it spring from some other well? Benedetto Varchi (see p. 330) defines jealousy rather circularly as "a kind of suspicious Care, or a careful kind of Suspicion" (p. 332). Although his *Blazon of Jealousy* outlines many types of jealousy, Varchi agrees with Robert Burton (see p. 335) in highlighting sexual jealousy as "furious passion . . . most eminent in men" (3.3.1.1). Both writers struggle to separate jealousy from love even as they acknowledge their intricate connection. Burton, for example, proclaims jealousy as a "bastard-branch, or kind of Love-Melancholy" (3.3.1.1). Just as Varchi's investigations of jealousy rely on humoral theory, often seeing women and foreigners (e.g., Turks and Italians) as more susceptible to jealousy, several scholars have noted how frequently John Leo Africanus identifies certain African groups as excessively jealous, and readers might want to pay attention to the causes of jealousy given in the contextual materials as well as the differing views on jealousy expressed in *Othello*. Natasha Korda points out that many texts on jealousy reveal it as "a symptom of the curiosity, greed, and covetousness that arise from the institution of private property" (130) and cautions that these writers may be projecting onto others issues that are sources of anxiety within their own culture (129). Readers might use her insight to interrogate other characters' relationships to love and jealousy: What characterizes Roderigo's desire for Desdemona? What does Iago mean when he says of Desdemona: "Now, I do love her too, / Not out of absolute lust . . . But partly led to diet my revenge" (2.1.271–74)?

THOMAS BUONI

# *From* Problems of Beauty and All Human Affections

*1606*

Almost all writers on the passions question the role of gifts or tokens in inciting love. It is unclear, however, how much of their concern springs from a general interest in the workings of the material world on the immaterial self and how much from concerns with covetousness and private property. How does Buoni's understanding of the efficacy of love tokens compare with Brabantio's? How can we relate it to stories about the handkerchief? If gifts are substitutes for or signs of the beloved, the reader might consider how Buoni's ideas about gifts resonate with the use of tokens in the military (see Chapter 4, p. 310).

## WHY DO LOVERS SO MUCH ESTEEM THE GIFTS OF THEIR BELOVED?

*Problem 60*

*Perhaps* because they see I know not what kind of grace to shine and show itself in that gift which cometh from that they best *Love*, the which they esteem so much the more by how much it seemeth to present the excellent and honorable qualities of the giver. *Or perhaps* because those gifts are as rich pledges of that grace and favor whereby they may easily obtain to the possession of that they *Love*. And therefore, as they that have anything in their custody, either in value or Beauty extraordinary, with an extraordinary heed and care look unto it, so they prizing these gifts above all their earthly riches do likewise above all take care to keep them. *Or perhaps* that they might thereby show and give testimony that if they have that thing in so high esteem that cometh from their beloved, in how much more the person that sent it, who doth as far exceed the gift in value, as the substance the shadow, and a perfect, an appearing good.

---

Thomas Buoni, *Problems of Beauty and All Human Affections*, trans. S. L. (London, 1606), 124–25.

→ BENEDETTO VARCHI

# *From* The Blazon of Jealousy

*1615*

*Translated by Robert Tofte*

Robert Tofte's (bap. 1562, d. 1619/20) translation of Benedetto Varchi's (1502–1565) *Lettura . . . della gelosia* (1545) almost overwhelms Varchi's initial lecture with autobiographical musings, amplifications, and other asides (see Figure 31). In renaming the text a "blazon," Tofte taps into a very specific rhetoric of display (to *blazon* is to publish widely or to describe in vivid and eloquent detail). He uses Varchi to create a specifically English version of continental theories of jealousy (Korda 137). As you read, pay attention to Tofte's annotations. What kind of conversation does he have with Varchi (and with his English readers)? Varchi sees jealousy springing from four possible causes: pleasure, passion, property, and honor. This excerpt focuses on honor.

Lastly, Jealousy cometh in respect of a man's° Reputation and Honor, according as his nature is, or as his Breeding hath been, or after the fashion and manner of the Country in which he is born and liveth, because (in this point) diverse are the opinions of men and as contrary are the Customs of Countries, whereupon they say that the Southern Nations,ᴾ and such as dwell in hot Regions are very Jealous; either because they are much given and inclined unto Love naturally: or else for that they hold it a great disparagement

°Honor is the Reputation and Credit or the good name and Fame of a Man, which the generous Spirit prizeth at so high a rate as before he will have the same eclipsed, he will lose all his wealth, yea, and his dearest life too, according unto the saying of a certain grave and wise Gentleman:

> *Untainted* Honor *(not long life) the treasure is*
> *Which noble Minds do hold to be their chiefest bliss.*

ᴾThe Persians were wont to be so jealous of their Wives, as they never suffered them to go abroad but in Wagons close shut; but at this day the Italian is counted the man that is most subject to this vice, the sallow complexioned fellow with a black beard, being he that is most prone as well to suspect as to be suspected about Women's matters, according to the old saying:

> *To a Red man read thy Read,*
> *With a Brown man break thy Bread,*
> *At a Pale man draw thy Knife,*
> *From a Black man keep thy Wife.*

Which we expound after this manner:

> *The Red is wise, the Brown trusty,*
> *The Pale envious, the Black lusty.*

Benedetto Varchi, *The Blazon of Jealousy*, trans. Robert Tofte (London, 1615), 21–24, 56–58.

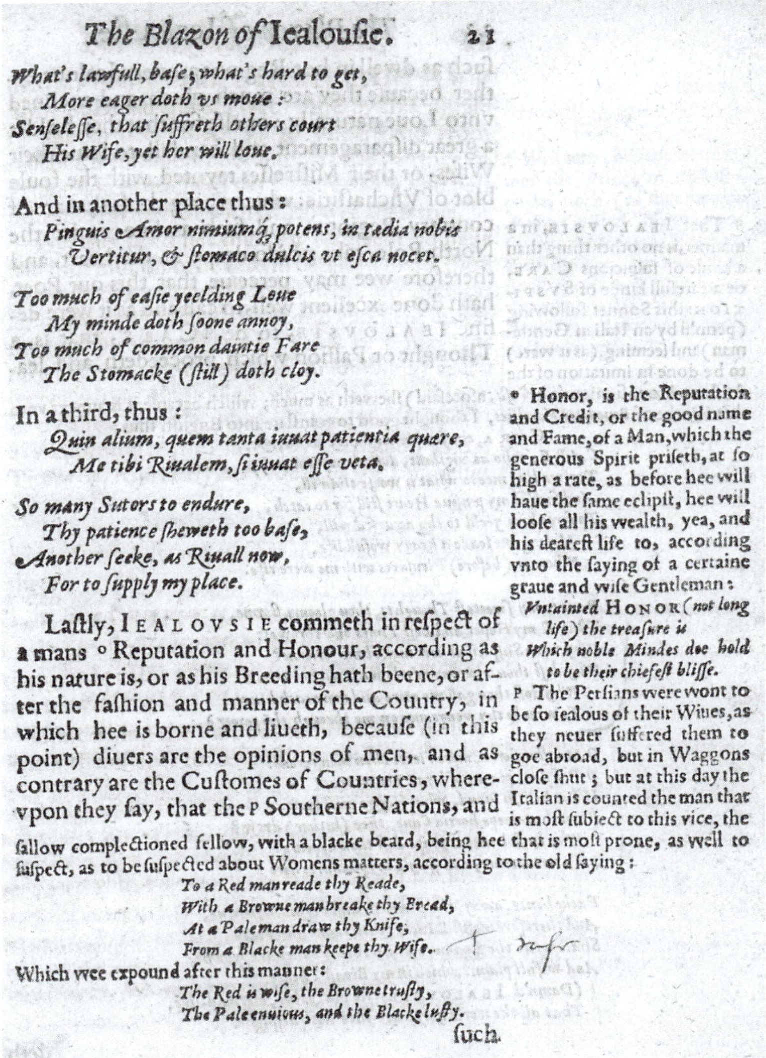

The Blazon of Iealousie. 21

*What's lawfull, base; what's hard to get,*
*More eager doth vs moue:*
*Senselesse, that suffreth others court*
*His Wife, yet her will loue.*

And in another place thus:

*Pinguis Amor nimiumq́, potens, in tædia nobis*
*Vertitur, & stomaco dulcis vt esca nocet.*

*Too much of easie yeelding Loue*
*My minde doth soone annoy,*
*Too much of common daintie Fare*
*The Stomacke (still) doth cloy.*

In a third, thus:

*Quin alium, quem tanta iuuat patientia quære,*
*Me tibi Riualem, si iuuat esse veta.*

*So many Sutors to endure,*
*Thy patience sheweth too base,*
*Another seeke, as Riuall now,*
*For to supply my place.*

Lastly, IEALOVSIE commeth in respect of a mans ° Reputation and Honour, according as his nature is, or as his Breeding hath beene, or after the fashion and manner of the Country, in which hee is borne and liueth, because (in this point) diuers are the opinions of men, and as contrary are the Customes of Countries, wherevpon they say, that the P Southerne Nations, and sallow complectioned fellow, with a blacke beard, being hee that is most prone, as well to suspect, as to be suspected about Womens matters, according to the old saying:

*To a Red man reade thy Reade,*
*With a Browne man breake thy Bread,*
*At a Pale man draw thy Knife,*
*From a Blacke man keepe thy Wife.*

Which wee expound after this manner:

*The Red is wise, the Browne trusty,*
*The Pale enuious, and the Blacke lusty.*

such

° Honor, is the Reputation and Credit, or the good name and Fame, of a Man, which the generous Spirit priseth, at so high a rate, as before hee will haue the same eclipst, hee will loose all his wealth, yea, and his dearest life to, according vnto the saying of a certaine graue and wise Gentleman:

*Vntainted* HONOR *(not long life) the treasure is*
*Which noble Mindes doe hold to be their chiefest blisse.*

P The Persians were wont to be so iealous of their Wiues, as they neuer suffered them to goe abroad, but in Waggons close shut; but at this day the Italian is counted the man that is most subiect to this vice, the

FIGURE 31 *Page 21, from Benedetto Varchi,* The Blazon of Jealousy, *translated by Robert Tofte (1615).*

and scandal to have their Wives or their Mistresses tainted with the foul blot of Unchastity: which thing those that are of contrary Regions and such as live under the North Pole take not so deep at the heart, and therefore we may perceive that this our Poet hath done excellent well to call and as it were define Jealousy to be Care,[q] that is, a Thought or Passion which proceedeth and leadeth on Fear, which is as much to say, as if it came of Dread and Suspect. And by this phrase of speech, he giveth us to understand from whence it springeth, because (as the Prince of Philosophers[R] teacheth us) we are easily and best nourished with that with which we are born.

Neither doth he think it sufficient to have said thus much, but he addeth besides (*Cresci* [which means] thou groweth or increaseth), which word no doubt is set down by him, with great and excellent judgment, by reason that Jealousy may (as other like Qualities) increase or diminish, and it increaseth or diminisheth through four things, or means, to wit: 1. According to the Persons; 2. According to the Places; 3. According to the Times; 4. And lastly, according to the Business taken in hand.

The persons, by means whereof Jealousy increaseth or decreaseth, are in a manner always three.

1. The Party that is Jealous.
2. His Mistress, over whom he is Jealous.
3. The Person whom he suspecteth, and therefore is Jealous of him.

Concerning the Party that is Jealous: such as know themselves to be destitute[S] and deprived

[q]That Jealousy, in a manner, is no other thing than a kind of suspicious Care, or a careful kind of Suspicion . . .

[R]Well may *Aristotle* be termed the Prince of Philosophers, since (as the famous *Averrois* writeth) Nature meant (when Aristotle was born) to show the utmost proof of all her strength and power, so that what was possible for a mortal man to know, so much did he understand.

[S]Indeed I am of the opinion, that the most worthless persons are always most subject to this infectious Disease of Jealousy, as Mr. *George Wither* rightly saith.

*There is None Jealous I durst pawn my life,*
*But he that hath defiled another's Wife:*
and commonly, *Mala Mens malus Animus,* An ill Disposition breeds an ill suspicion.
*And for that he himself hath gone astray,*
*He straight-way thinks his Wife will tread that way.*

of every good Quality and Virtue, and that find themselves to be little (or nothing at all) favored or respected of their Mistresses and Ladies, swallow down more easily, and sooner, this poison than others do. A Testimonial of which Mr. John Bocchus[1] setteth down most judiciously (as is his wonted manner) in the ninth Tale of his seventh *Giornata* or day's Work, in the person of Annigucchio *Berlinghieri*,[T] as everyone may perceive that will take the pains to read the same. Besides, it importeth very much to know of what nature the Jealous man is, because if he be naturally suspicious, he then will take everything in the worse sense, interpreting all whatsoever he either heareth or seeth in a sinister and bad sense or meaning, and so his Disease (in time) cometh to be desperate. . . .

And certainly it cannot be denied, but that many senseless and brute beasts are Jealous, as is apparently seen in Bulls, in Swans,[Q] in Lions, in Doves, in Hens, and such like. Besides, me thinks, it is as natural a thing for a man to be Jealous, as to desire to engender, and beget that which is like to himself, which is the most natural thing (as *Aristotle* avoucheth in his second Book *De Anima*) that living creatures can do. And this they do, that they might (as he allegeth oftentimes) in some sort, participate and come near unto divine Nature, as much and after the best manner they shall be able.

The best counsel therefore I can give to these kinds of suspicious Brains, is to possess their souls with patience, considering it is the best Salve for this Sore, and to give over this frantic Malady, following this good Counsel.

*Thy Wife being fair, be not thou Jealous,*
*Because Suspicion cures not women's Follies.*

[T]See this Tale in Boccaccio's *Decameron*, and in his seven *Giornata*, the Argument whereof is briefly thus: *Annigucchio*, a rich Merchant of *Florence*, being jealous of his fair wife, perceived how she used to tie a small line or thread about one of her feet when she went to bed, whereupon he one night finding his Rival to pull the same, leapt out of his Bed with his Sword drawn to follow him, and she, seeing that her devise was descried, got her maid to lie in her place in the bed, whom her Husband coming back (for he could not overtake the foresaid Fellow) beat most pitifully, and that done, set his Wife's kindred to see her in that pitiful taking, but when they saw it was another and not their kinswoman, they began to swagger with him, and she to rail at him, for calling her good name in question, whereupon he being outfaced by his Wife, and the rest, that he was drunk, was glad to ask her forgiveness, as if he had done her great wrong, and, after that, never durst find fault with her more, but suffered her to have her will and take her pleasure where she thought good and liked best.

[Q]The Tale of the Swan, about *Windsor*, finding a strange Cock with his Mate, and how far he swam after the other to kill it, and then returning back, slew his Hen also (this being a certain truth, and not many years done upon this our Thames) is so well known to many Gentlemen, and to most Watermen of this River, as it were needless, to use any more words about the same. . . .

---

[1] *John Bocchus*: Italian poet Giovanni Boccaccio, author of *The Decameron*, a collection of 100 stories. [Hall]

Now if any shall doubt whether Jealousy be a natural thing or no, or (if it being so) why then should it be condemned and blamed so much (considering that according to *Aristotle's* rule, none ought either to be praised or blamed for anything they do through the secret instinct of Nature, they being as it were indifferent (as we may term them). To them I answer this: we condemn not Jealousy itself, but the Excess,[R] and the too too much of the same, as we find not fault with eating and drinking moderately, and other such natural desires; but the abuse thereof, through too much gluttony. Surfeiting, Quaffing, and Drunkenness, being that which we blame and disallow of, and therefore if any shall be Jealous with discretion (and not without great and important cause), observing a true and temperate decorum in the Time, the place, the person, and the cause, as is fit and convenient for him; especially, if it shall concern his own reputation and credit, or the good name of his Mistress, or Wife, he is not to be discommended at all.

[R]Here the Author showeth his opinion as concerning Jealousy because he would not be mistaken, condemning this foolish and suspicious Humor; taken or conceited upon no occasion or cause given, by many men over-rashly and to the utter overthrow, many times of themselves, and of such as they love and affect most dearly, wishing the golden Mean, that is, the Mediocrity or Virtue herein, to be used by everyone, and that also with great Discretion and Judgment, remembering always this Lesson.

*'Tis fast goodwill, and gentle courtesies,*
*Reclaims a Woman, and not watching eyes;*
*For where Suspect directeth forward wills,*
*Beauty's sweet dalliance with delight it kills:*
*And where a Man is Jealous without cause,*
*The Woman good, for to be bad (oft) draws.*

→ **ROBERT BURTON**

## *From* Anatomy of Melancholy                                     *1632*

Complexion theory's never-quite-achieved ideal was a temperate body consisting of a perfect balance of wet, dry, cold, and hot qualities. These conditions
coincided with humoral theory's concern with the balance of bodily fluids:
blood, phlegm, choler or yellow bile, and melancholy or black bile. In neither
schema are these states absolute or equal; under the hierarchy of Aristotelian
thought, the dry and hot states associated with men were superior and more
conducive to courage and rational behavior than the wet and cold states associated with women. Within such frameworks, a person would be understood to
have a cold complexion or phlegmatic constitution in relation to others of his
nation or climate. On the one hand, the basic complexion remains the same
from birth, even though it can alter with any number or factors: illness, age, climate, and so on (to this day, one might still speak of a choleric, or angry, individual). On the other hand, the humoral balance might change more frequently
with specific stimuli (diet, illness, injury, etc.) and will in turn alter a person's
native complexion.

Much humoral and medical theory was concerned with prescriptive advice
on ameliorating the effects of humoral imbalance. Othello offers such advice to
Desdemona: "Hot, hot, and moist. This hand of yours requires / A sequester
from liberty, fasting and prayer" (3.4.33–34). Her hot and moist hand, straying
from the temperate ideal, requires "treatment" consisting of physical and moral
practice. Robert Burton's (1577–1640) massive *Anatomy of Melancholy* follows this
form, offering advice on resisting jealousy. Modeled on contemporary medical
treatises, it rather humorously dissects the forms, causes, and manifestations of
melancholy, a disease of great interest to intellectuals because of its association
with creativity. The following excerpt comes from the third book on love and
religious melancholy in an expanded edition. How does Burton's description of
love compare with descriptions of marriage in Chapter 3? How is his cure for
jealousy influenced by ideas about women's sexuality?

### SYMPTOMS OF JEALOUSY

Of all passions . . . Love is most violent, and of those bitter potions which
this Love-Melancholy affords, this bastard jealousy is the greatest, as appears by those prodigious Symptoms which it hath and that it produceth.
For besides *Fear* and *Sorrow*, which is common to all Melancholy, anxiety
of mind, suspicion, aggravation, restless thoughts, paleness, meagerness,
neglect of business, and the like, these men are farther yet misaffected, and

---

Robert Burton, *Anatomy of Melancholy* (London, 1632), 608–11, 617.

in an higher strain. 'Tis a more vehement passion, a more furious perturbation, a bitter pain, a fire, a pernicious curiosity, a gall corrupting the honey of our life, madness, vertigo, plague, hell: they are more than ordinarily disquieted, they lose *bonum pacis*,[1] as *Chrysostom*[2] observes, and though they be rich, keep sumptuous tables, be nobly allied, yet *misserrimi omnium sunt*,[3] they are most miserable: they are more than ordinarily discontent, more sad, . . . more than ordinarily suspicious. "Jealousy," saith *Vives*, "begets unquietness in the mind, night and day: he hunts after every word he hears, every whisper, and amplifies it to himself, (*as all melancholy men do in other matters*) with a most injust calumny of others, he misinterprets every thing [that] is said or done, most apt to mistake or misconstrue," he pries in every corner, follows close, observes to a hair . . . besides those strange gestures of staring, frowning, grinning, rolling of eyes, menacing, ghastly looks, broken pace, interrupt, precipitate, half turns. He will sometimes sigh, weep, sob for anger . . . swear and belie, slander any man, curse, threaten, brawl, scold, fight and sometimes again flatter, and speak fair, ask forgiveness, kiss and coll,[4] condemn his rashness and folly, vow, protest and swear he will never do so again; and then eftsoons,[5] impatient as he is, rave, roar, and lay about him like a mad man, thump her sides, drag her about perchance, drive her out of doors, send her home, he will be divorced forthwith, she is a whore, &c. By and by with all submiss complement,[6] entreat her fair, and bring her in again, he loves her dearly, she is his sweet, most kind and loving wife, he will not change, nor leave her for a kingdom; so he continues off and on, as the toy takes him, the object moves him, but most part brawling, fretting, unquiet he is, accusing and suspecting not strangers only, but Brothers and Sisters, Father and Mother, nearest and dearest friends. . . .

And through fear, conceives unto himself things almost incredible and impossible to be effected. As an Heron when she fishes, still prying on all sides; or as a Cat doth a Mouse, his eye is never off hers, he glotes[7] on him, on her, accurately observing on whom she looks, who looks at her, what she saith, doth, at dinner, at supper, sitting, walking, at home, abroad, he is the same, still enquiring, mandring,[8] gazing, listening, affrighted with every small object; why did she smile? Why did she pity him, commend him? Why did she drink twice to such a man? Why did she offer to kiss, to dance? &c. a whore, a whore, an arrant whore. . . . Though there be no danger at all, no cause of suspicion, she live in such a place, where *Messalina*[9] herself

[1] *bonum pacis*: the good of peace.   [2] *Chrysostom*: John Chrysostom (374–407 C.E.), Syrian preacher who valued asceticism.   [3] *misserrimi omnium sunt*: they are the most wretched of all.   [4] **coll**: hug.   [5] **eftsoons**: soon after.   [6] **submiss complement**: quiet or subdued flattery.   [7] **glotes**: looks or gazes askance.   [8] **mandring**: grumbling or muttering.   [9] *Messalina*: third wife of the emperor Claudius with a reputation for promiscuity and political scheming.

could not be dishonest if she would, yet he suspects her as much as if she were in a bawdy house, some Prince's Court, or in a common Inn, where all comers might have free access. He calls her on a sudden all to naught, she is a strumpet, a light huswife, a bitch, an arrant whore. No persuasion, no protestation can divert this passion, nothing can ease him, secure, or give him satisfaction. It is most strange to report what outrageous acts by men and women have been committed in this kind, by women especially, that will run after their husbands into all places, and companies. . . . But women are sufficiently curbed in such cases, the rage of men is more eminent, and frequently put in practice. See but with what rigor those jealous husbands tyrannize over their poor wives, in *Greece, Spain, Italy, Turkey, Africa, Asia,* and generally over all those hot countries. . . .

## CURE OF JEALOUSY

I could willingly wink at Lady's faults, but that I am bound by the laws of history to tell the truth. I speak not of our times all this while, we have good, honest, virtuous men and women, whom fame, zeal, fear of God, religion and superstition contains, and yet for all that, we have too many knights of this order, so dubbed by their wives, many good women abused by dissolute husbands. In some places and such persons you may as soon enjoin them to carry water in a Sieve,[10] as to keep themselves honest. What shall a man do now in such a case? What remedy is to be had, how shall he be eased? By suing a divorce? That is hard to be affected . . . they carry the matter so cunningly, that though it be as common as Simony,[11] as clear and as manifest as the nose in a man's face, yet it cannot be evidently proved. . . . She will hardly be surprised by her husband, be he never so wary. Much better than to put it up, the more he strives in it, the more he shall divulge his own shame; make a virtue of necessity, and conceal it: Yea but the world takes notice of it, 'tis in every man's mouth, let them talk their pleasure, of whom speak they not in this sense? From the highest to the lowest they are thus censured all, there is no remedy then but patience.

---

[10] **carry water in a sieve:** an allusion to the story of the Roman vestal virgin who proved her chastity by carrying water in a sieve.    [11] **Simony:** buying or selling church pardons or offices.

→ FRANCIS BACON

# *From* The Essays or Counsels, Civil and Moral    *1625*

Not only does passion transform the body and spirit but it also affects the world beyond the individual. The imagination is a particularly important agent in this regard because it has a profound power over both humors and spirits. In his *Anatomy of Melancholy*, Robert Burton notes that humors and the imagination act in concert, "for when once the humors are stirred, and the imagination mis-affected . . . many such absurd symptoms will accompany, even madness it self" (3.3.4.1). Any number of early modern texts attest to the abilities of the imagina-tion to alter physical states. For instance, medical treatises are rife with tales of women whose birth was affected by something seen during conception or preg-nancy. The black Ethiopian queen Chariclea was said by the writer Ariosto to give birth to a white child because she saw a picture of a white man during con-ception.

In extreme cases, the force of passion is so great that "the victim personifies and objectifies his passion as if it had an independent life of its own" (Roach 48). In his essay "Of Envy," Francis Bacon (1561–1626) offers an excellent example of the materiality of the emotions. How does Bacon describe the workings of envy on both the envier and the object of his emotion? Why does envy in particular have such an effect on its object? How much of envy springs from social distinc-tions like class? Can it be said that Iago transfers his jealousy of Cassio to Othello?

## CHAPTER 9

*Of Envy*

There be none of the *Affections* which have been noted to fascinate, or bewitch, but *Love* and *Envy*. They both have vehement wishes; they frame themselves readily into Imaginations and Suggestions; And they come eas-ily into the Eye, especially upon the presence of the Objects, which are the Points that conduce to Fascination, if any such thing there be. We see, like-wise, the Scripture calleth *Envy* an *Evil Eye*: and the Astrologers call the evil Influences of the Stars *Evil Aspects*; So that still there seemeth to be acknowledged in the Act of *Envy* an Ejaculation, or Irradiation of the Eye. Nay, some have been so curious as to note that the Times when the Stroke or Percussion of an *Envious Eye* doth most hurt are when the *Party envied* is beheld in Glory, or Triumph; For that sets an Edge upon *Envy*; And

Francis Bacon, *The Essays or Counsels, Civil and Moral, of Francis Lo Verulam Viscount St. Alban* (London, 1625), 40–50.

besides, at such times, the spirits of the *person Envied* do come forth, most into the outward Parts, and so meet the Blow. . . .

A man that hath no virtue in himself ever *envieth* Virtue in others. For Men's Minds will either feed upon their own Good or upon others' Evil; and who wanteth the one will prey upon the other; And who so is out of Hope to attain to another's Virtue will seek to come at even hand by Depressing another's Fortune.

A man that is Busy, and Inquisitive, is commonly *Envious.* Therefore, it must needs be that he taketh a kind of play-pleasure in looking upon the Fortunes of others; Neither can he that mindeth but his own Business find much matter for *Envy.* For *Envy* is a Gadding Passion, and walketh the Streets, and doth not keep home. . . .

Lastly, near Kinsfolks, and Fellows in Office, and those that have been bred together are more apt to *Envy* their Equals, when they are raised. For it doth upbraid unto them their own Fortunes; And pointeth at them, and cometh oftener into their remembrance, and incurreth likewise more into the note of others: And *Envy* ever redoubleth from Speech and Fame. *Cain's Envy* was the more vile and Malignant toward his brother *Abel* because when his Sacrifice was better accepted, there was no Body to look on. . . .

Concerning *those that are more or less subject to Envy:* First, Persons of eminent Virtue, when they are advanced, are less *envied,* for their fortune seemeth but due unto them; and no man *Envieth* the Payment of a Debt, but Rewards, and Liberality, rather. Again, *Envy* is ever joined with the Comparing of a Man's Self; And where there is no Comparison, no *Envy;* And therefore Kings are not *envied* but by Kings. . . .

*Persons* of Noble Blood are less *envied* in their Rising: For it seemeth but Right done to their Birth. Besides, there seemeth not much added to their Fortune; and *Envy* is as the Sunbeams that beat hotter upon a Bank or steep rising Ground than upon a flat. And for the same reason, those that are advanced by degrees are less *envied* than those that are advanced suddenly, and *per saltum.*[1]

Those that have joined with their Honor, great Travels, Cares, or Perils are less subject to *Envy.* For Men think that they earn their Honors hardly, and pity them sometimes; and *Pity* ever healeth *Envy;* Wherefore, you shall observe that the more deep and sober sort of Politic persons, in their Greatness, are ever bemoaning themselves, what a Life they lead; Chanting a *Quanta patimur.*[2] Not that they feel it so, but only to abate the Edge of *Envy.* . . . And nothing doth extinguish *Envy* more than for a great Person to preserve all other inferior Officers, in their full Rights and Preeminences

---

[1] *per saltum:* at a leap; in one fell swoop.    [2] *Quanta patimur:* how much we suffer.

of their Places, for by that means there be so many Screens between him and *Envy*.

. . . As we said in the beginning, that the Act of *Envy* had somewhat in it of *Witchcraft*; so there is no other Cure of *Envy* but the cure of *Witchcraft*: And that is to remove the *Lot* (as they call it) and to lay it upon another. For which purpose, the wiser Sort of great Persons bring in ever upon the Stage somebody upon whom to derive the *Envy* that would come upon themselves; Sometimes upon Ministers and Servants; Sometimes upon Colleagues and Associates; and the like. And for that turn, there are never wanting some Persons of violent and undertaking Natures who so they may have Power, and Business, will take it at any Cost.

Now to speak of Public *Envy*. There is yet some good in *Public Envy*; whereas in *Private*, there is none. For *Public Envy* is as an *Ostracism* that eclipseth Men when they grow too great. And therefore, it is a Bridle also to Great Ones to keep them within Bounds.

This *Envy*, being in the Latin word *Invidia*, goeth in the Modern languages by the name of *Discontentment*; Of which we shall speak in handling *Sedition*. It is a disease, in a State, like to Infection. For as Infection spreadeth upon that which is sound and tainteth it; So when envy is gotten once into a State, it traduceth[3] even the best Actions thereof and turneth them into an ill Odor. . . .

We will add this, in general, touching the Affection of *Envy*, that of all other Affections, it is the most importune and continual. For of other *Affections*, there is occasion given but now and then. And therefore, it was well said, *Invidia festos dies non agit.*[4] For it is ever working upon some or other. And it is also noted that *Love* and *Envy* do make a man pine, which other Affections do not, because they are not so continual. It is also the vilest Affection, and the most depraved; For which cause, it is the proper Attribute of the Devil, who is called *The Envious Man, that soweth tares amongst wheat by night.* As it always cometh to pass that *Envy* worketh subtly and in the dark; And to the prejudice of good things, such as is the *Wheat.*

---

[3] **traduceth:** modifies, dishonors, perverts.  [4] *Invidia festos dies non agit:* envy takes no holidays.

# CHAPTER 6

# *Encounters with Othello*

—————————————————— ✝ ——————————————————

"Speak of Me as I Am," artist Fred Wilson's U.S. pavilion for the 2003 Venice Biennale (a contemporary art show held every two years in Venice), featured a video installation, *September Dream*: four video monitors showed edited extracts from different film versions of *Othello* (see Figure 32). This multiplication of the play is also a splitting and reversal that forces the audience to move across different actors' interpretations of the story. Even as it draws the audience into a seemingly familiar tale, the installation estranges its viewers; each version wordlessly unwinds in a continual backward loop from Desdemona's murder and Othello's suicide. While the pavilion's title evokes *Othello*, the video title reminds viewers of the televisual impact of the September 11, 2001, terrorist attacks, after which millions saw the same image of destruction played out over and over on TV monitors across the world (see Erickson, "Respeaking"). Thus, in Wilson's work the intimate horror of domestic murder is overlaid by a nation's horror, both scenes of destruction wrought by collisions of difference. Both the fictive murder seen on the screens and the actual murders in memory bring out in an audience the desire to undo, to move back to a state of innocence — even as the installation refuses to offer Shakespeare as a source of comfort (Erickson, "Respeaking" 8).

Wilson's work is what Shakespearean scholars call an appropriation, an artist's rewriting or citation of Shakespeare and his texts to serve his or her

FIGURE 32 *Detail of video installation,* September Dream, *by Fred Wilson (2003). This photograph represents the video installation as it traveled through the United States. Each monitor shows an edited six-minute extract from different film versions of* Othello. *In the original Venice Biennale installation the four videos were of slightly different lengths and ran on separate channels.*

own vision. Wilson talks back, not just to *Othello* and Shakespeare but also to *Othello's* most famous performers and directors in cinema. Using the last famous blackface film version of the play by Laurence Olivier, Wilson forces attention on the constructedness of the Moor, on Othello as a European image of a black man, one developed from the desires and fantasies of the representing culture. The entire installation foregrounds the invisibly ubiquitous presence of Moors in Venetian art and architecture. Venice, England, and the United States each become part of the larger history of *Othello*. As in his previous work, Wilson uses film to "reverse history" (Hoban), to uncover a buried or ignored past through juxtaposition and artful rearrangements of its material artifacts.

Like Wilson, other artists and writers over the centuries have tapped into the potential of Shakespeare's *Othello* (itself an appropriation of Cinthio's novella), each one approaching the play with concerns provoked by his or her personal history and cultural moment. Such adaptations seem to have begun soon after the play went into print: there is some disputed evidence of an *Othello* ballad appearing in the mid-seventeenth century (Furness 398–402). Often readers and viewers approach these revisions or rewritings thinking only of the relationship between the modern author and Shakespeare. However, artists' appropriations are almost never simply that two-dimensional. Christy Desmet reminds us, "Something happens when Shakespeare is appropriated, and both the subject (author) and object (Shakespeare) are changed in the process" (4); moreover, between the author and object, between the artist and Shakespeare, a number of cultural contexts (local history, gender, postcolonial condition, literary and cultural climate) influence the encounter. For example, Wilson's encounter is shaped by his vision of Venice, but also by 9/11. Like Wilson, film and stage directors have negotiated their relations to each other and to their predecessors as well as to Shakespeare (Starks).

The "bardolotry" that envelops Shakespeare today — the worship of Shakespeare as the Bard, or great poet — is the product of the institutionalization of his works as high art, or as a form of "cultural capital," that began in the nineteenth century.[1] Shakespeare's elevated stature means that not just a body of work but the concept of "Shakespeare" itself (which includes pervasive references to him and his works throughout the culture) has become a symbolic commodity that individuals can draw on for social distinction or cultural and material reward (Guillory ix). However, "Shakespeare" serves not only as a vehicle for social privilege but also as a site for addressing many complex social issues. Desmet notes that " 'Shakespeare' is circulated through different ages and social strata, in turn accruing and conferring symbolic value on cultural projects from both highbrow and lowbrow culture . . . and sometimes both together" (5).

In addition to drawing from the circulation of Shakespeare in the culture, Shakespearean performance and other forms of appropriation can rely on viewers' extremely personal identification with a character (Desmet 7; Chatterjee and Singh). Paul Robeson's performances at times drew energy from his equation of Othello's circumstances with his own personal experiences of racism. In contrast, the protagonist of Tayeb Salih's novel *Season of Migration to the North* (see p. 375), Mustapha Sa'eed, refuses to identify with Othello, but in the disaffiliation reveals the power of Orientalist visions of Arab and African men that Shakespeare's play makes possible.

---

[1] For more on the institutionalization of Shakespeare, see Bate; Bristol; Taylor. For the emerging distinctions between "high" and "low" or mass culture, see Levine. For a critique of these distinctions, see Albanese.

Writers often attempt to dismantle Shakespeare's authority by "talking back." Feminist bell hooks adopts the term "talking back" from her childhood to name a politically engaged feminist criticism: "In the world of the southern black community I grew up in, 'back talk' and 'talking back' meant speaking as an equal to an authority figure. It meant daring to disagree and sometimes it just meant having an opinion" (5). Feminism is not the only means of talking back. Thomas Cartelli points to the oppositional voices that speak against "Shakespearean drama's underwriting of class-based or imperialist agendas" (1). Oppositional authors take umbrage with critical tradition; they historicize and complicate assumptions that critics and viewers make about Shakespeare, as well as assumptions *Othello* makes about culture and society. Though Richard Wright's *Black Boy* and Amiri Baraka's *Dutchman* (neither of which is included here) indirectly speak to *Othello* by addressing racism in encounters between black men and white women, Derek Walcott (see p. 380) and Tayeb Salih (see p. 375) directly question the play's representation of black and African masculinity.

Many artists have poked fun at a range of authority figures through an association with the authority of Shakespeare. For example, when studying how Alexander Do Mar's illustration (see p. 365) derides Shakespeare's elevation of Othello as a noble Moor, one might also examine what it has to say about the culture's elevation of Shakespeare and the artist Rembrandt in the nineteenth century. Still other artists make visible relations that are muted or invisible in the primary text. Although not included in this volume, Djanet Sears' *Harlem Duet*, Nadine Gordimer's *My Son's Story*, and Caryl Phillips' *The Nature of Blood* question the absence of black women from Shakespeare's vision.

The texts in this chapter encourage readers to consider how the artist's encounter with Shakespeare introduces larger social, cultural, and political issues. While there are critical readings of *Othello* by Thomas Rymer, Charlotte Ramsey Lennox, and William Winter, readers should think of all encounters (including their own) as commentaries on or interpretations of both Shakespeare's play and the artist's vision. Thus, both critic Charlotte Lennox and playwright Paula Vogel question Shakespeare's conception of Emilia. Ask yourself how historical circumstances shape the artist's or critic's approach to the play. For example, as you read through the Rymer–Lennox disagreement about the plausibility of the marriage (see pp. 345–49), you might think about how the terms of the debate may be informed by England's immersion in the Atlantic slave trade at the end of the seventeenth century. The selection by William Winter (see p. 349) was written at the height of the bronze age of *Othello* in theater (see p. 24), out of a theatrical practice shaped in large part by a solidifying of stereotypes of black men. How do the terms Rymer and Lennox use to speak of color, class, and character differ from Winter's? How might those differences relate to the moments in which each writer lived?

Readers should also note emphases that are different in the appropriation than in the original; that is, are there figures who are more visible or who express opinions that counter your sense of their character from the play? Paula Vogel's feminist encounter (see p. 353) creates a relationship between Bianca and Desdemona not seen in Shakespeare's play: Vogel heightens class conflict as well as bonds between women. Both the talking back to and the borrowing from Shakespeare in all of these works are evidence of the fact that "Shakespeare is not a fixed object, some physically determinate piece of marble" (Williams 84); rather the author and his works shift, change, and re-solidify in response to cultural and historical conditions — and to the personal experience of the artists and audiences who encounter Shakespeare.

## Critical Encounters

→ THOMAS RYMER

## *From* A Short View of Tragedy                          *1693*

Now notorious, *A Short View of Tragedy* is one of the earliest extended attacks on Shakespeare's work. Stringently applying the neoclassical principles of art popular in his day (particularly the observance of the Aristotelian unities of time, place, and action), Thomas Rymer (1641–1713) specifically complains that in Shakespeare's tragedies "the Words and Action are seldom akin, generally are inconsistent, at cross purposes, embarrass and destroy each other" (Vickers 2:25). *Othello* in particular violates neoclassical rules proclaiming that a play should represent no more than one day and one geographical place. Rymer also harshly criticizes the play's blend of comic and tragic structures. His literal-minded attack was widely read, forcing other critics to either redefine neoclassical principles or defend Shakespeare as a brilliant exception to the rules. What are Rymer's views on race? On women's sexuality? How might those opinions have affected his view of the play's effectiveness as a tragedy?

Thomas Rymer, *A Short View of Tragedy* (London, 1693), 87–88, 91–92, 130–31, 146.

# From *A Short View of Tragedy*

## OTHELLO: A BLOODY FARCE

*S*hakespeare alters it [Cinthio's play] from the Original in several particulars, but always, unfortunately, for the worse. He bestows a name on his *Moor* and styles him the Moor of *Venice*: a Note of preeminence, which neither History nor Heraldry can allow him. *Cinthio*, who knew him best, and whose creature he was, calls him simply a *Moor*. . . . We say the Piper of *Strasburgh*; the Jew of *Florence*; and, if you please, the Pindar of *Wakefield*: all upon Record, and memorable in their Places. But we see no such Cause for the *Moor's* preferment to that dignity. And it is an affront to all Chroniclers, and Antiquaries, to top up on 'um a *Moor*, with that mark of renown who yet had never fallen within the Sphere of their Cognizance. . . . Then is the Moor's *Wife*, from a simple Citizen, in *Cinthio*, dressed up with her Topknots and raised to be *Desdemona*, a Senator's Daughter. All this is very strange and therefore pleases such as reflect not on the improbability.

Whatever rubs or difficulty may stick on the Bark, the Moral, sure, of this Fable is very instructive. I. First, This may be a caution to all Maidens of Quality how, without their Parents' consent, they run away with blackamoors. . . . Secondly, This may be a warning to all good Wives, that they look well to their Linen. Thirdly, This may be a lesson to Husbands, that before their Jealousy be Tragical, the proofs may be Mathematical. *Cinthio* affirms that *She was not overcome by a Womanish Appetite, but by the Virtue of the Moor.* It must be a good-natured Reader that takes *Cinthio's* word in this case, tho' in a Novel. *Shakespeare*, who is accountable both to the *Eyes*, and to the *Ears*, and to convince the heart of an Audience, shows that *Desdemona* was won, by hearing *Othello* talk. . . . This was the Charm, this was the philtre,[1] the love-powder that took the Daughter of this Noble Venetian. This was sufficient to make the Blackamoor White, and reconcile all, tho' there had been a Cloven-foot into the bargain. . . .

The Character of that State is to employ strangers in their Wars; But shall a Poet thence fancy that they will set a Negro to be their General; or trust a *Moor* to defend them against the *Turk*? With us a Blackamoor might rise to be a Trumpeter; but *Shakespeare* would not have him less than a Lieutenant-General. With us a *Moor* might marry some little drab or Small-coal Wench.[2] *Shakespeare*, would provide him the Daughter and Heir of some great Lord or Privy-Councilor: And all the town should reckon it a very suitable match. Yet the English are not bred up with that hatred and

---

[1] **philtre:** love potion.    [2] **Small-coal Wench:** seller of charcoal.

aversion to the *Moors* as are the Venetians, who suffer by a perpetual Hostility from them. . . . The *Characters* or Manners, which are the second part in a Tragedy, are not less unnatural and improper, than the Fable was improbable and absurd. . . . His [Othello's] Love and Jealousy are no part of a Soldiers Character, unless for Comedy. But what is most intolerable is *Iago*. He is no Blackamoor Soldier, so we may be sure he should be like other Soldiers of our acquaintance; yet never in Tragedy, nor in Comedy, nor in Nature was a Soldier with his Character. . . .

The Moor has nobody to take his part, no body of his Color. *Ludovico* has the new Governor *Cassio* and all his Countrymen Venetians about him. What Poet would give a villainous Blackamoor this Ascendant?[3] What Tramontain[4] could fancy the Venetians so low, so despicable, or so patient? This outrage to an injured Lady, the *Divine Desdemona*, might in a colder Climate have provoked somebody to be her Champion: but the Italians may well conclude we have a strange Genius for Poetry. In the next Scene *Othello* is examining the supposed Bawd; then follows another storm of horror and outrage against the poor Chicken, his Wife. Some Drayman or drunken Tinker might possibly treat his drab at this sort of rate, and mean no harm by it: but for his excellency, a My Lord General, to Serenade a Senator's Daughter with such a volley of scoundrel filthy Language is sure the most absurd Maggot that ever bred from any Poet's addled Brain. . . .

> Desdemona. O good *Iago*
> What shall I do to win my Lord again?

No woman bred out of a Pigsty, could talk so meanly. And this, she is called to Supper with *Othello, Ludovico* &c. after that comes a filthy sort of Pastoral Scene, where the *Wedding Sheets*, and Song of *Willow*, and her Mother's Maid, poor *Barbara*, are not the least moving things in this entertainment. . . .

There is in this Play some burlesque, some humor, and ramble of Comical Wit, some show and some *Mimicry* to divert the spectators: but the tragical part is plainly none other than a Bloody Farce, without salt or savor.

---

[3] **Ascendant:** superiority.  [4] **Tramontain:** foreigner (with connotation of uncouth or barbarous).

# *From* Shakespeare Illustrated

*1754*

Novelist and writer Charlotte Ramsey Lennox (1729–1804) produced the first full-length study of Shakespeare in literary history, *Shakespeare Illustrated.* She compiled this collection of sources and commentary during an era newly invested in authorial property and "unique conceptualization," the idea that exemplary literary works are those that are wholly original and unique to the individual author (Gallagher 158); thus, she is at times quite negative, finding Shakespeare's plays inferior to the original "novels" of Cinthio (Kramnick). She does, nonetheless, defend *Othello* against Rymer. How do the two authors approach Shakespeare's appropriation of Cinthio? How are their ideas on race, ethnicity, and gender negotiated in their appraisal of both authors?

But on the other hand *Shakespeare* has made a very ill use of the Lieu-tenant's Wife. . . . (128)

Emilia pronounces him jealous, perceives the Loss of that fatal Hand-kerchief, confirms some Suspicions he had entertained, and though she loves her Mistress to Excess, chooses rather to let her suffer all the bad Con-sequences of his Jealousy than confess she had taken the Handkerchief, which might have set all right again; and yet this same Woman, who could act so base and cruel a Part against her Mistress, has no greater Care in dying than to be laid by her Side. . . .

The Character of *Iago*, says this Critic [Rymer], is against common Sense and Nature. "*Shakespeare* would pass upon us a close, dissembling, false, insinuating Rascal, instead of an open-hearted, frank, plain dealing Soldier; a Character constantly worn by them for some Thousands of Years in the World." The Soldiers are indeed greatly obliged to Mr. *Rymer* for this Assertion, but though it may in general be true, yet surely it is not absurd to suppose that some few Individuals amongst them may be close dissembling Villains.

*Iago* was a Soldier, it is true, but he was also an *Italian*; he was born in a Country remarkable for the deep Art, Cruelty, and revengeful Temper of its Inhabitants. To have painted an *Italian* injured, or under a Suspicion of being injured, and not to have shown him revengeful, would have been mis-taking his Character. . . .

*Cinthio* indeed makes *Iago* not only urge *Othello* to the Murder of his Wife, but is himself the Perpetrator of it; this seems still more absurd. . . .

---

Charlotte Ramsey Lennox, *Shakespeare Illustrated* (London, 1754), 128–31, 133–34.

But he [Shakespeare] has greatly improved on the Novelist by making him jealous of the Moor with his own Wife; this Circumstance being sufficient, in an *Italian* especially, to account for the Revenge he takes on *Othello*, though his Barbarity to *Desdemona* is still unnatural. . . .

The Character of *Desdemona* fares no better in Mr. *Rymer's* Hands than that of *Iago*; her Love for the Moor, he says, is out of Nature.

Such Affections are not very common indeed; but a very few Instances of them prove that they are not Impossible; and even in *England* we see some very handsome Women married to Blacks, where their Color is less familiar than at *Venice*; besides the *Italian* Ladies are remarkable for such Sallies of irregular Passions. . . .

The Outlines of *Iago*, *Desdemona*, and *Cassio's* Characters are taken from the Novel; but that of *Othello* is entirely the Poet's own. In *Cinthio* we have a Moor, valiant indeed as we are told, but suspicious, sullen, cunning, obstinate and cruel. Such a Character married to the fair *Desdemona* must have given Disgust on the Stage; the Audience would have been his Enemies, and *Desdemona* herself would have sunk into Contempt for choosing him.

With what Judgment then has *Shakespeare* changed the horrid *Moor* of *Cinthio* into the amiable *Othello*, and made the same Actions which we detest in one, excite our Compassion in the other!

The Virtues of *Shakespeare's Moor* are no less characteristic than the Vices of *Cinthio's*; they are the wild Growth of an uncultivated Mind, barbarous and rude as the Clime he is born in; thus, his Love is almost Frenzy, his Friendship Simplicity; his Justice cruel; and his Remorse Self-Murder.

→ **WILLIAM WINTER**

## *From Othello*: As Presented by Edwin Booth  *1911*

William Winter (1836–1917) was one of the most influential American drama critics of the nineteenth century, and his work provides an excellent illustration of how the era exalted Shakespeare. Winter disliked extremes in acting, including emotional extremes (Watermeier 15), and this may have influenced his judgment that *Othello* was an aberration among Shakespeare's tragedies. His preface declares that "the total effect of the tragedy is hard, unrelieved, harrowing pain" (3). Lacking the ability to evoke exalted or sublime feelings in the audience, *Othello*, he claimed, should nonetheless still be considered great because it "was

William Winter, ed., *Shakespeare's Tragedy of* Othello: *As Presented by Edwin Booth* (Philadelphia: The Penn Publishing Company, 1911), p. 121.

needful to the completeness of Shakespeare's transcript of mankind" (3). The passage included here is from the play's appendix, which also includes extracts on Moors from a contemporary encyclopedia, as well as comments by Shakespeare editor Charles Knight and poet Samuel Taylor Coleridge to support his argument.

# From Othello: *As Presented by Edwin Booth*

## VII. THE COLOR OF OTHELLO

It used to be the practice of the stage to paint the Moor quite black — to present him, in fact, as a Negro. There are expressions in the text which, taken literally, and without allowance for the moods and attitude of the speakers, would afford a warrant for this practice. But, — since to make Othello a Negro is to unpoetize the character, and to deepen whatever grossness may already subsist in the subject of the tragedy, — it seems the better way to remember that poetry has a privilege to idealize all it touches, and that expressions of opinion are not statements of fact — and may therefore be disregarded. The persons who call the Moor "thick lips" and "the black Othello" are not his friends — to state it mildly. Besides, there is a clearly marked difference between a Moor and a Negro. The Moor should be painted a pale cinnamon color, which is at once truthful and picturesque. Shakespeare has, in my opinion, Anglicized the whole affair, leaving nothing barbaric in Othello but his capacity of animal delirium. He gets his terrible catastrophe, however, by means of this — ending a frightful storm of frenzy with a dread calm which is extremely awful; and he gets a splendid effect of contrast in the elements of color and nationality.

Staging Women

→ THOMAS JORDAN

## *From* The Nursery of Novelties in a Variety of Poetry

*1665*

London's poet laureate Thomas Jordan (c. 1612–1685) began his career on the London stage during the mid-seventeenth century and made his living both acting and composing verse and broadsides. As a former boy actor, he would have played women's roles himself and perhaps had a particular interest in the most radical change in English theater in the Restoration — the use of actresses on the public stage. Jordan's prologue marks the performance of *Othello* by the King's Company on December 8, 1660, that is thought to be the debut of actresses in the professional theater (Howe 4). How does Jordan assume the audience will react to the actress? Is there a connection between the views of actresses and views of Desdemona?

Play on the Stage, where all eyes are upon her,
Shall we count that a crime *France* calls an honor
In other Kingdoms Husbands safely trust 'um,
The difference lies only in the custom;
And let it be our custom I advise,      5
I'm sure this Custom's better than th'Excise,
And may procure us custom, hearts of flint
Will melt in passion when a woman's in't.
     But Gentlemen you that as judges sit
     In the Star-Chamber[1] of the house the Pit;      10
Have modest thoughts of her, pray do not run
To give her visits when the Play is done,
With damn me, your most humble Servant Lady,
She knows the things as well as you it may be:
Not a bit there dear Gallants, she doth know      15
Her own deserts, and your temptations too.

---

[1] **Star-Chamber:** an English court that came to be a symbol of an arbitrary and oppressive court.

---

Thomas Jordan, *The Nursery of Novelties in a Variety of Poetry* (London, 1665), 22–23.

But to the point, in this reforming age
We have intents to civilize the Stage.
Our women are defective, and so siz'd
You'd think they were some of the Guard disguis'd;[2]                    20
For (to speak truth) men act, that are between
Forty and fifty, Wenches of fifteen;
With bone so large, and nerve so incompliant,[3]
When you call *Desdemona*, enter Giant;
We shall purge every thing that is unclean,                              25
Lascivious, scurrilous, impious or obscene;
And when we've put all things in this fair way
*Barebones*[4] himself may come to see a Play.

## EPILOGUE

And how d'ye like her, come what is't ye drive at,
She's the same thing in public as in private;                           30
As far from being what you call a Whore,
As *Desdemona* injur'd by the Moor?
Then he that censures her in such a case
Hath a soul blacker than *Othello's* face:
But Ladies what think you, for if you tax                               35
Her freedom with dishonor to your Sex,
She means to act no more, and this shall be
No other Play but her own Tragedy;
She will submit to none but your commands,
And take Commission only from your hands.                               40

---

[2] **Guard disguis'd:** possibly a regiment of the New Model Army, England's first professional army formed under Oliver Cromwell in 1645.   [3] **incompliant:** unyielding.   [4] ***Barebones:*** Oliver Cromwell, whose protectorate enforced stringent prohibitions against theater during the Commonwealth period.

→ PAULA VOGEL

# *From* Desdemona: A Play about a Handkerchief    *1994*

Pulitzer Prize winner Paula Vogel (b. 1951) foregrounds the women's relations in *Othello* in her *Desdemona: A Play about a Handkerchief*. Perhaps because of its violent disruption of audience sympathy for Desdemona, Vogel's play hasn't been performed as frequently as her other works. In emphasizing class and material differences between women, she challenges any idealized view of female loyalty. The play dramatizes the depth of Othello's fears: Vogel's Desdemona is unfaithful with every man in the play except Cassio. How does the focus on Desdemona's sexual adventurism force the audience to question the roles of women in both Shakespeare's world and their own?

## Scene II

*Emilia eats her lunch. Desdemona plays in a desultory fashion with a toy. Then, frightened.*

DESDEMONA:    Emilia — have you ever deceived your husband Iago?

EMILIA:    (*With a derisive snort.*) That's a good one. Of course not, miss — I'm an honest woman.

DESDEMONA:    What does honesty have to do with adultery? Every honest man I know is an adulterer . . . (*Pause.*) Have you ever thought about it?

EMILIA:    What is there to be thinkin' about? It's enough trouble once each Saturday night, than to be lookin' for it. I'd never cheat, never, not for all the world I wouldn't.

DESDEMONA:    The world's a huge thing for so small a vice.

EMILIA:    Not my world, thank you — mine's tidy and neat and I aim to keep it that way.

DESDEMONA:    Oh, the world! Our world's narrow and small, I'll grant you — but there are other worlds — worlds that we married women never get to see.

EMILIA:    Amen — and don't need to see, I should add.

DESDEMONA:    If you've never seen the world, how would you know? Women are clad in purdah,[1] we decent, respectable matrons, from the cradle to the altar to the shroud . . . bridled with linen, blinded with lace . . . These very walls are purdah.

---

[1] **purdah:** a practice requiring women to cover their bodies in public.

Paula Vogel, *Desdemona: A Play about a Handkerchief* (New York: Dramatists Play Service, 1994), 19–20.

EMILIA:   I don't know what this thing called "purr-dah" means, but if it stands for dressing up nice, I'm all for it. . . .

DESDEMONA:   I remember the first time I saw my husband and I caught a glimpse of his skin, and oh, how I thrilled. I thought — aha — a man of a different color. From another world and planet. I thought — if I marry this strange dark man, I can leave this narrow little Venice with its whispering piazzas behind — I can escape and see other worlds. (*Pause.*) But under that exotic facade was a porcelain white Venetian.

EMILIA:   There's nothing wrong with Venice; I don't understand why Madam's all fired up to catch Cyprus Syph and exotic claps.

DESDEMONA:   Of course you don't understand. But I think Bianca does. She's a free woman — a new woman, who can make her own living in the world — who scorns marriage for the lie that it is.

EMILIA:   I don't know where Madam's getting this new woman hog-wash, but no matter how you dress up a cow, she's still got udders. Bianca's the eldest one of six girls, with teeth so horsy she could clean 'em with a hoof pick, and so simple she has to ply the trade she does! That's what your Miss Bianca is!

DESDEMONA:   Bianca is nothing of the sort. She and I share something common in our blood — that desire to know the world. I lie in the blackness of the room at her establishment . . . on sheets that are stained and torn by countless nights. And the men come into that pitch-black room — men of different sizes and smells and shapes, with smooth skin — with rough skin, with scarred skin. And they spill their seed into me, Emilia — seed from a thousand lands, passed down through generations of ancestors, with genealogies that cover the surface of the globe. And I simply lie still there in the darkness, taking them all into me; I close my eyes and in the dark of my mind — oh, how I travel!

## Blackface Minstrelsy

According to several scholars of American popular culture, American theater in the nineteenth century witnessed a lengthy, public, and often contentious divorce whose implications have lasted until our own day. Theatrical performances, previously experienced across a broad range of classes and in a number of venues, split into two categories: elite, almost sacred events attended for cultural enrichment, and popular events attended for enjoyment and escape (Levine; Taylor). Shakespeare was the fought-over child of this fractured union. Gary Taylor suggests that he was "commandeered by [high] culture" (203). However, even as William Winter (see p. 349) and other elite commentators struggled to elevate Shakespeare as the Bard whose sacred poetry embodied the highest and most universal ideals of Western culture, entertainers like Thomas Dartmouth "T. D." Rice performed a version of Shakespeare that was public property, enjoyed in a range of popular entertainments — burlesques, parodies, and travesties. These seemingly irreconcilable differences around the same Shakespeare reflected larger pressures in American culture. *Othello*, which traveled in American culture as both tragedy and comedy, was so in demand that it became known as "Shakespeare's American Play" (Edelstein 179). While audiences wept at its pathos in conventional performances, they laughed at its comic transformation in blackface minstrel shows (often in the same venue); these forms spoke to each other and addressed important cultural concerns about sexuality, race, and culture.

Dramatic performance in blackface makeup has been an integral part of European vernacular entertainment for centuries — including "highbrow" performances of *Othello*. However, the comparatively "lowbrow" form of blackface minstrelsy was a specific cultural phenomenon that manifested a particular and degraded relationship to black culture and black slavery. Eric Lott characterizes this relationship as one of "love & theft," a combination of attraction and fear: ridicule and caricature emphasized the difference between black and white workers and "improbably threatening or startlingly sympathetic racial meanings were simultaneously produced and dissolved" (234). Popular contemporary accounts of the origins of blackface minstrelsy in the United States are themselves narratives of American racial politics; scholars have many theories about its roots in centuries-old vernacular traditions of blackface — English folk dramas, morris dances, burlesques, harlequinade, and commedia dell'arte (Chambers; Cockerell; Needham; Woodbridge, *Scythe*). Still others debate the degree and manner of minstrelsy's appropriation of actual black cultural forms such as melodies, slave songs, and urban festivals (Huggins 249; Lhamon). While many commentators condemned these "Ethiopian operas," their many fans (including Mark Twain) lauded minstrelsy as the first truly American art form; it was in any case America's most popular antebellum entertainment, lasting from the 1830s well into the era of film and beyond.[1]

Blackface minstrelsy was rooted in the distortion and commodification of black bodies — its performers blackened their skin, drew cavernous red mouths for themselves, and used exaggerated dialect and gesture. The performances consisted of a range of theatrical practices: folk music and dance,

---

[1] Sacks notes that minstrelsy remained an important aspect of rural popular entertainment into the mid-twentieth century.

parodies of formal oratory, use of slang and cant terms, female imperson-ation, and improvisation. Its content relied on sexual (often homoerotic) license as well as on myths of the Old South and the alleged closeness of African Americans to nature. Originally, minstrelsy was performed as an entr'acte — an interlude between acts or after a longer theatrical perfor-mance — or with other entertainments in circuses, museums, and vaude-villes. For example, some reports suggest that T. D. Rice first "jumped Jim Crow" in New York after an Edwin Booth/Thomas Hamblin *Othello* (Odell 3:631). Such theatrical moments call into question what it means to perform an interracial tragedy and then transform it into a comedy through racial caricature. Originally a short form that preferred spectacle over narrative, minstrelsy was later seen in incarnations that mimicked known stories in a longer form of "darkey dramas" (MacDonald n7), which were no less histri-onic. Although Desdemona in Rice's *Otello* was played by a white woman, white men playing the "negro wench" was a popular aspect of minstrelsy (Allen 164–70; Engle 68; Lott 159–68), and in these shorter versions, she would have been played by a cross-dressed man. Given that the shorter minstrels and performance of minstrel songs was one of a number of set pieces performed by a few men, it is possible that the earlier short *Othello* minstrels featured cross-dressed Desdemonas in blackface.

Blackface minstrelsy both was shaped by and commented on major political, social, and theatrical transformations as Americans struggled with a variety of social and ideological changes: an increasing emphasis on capital and enterprise as American ideals; a growing urban elite with anxieties about the performance of status (Huggins 271–75); vocal debate about move-ment into the American frontier (Saxton 16–17); more vocal and stringent prohibitions against racial intermarriage, or amalgamation (Collins); the rebellion and emancipation of West Indian slaves in England and rising abolitionist sentiment in the American North; and a developing "Cult of True Womanhood" (Welter). Minstrelsy burst into public consciousness at the same time as the institutionalization of Shakespeare, the bronze age of *Othello* performance, attacks on African American theater, and the electrify-ing appearance of Ira Aldridge, the first major African American actor on the English stage.

Many scholars of blackface note that the form was a recognized way for attacking elite pretension and power. Even though it was clearly a competi-tion over the meanings of whiteness that "provided a convenient mask through which to voice class resentments" (Lott 68), nonetheless, it did not merely look upward. Blackface minstrelsy literally denigrated black aspira-tions for freedom and agency; it allowed white working classes to carve out a space for themselves that distinguished them from their social superiors and from other, mostly racialized, groups deemed socially inferior. Within this realm performers were allowed to act on forbidden impulses and behaviors while at the same time frowning on them as characteristic of African Americans and other ethnic groups. Minstrelsy, like other forms of burlesque, mocked the pretension and illusions of bardolotry and seemingly elite forms (see Bristol); however, as a privileged forum for speaking about race, sexuality, and social movement, blackface *Othellos* produced varied and often contradictory meanings. Rice may have danced Jim Crow and recited his *Othello* ballad at traditional performances of the play. Meanwhile, Ira Aldridge also blackened up and jumped Jim Crow after his Shakespeare performances in England, but as part of a plea for contributions to his abolitionist activities.

Along these lines, one might want to think of numerous comic and tragic *Othellos* circulating in the nineteenth century, each speaking in different ways to cultural concerns about sexuality, race, and culture. Clearly *Othello's* themes proved fertile ground for the exploration of ideals of racial difference: both canonical Shakespeare performances and their blackface counterparts circulated and were energized by theories of racial hierarchy and related fears of racial "pollution" through miscegenation (Collins 2ff.). The nineteenth century was also the heyday of scientific racism and its related fears of black sexual appetite as a potential threat to the white race. Aligned with growing fears of the sexuality of black men, the same industrializing and urbanizing forces that galvanized blackface supported an ideal of white femininity, one of asexual purity, "an image of frail and mindless femininity," cloistered in the home (Giddings 54). Desdemona's disobedience and self-assertion become sites of contestation between different theatrical forms. (For example, compare the Do Mar illustration of her murder, Figure 34, p. 365, with the more conventional images throughout the volume.) Her desire, always existing uneasily in the text and all but disappearing in traditional theater, is heightened and mocked on the minstrel stage. Given the views on sexuality in the texts presented here, readers will want to consider the startling appearance of Othello and Desdemona's unnamed son in Rice's *Otello* (p. 366) as well as how the performance of black bodies in the illustrations and texts speaks to anxieties about whiteness.

→ Desdemonum: An Ethiopian Burlesque,
in Three Scenes
*1874*

With minstrelsy's popularity firmly established, nineteenth-century publishers flooded the market with cheap songbooks and scripts like Alexander Do Mar's *Othello: An Interesting Drama, Rather!* (1850) and *Desdemonum: An Ethiopian Burlesque, in Three Scenes* (1874): "little lyric volumes of racist mass caricature" (Lott 171), which were later in the century enjoyed by striving white middle-class families who preferred the propriety of the hearth over the boisterous atmosphere of the popular theater or burlesque house, but who still wished to have access to its entertainment. *Desdemonum*, like some other plays, was most likely published many years after its original performance. *Othello* was among the most popular blackface and burlesque adaptations of Shakespeare (Collins, Edelstein, Lanier, MacDonald). It may be useful to think about why so many of such performances needed to show the actual elopement from the house (a scene never staged in the original) in ways reminiscent of Jessica's flight in *The Merchant of Venice*.

Several texts associate Othello with foreign slavery in different ways, often making him Haitian or Jamaican and thereby linking him to well-known cases of Caribbean slave rebellion. Many draw upon popular anti-Irish sentiments. They often end with morals: the *Othello Travestie* (not included here) concludes, "The fair sex should never wed the black." How do the minstrel performances included here, render the tragedy comic in both form and content? How does that comedy then deal with all forms of appetite, not simply sexual ones? What is the effect of the combination of mock-Latinate language and made-up folk dialect in *Desdemonum*? Consider Figure 33: What does the cover image of a huge, grinning black head on a stage suggest? What is the reader being invited into?

---

*Desdemonum: An Ethiopian Burlesquer, in Three Scenes* (New York, 1874), 1–8.

FIGURE 33 *Front cover, from* Desdemonum: An Ethiopian Burlesque, in Three Scenes *(1874).*

## *Desdemonum*

CHARACTERS

OTELLER
IAGUM
CASHUM
RODERIGUM
BRABANTIUM
JUDGE
DESDEMONUM
*Musicians, Officers, &c., &c.*

COSTUMES

*Burlesque costumes of Othello.*

PROPERTIES

*Tamborine — Banjo — Rope — Ladder — Door bell, to ring outside —
Judge's bench, railing and witness box for Scene II. — Sofa — Cushions —
2 chairs — Dagger — Handkerchief.*

## SCENE I. — A STREET IN WENNICE. HOUSE OF BRABANTIUM, WITH PRACTICAL [OPERABLE] WINDOW, R. H. NIGHT.

*Enter* OTELLER, *L., with tambourine, and musicians, who serenade and retire.*

Duet.

OTELLER:

Wake, Desdemonum, see de risin' moon,
Ebrybody's snorin', nightingale's in tune;
Trow aside your lattice, show your lubly phiz;
Sing a song of welcome, while I go troo my biz!

DESDEMONUM: (*At casement.*)

'Tel, my duck, I hear you; daddy's gone to bed.
Fotch along your ladderum, I'm de gal to wed!
Since burnt-cork am de fashion, I'll not be behind —
I'll see Oteller's wisage in his highfalutin' mind.

BOTH:

De hour am propitious — come, my darlin' flame!
Dey say dat in de dark all cullers am de same.

(*Oteller throws her a rope ladder. She descends. They embrace.*)

Air.

DESDEMONUM:

When my soldier returns, full ob fame from de wars,
All cubbered wid honor and glory and scars,
Den how happy' I feel, and his arms round me steal,
And as I feel his kisses my brains fairly reel.

Air.

OTELLER:

Now sheath'd be my sword,
And to beauty
Let duty, let duty gib way.
Take de laurel from my brow,
     Wreathe it round wid roses now,
     And luft's go before de priest widout delay.

*They dance off L.*

*Roderigum and Iagum steal on R.*

IAGUM:

What's de matter, Rodereegum?
Got de mulligrub?[1]
Look so pale about de gills,
Guess you are in lub.

RODERIGUM:

She's gib me de mitten,[2]
And disconsolate I'm gittin';
Great mind to go and drown myself
In some old washing-tub.

IAGUM:

Drown cats and blind puppies!
Dere's fish in de sea
Just as good as any
In de market dat be!

RODERIGUM:     (*Producing banjo.*)
Yet one more dose my lub I'll gib?

---

[1] *mulligrub:* a fit of depression, low spirits. Also, stomachache.     [2] *gib me de mitten:* rejected me as a suitor.

Uf dat don't fotch her, dam if I lib! (*Sees ladder.*)
De jig's up for good — dat ladder tells de tale.

IAGUM: (*Picks up Oteller's hat.*)    It's dat nigger Oteller.
Let's kick up a gale!

(*Rings door bell fiercely, while Roderigum pounds. Brabantium puts head out of window.*)

BRABANTIUM:    Who dat makin' fuss dar?

RODERIGUM:    Desdemonum's cut her stick.[3]

BRABANTIUM:    Ring de bell and beat de gong,
I'll make Oteller sick!

ALL:
Ring de bell and beat de gong,
Fotch your swords an' guns along,
While I sing a little song —
My darter's cut her stick!

# Scene 2. — The Court-room at the Tombs. Judge on the Bench. Crowd Standing Round. Hum of Voices.

JUDGE:
Take off your hats, quit buzzin',
Fotch in dat hulky nig;
While de goose am cookin',
Guess I'll dance a jig. (*Dances a breakdown.*)[4]

*Enter officers with Oteller, Brabantium, etc., R.*

JUDGE:    Brabantium, what's de matter, dat you look so blue?

BRABANTIUM:    Dat darky's stole my darter, but de act I'll make him rue.

JUDGE:
To this what says Oteller?

OTELLER:
Judge, de fact am so;
De gal, you see, got struck wid me,
And would to parson go,
I ain't much on de talk,
but when fightin's round I'm der
Knock de chip from off my shoulder, and for bloody work prepare!

---

[3] **cut her stick:** deserted (perhaps with a sexual connotation).    [4] *breakdown:* a popular dance associated with African American slaves.

BRABANTIUM:

He's bewitched her, dat's de matter; come de Hoodoo on de gal.
He's played de black art on her, and Iagum is his pal.
Let him gub me back my darter, gub my Desdy back to me,
And send him to de Island, whar such fellers ought to be.

JUDGE:

We'll hear de girl's opinion. See, she comes dis way.
Now, Desdemonum, what you got to say?

*Enter Desdemonum, R.*

Song.

DESDEMONUM:

When duty calls; de wise gib ear —
Dat principle I freely own.
My husband's claim in law holds good.
I owe my faith to him alone.

BRABANTIUM:

To dat Jamaica nig? Why, gal, you're blind.

DESDEMONUM:

I see de feller's wisage in his mind;
Beauty's but skin deep anyhow, you know.

BRABANTIUM:

Well, since you've done de mischief you kin go;
But keep your eye peeled, Moor, nor cuckold be —
She's humbugged her old daddy, and may thee.

*(Exeunt severally, R. and L.)*


## SCENE 3. — A CHAMBER IN THE HOUSE OF OTELLER. SOFA, CUSHIONS, TWO CHAIRS.

*Enter Iagum, R., with a handerkerchief.*

IAGUM:

Now for de nex' t'ing on de peppergram.
Dis han'kerchum I foun' upon de stairs
Oteller gave to Desde. I'll convey it
Straightway to Michael Cashum. Then Oteller
I'll pump so full of stories he'll be jealous.
Sack Mr. Cashum, and I'll git his place.                    *(Exit L.)*

*Enter Oteller., L., meeting Desdemonum.*

DESDEMONUM:   My dear Oteller, dinner's on de table.

OTELLER: (*Aside.*)   How cool she takes it. Whar's dat han'kerchum dat an Egyptian to my mudder gib?

DESDEMONUM:   Bodder de han'kerchum; come, git your hash.

OTELLER:   De han'kerchum!

DESDEMONUM:   Your hash, I say, is ready.

OTELLER:   I'll settle Cashum's hash. You gub it to him.
Jus' now, I seen him wipe his mouf wid it.

DESDEMONUM:   It's no such t'ing ! I drop it on de stairs.

OTELLER:   Den say your prayers and die. De han'kerchum! De han'kerchum!

*(Draws her, kicking, to sofa.)*

Song.

DESDEMONUM:

Good-bye, husband; good-bye, dad,
To go off this way's quite too bad.
Let's have one squall before I slide,
And den to go I'm satisfied!

*(He smothers her with the cushions.)*

OTELLER:

Now, come in all;
For one last look
Ere black Oteller's life is took.

CASHUM:

Dere's some foul lie been goin' round,
Dis 'kerchief on de stairs I found,
And used it but my nose to blow

OTELLER:

Den dere's an end to all my woe.
Fiddlers, scrape! and fifers, play!
For here's the deuce and all to pay!

*(Stabs himself and falls on Desdemonum's body. The characters join hands and dance around them. Oteller and Desdemonum get up and join in. Tableau.[5])*

---

[5] *Tableau*: this dramatic convention of creating "living pictures" on stage was an especially popular way to close acts or scenes in nineteenth-century theater (Meisel 48). Mimicking conventions of painting (and in some cases with a giant picture frame on stage), the actors froze in set poses. It is possible that the actors here are mimicking popular painted images of *Othello*.

FIGURE 34 *Othello 5.2, from Alexander Do Mar,* Othello, An Interesting Drama, Rather! *(1850). Do Mar's verse* Othello *advertised itself as having "illustrations after Rembrandt," perhaps both capitalizing on and satirizing the nineteenth-century idealization of the seventeenth-century artist Rembrandt van Rijn. In her struggle, Desdemona's posture draws attention to Othello's exaggerated features. How does this portrayal of 5.2 differ from the illustrations of scene 5.2 in the introduction (Figures 1 and 5 on pages 7 and 17)?*

→ THOMAS DARTMOUTH RICE

## *From* Otello: A Burlesque Opera                    *1853*

The career of Thomas Dartmouth Rice (1808–1860), an originator of blackface
minstrelsy known as Daddy or T. D. who created the Jump Jim Crow dance,
demonstrates the arc of early minstrelsy. Rice began as a regional performer
who, according to an apocryphal account, first "jumped Jim Crow" by imitating
a disabled black man he saw in Cincinnati. Allegedly adapting black songs and
dances witnessed in travels through the South and on the western frontier, Rice,
like Daniel Emmett and other performers, brought to New York and other
urban stages an entertainment form that released the fears and fantasies of
urban white working-class men through the "thrill and stench of racial difference" (Jefferson H1). Major innovators and stars like Rice were in much
demand and highly paid; minstrelsy had become a big business and was so pervasive a means for representing blackness that actual African-descended performers sometimes "blacked up" to get work on the stage. Rice's *Otello* was
seemingly first performed with an hour-long *Uncle Tom's Cabin* in 1854. Rice
performed several versions of *Othello* over his career, including a short ballad
typical of earlier minstrel forms as well as the longer *Otello* performance excerpted here. Exhibiting hubris in the face of a master text, Rice's ballad (not
included here) concluded: "The tale is writ in Shakespeare's lyric finis, / But his
account is not as good as mine is."

[*Recitative*] Most potent, grabe, and reberand Signiors, my bery noble and
    approbed good Massas: Dat I hab tuck away dis old man's dater[1] — is
    true and no mistake. True, I's married her. De bery head and tail ob my
    offence hab dis extent no more. Rude am I in talk. I cannot chat like
    some folks for, since a piccanniny[2] two years old, I'b alway been in rows
    and spreezes.[3] Yet, by your gracious patience, I'll tell you how I won his
    darter.
ALL:    Hear him! Hear him! Hear him!
DUKE:   Silence — Say it, Otello.

    *Music // Air: Ginger Blue*[4]

---

[1] **dater:** daughter.    [2] **piccanniny:** in the United States, a derogatory term for a child of black
African descent.    [3] **rows and spreezes:** fights and (often drunken) frolicking.    [4] ***Ginger Blue:*** a
popular song; Ginger Blue was a stock plantation minstrel character (Allen 171–73).

---

Thomas Dartmouth Rice, *Otello: A Burlesque Opera* (New York, 1853; NYPL mss NCOF+),
11–23.

[OTELLO:]
Her farder lub'd me well
And he say to me one day,
Otello won't you come wid me and dine?
As I whar rader sharp set,[5]
Why, bery well, I say,
I'll be up to de trough Sar, in time.
We had terrapins,[6] Chicken Stew,
and nice punking Pie,
And a dish filled with nice Macaroni,
And last not least come de fried sassenges,
All cooked by de fair Desdemona.

*2nd Verse*

When de dinner it was ober,
And de whiskey flew about,
And de old Man was high in his glory,
He axed me to sing a song,
Fore the company put out.
Or else would I tell again my story
Ob de sprees[7] dat I got in
And de scrapes dat I get out
And how often run away when leff loose
And how dat I got free
From de Southern Slabery
And how often was I in de Calaboose.[8]

*3rd Verse*

Now dese tings to hear,
Desdemona cocked her ear
And wisht Heaben hab made
Her sich a nigger.
But den de house affairs
Would call her down stairs
War she'd sit in de corner
Cry and snigger.
My story being done

---

[5] *As I whar rader sharp set*: as I was rather hungry.    [6] **terrapins**: turtles famous for their delicate flesh.    [7] **sprees**: bouts of drinking; boisterous behavior.    [8] **Calaboose**: prison

She only wished I had a son
And to tell this story
I would undo her.
Den she wink and blink at me
And I did de same to she.
And upon dis suit, Sar, I won her.

BRABANTIO:

'Tis all a lie, told to defraud the bench
Please you, order some one fetch the wench
That she may here confront him face to face.

OTELLO:    Ancient conduct her, bring her — you best know de place.

*Exeunt Iago and Roderigo, L.H.*

BRABANTIO:

And if she do confess — she first began
To throw sheep's eyes and ogle at the man;
If, as he says — she took these means to woo him
Why blow me tight if I don't give her to him.

*Enter Desdemona and Ladies, Iago and Roderigo.*

Oh here she is — my child — my darling child,
Your poor old father — has been almost wild.
But tell me — since you lost your poor dear mother,
Don't you love me dear more than any other?

DESDEMONA:

Why, my dear father — if I must be candid,[9]
You've loved your child as much as ever man did.
And as in duty bound, I loved or rather,
Worshipped my parent, but then you're my father.
I've followed the example of my mother,
Who loved her father — but left him for another.

BRABANTIO:    Madam, your mother never left her home.

DESDEMONA:

Pshaw! pshaw — confess the case now do, Sir, do.
Did she not give up all the world for you
And of her speculation[10] ne'er did rue.
I've only done as folks have done before
I've cut you all for this — my Blackamoor. [*Crosses to Otello.*]
He is my Husband. What's done can't be undone. . . .

OTELLO:    Don't fret, sweet Desdemona.

---

[9] **candid**: sincere; white (possible pun).    [10] **speculation**: commercial venture.

CHORUS:    Bravo, Bravo Bravissimo.

OTELLO [*2nd verse*]:
Black folks from sheer vexation
Will grumble at me a few
And call dis 'malgamation[11]
Well, I don't care *Damn* if they do. [*pause*]
If I hab no objection,
What de debils dat to dem
You can't help your complexion;
Nature made you as well as dem.

CHORUS:
Bravo Otello: he's a clever fellow
One so glorious, will be victorious.

OTELLO:    Don't fret, sweet Desdemony.

DESDEMONA:    Oh, oh, oh, oh, oh, oh,

OTELLO:    Don't fret, sweet Desdemony.

CHORUS:    Bravo, Bravo, Bravissimo.

DESDEMONA [*3rd verse*]:
Where's the use of getting married
If our husbands have to roam?
Far better to have tarried
A single life at home.
For, if this is a beginning,
I plain gin to see,
This thing called matrimony
Is not the thing crack'd up to be.

CHORUS:
Bravo Otello: He's a clever fellow
One so glorious, will be victorious. . . .


# CYPRUS.

*Enter Cassio R.H.*

CASSIO:
Faith then I wish Otello, safe and sound,
Was treading once again upon the ground
For while on terra firma all seems level
The sea beyon't is rolling like the devil [*gunfire*]
Sure thats the signal, then he's come at last.

---

[11] 'malgamation: amalgamation, term for interracial marriage.

*Enter Montano L.H.*

MONTANO:
A ship — a ship — has just her anchor cast
And one Iago's come.

CASSIO:
                 Iago said ye —
Then, by the powers — he's brought the Captain's lady.

MONTANO:    What, is Otello married? Why, how is this?

CASSIO:
And to as fine a gal as one could kiss
Mistress Iago's come too — for 'tis said,
She's to the bride, a sort of Lady's maid [*Laugh L.H.*]
By the hokey's and here they are.

[*Enter Desdemona, Emilia, ladies and child and Iago, L.H.*]

CASSIO:
Madam I wish you joy
Blood an zouns and whiskey,[12] what a bouncing boy!
Mistress Iago, I'm glad to see you, too.
Mister Iago, Sir, the same to you. [*Crosses to L.C.*]
For old acquaintance sake; give us a buss
Don't mind your husband he'll not raise a fuss. [*Kisses Emilia.*]

IAGO:
Oh, pile on a load or two; don't mind me, pray,
'Stead of her lip — would she'd give her tongue away.
She often blows me up — [13]

EMILIA:
                 You tell a lie.
I never blow you up, you fool, not I.
Except when you get into brawls and fights
And come home reeling every hour of the night.
You've killed my peace and almost broke my heart.
Oh, if I had some friend to take my part. [*Falls on Cassio's neck.*]
Wait 'til I get home! You say I scold you
I'll make the house, you wretch, too hot to hold you.

DESDEMONA:
I never hear her scold — nor think she can;
So don't you be so cross, you naughty man.

---

[12] **zouns and whiskey:** "zounds" (God's wounds), an epithet.   [13] **blows me up:** scolds.

What would you say of woman, if you could
Find one amongst us that was very good?

*Air, Yankee Doodle.*

IAGO:

I'll tell you. [*Cue for orchestra.*]
Now, she's that fair and never proud,
A gal so nice and cozy,
A smartish tongue — but never loud —
And lips so red and rosy
With lots of cash — but none too gay —
Just neat and not too dashy,
With locks just the flowers of May
And bonnet not too splashy.[14]

*2nd Verse*

The gal that being in a rage
And could keep down her dander;
One who in scandal won't engage
Nor go ahead on slander;
One who could think without a word.
Where do you think I'll find her?
One who a young man's footstep heard
And would not look behind her.
[*Spoken*] She'd be the critter that I see very clear.

DESDEMONA:     For what —

IAGO:     To pickle tripe and bottle ginger beer.

DESDEMONA:

Your wit and spleen are both surcharged in vapor[15]
You shan't write puffs for me in Bennett's paper.[16]

CASSIO:

Oh, don't you mind or care a fig about him.
Faith, he's a ladies man; the devil doubt him.

[*Takes her hand, both retire up.*]

---

[14] **splashy:** extravagant.     [15] **wit and spleen are both surcharged in vapor:** his wit and spleen (temper or melancholy) are so overloaded that they are up in smoke?     [16] **You shan't write puffs for me in Bennett's paper:** you won't write flattering reviews of me in the *New York Herald* (a paper published by James Bennett).

IAGO:

He takes her by the hand and slaps her shoulder,
I'll have you stranger yet ere you're much older.

*Otello sneezes without.*

The Moor! I swan,[17] I know him by his sneeze.
DESDEMONA:    Come then we'll go and meet him, if you please.

*Music and crush of Cymbals.*
*Enter Otello and attendants, L.H.*

OTELLO:

Oh, my fair warrior, I embrace dee thus!
Welcome! Honey, to de Town of Cyprus.

DESDEMONA:

Behold this pledge — your image here is seen.
Not this side, love, the other side I mean. [*Points to child's face.*]

*Otello takes the boy and kisses him.*

OTELLO [*to Cassio*]:

How do our old acquantaince of the Isle?
Honey you shall be well desired de while.

[17] swan: swear.

## Postcolonial Encounters

Although not quite the illustrative colonial subject like *The Tempest*'s Caliban, Othello has been used by artists to speak to many aspects of postcolonial conditions: exile, self-alienation, mimicry, desire, and, of course, race
and ethnicity. Critic Edward Said's landmark study, *Orientalism*, notes that
in *Othello* "the Orient and Islam are always represented as outsiders having a
special role to play *inside* Europe" (71). This "special role" of the outsider
within is of great interest to postcolonial writers who concern themselves
with cultures affected by imperial processes (Ashcroft et al. 2). Indeed, postcolonial literature emerges out of these experiences of colonization: it
emphasizes the difference between indigenous ways of seeing the world and
those of the original colonizing power. It often explores the tension between
the colony and the metropole, as well as those tensions created within subjects who move, geographically or psychologically, between the (former)
colony and the imperial center. Chapter 1 mentioned Ireland as England's

FIGURE 35   Othello No. 1, *by Hervé Télémaque (1960).*

earliest and most sustained colonial other. Critics Andrew Hadfield and Romana Wray note in different ways how *Othello* resonates with the Irish colonial experience (see Burnett and Wray).

Both Derek Walcott (b. 1930) and Tayib Salih (b. 1929) write out of home countries (St. Lucia and Sudan, respectively) formerly colonized by Britain to varying degrees. Like Haitian-born artist Hervé Télémaque (b. 1937), whose painting *Othello No. 1* (Figure 35) was created at the height of black power and artistic decolonization movements, the authors of the texts in this section reflect the values of an emerging politicized racial consciousness in art (Powell 130–32). Suggesting layers of fantasy and artifice within an almost fevered delirium, the painting shares with the printed texts an interrogation of *Othello*'s construction and, possibly, the multiple and alienated subjectivity of the colonial subject.

*Othello* resonates with concerns about language, education, and cultural assimilation that characterize much postcolonial literature (Ashcroft et al. 4). Just as some writers use Caliban from *The Tempest* as a figure for exploring the psychological effects of colonial education and rule, others use Othello as an archetype — that is, an original model — that allows them to explore issues of divided subjectivity and race. Colonization was not just an economic and political order; in its colonies, Britain established structures that made its cultural forms dominant over indigenous forms and created a native bureaucratic elite whose status relied on serving the empire and accepting its values. The word *mimicry* describes the condition of the colonial writer who, denied the value of his native experience and culture as "untrue" or "inferior," had to write "about material which lies at one remove from the significant experiences of the post-colonial world," using the language and forms of the colonizing power (Ashcroft et al. 88). Within this framework, readers might consider how these authors might understand Othello as one whose reality is constructed through his service to a foreign state. Jyotsna Singh notes that Tayeb Salih and other African writers "sought to historicize Othello's divided subjectivity as a 'mimic man'" (293); that is, they foreground the political conditions that generate the psychic splitting in the play.

If within the play Othello reads as an archetypal postcolonial subject, Salih and other writers remind us that he is also a character created by a writer whose works come to serve a colonizing agenda. Not only did the institutionalization of the English language grow in tandem with the development of colonial bureaucracy but its standardization was in some cases part of England's imperialist agenda (Viswanathan). That language constructs the world and our experience of it becomes a particular point of crisis for writers from former English colonies who were raised in this system of education. Salih's protagonist, Mustapha Sa'eed, remembers formal education as an arm of colonial rule:

> That was the time when we first had schools. I remember now people were not keen about them and so the government would send its officials to scour the villages and tribal communities, while people would hide their sons — they thought of schools as being a great evil that had come to them with the armies of occupation. (20)

Within such colonial systems of education, the teaching of Shakespeare was and continues to be an important conduit for instilling European ideals of reason, civilization, and aesthetics. Many postcolonial writers talk back to Shakespeare as an authority figure from these education systems, while others use his works to counter colonial misrepresentations of local or indigenous histories and subjectivity.

Western readers often see Othello as a convert who reverts to an essential and inevitable barbarism; this common view is accompanied by an idealizing of Desdemona as a naive innocent (Singh 291). Critic Jyotsna Singh astutely directs our attention to this reading's stereotypical views of cultural difference which insist that African men are inherently hypersexual and prone to violence. In contrast, some postcolonial writers demand an attention to the colonial histories that shape native subjectivity and view the Othello-Desdemona relationship as a metaphor for colonial relations. The erotic engagement with Desdemona thus comes to represent the male postcolonial subject's engagement with and aggression toward the European world. How do the texts in this section place *Othello* within a context of colonization, racism, and gender struggle?

→ TAYEB SALIH

## *From* Season of Migration to the North      *1969*

Tayeb Salih (b. 1929) uses both form and content in his novel *Season of Migration to the North* to speak to the split conditions of post-coloniality. He has chosen an indigenous English genre — the novel — to write in Arabic the story of Mustapha Sa'eed, a man who moves from his village outside Khartoum to London (the heart of imperial power) and back again. While in London, Sa'eed is tried and released on the charge of killing Jean, his white English wife. Critic Barbara Harlow suggests that the novel works in the Arabic tradition of *mu aradeh*, "literally 'opposition,' 'contradiction,' but meaning here a formula whereby one person will write a poem, and another will retaliate by writing along the same lines, but reversing the meaning" (162). The novel seems to talk back to Shakespeare and his *Othello*, particularly forcing the reader's attention to the fantasies that propel racism (S. Hall, "Why Fanon?" 21). How does Sa'eed make use of *Othello*? How are his sexual encounters an attempt to avenge the colonizing process? The novel is also intensely concerned with the psychic divisions of African men under colonial rule and with the Western ideal's false promise of a unified subject. In this excerpt, Sa'eed is telling the novel's narrator the story of his life in London. While Sa'eed is a double of Othello, the novel's narrator is also a double of Sa'eed — "in both the telling and their reciprocal effects, . . . they become inseparable" (Harlow 170).

Thirty years. The willow trees turned from white to green to yellow in the parks; the cuckoo sang to the spring each year. For thirty years the Albert Hall was crammed each night with lovers of Beethoven and Bach, and the presses brought out thousands of books on art and thought. The plays of Bernard Shaw were put on at The Royal Court and The Haymarket. Edith

Tayeb Salih, *Season of Migration to the North* (Oxford: Heinemann, 1969), 36–42.

Sitwell was giving wings to poetry and The Prince of Wales's Theatre pulsated with youth and bright lights. The sea continued to ebb and flow at Bournemouth and Brighton, and the Lake District flowered year after year. The island was like a sweet tune, happy and sad, changing like a mirage with the changing of the seasons. For thirty years I was a part of all this, living in it but insensitive to its real beauty, unconcerned with everything about it except the filling of my bed each night.

Yes. It was summer — they said that they had not known a summer like it for a hundred years. I left my house on a Saturday, sniffing the air, feeling I was about to start upon a great hunt. I reached Speakers' Corner in Hyde Park. It was packed with people. I stood listening from afar to a speaker from the West Indies talking about the color problem. Suddenly my eyes came to rest on a woman who was craning her neck to catch a glimpse of the speaker so that her dress was lifted above her knees exposing two shapely, bronzed legs. Yes, this was my prey. I walked up to her, like a boat heading toward the rapids. I stood beside her and pressed up close against her till I felt her warmth pervading me. I breathed in the odor of her body, that odor with which Mrs. Robinson had met me on the platform of Cairo's railway station. I was so close to her that, becoming aware of me, she turned to me suddenly. I smiled into her face — a smile the outcome of which I knew not, except that I was determined that it should not go to waste. I also laughed lest the surprise in her face should turn to animosity. Then she smiled. I stood beside her for about a quarter of an hour, laughing when the speaker's words made her laugh — loudly so that she might be affected by the contagion of it. Then came the moment when I felt that she and I had become like a mare and foal running in harmony side by side. A sound, as though it were not my voice, issued from my throat: "What about a drink, away from this crowd and heat?" She turned her head in astonishment. This time I smiled — a broad innocent smile so that I might change astonishment into, at least, curiosity. Meanwhile I closely examined her face: each one of her features increased my conviction that this was my prey. With the instinct of a gambler I knew that this was a decisive moment. At this moment everything was possible. My smile changed to a gladness I could scarcely keep in rein as she said: "Yes, why not?" We walked along together; she beside me, a glittering figure of bronze under the July sun, a city of secrets and rapture. I was pleased she laughed so freely. Such a woman — there are many of her type in Europe — knows no fear; they accept life with gaiety and curiosity. And I am a thirsty desert, a wilderness of southern desires. As we drank tea, she asked me about my home. I related to her fabricated stories about deserts of golden sands and jungles where non-existent animals called out to one another. I told her that the streets of my country teemed with elephants and lions and that during siesta time crocodiles crawled through it. Half-credulous, half-disbelieving, she listened to me, laughing and closing her eyes, her cheeks reddening. Sometimes she would hear me out in silence, a Christian sympathy in her eyes. There came a moment when I felt I had been transformed in her eyes into a naked, primitive creature, a spear in one hand and arrows in the other, hunting elephants and lions in the jungles. This was fine. Curiosity had changed to gaiety, and gaiety to sympathy, and when I stir the still pool in its depths the sympathy will be transformed into a desire upon whose taut strings I shall play as I wish. "What race are you?" she asked me. "Are you African or Asian?"

"I'm like Othello — Arab-African," I said to her.

"Yes," she said, looking into my face. "Your nose is like the noses of Arabs in pictures, but your hair isn't soft and jet black like that of Arabs."

"Yes, that's me. My face is Arab like the desert of the Empty Quarter,[1] while my head is African and teems with a mischievous childishness."

"You put things in such a funny way," she said laughing.

The conversation led us to my family, and I told her — without lying this time — that I had grown up without a father. Then, returning to my lies, I gave her such terrifying descriptions of how I had lost my parents that I saw the tears well up in her eyes. I told her I was six years old at the time when my parents were drowned with thirty other people in a boat taking them from one bank of the Nile to the other. Here something occurred which was better than expressions of pity; pity in such instances is an emotion with uncertain consequences. Her eyes brightened and she cried out ecstatically:

"The Nile."

"Yes, the Nile."

"Then you live on the banks of the Nile?"

"Yes. Our house is right on the bank of the Nile, so that when I'm lying on my bed at night I put my hand out of the window and idly play with the Nile waters till sleep overtakes me."

Mr. Mustafa, the bird has fallen into the snare. The Nile, that snake god, has gained a new victim. The city has changed into a woman. It would be but a day or a week before I would pitch tent, driving my tent peg into the mountain summit. You, my lady, may not know, but you — like Carnarvon[2] when he entered Tutankhamen's tomb — have been infected with a deadly disease which has come from you know not where and which will bring

---

[1] The Empty Quarter: the Rub al Khali in Saudi Arabia. One of the largest sand deserts in the world.   [2] Carnarvon: Lord Carnarvon was the wealthy English aristocrat who financed Howard Carter's search for Tutankhamen's tomb. Carnarvon died within weeks of the official opening of the tomb.

about your destruction, be it sooner or later. My store of hackneyed phrases is inexhaustible. I felt the flow of conversation firmly in my hands, like the reins of an obedient mare: I pull at them and she stops, I shake them and she advances; I move them and she moves subject to my will, to left or to right.

"Two hours have passed without my being aware of them," I said to her. "I've not felt such happiness for a long time. And there's so much left for me to say to you and you to me. What would you say to having dinner together and continuing the conversation?"

For a while she remained silent. I was not alarmed for I felt that satanic warmth under my diaphragm, and when I feel it I know that I am in full command of the situation. No, she would not say no. "This is an extraordinary meeting," she said. "A man I don't know invites me out. It's not right, but —" She was silent. "Yes, why not?" she then said. "There's nothing to tell from your face you're a cannibal."

"You'll find I'm an aged crocodile who's lost its teeth," I said to her, a wave of joy stirring in the roots of my heart. "I wouldn't have the strength to eat you even if I wanted to." I reckoned I was at least fifteen years her junior, for she was a woman in the region of forty, whose body — whatever the experiences she had undergone — time had treated kindly. The fine wrinkles on her forehead and at the corners of her mouth told one not that she had grown old, but that she had ripened.

Only then did I ask her name.

"Isabella Seymour," she said.

I repeated it twice, rolling it round my tongue as though eating a pear.

"And what's *your* name?"

"I'm — Amin. Amin Hassan."

"I shall call you Hassan."

With the grills and wine her features relaxed and there gushed forth — upon me — a love she felt for the whole world. I wasn't so much concerned with her love for the world, or for the cloud of sadness that crossed her face from time to time, as I was with the redness of her tongue when she laughed, the fullness of her lips and the secrets lurking in the abyss of her mouth. I pictured her obscenely naked as she said: "Life is full of pain, yet we must be optimistic and face life with courage."

Yes, I now know that in the rough wisdom that issues from the mouths of simple people lies our whole hope of salvation. A tree grows simply and your grandfather has lived and will die simply. That is the secret. You are right, my lady: courage and optimism. But until the meek inherit the earth, until the armies are disbanded, the lamb grazes in peace beside the wolf and the child plays water-polo in the river with the crocodile, until that time of happiness and love comes along, I for one shall continue to express myself in this twisted manner. And when, puffing, I reach the mountain peak and implant the banner, collect my breath and rest — that, my lady, is an ecstasy greater to me than love, than happiness. Thus I mean you no harm, except to the extent that the sea is harmful when ships are wrecked against its rocks, and to the extent that the lightning is harmful when it rends a tree in two. This last idea converged in my mind on the tiny hairs on her right arm near to the wrist, and I noticed that the hair on her arms was thicker than with most women, and this led my thoughts to other hair. It would certainly be as soft and abundant as cypress-grass on the banks of a stream. As though the thought had radiated from my mind to hers she sat up straight. "Why do you look so sad?" she said.

"Do I look sad? On the contrary, I'm very happy."

The tender look came back into her eyes as she stretched out her hand and took hold of mine. "Do you know that my mother's Spanish?" she said.

"That, then, explains everything. It explains our meeting by chance, our spontaneous mutual understanding as though we had got to know each other centuries ago. Doubtless one of my forefathers was a soldier in Tarik ibn Ziyad's army. Doubtless he met one of your ancestors as she gathered in the grapes from an orchard in Seville. Doubtless he fell in love with her at first sight and she with him. He lived with her for a time, then left her and went off to Africa. There he married again and I was one of his progeny in Africa, and you have come from his progeny in Spain."

These words, also the low lights and the wine, made her happy. She gave out throaty, gurgling laughs.

"What a devil you are!" she said.

For a moment I imagined to myself the Arab soldiers' first meeting with Spain:[3] like me at this instant sitting opposite Isabella Seymour, a southern thirst being dissipated in the mountain passes of history in the north. However, I seek not glory, for the likes of me do not seek glory.

After a month of feverish desire I turned the key in the door with her at my side, a fertile Andalusia; after that I led her across the short passageway to the bedroom where the smell of burning sandalwood and incense assailed her, filling her lungs with a perfume she little knew was deadly. In those days, when the summit lay a mere arm's length away from me, I would be enveloped in a tragic calm. All the fever and throbbing of the heart, the strain of nerves, would be transformed into the calm of a surgeon as he opens up the patient's stomach. I knew that the short road along which we walked together to the bedroom was, for her, a road of light redolent with the aroma of magnanimity and devotion, but which to me was the last step

---

[3] the Arab soldiers' first meeting with Spain: a reference to the Muslim conquest of Spain.

before attaining the peak of selfishness. I waited by the edge of the bed, as though condensing that moment in my mind, and cast a cold eye at the pink curtains and large mirrors, the lights lurking in the corners of the room, then at the shapely bronze statue before me. When we were at the climax of the tragedy she cried out weakly, "No. No." This will be of no help to you now. The critical moment when it was in your power to refrain from taking the first step has been lost. I caught you unawares; at that time it was in your power to say "No." As for now the flood of events has swept you along, as it does every person, and you are no longer capable of doing anything. Were every person to know when to refrain from taking the first step many things would have been changed. Is the sun wicked when it turns the hearts of millions of human beings into sand-strewn deserts in which the throat of the nightingale is parched with thirst? Lingeringly I passed the palm of my hand over her neck and kissed her in the fountain-heads of her sensitivity. With every touch, with every kiss, I felt a muscle in her body relax; her face glowed and her eyes sparkled with a sudden brightness. She gazed hard and long at me as though seeing me as a symbol rather than reality. I heard her saying to me in an imploring voice of surrender "I love you," and there answered her voice a weak cry from the depths of my consciousness calling on me to desist. But the summit was only a step away, after which I would recover my breath and rest. At the climax of our pain there passed through my head clouds of old, far-off memories, like a vapor rising up from a salt lake in the middle of the desert. She burst into agonized, consuming tears, while I gave myself up to a feverishly tense sleep.

→ DEREK WALCOTT

# Goats and Monkeys

1965

Born in St. Lucia, then a British dependency, poet and playwright Derek Walcott (b. 1930) has been one of the Caribbean's most lauded voices, noted for his explorations of Caribbean multivocality and exile. His fellow Nobel laureate Joseph Brodsky famously proclaimed that the West Indies "were discovered by Columbus, colonized by the British, and immortalized by Walcott" (41). "Goats and Monkeys'" first appeared in *The Castaway and Other Poems* (1965), a collection that draws on the themes of wandering, exile, and isolation that appear frequently in Walcott's later meditations on the search for home in a

Derek Walcott, "Goats and Monkeys," in *Collected Poems 1948–1984* (New York: Ferrar, Straus and Giroux, 1986).

divided world. The appearances of Robinson Crusoe and Caliban are only the most obvious signs of his extended dialogue with European tradition in *The Castaway*. "Goats and Monkeys" amplifies the collection's sense that we are "castaway in a meaningless universe" (King 220). Walcott's poem suggests that Othello is a European projection of male anxieties over female sexuality onto blackness (King 200). Its images of eclipse and chaos might be compared with those found in seventeenth-century poems on miscegenation (K. Hall, *Things* 269–90; Tokson 26–30), as well as with the frenzy and tumult of Télémaque's painting (see p. 373).

> . . . even now, an old black ram
> is tupping your white ewe.
> — *Othello*

The owl's torches gutter. Chaos clouds the globe.
Shriek, augury! His earthen bulk
buries her bosom in its slow eclipse.
His smoky hand has charred
that marble throat. Bent to her lips,                                   5
he is Africa, a vast, sidling shadow
that halves your world with doubt.
"Put out the light," and God's light is put out.

That flame extinct, she contemplates her dream
of him as huge as night, as bodiless,                                   10
as starred with medals, like the moon
a fable of blind stone.
Dazzled by that bull's bulk against the sun
of Cyprus, couldn't she have known
like Pasiphaë,[1] poor girl, she'd breed horned monsters?               15
That like Euyridice,[2] her flesh a flare
traveling the hellish labyrinth of his mind
his soul would swallow hers?

Her white flesh rhymes with night. She climbs, secure.

Virgin and ape, maid and malevolent Moor,                              20
their immoral coupling still halves our world.

---

[1] **Pasiphaë:** wife of King Minos; she fell in love with a bull and gave birth to the Minotaur, a monster with the head of a bull and the body of a man.  [2] **Eurydice:** wife of Orpheus. In leading her back from Hades, Orpheus lost faith and looked back at her, thus losing her to the underworld.

He is your sacrificial beast, bellowing, goaded,
a black bull snarled in ribbons of its blood.
And yet, whatever fury girded
on that saffron-sunset turban, moon-shaped sword                    25
was not his racial, panther-black revenge
pulsing her chamber with raw musk, its sweat,
but horror of the moon's change,
of the corruption of an absolute,
like a white fruit                                                  30
pulped ripe by fondling but doubly sweet.

And so he barbarously arraigns the moon
for all she has beheld since time began
for his own night-long lechery, ambition,
while barren innocence whimpers for pardon.                         35

And it is still the moon, she silvers love,
limns lechery and stares at our disgrace.
Only annihilation can resolve
the pure corruption in her dreaming face.

A bestial, comic agony. We harden                                   40
with mockery at this blackamoor
who turns his back on her, who kills
what, like the clear moon, cannot abhor
her element, night; his grief
farcically knotted in a handkerchief                                45
a sibyl's
prophetically stitched remembrancer
webbed and embroidered with the zodiac,
this mythical, horned beast who's no more
monstrous for being black.                                          50

# Bibliography

><-

## Primary Sources

Bacon, Francis. *The Essays or Counsels, Civil and Moral, of Francis Lo Verulam Viscount St. Alban.* London, 1625.

Barret, Robert. *The Theory and Practice of Modern Wars.* London, 1598.

Best, George. *A True Discourse of the Late Voyages of Discovery for the Finding of a Passage to Cathaya by the Northwest . . .* London, 1578.

Buoni, Thomas. *Problems of Beauty and All Human Affections.* Trans. S. L. London, 1606.

Burton, Robert. *Anatomy of Melancholy.* London, 1638.

Castiglione, Baldassare. *The Book of the Courtier.* Trans. Thomas Hoby. London, 1636.

Church of England. "A Form to be used in Common Prayer, every Sunday, Wednesday, and Friday, through the Whole Realm: To Excite and Stir all Godly People to Pray unto God for the Preservation of those Christians and their Countries, that are now invaded by the Turk in Hungary, or elsewhere." *Liturgical Services: Liturgies and Occasional Forms of Prayer Set Forth in the Reign of Queen Elizabeth.* Ed. William Keatinge Clay. Cambridge: Cambridge UP, 1847. 527–35.

Cinthio [Giovanni Battista Giraldi]. *Gli Hecatommithi. Narrative and Dramatic Sources of Shakespeare.* Ed. Geoffrey Bullough. London: Routledge and Kegan Paul; Columbia UP, 1957–75.

Contarini, Gaspar. *The Commonwealth and Government of Venice*. Trans. Lewis Lewkenor. London, 1599.

Coryate, Thomas. *Coryats Crudities; Hastily Gobbled Up in Five Months Travels in France, Savoy, Italy, . . . Switzerland &c.* London, 1611.

*The Cuckold's Haven.* London, 1638.

*Desdemonum: An Ethiopian Burlesque, in Three Scenes.* New York: Happy Hours Co., 1874.

Digges, Thomas and Leonard. *An Arithmetical Military Treatise, Named Stratioticos.* London, 1579.

Do Mar, Alexander. *Othello: An Interesting Drama, Rather! With Illustrations After Rembrandt.* London: J. L. Marks, 1850.

Elizabeth I. "Edict Arranging for the Expulsion from England of Negroes and Blackamoors." 1601. *Tudor Royal Proclamations.* New Haven: Yale UP, 1964.

Fletcher, Giles, the Elder. *Policy of the Turkish Empire*, London, 1597.

Geneva Bible. London, 1602.

Hughes, Charles, ed. *Shakespeare's Europe, A Survey of the Condition of Europe at the end of the 16th century*, being unpublished chapters of Fynes Moryson's Itinerary (1617). 2nd ed. New York: B. Blom, 1967.

James VI and I. *The Lepanto.* In *Reading Monarchs' Writing: The Poetry of Henry VII, Mary Stuart, Elizabeth I and James VI/I.* Ed. Peter C. Herman. Arizona: Arizona Center for Medieval and Renaissance Studies, 2002.

Jordan, Thomas. *The Nursery of Novelties in a Variety of Poetry.* London, 1655.

Knolles, Richard. *The General History of the Turks from the first Beginning of that Nation to the Rising of the Ottoman Family: With all the Notable Expeditions of the Christian Princes Against Them.* London, 1603.

"A Lamentable Ballad of the Tragical End of a Gallant Lord and a Virtuous Lady, with the Untimely End of Their Two Children, Wickedly Performed by a Heathenish Blackamoor Their Servant; The Like Never Heard Of." 1660? *The Roxburghe Ballads.* Ed. William Chappell. Vol. 2. 1869; New York: AMS Press, 1966.

La Primaudaye, Pierre de. *The French Academy.* Trans. Thomas Bowe. London, 1586.

Lennox, Charlotte Ramsey. *Shakespeare Illustrated.* London, 1754.

Leo Africanus, John. *A Geographical History of Africa.* Trans. John Pory. London, 1600.

Linschoten, Jan Huyghen van. *His Discourse of Voyages into the East and West Indies Divided into Four Books.* London, 1598.

Luther, Martin. *A Commentary of M. Doctor Martin Luther upon the Epistle of S. Paul to the Galatians.* London, 1575.

Martyr, Peter. *The Decades of the New World or West India.* Trans. Richard Eden. London, 1555.

Moryson, Fynes. See Charles Hughes.

Parker, Martin. *The Married Man's Lesson: Or, A Dissuasion from Jealousy.* London, 1624.

*Policy of the Turkish Empire*, London, 1597.

Proctor, Thomas. *Of the Knowledge and Conduct of Wars*. London, 1578.

Rice, Thomas Dartmouth. *Otello: A Burlesque Opera*. New York, 1853 (NYPL mss NCOF+ ).

Rymer, Thomas. *A Short View of Tragedy*. London, 1693.

Salih, Tayeb. *Season of Migration to the North*. Oxford: Heinemann, 1969.

Ste. B. *Counsel to the Husband: To the Wife Instruction . . .* London, 1608.

Styward, Thomas. *The First Book of Martial Discipline*. London, 1581.

Taylor, John. *A Valorous and Perilous Sea-fight Fought with Three Turkish Ships*. London, 1640.

Udall, Nicholas. *Respublica. Recently Recovered "Lost" Tudor Plays with Some Others*. Ed. John S. Farmer. New York: Barnes and Noble, 1966.

Varchi, Benedetto. *The Blazon of Jealousy*. Trans. Robert Tofte. London, 1615.

Vives, Juan Luis. *Instruction of a Christian Gentlewoman*. London, 1557.

Vogel, Paula. *Desdemona: A Play about a Handkerchief.* New York: Dramatists Play Service, 1994.

Walcott, Derek. "Goats and Monkeys." *Collected Poems 1948–1984*. London: Farrar, Straus and Giroux, 1986.

Whately, William. *A Bride-bush: Or, A Wedding Sermon*. London, 1617.

Winter, Willam. *Shakespeare's Tragedy of Othello: As Presented by Edwin Booth*. Philadelphia: Penn Publishing Company.

Woolley, Hannah. *The Gentlewoman's Companion: Or, A Guide to the Female Sex . . .* London, 1675.

Wright, Thomas. *The Passions of the Mind in General*. Ed. William Webster Newbold. New York: Garland, 1986.

## Secondary Sources

Albanese, Denise. "Black and White, and Dread All Over: The Shakespeare Theatre's 'Photonegative' *Othello* and the Body of Desdemona." *Othello: William Shakespeare*. Ed. Lena Cowen Orlin. Basingstoke: Palgrave Macmillan, 2004. 220–49.

Allen, Robert Clyde. *Horrible Prettiness: Burlesque and American Culture*. Chapel Hill: U of North Carolina P, 1991.

Amussen, Susan Dwyer. *An Ordered Society: Gender and Class in Early Modern England*. New York: Columbia UP, 1993.

Anderson, Ruth Leila. *Elizabethan Psychology and Shakespeare's Plays*. New York: Haskell House, 1964.

Andrea, Bernadette. "Assimilation or Dissimulation? Leo Africanus's *Geographical Historie of Africa* and the Parable of Amphibia." *Ariel: A Review of International English Literature*. 32.3 (July 2001): 7–29.

——. "Black Skin, the Queen's Masques: Africanist Ambivalence and Feminine Author(ity) in the Masques of *Blackness* and *Beauty*." *English Literary Renaissance* 29.2 (Spring 1999): 246–81.

———. "Pamphilia's Cabinet: Gendered Authorship and Empire in Lady Mary Wroth's *Urania*." *ELH* 68 (2001): 335–58.

Andreas, James R. "The Curse of Cush: Othello's Judaic Ancestry." *Othello: New Critical Essays*. Ed. Philip C. Kolin. New York: Routledge, 2002. 169–87.

———. "*Othello*'s African-American Progeny." *South Atlantic Review* 57.4 (1992): 39–57.

Anthias, Floya, and Nira Yuval-Davis. "Women and the Nation-State." *Nationalism*. Ed. John Hutchinson and Anthony D. Smith. Oxford: Oxford UP, 1994.

Anzaldúa, Gloria. *Borderlands/La Frontera*. San Francisco: Aunt Lute Books, 1987.

Ashcroft, Bill, Gareth Griffiths, and Helen Tiffin, eds. *The Empire Writes Back: Theory and Practice in Post-Colonial Literatures*. New York: Routledge, 1989.

Atil, Esin, ed. *Süleymanname: The Illustrated History of Süleyman the Magnificent*. Washington, DC: National Gallery of Art; New York: H. N. Abrams, 1986.

Bach, Rebecca Ann. "Shakespeare and Renaissance Literature Before Heterosexuality." New York: Palgrave, forthcoming 2007.

Bacon, Francis. *The Essayes or Counsels, Civill and Morall*. Ed. Michael Kiernan. Cambridge: Harvard UP, 1985.

Barbaro, Francesco. *Of Wifely Duties*. Trans. Benjamin G. Kohl. *The Earthly Republic: Italian Humanists on Government and Society*. Ed. Benjamin G. Kohl and Ronald G. Witt with Elizabeth Welles. Philadelphia: U of Pennsylvania P, 1991, 1978. 189–228.

Bartels, Emily C. "Making More of the Moor: Aaron, Othello, and Renaissance Refashionings of Race." *Shakespeare Quarterly* 41 (1990): 433–54.

———. "*Othello* and Africa." *William and Mary Quarterly* 3rd ser., 54.1 (January 1997): 45–64.

Barthelemy, Anthony Gerard, ed. *Black Face Maligned Race: The Representation of Blacks in English Drama*. Baton Rouge: Louisiana State UP, 1987.

———, ed. *Critical Essays on Shakespeare's* Othello. New York: G. K. Hall, 1994.

Bate, Jonathan. *Shakespeare Constitutions: Politics, Theatre, Criticism, 1730–1830*. Oxford: Clarendon, 1989.

Baumer, Franklin L. "England, the Turk, and the Common Corps of Christendom." *American Historical Review* 50 (1994): 26–42.

Berlin, Ira. *Many Thousands Gone: The First Two Centuries of Slavery in North America*. Cambridge: Harvard UP, 1998.

Berger, Thomas L. "The Second Quarto of *Othello* and the Question of Textual 'Authority.'" *Othello: New Perspectives*. Ed. Kent Cartwright and Virginia Mason Vaughan. Madison, NJ: Fairleigh Dickinson UP, 1991. 26–47.

Bethell, S. L. "Shakespeare's Imagery: The Diabolic Images in *Othello*." *Shakespeare Survey* 5 (1952): 62–80.

Blake, John William. *Europeans in West Africa, 1450–1560*. London: Hakluyt Society, 1942.

Blakely, Allison. *Blacks in the Dutch World: The Evolution of Racial Imagery in a Modern Society.* Bloomington: Indiana UP, 1993.

Bland, Sheila Rose. "How I Would Direct *Othello.*" *Othello: New Essays by Black Writers.* Ed. Mythili Kaul. Washington, DC: Howard UP, 1996. 29–41.

Blount, Henry. *A Voyage into the Levant.* Ed. Gerald MacLean. *Travel Knowledge: European Discoveries in the Early Modern Period.* Ed. Ivo Kamps and Jyotsna Singh. New York: Palgrave. 79–84.

Boose, Lynda E. "'The Getting of a Lawful Race': Racial Discourse in Early Modern England and the Unrepresentable Black Woman." *Women, "Race," and Writing in the Early Modern Period.* Ed. Margo Hendricks and Patricia Parker. London: Routledge, 1994. 35–54.

——. "Othello's Handkerchief: 'The Recognizance and Pledge of Love.'" *Critical Essays on Shakespeare's* Othello. Ed. Anthony Gerard Barthelemy. New York: G. K. Hall, 1994. 55–67.

Bradshaw, Graham. "Obeying the Time in *Othello*: A Myth and the Mess It Made." *English Studies: A Journal of English Language and Literature.* 73.3 (June 1992): 211–28.

Braude, Benjamin. "The Sons of Noah and the Construction of Ethnic and Geographical Identities in the Medieval and Early Modern Periods." *William and Mary Quarterly* 3rd ser., 54.1 (January 1997): 103–42.

Braudel, Ferdnand. *The Mediterranean and the Mediterranean World in the Age of Philip II.* New York: Harper & Row, 1966. 2 vols.

Bray, Alan. *Homosexuality in Renaissance England.* New York: Columbia UP, 1995.

Bristol, Michael. *Big-Time Shakespeare.* New York: Routledge, 1996.

Brodsky, Joseph. "On Derek Walcott." *New York Review of Books* 10 November 1983. 39–41.

Brotton, Jerry. *Trading Territories: Mapping the Early Modern World.* London: Reaktion Books, 1997.

——, and Lisa Jardine. *Global Interests: Renaissance Art between East and West.* Ithaca: Cornell UP, 2000.

Bullough, Geoffrey. *Narrative and Dramatic Sources of Shakespeare.* Vol. 7. New York: Columbia UP, 1957.

Burnett, Mark Thornton. *Masters and Servants in English Renaissance Drama and Culture: Authority and Obedience.* New York: St. Martin's, 1997.

——, and Ramona Wray, eds. *Shakespeare and Ireland: History, Politics, Culture.* New York: St. Martin's, 1997.

Burton, Jonathan. *Traffic and Turning: Islam and English Drama, 1579–1624.* Newark: U of Delaware P, 2005.

Cahill, Patricia. *"Tales of Iron Wars": Martial Bodies and Manly Economies in Elizabethan Culture.* Diss. Columbia U, 2000.

Callaghan, Dympna. "Looking Well to Linens: Women and Cultural Production in *Othello* and Shakespeare's England." *Marxist Shakespeares.* Eds. Jean E. Howard and Scott Cutler Shershow. London, New York: Routledge, 2001. 53–81.

——. "'Othello was a White Man': Properties of Race on Shakespeare's Stage." *Alternative Shakespeares.* Ed. Terence Hawkes. Vol. 2. London: Routledge, 1996: 192–95.

——. *Romeo and Juliet: Texts and Contexts.* New York: Bedford/St. Martin's, 2003.

Campbell, Mary B. *The Witness and the Other World: Exotic European Travel Writing, 400–1600.* Ithaca: Cornell UP, 1988.

Capp, Bernard. "Separate Domains? Women and Authority in Early Modern England." *The Experience of Authority in Early Modern England.* Ed. Paul Griffiths et al. New York: St. Martin's, 1996. 117–45.

Carlson, Marvin A. *The Italian Shakespearians: Performances by Ristori, Salvini, and Rossi in England and America.* Washington, DC: Folger Books, 1985.

Cartelli, Thomas. *Repositioning Shakespeare: National Formations, Postcolonial Appropriations.* London: Routledge, 1999.

Cartwright, Kent, and Virginia Mason Vaughan, eds. *Othello: New Perspectives.* Madison, NJ: Fairleigh Dickinson UP, 1991.

Cary, Elizabeth. *The Tragedy of Mariam, the Fair Queen of Jewry, with The Lady Falkland: Her Life.* Ed. Margaret W. Ferguson and Barry Weller. Berkeley: U of California P, 1994.

Chambers, E. K. *The Medieval Stage.* Vol 2. Oxford: Clarendon, 1903.

Chatterjee, Sudipto, and Jyotsna G. Singh. "Moor or Less? The Surveillance of Othello, Calcutta, 1848." *Shakespeare and Appropriation.* Ed. Christy Desmet and Robert Sawyer. Routledge: London, 1999. 65–82.

Chettle, Henry. *The Tragedy of Hoffman.* London, 1603.

Cockerell, Dale. *Demons of Disorder: Early Blackface Minstrels and Their World.* Cambridge: Cambridge UP, 1997.

Coles, Paul. *The Ottoman Impact on Europe.* London: Thames & Hudson, 1968.

Collins, Kris. "White-Washing the Black-a-Moor: *Othello*, Negro Minstrelsy and Parodies of Blackness." *Journal of American Culture* 19.3 (Fall 1996): 87–101.

Comensoli, Viviana. "Music, *The Book of the Courtier*, and Othello's Soldier-ship." *The Italian World of English Renaissance Drama: Cultural Exchange and Intertextuality.* Ed. Michele Marrapodi. Newark: U of Delaware P, 1999. 89–105.

Condé, Maryse. "'Neg Pa Bon'" ('Nigger No Good'). In *Othello: New Essays by Black Writers.* Ed. Mythili Kaul. Washington, DC: Howard UP, 1996. 83–90.

Cowhig, Ruth. "Actors Black and Tawny in the Role of Othello — and Their Critics." *Theatre Research International* 4 (1979): 133–46.

——. "Blacks in English Renaissance Drama and the Role of Shakespeare's Othello." *The Black Presence in English Renaissance Literature.* Ed. David Dabydeen. Manchester, UK: Manchester UP, 1985. 1–26.

D'Amico, Jack. *The Moor in English Renaissance Drama.* Tampa: U of South Florida P, 1991.

——. *Shakespeare and Italy: The City and the Stage*. Gainesville: UP of Florida, 2001.

Dash, Irene. *Wooing, Wedding and Power: Women in Shakespeare's Plays*. New York: Columbia UP, 1981.

Davis, Ralph. "England and the Mediterranean, 1570–1670." *Essays in the Economic and Social History of Tudor and Stuart England*. Ed. F. J. Fisher. Cambridge: Cambridge UP, 1961. 117–37.

Desmet, Christy. "Introduction." *Shakespeare and Appropriation*. Ed. Christy Desmet and Robert Sawyer. London: Routledge, 1999. 1–14.

de Somogyi, Nick. *Shakespeare's Theatre of War*. Aldershot, Eng.: Ashgate, 1998.

DiGangi, Mario. *The Homoerotics of Early Modern Drama*. Cambridge: Cambridge UP, 1997.

Draper, John W. "Shakespeare and Florence and the Florentines." *Italica* 23.4 (December 1946): 287–93.

Dunn, Diana, ed. *War and Society in Medieval and Early Modern Britain*. Liverpool: Liverpool UP, 2000.

Dusinberre, Juliet. *Shakespeare and the Nature of Women*. London: Macmillan, 1975.

Edelstein, Tilden G. "*Othello* in America: The Drama of Racial Intermarriage." *Region, Race and Reconstruction*. Ed. J. Morgan Kousser. Oxford: Oxford UP, 1982.

Eltis, David. *The Military Revolution in Sixteenth-Century Europe*. New York: St. Martin's, 1995.

Elyot, Thomas. *Bibliotheca Eliotae*. London, 1548.

Engle, Gary D. *This Grotesque Essence: Plays from the American Minstrel Stage*. Baton Rouge: Louisiana State UP, 1978.

Engler, Balz. "How Shakespeare Revised *Othello*." *English Studies* 57 (1976): 515–21.

Erickson, Peter. "Images of White Identity in *Othello*." *Othello: New Critical Essays*. Ed. Philip C. Kolin. New York: Routledge, 2002. 133–46.

——. "Respeaking Othello in Fred Wilson's *Speak of Me as I Am*." *Art Journal* 64.2 (2005): 4–19.

Everett, Barbara. "'Spanish' Othello: The Making of Shakespeare's Moor." *Shakespeare Survey* 35 (1982): 101–12.

Fanon, Franz. *The Wretched of the Earth*. Trans. Constance Farrington. New York: Grove, 1968.

Floyd-Wilson, Mary. *English Ethnicity and Race in Early Modern Drama*. Cambridge: Cambridge UP, 2003.

Frye, Susan. "Staging Women's Relations to Textiles." *Early Modern Visual Culture: Representation, Race and Empire in Renaissance England*. Ed. Peter Erickson and Clark Hulse. Philadelphia: U of Pennsylvania P, 2000. 215–50.

Fryer, Peter. *Staying Power: The History of Black People in Britain*. London: Pluto, 1984.

Fuller, Mary C. "English Turks and Resistant Travelers: Conversion to Islam and Homosocial Courtship." *Travel Knowledge: European Discoveries in the Early Modern Period.* Ed. Ivo Kamps and Jyotsna Singh. New York: Palgrave, 2001. 66–73.

Fumerton, Patricia. *Cultural Aesthetics: Renaissance Literature and the Practice of Social Ornament.* Chicago: Chicago UP, 1991.

Furness, Horace Howard, Ed. *Othello.* New York: Dover, 1963.

Gallagher, Catherine. *Nobody's Story: The Vanishing Acts of Women Writers in the Marketplace, 1670–1820.* Berkeley: U of California P, 1994.

Garner, Shirley Nelson, and Madelon Sprengnether, eds. *Shakespearean Tragedy and Gender.* Indianapolis: Indiana UP, 1996.

Gaukroger, Stephen, ed. *The Soft Underbelly of Reason: The Passions in the Seventeenth Century.* London: Routledge, 1998.

Genster, Julia, "Lieutenancy, Standing in, and Othello." *ELH* 57.4 (1990): 785–809.

Giddings, Paula. *When and Where I Enter: The Impact of Black Women on Race and Sex in America.* New York: Morrow, 1984.

Gillies, John. *Shakespeare and the Geography of Difference.* Cambridge: Cambridge UP, 1994.

———, and Virginia Mason Vaughan, eds. *Playing the Globe: Genre and Geography in English Renaissance Drama.* Madison, NJ: Fairleigh Dickinson UP, 1998.

Goffman, Daniel. *The Ottoman Empire and Early Modern Europe.* New York: Cambridge UP, 2002.

Goldberg, Jonathan, ed. *Queering the Renaissance.* Durham: Duke UP, 1994.

Gowing, Laura. *Domestic Dangers : Women, Words, and Sex in Early Modern London.* Oxford: Oxford UP, 1996.

Greenblatt, Stephen. *Marvelous Posessions: The Wonder of the New World.* Chicago: U of Chicago P, 1992.

———. *Renaissance Self-Fashioning.* Chicago: U of Chicago P, 1980.

Grennan, Eamon. "The Women's Voices in *Othello*: Speech, Song, Silence." *Shakespeare Quarterly* 38.3 (Autumn 1987): 275–92.

Griffin, Eric. "Un-sainting James: Or *Othello* and the 'Spanish Spirits' of Shakespeare's Globe." *Representations* 62 (Spring 1998): 58–99.

Guillory, John. *Cultural Capital: The Problem of Literary Canon Formation.* Chicago: U of Chicago P, 1993.

Gundersheimer, Werner. "'The Green-Eyed Monster': Renaissance Conceptions of Jealousy." *Proceedings of the American Philosophical Society* 137.3 (September 1993): 322–31.

Gurr, Andrew, and Mariko Ichikawa. *Staging in Shakespeare's Theaters.* Oxford: Oxford UP, 2000.

Hacker, Barton C. "Women and Military Institutions in Early Modern Europe: A Reconnaissance." *Signs* 6.4 (Summer 1981): 643–71.

Hakluyt, Richard, ed. *The Principal Navigations, Voyages, Traffiques and Discoveries of the English Nation.* London, 1599. 3 vols.

Hale, J[ohn] R[igby]. *The Art of War and Renaissance England.* Washington, DC: Folger Shakespeare Library, 1961.

Hall, Kim F. "Guess Who's Coming to Dinner? Colonization and Miscegenation in *The Merchant of Venice.*" *Renaissance Drama* (1992): 87–111.

——. "Object into Object?: Some Thoughts on the Presence of Black Women in Early Modern Culture." *Early Modern Visual Culture: Representation, Race and Empire in Renaissance England.* Ed. Peter Erickson and Clark Hulse. Philadelphia: U of Pennsylvania P, 2000. 346–79.

——. "*Othello* and the Problem of Race" *Blackwell Companions to Shakespeare.* Vol. 1. Ed. Richard Dutton and Jean Howard. London: Blackwell, 2003. 4 vols.

——. "Reading What Isn't There: 'Black' Studies in Early Modern England?" *Stanford Humanities Re/View* 3.1 (1993): 23–33.

——. *Things of Darkness: Economies of Race and Gender in Early Modern England.* Ithaca: Cornell UP, 1995.

Hall, Stuart. "Subjects in History: Making Diasporic Identities." *The House That Race Built: Black Americans, U.S. Terrain.* Ed. Wahneema Lubiano. New York: Pantheon, 1997. 289–300.

——. "Why Fanon? Why Now? Why *Black Skin, White Masks?*" *The Fact of Blackness: Frantz Fanon and Visual Representation.* Ed. Alan Reed. Seattle: Bay Press, 1996.

Hammill, Graham. "The Epistemology of Expurgation: Bacon and the Masculine Birth of Time." *Queering the Renaissance.* Ed. Jonathan Goldberg. Durham: Duke UP, 1994. 236–52.

Harlow, Barbara. "Othello's Season of Migration." *Edebiyat: The Journal of Middle Eastern Literatures* 4.2 (1979): 157–75.

Harris, Bernard. "A Portrait of a Moor." *Shakespeare Survey* 11 (1958): 85–89.

Harris, Jonathan Gil, and Natasha Korda. *Staged Properties in Early Modern English Drama.* Cambridge: Cambridge UP, 2002.

Helgerson, Richard. *Adulterous Alliances: Home, State, and History in Early Modern European Drama and Painting.* Chicago: U of Chicago P, 2000.

Henderson, Katherine Usher, and Barbara F. McManus. *Half Humankind: Contexts and Texts of the Controversy about Women in England, 1540–1640.* Urbana: U of Illinois P, 1985.

Hendricks, Margo. "'The Moor of Venice,' Or the Italian on the Renaissance English Stage." *Shakespearean Tragedy and Gender.* Ed. Shirley Nelson Garner and Madelon Sprengnether. Indianapolis: Indiana UP, 1996. 193–209.

——, and Patricia Parker, eds. *Women, "Race," and Writing in the Early Modern Period.* London: Routledge, 1994.

Hess, Andrew C. "The Battle of Lepanto and Its Place in Mediterranean History." *Past and Present* 57 (November 1972): 53–73.

Hill, Errol. *Shakespeare in Sable: A History of Black Shakespearean Actors.* Amherst: U of Massachusetts P, 1984.

Hoban, Phoebe. "The Shock of the Familiar." *New York Magazine* 28 July 2003.

Hodgdon, Barbara. "Race-ing Othello, Re-engendering White-Out." *Shakespeare the Movie: Popularizing the Plays on Film, TV, and Video*. Ed. Lynda Boose and Richard Burt. London: Routledge, 1997. 23–44.

Hoenselaars, A. J. "Italy Staged in English Renaissance Drama." *Shakespeare's Italy: Functions of Italian Locations in Renaissance Drama*. Ed. Michele Marrapodi, A. J. Hoenslaars, Marcello Capuzzo, and L. Falzon Stantucci. Manchester: Manchester UP, 1993. 30–48.

Honigmann, E. A. J. *The Texts of "Othello" and Shakespearean Revision*. London and New York: Routledge, 1996.

hooks, bell. *Talking Back: thinking feminist • thinking black*. Boston: South End, 1989.

Howard, Jean. "Gender on the Periphery." *Shakespeare and the Mediterranean*. Ed. Tom Clayton, Susan Brock, and Vicente Forés. Newark: U of Delaware P, 2004. 344–62.

Howe, Elizabeth. *The First English Actresses: Women and Drama, 1660–1700*. Cambridge: Cambridge UP, 1992.

Howell, Martha. *The Marriage Exchange: Property, Social Place, and Gender in Cities of the Low Countries, 1300–1550*. Chicago: U of Chicago P, 1998.

Hulfton, Olwen. *The Prospect Before Her: A History of Women in Western Europe 1500–1800*. New York: Knopf, 1996.

Huggins, Nathan. *Harlem Renaissance*. New York: Oxford UP, 1971.

Hull, Suzanne W. *Chaste, Silent & Obedient: English Books for Women, 1475–1640*. San Marino: Huntington Library, 1982.

Hunter, G. K. *Dramatic Identities and Cultural Tradition: Studies in Shakespeare and His Contemporaries*. Liverpool: Liverpool UP, 1978.

——. *Othello and Colour Prejudice*. London: Oxford UP, 1967.

Hyman, Earle. "*Othello* or, Ego in Love, Sex and War." *Othello: New Essays by Black Writers*. Ed. Mythli Kaul. Washington, DC: Howard UP, 1996. 23–28.

James I. *The Political Works of James I*. Ed. Charles Howard McIlwain. New York: Russell and Russell, 1965.

James, Henry. *The Scenic Art; Notes on Acting & the Drama, 1872–1901*. New York: Hill and Wang, 1957.

James, Susan. *Passion and Action: The Emotions in Seventeenth Century Philosophy*. Oxford: Clarendon, 1997.

Jardine, Lisa. "'Why Should He Call Her Whore?': Defamation and Desdemona's Case." *Addressing Frank Kermode: Essays in Criticism and Interpretation*. Ed. M. Warner and M. Tudeau-Clayton. New York: Macmillan, 1991. 124–53.

Jefferson, Margo. "Seducified by a Minstrel Show." *New York Times* 22 May 1994: H2.

Jennings, Ronald C. *Christians and Muslims in Ottoman Cyprus and the Mediterranean World, 1571–1640*. New York: New York UP, 1993.

Johnson, Lemuel A. *Shakespeare in Africa (and Other Venues): Import and the Appropriation of Culture*. Lawrenceville, NJ: Africa World Press, 1996.

Jones, Emyrs. "*Othello*, Lepanto and the Cyprus Wars." *Shakespeare Survey* 21 (1968): 47–52.

Jones, Eldred D. *The Elizabethan Image of Africa*. Charlottesville: UP of Virginia, 1971.

Kamps, Ivo, and Jyotsna G. Singh, eds. *Travel Knowledge: European Discoveries in the Early Modern Period*. New York: Palgrave, 2001.

Kaplan, M. Lindsay. *The Merchant of Venice: Texts and Contexts*. New York: Bedford/St. Martin's, 2002.

Kaplan, Paul H. D. "The Earliest Images of *Othello*." *Shakespeare Quarterly* 39.2 (Summer 1988): 171–86.

Kaul, Mythili, ed. *Othello: New Essays by Black Writers*. Washington, DC: Howard UP, 1996.

Kelly-Gadol, Joan. "Did Women Have a Renaissance?" *Becoming Visible: Women in European History*. Ed. Renate Bridenthal and Claudia Koonz. Boston: Houghton Mifflin: 1977.

Kennedy, Gwynne. *Just Anger: Representing Women's Anger in Early Modern England*. Carbondale: Southern Illinois UP, 2000.

Kenseth, Joy, ed. *The Age of the Marvelous*. Hanover, NH: Hood Museum of Art, Dartmouth College, 1991.

King, Bruce. *Derek Walcott: A Caribbean Life*. Oxford: Oxford UP, 2000.

Kirsch, Arthur C. *Jacobean Dramatic Perspectives*. Charlottesville: UP of Virginia, 1972.

———. *The Passions of Shakespeare's Tragic Heroes*. Charlottesville: UP of Virginia, 1990.

Klein, Joan Larsen, ed. *Daughters, Wives & Widows: Writings by Men about Women and Marriage in England, 1500–1640*. Urbana: U of Illinois P, 1992.

Kolin, Philip C., ed. *Othello: New Critical Essays*. New York: Routledge, 2002.

Korda, Natasha. *Shakespeare's Domestic Economies: Gender and Property in Early Modern England*. Philadelphia: U of Pennsylvania P, 2002.

Kramnick, Jonathan Brody. *Making the English Canon: Print-Capitalism and the Cultural Past, 1700–1770*. Cambridge: Cambridge UP, 1992.

Kwei-Armah, Kwame. "My Problem with the Moor." *Guardian* 7 April 2004.

Lanier, Douglas. "Minstrelsy, Jazz, Rap: Shakespeare, African American Music, and Cultural Legitimation." *Borrowers and Lenders: The Journal of Shakespeare and Appropriation*. Vol. 1. <http://atropos.english.uga.edu/cocoon/borrowers/request?id=282285>.

Leonard, William. *Masquerade in Black*. Metuchen, NJ: Scarecrow, 1986.

Lester, Julius. *Othello, a Novel*. New York: Scholastic, 1995.

Levine, Lawrence W. *Highbrow/Lowbrow: The Emergence of Cultural Hierarchy in America*. Cambridge: Harvard UP, 1988.

Lhamon, William T., ed. *Jump Jim Crow: Lost Plays, Lyrics, and Street Prose of the First Atlantic Popular Culture*. Cambridge: Harvard UP, 2003.

Lieblein, Lenore. "The Context of Murder in English Domestic Plays, 1590–1610." *Studies in English Literature* 23 (1983): 177–96.

Little, Arthur L., Jr. *Shakespeare Jungle Fever: National-Imperial Re-Visions of Race, Rape and Sacrifice.* Stanford: Stanford UP, 2000.

Liu, Tessie. "Race." *A Companion to American Thought.* Ed. R. W. Fox and J. Klopperman. Oxford: Blackwell. 564–67.

Lodge, Thomas, *A Fig for Momus. . . .* London: 1595.

Logan, Oliver. *Culture and Society in Venice, 1470–1790: The Renaissance and Its Heritage.* New York: Scribner. 1972.

Loomba, Ania. "'Delicious Traffick': Alterity and Exchange on Early Modern Stages." *Shakespeare Survey: An Annual Survey of Shakespeare Studies and Production* 52 (1999): 201–14.

——. *Race, Gender, Renaissance Drama.* Manchester: Manchester UP, 1989.

——. "Sexuality and Racial Difference." *Critical Essays on Shakespeare's* Othello. Ed. Anthony Gerard Barthelemy. New York: G. K. Hall, 1994. 162–86.

Lott, Eric. *Love and Theft: Blackface Minstrelsy and the American Working Class.* New York: Oxford UP, 1995.

Lupton, Julia Reinhard. "Othello Circumcised: Shakespeare and the Pauline Discourse of Nations." *Representations* 57 (1997): 73–89.

MacDonald, Ann-Marie. *Goodnight Desdemona (Good Morning Juliet).* Toronto: Playwrights Canada Press, 1998.

MacDonald, Joyce Green. "Acting Black: *Othello, Othello* Burlesques, and the Performance of Whiteness." *Theater Journal* 46 (1979): 133–46.

——. *Women and Race in Early Modern Texts.* Cambridge: Cambridge UP, 2002.

Mafe, Diana Adesola. "From Ogun to Othello: (Re)Acquainting Yoruba Myth and Shakespeare's Moor." *Research in African Literatures* 35.3 (2004): 46–61.

Marcus, Leah S. "The Two Texts of 'Othello' and Early Modern Constructions of Race." *Textual Performances: The Modern Reproduction of Shakespeare's Drama.* Ed. Lukas Erne and Margaret Jane Kidnie. Cambridge: Cambridge UP, 2004. 21–36.

Mark, Peter. "European Perceptions of Black Africans in the Renaissance." *Africa and the Renaissance: Art in Ivory.* Ed. Susan Vogel et al. New York: Center for African Art, 1988. 21–32.

——. *Africans in European Eyes: The Portrayal of Black Africans in Fourteenth and Fifteenth Century Europe.* Syracuse, NY: Maxwell School of Citizenship and Public Affairs, Syracuse U, 1974.

Masters, Bruce. *The Origins of Western Economic Dominance in the Middle East: Mercantilism and the Islamic Economy in Aleppo, 1600–1750.* New York: New York UP, 1988.

Matar, Nabil I. *Turks, Moors and Englishmen in the Age of Discovery.* New York: Columbia UP, 1999.

McIntosh, Marjorie. "Servants and the Household Unit in an Elizabethan English Community." *Journal of Family History* 9 (1984): 3–23.

McLaren, Anne. "Monogamy, Polygamy and the True State: James I's Rhetoric of Empire." *History of Political Thought* XXV.3 (2004): 446–80.

McMillin, Scott, Ed. *The First Quarto of Othello.* Cambridge: Cambridge UP, 2001.

McPherson, David C. *Shakespeare, Jonson and the Myth of Venice.* Newark: U of Delaware P, 1990.

Meisel, Martin. *Realizations: Narrative, Pictorial, and Theatrical Arts in Nineteenth Century England.* Princeton: Princeton UP, 1983.

Muldrew, Craig. "'A Mutual Assent of Her Mind'? Women, Debt, Litigation and Contract in Early Modern England." *History Workshop Journal* 55 (Spring 2003): 47–72.

——. *The Economy of Obligation: The Culture of Credit and Social Relations in Early Modern England.* New York: St. Martin's, 1998.

Mulryne, J. R. "History and Myth in *The Merchant of Venice.*" *Shakespeare's Italy: Functions of Italian Locations in Renaissance Drama.* Ed. Michele Marrapodi, A. J. Hoenslaars, Marcello Capuzzo, and L. Falzon Stantucci. Manchester: Manchester UP, 1993. 87–99.

Needham, Joseph. "The Geographical Distribution of English Ceremonial Dance Traditions." *Journal of the English Folk Dance and Song Society* 3.1 (1936): 1–45.

Neill, Michael. "'His Master's Ass': Slavery, Service and Subordination in *Othello.*" *Shakespeare and the Mediterranean.* Ed. Tom Clayton, Susan Brock, and Vicente Forés. Newark: U of Delaware P, 2004. 215–29.

——. *Putting History to the Question: Power, Politics, and Society in English Renaissance Drama.* New York: Columbia UP, 2000.

Neely, Carol Thomas. *Broken Nuptials in Shakespeare's Plays.* New Haven: Yale UP, 1985

Newbold, William Webster. General Introduction. *The Passions of the Mind in General.* By Thomas Wright. New York: Garland, 1986. 3–50.

Newman, Karen. "'And Wash the Ethiope White': Femininity and the Monstrous in *Othello.*" *Critical Essays on Shakespeare's* Othello. Ed. Anthony Gerard Barthelemy. New York: G. K. Hall, 1994. 124–43.

Odell, George, ed. *Annals of the New York Stage.* 15 vols. New York: Columbia UP, 1927–49.

Oldridge, Darren. *The Devil in Early Modern England.* Stroud: Sutton, 2000.

Omi, Michael, and Howard Winant. *Racial Formation in the United States: From the 1960s to the 1980s.* New York : Routledge & Kegan Paul, c. 1986.

Orkin, Martin. "*Othello* and the Plain Face of Racism." *Shakespeare Quarterly* 38.2 (1987): 166–88.

Orlin, Lena Cowen. "Implicating *Othello.*" *Shakespearean Tragedy and Gender.* Ed. Shirley Nelson Garner and Madelon Sprengnether. Bloomington: Indiana UP, 1996. 171–92.

——, ed. *Othello: William Shakespeare.* New York: Palgrave Macmillan, 2004.

——. *Private Matters and Public Culture in Post-Reformation England.* Ithaca: Cornell UP, 1994.

Ortelius, Abraham. *Abraham Ortelius His Epitome of the Theatre of the World.* London, 1603.

Oz, Avraham. "Dobbin on the Rialto: Venice and the Division of Identity." *Shakespeare's Italy: Functions of Italian Locations in Renaissance Drama.* Ed. Michele Marrapodi, A. J. Hoenslaars, Marcello Capuzzo, and L. Falzon Stantucci. Manchester: Manchester UP, 1993. 185–212.

Parker, Patricia. "Fantasies of 'Race' and 'Gender': Africa, *Othello* and Bringing to Light." *Women, "Race," and Writing in the Early Modern Period.* Ed. Margo Hendricks and Patricia Parker. London: Routledge, 1994. 84–100.

Paster, Gail Kern. *The Body Embarrassed: Drama and the Disciplines of Shame in Early Modern England.* Ithaca: Cornell UP, 1993.

——. *Humoring the Body: Emotions and the Shakespearean Stage.* Chicago: U of Chicago P, 2004.

Pechter, Edward. *Othello and Interpretive Traditions.* Iowa City: U of Iowa P, 1999.

Pfister, Manfred. "Shakespeare and Italy, or, the Law of Diminishing Returns." *Shakespeare's Italy: Functions of Italian Locations in Renaissance Drama.* Ed. Michele Marrapodi, A. J. Hoenslaars, Marcello Capuzzo, and L. Falzon Stantucci. Manchester: Manchester UP, 1993. 295–304.

Platt, Peter G. *Reason Diminished: Shakespeare and the Marvelous.* Lincoln: U of Nebraska P, 1997.

——. "'The Meruailouse Site': Shakespeare, Venice, and Paradoxical Stages." *Renaissance Quarterly* 54.1 (2001): 121–54.

Potter, Lois. *Othello.* New York: Palgrave, 2002.

Powell, Richard J. *Black Art and Culture in the 20th Century.* London: Thames and Hudson, 1997.

Pratt, Mary Louise. *Imperial Eyes: Travel Writing and Transculturation.* London: Routledge, 1992.

Quarshie, Hugh. "Second Thoughts on Playing *Othello*." *Black Othellos.* July 2004. <http://www.rsc.org.uk/othello/learning/othello.html>.

Riggs, Marlon T. *Ethnic Notions.* San Francisco: California Newsreel, 1986, videocassette.

Roach, Joseph. *The Player's Passion: Studies in the Science of Acting.* Newark: U of Delaware P, 1985.

Robeson, Paul. *Paul Robeson Speaks: Writings, Speeches, Interviews, 1918–1974.* Ed. Philip S. Foner. Larchmont, NY: Brunner/Mazel, 1978.

Rosenburg, Marvin. *The Masks of Othello: The Search for the Identity of Othello, Iago and Desdemona by Three Centuries of Actors and Critics.* Newark: U of Delaware P, 1992.

Rose, Mary Beth. *The Expense of Spirit: Love and Sexuality in English Renaissance Drama.* Ithaca: Cornell UP, 1988.

Ross, Lawrence J. "The Meaning of Strawberries in Shakespeare." *Studies in the Renaissance* 7 (1960): 225–40.

Royster, Francesca. "The End of Race and the Future of Early Modern Cultural Studies." *Shakespeare Studies* 26 (1988): 59–69.

Rymer, Thomas. *The Critical Works of Thomas Rymer.* Ed. C. A. Zimansky. New Haven: Yale UP, 1956.

Sacks, Howard L. "Cork and Community: Postwar Black Minstrelsy in the Rural Midwest." *Theatre Survey* 41.2 (November 2000): 21–50.

Said, Edward. *Orientalism.* New York: Vintage, 1978.

Sanders, Norman. *Othello: The New Cambridge Shakespeare.* Cambridge: Cambridge UP, 1984.

Saxton, Alexander. "Blackface Minstrelsy and Jacksonian Ideology." *American Quarterly* 27 (1975): 3–28.

Scot, Reginald. *The Discoverie of Witchcraft.* London, 1584.

Scott, Joan Wallach. *Gender and the Politics of History.* New York: Columbia UP, 1999.

Scragg, Leah. "Iago — Vice or Devil?" *Shakespeare Survey* 21 (1968): 53–66.

Seward, Anna. *The Poetical Works.* Vol 2. London, 1810.

Shakespeare, William. *The Complete Works of Shakespeare.* Ed. Gary Taylor and Stanley Wells. Oxford: Clarendon, 1988.

———. *Othello: A New Variorum Edition.* Ed. Horace Howard Furness. Vol. 6. Philadelphia: Lippincott, 1886.

———. *Othello.* Ed. Julie Hankey. Bristol: Bristol Classical, 1987.

———. *Othello.* Ed. E. A. J. Honigmann. Walton-on-Thames: Nelson, 1997.

Shannon, Laurie. *Sovereign Amity: Figures of Friendship in Shakespearean Contexts.* Chicago: U of Chicago P, 2002.

Shapiro, James S. *Shakespeare and the Jews.* New York: Columbia UP, 1996.

Siemon, James R. "'Nay, That's Not Next': *Othello* V.ii. in Performance, 1760–1900." *Shakespeare Quarterly* 37.1 (Spring 1986): 38–51.

Singh, Jyotsna. "Othello's Identity, Postcolonial Theory, and Contemporary Rewritings of *Othello.*" *Women, "Race," and Writing in the Early Modern Period.* Ed. Margo Hendricks and Patricia Parker. London: Routledge, 1994. 287–99.

Siraisi, Nancy G. *Medieval and Early Renaissance Medicine: An Introduction to Knowledge and Practice.* Chicago: U of Chicago P, 1990.

Smith, Alan K. "Fraudomy: Reading Sexuality and Politics in Burchiello" *Queering the Renaissance.* Ed. Jonathan Goldberg. Durham: Duke UP, 1994. 84–106.

Smith, Ian. "Barbarian Errors: Performing Race in Early Modern England." *Shakespeare Quarterly* 49.2 (Summer 1998): 168–86.

———. "The Queer Moor: Race and Sexuality in *Othello.*" Unpublished essay.

Smith, Henry. *A Preparative to Marriage.* London, 1591.

Snyder, Susan. *The Comic Matrix of Shakespeare's Tragedies: Romeo and Juliet, Hamlet, Othello, and King Lear.* Princeton: Princeton UP, 1979.

———. *Othello: Critical Essays.* New York: Garland, 1988.

Sofer, Andrew. *The Stage Life of Props.* Ann Arbor: U of Michigan P, 2003.

———. "Felt Absences: The Stage Properties of *Othello*'s Handkerchief." *Comparative Drama* 31.3 (Fall 1997): 367–93.

Sohmer, Steve "The 'Double Time' Crux in *Othello* Solved." *English Literary Renaissance* 32.2: 214–38.

Sowernam, Ester. *Ester Hath Hang'd Haman: Or an Answer to a Lewd Pamphet, Entituled, the Arraignment of Women with the Arraignment of Lewd, Idle, Froward, and Vnconstant Men, and Husbands. . . .* London: 1617.

Spivack, Bernard. *Shakespeare and the Allegory of Evil: The History of a Metaphor in Relation to His Major Villains.* New York: Columbia UP, 1958.

Stanton, Kay. "'Made to write 'whore' upon?': Male and Female Use of the Word 'Whore' in Shakespeare's Canon." *A Feminist Companion to Shakespeare.* Ed. Dympna Callaghan. London: Blackwell, 2000. 81–102.

Stallybrass, Peter. "Patriarchal Territories: The Body Enclosed." *Rewriting the Renaissance: The Discourses of Sexual Difference in Early Modern Europe.* Ed. Margaret W. Ferguson, Maureen Quilligan, and Nancy J. Vickers. Chicago: U of Chicago P, 1986. 123–42.

Starks, Lisa S. "The Displaced Body of Desire: Sexuality in Kenneth Branaugh's *Hamlet.*" *Shakespeare and Appropriation.* Ed. Christy Desmet and Robert Sawyer. London: Routledge, 1999. 160–78.

Stone, Lawrence. *The Family, Sex and Marriage in England, 1500–1800.* New York: Harper & Row, 1977.

Suzman, Janet. Interview with Joan Blakewell. BBC. 2000. <http://www.bbc.co.uk/religion/programmes/belief/scripts/beliefsuzman.html>.

Taylor, Gary. *Reinventing Shakespeare: A Cultural History, from the Restoration to the Present.* New York: Weidenfeld & Nicolson, 1989.

Teague, Francis. *Shakespeare's Speaking Properties.* Lewisburg: Bucknell UP, 1991.

Thompson, Ann, and Sasha Roberts, eds. *Women Reading Shakespeare, 1660–1900: An Anthology of Criticism.* Manchester: Manchester UP, 1997.

Tokson, Elliot H. *The Popular Image of the Black Man in English Drama, 1550–1688.* Boston: G. K. Hall, 1982.

Traub, Valerie. *The Renaissance of Lesbianism in Early Modern England.* Cambridge: Cambridge UP, 2002.

Underdown, David. "The Taming of the Scold: The Enforcement of Patriarchal Authority in Early Modern England." *Order and Disorder in Early Modern England.* Eds. Anthony Fletcher and John Stevenson. New York: Cambridge UP, 1985.

Trexler, Richard C. *Public Life in Renaissance Florence.* Ithaca: Cornell UP, 1991.

Vaughan, Virginia. *Othello: A Contextual History.* Cambridge: Cambridge UP, 1994.

Viswanathan, Gauri. *Masks of Conquest: Literary Study and British Rule in India.* New York: Columbia UP, 1989.

Vickers, Brian. *Shakespeare: The Critical Heritage.* Vol. 1. London: Routledge, 1974.

Vitkus, Daniel J., ed. *Three Turk Plays from Early Modern England:* Selimus, A Christian Turned Turk, *and* The Renegade. New York: Columbia UP, 2000.

———. *Turning Turk: English Theater and the Multicultural Mediterranean, 1570–1630.* New York: Palgrave, 2003.

Walker, Greg. *The Politics of Performance in Early Renaissance Drama*. Cambridge: Cambridge UP, 1998.

Wallace, Michelle. "Variations on Negation and the Heresy of Black Feminist Creativity." *Reading Black, Reading Feminist: A Critical Anthology*. Ed. Henry Louis Gates, Jr. New York: Penguin, 1990. 52–68.

Walvin, James. *The Black Presence: A Documentary History of the Negro in England, 1555–1860*. London: Orbach and Chambers, 1971.

Watermeier, Daniel J., ed. *Between Actor and Critic: Selected Letters of Edwin Booth and William Winter*. Princeton: Princeton UP, 1971.

Watt, Jeffery R. *The Making of Modern Marriage: Matrimonial Control and the Rise of Sentiment in Neuchatel, 1550–1800*. Ithaca: Cornell UP, 1992.

Webster, Margaret. *Don't Put Your Daughter on the Stage*. New York: Knopf, 1972.

Welter, Barbara. "The Cult of True Womanhood: 1820–1860." *American Quarterly* 18.2 (1966): 151–74.

Whigham, Frank. *Ambition and Privilege: The Social Tropes of Elizabethan Courtesy Theory*. Berkeley: U of California P, 1984.

Wiesner, Merry. *Women and Gender in Early Modern Europe*. New York: Cambridge UP, 2000.

Willan, T. S. *Studies in Elizabethan Foreign Trade*. Manchester: Manchester UP, 1959.

Williams, Patricia. *The Alchemy of Race and Rights: Diary of a Law Professor*. Cambridge: Harvard UP, 1991.

Wilson, Fred, and Kathleen Goncharov. *Speak of Me as I Am*. United States Pavillion, 50th Venice Biennale. 2003. Presented by the Massachusetts Institute of Technology, List Visual Arts Center.

Wiltenburg, Joy. *Disorderly Women and Female Power in the Street Literature of Early Modern England and Germany*. Charlottesville: UP of Virginia, 1992.

Woodbridge, Linda. *The Scythe of Saturn: Shakespeare and Magical Thinking*. Urbana: U of Illinois P, 1994.

——. *Women and the English Renaissance: Literature and the Nature of Womankind, 1540 to 1620*. Urbana: U of Illinois P, c. 1984.

Würzbach, Natascha. *The Rise of the English Street Ballad, 1550–1650*. Trans. Gayna Walls. Cambridge: Cambridge UP, 1990.

Yachnin, Paul. "Magical Properties: Vision, Possession, and Wonder in *Othello*." *Theatre Journal* 48.2 (1996): 197–208.

Zhiri, Oumelbanine. "Leo Africanus's *Description of Africa*." *Travel Knowledge: European Discoveries in the Early Modern Period*. Ed. Ivo Kamps and Jyotsna G. Singh. New York: Palgrave, 2001. 258–66.

Ziegler, Georgiana. "My Lady's Chamber: Female Space, Female Chastity in Shakespeare." *Textual Practice* 4.1 (Spring 1990): 73–100.

*Acknowledgments*

INTRODUCTION

Figure 1. Engraving of *Othello* Act 5.2, by Henry Singleton (1839?). Reprinted by permission of the Folger Shakespeare Library, Washington, DC.

Figure 2. Quarto *Othello* (Q1) 5.2 (1622). Reprinted by permission of the Folger Shakespeare Library, Washington, DC.

Figure 3. Folio *Othello* (F) 5.2 (1623). Reprinted by permission of the Folger Shakespeare Library, Washington, DC.

Figure 5. Engraving of *Othello* Act 5.2, by John Massey Wright/Timothy Stansfield Engleheart. Reprinted by permission of the Folger Shakespeare Library, Washington, DC.

Figure 6. Edmund Kean as Othello. Reprinted by permission of the Folger Shakespeare Library, Washington, DC.

Figure 7. Tomasso Salvini as Othello. Reprinted by permission of the Folger Shakespeare Library, Washington, DC.

Figure 8. Mr. Aldridge as Othello, from the Michael Booth Collection. Reprinted by permission of Newcastle University, Australia.

Figure 9. Paul Robeson and Mary Ure in *Othello* (1959). Reprinted by permission of AP/WIDE WORLD PHOTOS.

Figure 10. Patrick Stewart as Othello and Patrice Johnson as Desdemona in the Shakespeare Theatre Company's 1997–1998 production of William Shakespeare's *Othello*, directed by Jude Kelly. Photo by Carol Pratt. Reprinted by permission of Carol Pratt. Reprinted by permission of Barry M. Colfelt, Director of Public Relations and Marketing, Shakespeare Theatre Company, Washington, DC.

Giraldi Cinthio, *Gli Hecatommithi di M. Giovanbattista Giraldi Cinthio nobile ferrarese* (1566), from *Narrative and Dramatic Sources of Shakespeare*, ed. Geoffrey Bullough (New York, NY: Columbia UP, 1975). Reprinted by permission of Columbia University Press.

*Othello, The Moor of Venice* from *The Complete Works of Shakespeare*, 4th ed. Ed. David Bevington. Copyright © 1997 by Addison-Wesley Educational Publishers, Inc. Reprinted by permission of Pearson Education, Inc.


CHAPTER I

Figure 11. *Baptism of the Eunuch* (1626), by Rembrandt van Rijn. Reprinted by permission of Museum Catharijneconvent, Utrecht.

Figure 12. Engraving of Act 5.2, by George Noble, from a painting by Josiah Boydell for The Boydell Gallery (1800). Reprinted by permission of the Folger Shakespeare Library, Washington, DC.

Figure 13. *The Adoration of the Magi*, by Peter Paul Rubens. Reprinted by permission of the Folger Shakespeare Library, Washington, DC.

Figure 14. A Moor, from Cesare Vecellio, *Degli habiti antichi et moderni di diverse parti del mondo* (1598). Reprinted by permission of the Folger Shakespeare Library, Washington, DC.

Figure 15. Portrait of Abd el Ouahed ben Messaoud ben Mohammed Anoun (1600), Moroccan Ambassador to Queen Elizabeth I. Reprinted by permission of The University of Birmingham Collections.

Figure 16. "Aethiopem lavare," by Geffrey Whitney, from *A Choice of Emblems* (1586). Reprinted by permission of the Folger Shakespeare Library, Washington, DC.

Queen Elizabeth I, List of Royal Proclamations, Edict Arranging for the Expulsion from England of Negroes and Blackamoors (1601). From *Tudor Royal Proclamations* (New Haven: Yale University Press, 1964–69).

Church of England, "A Form to be used in Common Prayer, every Sunday, Wednesday, and Friday, through the Whole Realm: To Excite and Stir all godly people to pray unto God for the Preservation of those Christians and their Countries, that are now invaded by the Turk in Hungary, or elsewhere," *Liturgical services: Liturgies and Occasional Forms of Prayer set forth in the Reign of Queen Elizabeth*, ed. William Keatinge Clay (Cambridge: Cambridge University Press, 1847), 527–35.

Figure 17. Woodcut illustrating the ballad "The Lady and the Blackamoor," from *The Roxburghe Ballads*. Reprinted by permission of the British Library, C.20.f.7 (220).

Figure 18. Fresco of Saint James Riding over the Corpses of Saracens, from Il Sodoma (Giovanni Antonio Bazzi, Il Sodoma), Spanish Chapel, S. Spirito, Siena, Italy. Reprinted by permission of Alinari/Art Resource, NY.

Figure 19. Frontispiece, from Michel Baudier, *Inventaire de l'histoire generalle des Turcz* (1631). Photo courtesy of the Rare Book Division of the Library of Congress.

Figure 20. Frontispiece, from Richard Knolles, *The General History of the Turks* (1603). Reprinted by permission of the Folger Shakespeare Library, Washington, DC.

Figure 21. Osman, from Philip Lonicer, *Chronicorum Turcicorum* (1578). Photo courtesy of the Rare Book Division of the Library of Congress.

CHAPTER 2

Figure 22. Detail from *The Geography Lesson*, by Andreas Capella (1776). Photo reprinted by permission of Paul H. D. Kaplan.

Figure 23. The City-State of Venice, from Pietro Bertelli, *Theatrum Urbium Italicarum* (1599). Reprinted by permission of the Folger Shakespeare Library, Washington, DC.

Figure 24. Detail from *The Healing of a Madman*, by Vittorio Carpaccio (c. 1496). Copyright © David Lees/Corbis.

Fynes Moryson, *Unpublished Chapters of Fynes Moryson's Itinerary* (1617), in *Shakespeare's Europe*, 2nd ed., Ed. Charles Hughes (New York: Benjamin Blom, Inc., 1967), pp. 132, 163–165.

Figure 25. Engraving of Thomas Coryate with Venetian courtesan Margarita Emiliana, from Thomas Coryate, *Coryat's Crudities; Hastily Gobled Up in Five Months Travels* (1611). Reprinted by permission of the Folger Shakespeare Library, Washington, DC.

Figure 26. Map of Ottoman Empire, from Abraham Ortelius, *Epitome of the Theater of The World* (1570). Reprinted by permission of the Folger Shakespeare Library, Washington, DC.

Excerpts from "His Majesties Lepanto, or Heroicall Song," edited and modernized by Peter C. Herman, from *Reading Monarchs Writing: The Poetry of Henry VIII, Mary Stuart, Elizabeth I, and James VI/I*, edited by Peter C. Herman, MRTS vol. 234 (Tempe, AZ, 2002), lines 77–150, 269–284, 505–548. Copyright Arizona Board of Regents for Arizona State University. Reprinted with permission.

Figure 27. Procession of Venetian troops joining the Holy League, from Giacomo Franco, *Habiti d'huomeni et donne venetiane* (1609). Reprinted by permission of the British Library, C.48.h.11.

CHAPTER 4

Figure 28. *Battle of the Mohacs*, from *The Book of Suleyman*. Reprinted by permission of Topkapi Palace Museum, Turkey, H.1517, 220a.

Figure 29. "Snail" battle formation, from Thomas Styward, *The Pathway to Martial Discipline* (1581). Reprinted by permission of the Folger Shakespeare Library, Washington, DC.

CHAPTER 5

Figure 30. Title page, from Jean François Senault, *The Use of the Passions*, trans. Henry, Earl of Monmouth (London, 1649). Reprinted by permission of the Folger Shakespeare Library, Washington, DC.

Thomas Wright, *The Passions of the Mind in General* (1604), ed. William Webster Newbold (New York: Garland, 1986), pp. 94–96, 283–86. By permission of William Webster Newbold.

Figure 31. Page 21, from Benedetto Varchi, *The Blazon of Jealousy*, translated by Robert Tofte (1615). Reprinted by permission of the Folger Shakespeare Library, Washington, DC.

CHAPTER 6

Figure 32. Detail of video installation, *September Dream*, by Fred Wilson (2003). Four-channel video produced as part of *Speak of Me as I Am*, mixed media installation created for the U.S. Pavilion at the 50th Venice Biennale (June–November 2003). Photograph courtesy of PaceWildenstein, New York. Copyright © Fred Wilson, courtesy of PaceWildenstein, New York.

Paula Vogel, *Desdemona, A Play About a Handkerchief* (New York: Dramatists Play Service, 1994). Copyright © 1994 by Paula Vogel. Reprinted by permission of William Morris Agency, LLC on behalf of the Author.

Figure 33. Front Cover, from *Desdemonum: An Ethiopian Burlesque, in Three Scenes* (1874). Reprinted by permission of the Folger Shakespeare Library, Washington, DC.

Figure 34. Othello 5.2, from Alexander Do Mar, *Othello: An Interesting Drama, Rather!* (1850). Reprinted by permission of the Folger Shakespeare Library, Washington, DC.

Figure 35. *Othello No. 1*, by Hervé Télémaque (1960). Photographed for the UC Berkeley Art Museum by Benjamin Blackwell. Courtesy of the Regents of the University of California.

Tayeb Salih, pp. 37–39 from *Season of Migration to the North* (1969) by Tayeb Salih. Reprinted by permission of Harcourt Education.

Derek Walcott, "Goats and Monkeys," from *Collected Poems 1948–1984*. Copyright © 1986 by Derek Walcott. Reprinted by permission of Farrar, Straus and Giroux, LLC. Reprinted by permission of Faber and Faber Ltd.

# Index

DATE DUE

| | |
|---|---|
| MAY 1 6 2008 | |
| OCT 0 1 2008 | |
| APR 0 7 2010 | |
| MAY 1 3 2013 | |
| DEC 2 1 2018 | |
| DEC 2 2 2022 | |
| | |
| | |
| | |
| | |
| | |
| | |
| | |

DEMCO, INC. 38-2931